PENGUIN CLASSICS

THE WAY OF THE WORLD
AND OTHER PLAYS

WILLIAM CONGREVE was born in 1670 at Bardsey in Yorkshire. He came from a landed family and spent his early youth in Ireland, where his father served as a military officer. He was educated at Kilkenny School and Trinity College, Dublin, and at both places was a contemporary of Jonathan Swift. On coming to England, he entered the Middle Temple but does not appear to have practised law. As an undergraduate he probably wrote his novel, *Incognita*, of which Dr Johnson said that he would rather praise it than read it. His first play, *The Old Bachelor* (1693), was a great success and was followed by *The Double Dealer* (1693), *Love for Love* (1695) and *The Way of the World* (1700). He also wrote a tragedy, *The Morning Bride*. All of Congreve's plays were written before he was thirty. William Congreve died in 1729 and is buried in Westminster Abbey.

ERIC RUMP studied at Pembroke College, Cambridge, for his B.A. and at the University of Toronto for his Ph.D., and is now an Associate Professor in the English Department of Glendon College, York University, Toronto. He is the author of a number of articles on both Restoration and modern drama and has also edited a selection of Sheridan's comedies for Penguin Classics.

The Way of the World
and Other Plays

Edited by ERIC S. RUMP

THE OLD BACHELOR
THE DOUBLE DEALER
LOVE FOR LOVE
THE WAY OF THE WORLD

PENGUIN BOOKS

PENGUIN BOOKS

Published by the Penguin Group
Penguin Books Ltd, 80 Strand, London WC2R ORL, England
Penguin Group (USA) Inc., 375 Hudson Street, New York, New York 10014, USA
Penguin Group (Canada), 90 Eglinton Avenue East, Suite 700, Toronto, Ontario, Canada M4P 2Y3
(a division of Pearson Penguin Canada Inc.)
Penguin Ireland, 25 St Stephen's Green, Dublin 2, Ireland (a division of Penguin Books Ltd)
Penguin Group (Australia), 250 Camberwell Road, Camberwell, Victoria 3124, Australia
(a division of Pearson Australia Group Pty Ltd)
Penguin Books India Pvt Ltd, 11 Community Centre, Panchsheel Park, New Delhi – 110 017, India
Penguin Group (NZ), cnr Airborne and Rosedale Roads, Albany, Auckland 1310,
New Zealand (a division of Pearson New Zealand Ltd)
Penguin Books (South Africa) (Pty) Ltd, 24 Sturdee Avenue,
Rosebank, Johannesburg 2196, South Africa

Penguin Books Ltd, Registered Offices: 80 Strand, London WC2R ORL, England

www.penguin.com

This edition first published as *The Comedies of William Congreve* 1985
Published in Penguin Classics 2006

011

Introduction and Notes copyright © Eric S. Rump, 1985
All rights reserved

The moral right of the editor has been asserted

Printed in England by Clays Ltd, St Ives plc

ISBN-13: 978-0-141-44185-6

www.greenpenguin.co.uk

MIX
Paper from
responsible sources
FSC
www.fsc.org   FSC™ C018179

Penguin Books is committed to a sustainable
future for our business, our readers and our planet.
This book is made from Forest Stewardship
Council™ certified paper.

To
my late parents
with
love and gratitude

CONTENTS

INTRODUCTION

When Congreve, a teenager of nineteen, left Ireland for England in the spring of 1689, he may have intended to become a lawyer, for he enrolled as a student at the Middle Temple, though, as his friend Charles Gildon observed shortly afterwards, he had 'a wit of too fine a turn, to be long pleased with that crabbed, unpalatable study; in which the laborious, dull, plodding fellow, generally excells the more sprightly and vivacious wit'.[1] This 'wit' made its first appearance with the publication of his short novel *Incognita* (probably written while he was still a student at Trinity College, Dublin)[2] but, more importantly for his future career, it was during his early days in London that he became acquainted with the great literary figure of his day, John Dryden, a man then in his sixties. Quite how they first met is unknown, though by 1692 Congreve had contributed a verse translation of Juvenal's eleventh satire to the translations of Juvenal and Persius that were largely the work of Dryden himself, and this initial collaboration quickly developed into a firm friendship, for by the middle of the following year, Dryden, in a letter to his publisher Jacob Tonson, wrote that he was 'Mr Congreve's true lover and desire you to tell him, how kindly I take his often remembrances of me'.[3] It is to Dryden especially that credit must be given for encouraging Congreve to turn playwright.

In 1698, when Congreve was replying to Jeremy Collier's attacks

1. Charles Gildon, *The Lives and Characters of the English Dramatic Poets* (London, 1698).
2. For further biographical information, see John C. Hodges, *William Congreve* (New York, 1941).
3. Charles E. Ward (ed.), *The Letters of John Dryden* (Duke University Press, 1942), p. 59.

upon his plays,[4] he wrote that his first play, *The Old Bachelor*, was composed some years before it was acted and that it was largely undertaken 'to amuse myself in a slow recovery from a fit of sickness'.[5] This may well have been in the spring of 1689, when he was staying with his grandfather at Stretton Manor in Staffordshire shortly after his arrival from Ireland; the manuscript was then probably shown to Dryden in 1692 who, with typical generosity, declared that he had never seen 'such a first play in his life, but the author not being acquainted with the stage or the town, it would be a pity to have it miscarry for want of a little assistance: the stuff was rich indeed, it wanted only the fashionable cut of the town'.[6] Quite what suggestions Dryden and others, such as the playwright Thomas Southerne, who was also consulted, had to make have not been recorded but, according to Gildon, they were largely to do with the order of the scenes and the length of the play.[7] Once revised, the play was accepted by the only company then playing in London, the United Company,[8] and was probably in rehearsal by the closing months of 1692; the murder of one actor, William Mountfort, and the death of another, however, delayed the opening at the Theatre Royal, Drury Lane, until the March of 1693. As in any young playwright's fondest fancy, it proved a triumphant success and had, for those times, an extraordinary run of fourteen days.[9]

Congreve's knowledge of what Dryden calls 'the town' and indeed of the theatre in general must have been somewhat limited if

4. Jeremy Collier, *A Short View of the Immorality and Prophaneness of the English Stage* (1698). Collier's lengthy denunciation of Restoration drama had been published a few months earlier.

5. *Amendments to Mr Collier's False and Imperfect Citations* (London, 1698), p. 39.

6. John C. Hodges (ed.), *William Congreve: Letters and Documents* (London, 1964), p. 151.

7. Gildon, op. cit., p. 25.

8. The two companies licensed by Charles II shortly after his return to the throne in 1660 – the King's and the Duke's – had merged to form the United Company in 1682. They were to divide again, in 1695, while Congreve was still writing for the theatre.

9. For further information about the performances of Congreve's plays, see William van Lennep (ed.), *The London Stage*, Part One (1660–1700) (Carbondale, Illinois, 1965).

he first wrote the play when he was only nineteen, though, in addition to his own reading, he had access to the theatre while at Trinity College, Dublin, through the performances given at the Smock Alley Theatre. However, *The Old Bachelor* is probably best approached as a play in which a young, talented writer is content to re-explore the comic territory earlier mapped out by writers such as Etherege and Wycherley, but in so doing, is able to bring to that material a freshness and distinctiveness of accent that makes his first play something more than merely routine.

This is in part achieved through a graceful vigour in the writing that is established as early as the opening exchanges between Bellmour and Vainlove in which Bellmour, a typical rake, explores the familiar theme of the superiority of pleasure over business:

> Come come, leave business to idlers, and wisdom to fools; they have need of 'em. Wit be my faculty, and pleasure my occupation and let Father Time shake his glass. Let low and earthy souls grovel till they have worked themselves six foot deep into a grave. Business is not my element; I roll in a higher orb and dwell –
> VAINLOVE: In castles i'th'air of thy own building: that's thy element, Ned. Well as high as a flyer as you are, I have a lure may make you stoop.
> [*Flings a letter.*]

Moreover, Congreve also demonstrates in his first play his ability to give every character his or her own individual speech pattern. It is probably going too far to say, as some have, that even without the prefixes one could assign each speech to the appropriate character, but there is certainly no denying that there is a welcome variety in a play which includes, to name but a few, the breathless, fragmented speeches of Belinda, the snarling periods of Heartwell and the cloying babytalk of the Fondlewifes when, nominally at least, Laetitia is at her most loving.

Grace and charm may be displayed by the dialogue, but these are not necessarily the attributes of the world that dialogue reveals. The reference to the hawk and the lure in the quotation above is only a starting point for a series of references that suggest that 'civilized' as the social world may initially appear, there is something more brutal lurking not far below the surface. This emerges, in part, from the portrayal of women as creatures to be hunted.[10] Vainlove, for instance, sees them as 'hares' which he disturbs so Bellmour can 'course' them (p. 41), or as 'hares' which, given his strange sensibility, disappointingly do not flee but run into the mouths of the hounds (p. 83). Bellmour likewise sees them as 'partridges' which, once having been 'set' by Vainlove, he can then 'cover' (p. 44). Women, as well as being creatures to be hunted, are also seen as something to be eaten or devoured. Laetitia, for instance is 'a delicious morsel' (p. 41) for Bellmour, and Sharper describes Araminta to Vainlove as 'a delicious melon, pure and consenting ripe, and only waits thy cutting up' (p. 83). No doubt Bellmour's description of himself as a 'cormorant' (p. 42), a sea bird noted for its voracious appetite, could be connected with this set of references as well. Man may be the hunter, but he is likewise 'brutified', to use Fondlewife's splendid verb, at a number of points in the play. Vainlove is referred to as an ass, Bellmour an ape, Heartwell is described as an old fox that Silvia has successfully trapped and men generally can be stags whose horns, of course, suggest those of the cuckolded male. As Virginia Ogden Birdsall has suggested,[11] Sir Joseph's reference to the two best-known beast stories – Aesop's *Fables* and *Reynard the Fox* – may well provide a context for viewing much of what goes on in the play.

Setter's name alone would connect him with this area of the play, but more importantly he is one of a group whose success lies in their ability to present themselves convincingly as something they are not. The theme of deceit and disguise, of con-man and conned, is of course not new with Congreve, but it is something which he portrays in *The Old Bachelor* with youthful zest and, at times, almost dizzying complexity. It is Laetitia's letter to Vainlove, with its suggestion of an appropriate disguise, that first prompts Bellmour to temporarily abandon his 'half a score [of] mistresses' (p. 42) and disguise himself as Spintext. Of course, Laetitia soon sees through the disguise (though she is far from disappointed by what her discovery reveals), as does Fondlewife once he discovers that it is not

10. See also N. N. Holland, *The First Modern Comedies* (Harvard, 1959), chapter 13.
11. Virginia Ogden Birdsall, *Wild Civility* (Bloomington, Indiana, 1970), chapter 8.

a prayer book that Spintext has brought along with him but a copy of Scarron's *The Innocent Adultery*, but his continuing role as Spintext is important for the dénouement, for it is as Spintext that Bellmour performs the fake marriage between Heartwell and Silvia. If Bellmour is, in a sense, a substitute for Vainlove when he first visits Laetitia, then Sharper likewise is a substitute for Bellmour, for it is as Sir Joseph Wittol's rescuer (Bellmour in actuality) that Sharper presents himself when he first meets Sir Joseph, a substitution that the foolish Sir Joseph believes, along with the story of the lost £100. If Sir Joseph cannot see through Sharper, no more can Heartwell see through Silvia, for it is her convincing performance of child-like innocence that lures him into a hasty marriage. Not even Vainlove is as clear-sighted as one might expect, for he believes for a while that the letter from Araminta is genuine, whereas in fact it has been concocted by Silvia and Lucy. The only performance that nobody ever believes (except possibly Sir Joseph) is that of Bluffe as a figure of military valour, and the genuine heroes that he alludes to, such as Hannibal and Scipio Africanus, only serve in his case to underline the substantial gap between the fake and the real.

In a world of such shifting surfaces, there is at least one constant and that is money. Araminta and Belinda are contrasted in a number of ways: Araminta is loftily serious about love, while Belinda is not; Araminta is usually grave while laughter punctuates many of Belinda's speeches; Araminta is relatively honest and straightforward while a curious affectation tinges much of what Belinda has to say. But in one thing they are identical and that is in their fortunes. They are both seemingly free from any control by parents or guardians and so have within their own hands the not inconsiderable sum of £12,000 each. Bellmour announces at the outset that he is 'damnably in love' (p. 42) with Belinda, but how much that love is based on a realization of her wealth is a question raised quite early on in the play. In reply to Sharper's charge that Belinda is 'too proud, too inconstant, too affected, and too witty, and too handsome for a wife', Bellmour replies:

But she can't have too much money. – There's twelve thousand pound, Tom. – 'Tis true she is excessively foppish and affected, but in my conscience I believe the baggage loves me, for she never speaks well of me herself, nor suffers anybody else to rail at me. Then, as I told you, there's twelve thousand pound – hum – why, faith, upon second thoughts, she does not appear to be so very affected neither. (p. 43)

Of course Bellmour and Belinda do agree to get married by the end of the play – though the manner is curiously offhand – but how much the match should be seen as the successful outcome of fortune-hunting on Bellmour's part is never really made clear.

Silvia's misfortune is that while she has the capacity for love, she apparently does not have the cash. Before the opening of the play, she has fallen in love with Vainlove but she has also succumbed to the physical attractions of Bellmour. Her love for Vainlove, once rebuffed, sours into a cry for 'vengeance' (p. 65) but in passages like this, as with similar speeches from Mrs Loveit in Etherege's *Man of Mode*, there is the uncertainty of whether we are witnessing a character driven beyond the conventional comic boundaries or a character comically elevating herself on tragic stilts. She is, however, not readily at home in the world of deceit and disguise and it is only Lucy's promptings that persuade her to play the role of simple innocence that Heartwell desires. In consequence, Bellmour's curt dismissal of her as simply a 'whore' – he presumably bears some responsibility for her condition – and therefore an unsuitable partner for his 'friend' Heartwell (p. 101), seems unduly harsh and the provision of Wittol for her as a substitute husband a dubious reward indeed.

The question of what dramatic language is appropriate for comedy also briefly arises in connection with Heartwell. He is introduced to us as a 'pretended woman hater' (p. 42), so that much of the comedy lies in seeing one who prides himself on his knowledge of the world – 'I have baited too many of those traps to be caught in one myself' (p. 46) – being himself deceived by Silvia's performance. However, it is the teasing of him – one might almost say the tormenting of him – by the other characters in the final act and his response that suddenly make us look at him and them in a less coolly detached way:

How have I deserved this of you? Any of ye? Sir, have I impaired the honour
of your house, promised your sister marriage, and whored her? Wherein
have I injured you? (p. 112)[12]

Congreve could no doubt count on Betterton, the Olivier of his day,
bringing to such a speech his long experience in more serious roles
and it is in speeches such as this that a pointer might be found to the
ways in which Congreve would be extending his range in his second
play, *The Double Dealer*, which probably opened in the November of
the same year as *The Old Bachelor*, 1693.

Whereas Congreve had set much of his first play in the streets and
parks of contemporary London, he chose in his second to retreat
indoors and to set his play, with the exception of the scene in Lady
Touchwood's bedroom, entirely in the 'gallery' of Lord Touchwood's house. The reason for this, as he explains in his somewhat
angry preface, was that he wanted to write a 'true and regular
comedy' in which the three unities of time, place and action were
preserved with 'the utmost severity' (p. 122). In consequence there is,
with the exception noted above, the single 'gallery' setting; in place
of the variety of incidents in *The Old Bachelor*, there is a concen-
tration on Maskwell's plotting and the time that elapses on stage is
little more than three hours.

Although Congreve has deliberately confined himself to the
portrayal of a single section of the house, he nevertheless very
skilfully evokes the sense of a much larger place, so that, although we
do not see it, we become very aware of the size of Lord Touchwood's
mansion, of rooms beyond rooms in which the drama continues to
unfold, although we, as audience, can be privy to only part of it. The
play, for instance, opens not with people in the gallery, but with
people drifting into the gallery as they leave the nearby dining-room,
and as the play proceeds, we learn of back-stairs and concealed
doors, of quarters for the resident chaplain, of a garden large enough
for Brisk and Lady Froth to wander unobserved, of stables for a
coach and six, of an area for the ladies to take tea and of somewhere
else with an 'inviting couch' (p. 202) where Lord Froth can sleep out
part of the play. Yet for all this marvellous evocation of life in one of

12. See also Herbert Davis, *The Complete Plays of William Congreve* (Chicago, 1967),
p. 7.

the great houses, it remains curiously self-enclosed, the bustle of
contemporary London pushed far away beyond its enclosing walls.
Perhaps, indeed, it is not even in London, for the one reference we
get to an actual place – St Albans – provides no particular geo-
graphical location for it at all.

Such a change in setting is entirely appropriate for Congreve's
purposes in *The Double Dealer*, for he has chosen to portray a far
more socially elevated and interconnected group than in *The Old
Bachelor*. Although Sir Paul and Lady Touchwood, because of their
temperamental differences, may sometimes seem an odd pair to be
brother and sister, it is nevertheless that relationship which provides
the tie between the families of the Touchwoods and the Plyants, as
well as making Mellefont and Cynthia, through their proposed
marriage, the only possible means by which the two families can
remain united and their fortunes secure. For in Congreve's portrayal
of this group, there is an air of exhaustion, of impotence even – at
least in terms of the older males – that suggests that both families
have almost lost the vitality to reproduce themselves. Sir Paul, from
his first marriage, has only fathered the one daughter, Cynthia, and if
Lady Plyant has her way, will presumably not be producing any
further children, and although it is never stated that Lord Touchwood is impotent, there seems little doubt that he has abandoned any
hope of fathering children of his own. In consequence, the off-stage
dinner party at the beginning of the play, from which people start to
emerge slightly tipsy on the fashionably new champagne, is more
than a social gathering of old friends; it is a dynastic gathering to
ensure, through the signing of two documents, that the families of
the Touchwoods and the Plyants have a future as well as a past. For
Mellefont is, as Lord Touchwood explains in the final act, 'the alone
remaining branch of all our ancient family' (p. 191), just as Cynthia is
the only heiress for Sir Paul's 'good estate in the country, some
houses in town, and some money' (p. 163). Once the legal document
making Mellefont Lord Touchwood's heir has been signed, along
with the marriage contract between Mellefont and Cynthia, then the
two families can part, secure in the knowledge that their joint affairs
are once more on a secure base.

Rich and important as these two families may be, Congreve's

portrait of both them and their friends is far from a flattering one. Although not unintelligent or unlearned – Lady Froth, for instance, may know some Greek and can rattle off at least the names of the fashionable French critics – the constant striving for wit that never quite comes off and the literature that they produce reveals a triviality of mind that runs through much of the group. Lady Froth is perhaps the best example, for she is at work on what the seventeenth century would consider one of the noblest productions of the human mind, an epic or 'heroic' poem, but from the extracts that we are allowed to hear, it will clearly be an unintentional parody of that genre. Its dubious puns (Lord Froth is to become Spumoso), its tired classicism (the dairymaid is to be transformed into Thetis) and its broken-backed metre will require more than Brisk's commentary and notes to disguise its utter vacuity. Brisk, as well as being a commentator, is also a writer, though a writer who has difficulty in classifying his own work, for he is unclear about whether to define the one poem we hear as an 'epigram' or an 'epigrammatic sonnet' (p. 168), though he does attempt to allay any doubts by claiming it is 'satire'. The Froths, we are told, wrote excessively during their courtship, but Lord Froth seems to have now undertaken the role of the theatre critic who displays his insightfulness by going to comedies but never laughing in the hope that he may thereby 'mortify the poets' (p. 134). Even the chaplain, Saygrace, is not immune to this literary fever, for when Maskwell calls upon him in the final act he is valiantly struggling over the last line of an acrostic.

Literature may be the major preoccupation of at least one of the ladies in the play but most of them are preoccupied with something else as well. Jeremy Collier, in his *Short View of the Immorality and Prophaneness of the English Stage*, remarked that 'there are but four ladies in this play, and three of the biggest of them are whores'[13] and, blunt as this may be, it is also reasonably fair. Lady Plyant, for instance, is superficially concerned with her 'honour', and her 'niceness' is almost her husband's despair, for she has him nightly bundled up in blankets before being put to bed, but in the past, we are given to believe, this has not been the fate of other men, and it

13. Collier, op. cit., p. 12.

well might not have been for two of the men in the play. She is all too
ready to believe that Mellefont is in love with her, and although
protesting that her honour is 'infallible and uncomatible' (p. 149), she
leaves exactly the opposite impression, and once persuaded that the
rumours of his passion entail no more than 'profound respect'
(p. 134), she is quite prepared to transfer her affections to Careless and
to demonstrate them once they are concealed in the wardrobe. The
passionate love of the Froths is related to us early on in the play, but
this forms no barrier to her dalliance with Brisk and their withdrawal
to the garden for star-gazing and 'couplets'. Yet, for all Lord
Touchwood's ponderous moralizing in the closing lines of the play,
they remain unexposed and unpunished; that is reserved for Lady
Touchwood and Maskwell alone.

Lady Touchwood is in many ways a natural member of such an
aristocratic group, but an extended fissure runs through this play
which places Maskwell and her on one side and the rest on the other.
For Maskwell, it must be remembered, is neither titled nor a cus-
tomary associate of titled people in the way that Careless and Brisk
undoubtedly are. His actual position in the Touchwood household
is unclear, but from what we hear of Mellefont's earlier kindness
to him and from Lady Touchwood's reference to him as once being
'in the nature of a servant' (p. 137), it seems that he is somebody who
has risen within the household without ever becoming a fully fledged
member of it. In a private way he has, of course, since he is now
Lady Touchwood's lover; the action then, from Maskwell's point
of view, can be seen as the upwardly mobile young man's attempt to
finally and publicly break into that golden circle by replacing Mellefont
both as Lord Touchwood's heir and Cynthia's husband.

From Maskwell's desire for the money and the girl, from his
energy and his delight in disguise, may well come a reminder of
certain aspects of earlier Restoration comic 'heroes' such as
Etherege's Dorimant, but instead of being presented for our sardonic
amusement, he is depicted as a diminished Iago of the bedroom and
boudoir.[14] There are echoes of *Othello* as in Lord Touchwood's

14. Brian Corman has an interesting discussion of the divisions in this play in '"The
Mixed Way of Comedy": Congreve's *The Double Dealer*', *Modern Philology*, 71 (1974),
356–65.

demand for 'ocular proof' (p. 184); a number of the soliloquies are given to Maskwell; he, like Iago, can be seen as a kind of dramatist within the play and references to 'hell', 'fire' and 'damnation' can readily be found. In counterpoint to this, the dramatic language of Lady Touchwood, while not deriving from Shakespeare, can be seen to have an uneasy relationship – be it parody or echo – to the heightened language of Restoration tragedy writers such as Lee or even Dryden. It is Maskwell and Lady Touchwood alone who, amidst a flurry of disguised parsons, are dragged on stage, publicly exposed and condemned as 'strumpet' and 'villain' (p. 204). Yet all this takes place before the Froths, the Brisks, and the Plyants, who, in many ways, have behaved little differently, though, unlike Lady Touchwood, they have had the decency to confine their activities to members of their own circle.

The play finds its nominal centre in Mellefont and Cynthia, but with Maskwell assuming much of the energy of the earlier comic heroes – or even Bellmour in Congreve's first play – Mellefont's role is confined to one of trusting honesty, a combination of the good man and the gull. Unlike earlier comedies too, the courtship of Mellefont and Cynthia is over before the play begins, and although they attempt some of that witty raillery often associated with such comedies, as in their comparison of marriage to a game of bowls, it has an autumnal feel about it, as though its energy is almost depleted. Cynthia is clear-sighted – for much of the play indeed she has little to do beyond shrewdly observing what is going on around her – and Mellefont is kind-hearted, if slightly dull. Presumably it is in qualities such as these that we are directed to place our trust at the end of this experimental, 'serious' comedy.

If it was an experiment on Congreve's part, an experiment in a rather different sort of comedy, then it was one that was not received with the enthusiasm which greeted Congreve's first play. Dryden observed in one of his letters that it was 'much censured by the greater part of the town', though quickly added that it was 'defended only by the best judges, who, you know, are commonly the fewest'.[15] It was perhaps because of this public reaction that

15. Charles E. Ward (ed.), *The Letters of John Dryden* (Duke University Press, 1942), p. 63.

Congreve, in his third play, *Love for Love*,[16] returned to a somewhat more conventional comic structure.

The return, in part, can be seen in the creation of Valentine, who has connections both with the witty rakes of earlier Restoration plays and the figure of Bellmour in Congreve's own first comedy. However, for Valentine, much of that libertine life now lies in the past; it is only the introduction of the nurse with his child – as well as his unnerving remark about smothering it – that brings it to our attention at all. For, unlike Bellmour, he cannot start the play by making a choice between 'business' and 'pleasure', for he has almost completely run out of cash and credit, and is now bleakly confined to his rooms with only his servant, Jeremy, for company. His world is no longer the fashionable world of London's parks and playhouses but a world of deprivation and confinement; the deprivation underlined by Jeremy's spirited enlargement on the theme of famine and the confinement by the bailiff's remark that, in addition to Valentine, they have 'half a dozen gentlemen to arrest in Pall Mall and Covent Garden' (p. 224). All that is now left to him are his books – significantly he is now reading the Stoic Epictetus – and his 'wit', which he promises to display, to Jeremy's horror, by turning playwright. It is this concept of plays and playwrighting and all the attendant associations – role-playing, disguise etc. – that not only provides a context in which to view Valentine's development, but also that of a number of other characters as well.

For much of the social world that we see during the course of the play is rooted in the concept of acting out a role, the dynamics of which are perhaps most clearly seen in the relationship between Prue and Tattle. Prue is in some ways a younger version of Wycherley's Margery Pinchwife and, like her, is fresh from the country when we first encounter her as she bounds vigorously on stage to display to her step-mother the gifts that Tattle has given her. Once Tattle has her alone, he commences not only her seduction but also her education. He explains that her honesty and straightforwardness

16. This was the first play put on by Betterton's new company at the revived Lincoln's Inn Fields Theatre in the April of 1695, and it provided a splendid opening for the group with an initial run of thirteen days.

must be abandoned; that to be considered 'well bred' she must start lying as 'all well-bred persons lie' (p. 250), and somewhat in the manner of a director with an actor, he coaches her in her part until he feels she has got it right. Prue is a ready learner and takes on her new role with enthusiasm, but the play she thinks she is in is a rather old-fashioned one which will conclude with her marriage to Tattle. This is not the ending achieved, but although disappointed in her hopes of Tattle, there is no sense that she will revert to her former country ways.

Prue's male counterpart in the play is Ben; if she, in Mrs Frail's words, is a 'land-monster', then he is a 'sea-beast' (p. 230). Congreve may have had Ben in mind when he wrote in his essay 'Concerning Humour in Comedy' (1695) that 'one may almost give a receipt [sc. recipe] for the composition of such a character', but if so, he was being a little too dismissive of his own art, for Ben has more to do than merely provide the play with a little local colour. Like Prue, he is completely ignorant about city life, but unlike her he is in no way fascinated or attracted by it. His most appealing quality is his honesty, his inability to play roles, or, as he puts it, 'to look one way and to row another' (p. 262). He is straightforward in his dealings with Prue; he is ready to believe in Mrs Frail's affection for him; his promises of fidelity to her can be readily believed and though finally rejected by her once she knows he will not inherit Sir Sampson's estate, it is a rejection that allows him to return unscathed to his natural element. Throughout he behaves, as Maximillian Novak has pertinently suggested, like a sort of 'noble savage' suddenly let loose on the drawing-rooms of London.[17] Although he himself does not say so, it may have reinforced his growing conviction about the madness of the urban world when he sees two of that world's seemingly most accomplished role-players, Tattle and Mrs Frail, mistakenly getting married to one another while one is disguised as a friar and the other as a nun.

Hamlet is one of literature's most famous 'madmen' and it is to that role that Valentine primarily turns when he does indeed turn playwright, as he threatened in the first act, and both scripts and

17. Maximillian Novak, *William Congreve* (New York, 1971), p. 115.

performs the part of a madman in the fourth act of the play. The echoes of Shakespeare's play are there both verbally and visually, for Valentine is discovered in 'disorderly' dress, though draped upon a couch which somehow does not quite fit with one's memories of Elsinore. The casting of Betterton as Valentine may seem strange, for he was then just on sixty,[18] but it had the distinct advantage of allowing the period's most famous Hamlet to perform a fake Hamlet within the confines of a comedy. Fake though it may be, the performance is good enough to convince a number of the spectators on stage that it is genuine. Valentine's domineering father, Sir Sampson, is convinced by it, as is the lawyer, Buckram, and Valentine is thereby able to postpone the signing away of his inheritance. The normally perceptive Mrs Frail is convinced by it and is thus tricked into her marriage to Tattle. The one person, of course, that it does not convince is Angelica. Although she may have her doubts about anybody going mad for love, at least in a Restoration comedy, she is nevertheless prepared to believe Valentine until an injudicious wink on Scandal's part confirms her suspicions that what has been prepared for her is an elaborate masquerade, but a masquerade she decides will be kept going. Valentine may well wish to end the play in the fourth act ('the comedy draws towards an end') and with that in view to leave 'acting and be ourselves' (p. 292), but Angelica is determined that he will in some ways be mad indeed before that can come about.

Angelica's response to Valentine's play is to create another one of her own devising. Congreve supplies us with little background information about Angelica, but we do know that by Restoration standards she is very wealthy and that her fortune (£30,000) is in her own control. She has, Valentine tells us, been courted by others besides himself and although she has not encouraged him, it soon becomes clear that what she is doing is testing Valentine in an attempt to discover the sincerity or genuineness of his proclaimed love for her. In consequence, the play she devises is one in which she casts Sir Sampson in the role of her husband-to-be. Others more

18. Further discussion of this can be found in Peter Holland's illuminating book, *The Ornament of Action* (Cambridge, 1979), p. 226.

perspicacious than Sir Sampson might have had some doubts about the appropriateness of such a role, but given his inflated view of himself as somebody of almost heroic stature, it is a role he is easily lured into playing. Once under way in the fifth act, it is a play that the spectators on stage believe in too, including Scandal and Valentine, and it is because Valentine does believe it that he makes his splendid gesture of renunciation by signing away his inheritance for Angelica's benefit, a gesture that Scandal sees as demonstrating that Valentine is now genuinely mad as it must lead to his ruin. For Angelica, of course, it is the climax she had wished for in what she calls the 'trial' of his 'virtue' (p. 310), and once that trial has been passed, she can tear up the document, and reward his generosity of spirit with her hand and heart. It is a marvellously satisfying and exuberant conclusion to what is, in many ways, Congreve's sunniest play.

Congreve's final comedy, *The Way of the World* – his one tragedy, *The Mourning Bride*, had appeared to great acclaim in 1697 – was given its first performance in the March of 1700. Whereas in his two previous comedies, *The Double Dealer* and *Love for Love*, Congreve had used the relationships between two families as one of the structural means of organizing his drama, in *The Way of the World* he confines himself to just one. This, in part, explains the 'complexity' of the play, for with the exception of Mirabell and Marwood (and Petulant, too, if one wants to include the fools), everybody is in some way related to everybody else. Early on in the first act, Mirabell asks Fainall about his relationship to Sir Wilfull Witwoud, who is about to arrive on a visit from the country, and Fainall replies, in a speech no audience could surely be expected to follow:

. . . he is half brother to this Witwoud by a former wife, who was sister to my Lady Wishfort, my wife's mother. (p. 329)

Because of all this consanguinity, the audience, as though present at somebody else's family gathering, is on the outside and often only dimly aware of some of the underlying tensions, but it does slowly start to emerge that what we are witnessing is a battle for the Wishfort family, with Mirabell on one side and Fainall on the other, and a battle whose outcome will in part determine the nature of that family's life for the next generation at least. For if Mirabell wins it, there is hope that through his marriage to Millamant a more open and generous structure may emerge; if he loses to Fainall, it will not.

At present, much of the control of the family lies in the hands of the comically formidable Lady Wishfort, for her own husband, Sir Jonathan, is dead, as are her two sisters and their husbands. Although her actual appearance is daringly delayed by Congreve until the beginning of Act Three, in a splendid scene in which she is gulping cherry brandy while calling for 'paint' for her ageing face, her presence and power are felt from the very beginning through the references made to her by other characters. It is a power or control that she not only exercises in the present but has exercised in the past for some time as well. It has manifested itself in the education she designed for her daughter Arabella (Mrs Fainall) which was largely based on the principle of impressing upon her 'a young odium and aversion to the very sight of men' (p. 397). It has manifested itself as well in marriage arrangements, for she points out that Arabella's first husband, Languish, was her choice, and it is likewise a power she has over Millamant, for half of Millamant's fortune (a not inconsiderable £6,000) depends upon her marrying with Lady Wishfort's consent. It expresses itself, too, in the 'cabal' which she has set up and over which she presides; a group initially composed only of women, though, as Fainall tells us, they later decided to enrol one token man 'upon which motion Witwoud and Petulant were enrolled members' (p. 325). In her social appearance, her sense of herself is expressed in part through her attachment to 'decorum', an attachment which often manifests itself linguistically by a desperate search for the delicately appropriate phrase, as when she says to the (fake) Sir Rowland, 'I hope you do not think me prone to any iteration of nuptials' (p. 388). Of course there is a blindness in her to her own absurdity; a blindness which enables her to believe that Mirabell's protestations of affection are genuine and not, as they are, a convenient disguise to enable him to pursue her niece.

Fainall and Mirabell are the first characters we meet in the chocolate house at the beginning of Act One. They have just finished playing cards and Mirabell, perhaps significantly, has lost.[19] In terms

19. See Mary Wagoner, 'The Gambling Analogy in *The Way of the World*', *Tennessee Studies in Literature*, 13 (1968), 75–80.

of tone or attitude, it is difficult to make much distinction between them at this stage, though an early remark by Fainall, to the effect that if Mirabell had been more successful in his deception of Lady Wishfort then things would have remained in the 'state of nature' (p. 326), might suggest that, in Fainall's view, there lies beneath the surface of the nominally civilized world an essentially Hobbesian struggle for power and gratification. It is almost certain that Fainall's marriage to the then widowed Arabella Languish was prompted by motives no loftier than a desire for her money and his desire for further gratification is depicted through his adulterous affair with Mrs Marwood. That affair, it appears, was again partly motivated by Fainall's greed, and in a fascinating scene in Act Two, Congreve, no longer needing the heightened language of tragedy to depict their tortured affair, brilliantly extends the range of his art. Fainall's desires, however, are enlarged beyond Mrs Marwood to a desire for complete control of the Wishfort household, and by threatening to divorce his wife once he has found out about the earlier affair between Mirabell and her, he plans to take over his wife's fortune, Millamant's £6,000 and even control of Lady Wishfort herself. It is a threat only thwarted by Mirabell's production of an earlier deed that Mrs Fainall had given him while still a widow; without it, Fainall might well have had his way.

Although it may be initially difficult to distinguish between Fainall and Mirabell, the characters' similarities lie more in what we hear about Mirabell's past than what we see of him during the course of the play. Like some earlier Restoration comic 'heroes', he appears to have no family of his own and there may be a suggestion, as in Lady Wishfort's description of him as a 'spendthrift prodigal' (p. 357), that his own financial position is far from secure. More important, perhaps, at least for the modern reader or audience, is his treatment of Mrs Fainall, and, as far as recent commentators are concerned, opinion can range from seeing him as essentially a bounder to seeing him as little short of the perfect gentleman. The two of them, of course, had an affair while Arabella was still a widow, and Mirabell, in reply to her somewhat accusatory question of 'why did you make me marry this man' (p. 345), merely says that because of her suspected pregnancy, it was a marriage to save her

'reputation'. The question of why Mirabell did not save her reputation by marrying her himself, which is the question most of us want
to raise, is one that Mrs Fainall herself never asks, nor is it raised by
others in the play. At one point Foible refers to her as a 'pattern of
generosity' (p. 359), and perhaps it is by focusing on that quality and
Mirabell's equal honesty and trust in her in terms of his own affairs,
that Congreve invites us to see the difference between them and the
devious ways of Fainall and Mrs Marwood.

   For in the play itself, Mirabell, far from being a successful
schemer, is hardly ever in control of anything. His earlier pose as
Lady Wishfort's languishing lover has been uncovered by Mrs
Marwood; his disguising of his servant as his uncle, Sir Rowland,
also fails, and his attempts at a steady courtship of Millamant reduce
him at one point to feeling that he would be better off courting a
whirlwind. The characterization of Millamant has been praised by
many as subtle and charming: her playfulness, her rapidly changing
moods, can prove as delightful to an audience as they are baffling to
Mirabell. Beyond that, however, they may suggest, not just a
mercurial temperament, but a wariness on her part, a fear that love,
even Mirabell's love, may prove transient. Her independence is dear
to her and she is all too aware that there are losses as well as gains if
she does, as she puts it, agree to 'dwindle into a wife' (p. 380). In
consequence, the famous 'proviso' scene in the fourth act not only
dramatizes her final acceptance of that process of change or development but also, with its portrayal of the combination of personal
commitment and social form, builds into the play a perception of the
kind of life they will lead together once they are man and wife. With
Mirabell's mention of 'breeding' too, it may also suggest that in the
future beyond the play, their own personal fulfilment will find a
larger form in the renewal of the Wishfort family as well.

   The verve and inventiveness of *The Way of the World* provides no
evidence that Congreve felt that he had exhausted the possibilities of
comedy – indeed it leaves just the opposite impression – but at the
young age of thirty he was to cease writing comedies. It is true that
the play was not as well received as *Love for Love* but it was far from
being a failure and Congreve's ongoing connection with the stage, as
in his sharing with Vanbrugh the management of the new Queen's

Theatre in the Haymarket and his writing the text for the opera, *Semele*, first set by Eccles and later by Handel, might suggest that at the time he did not think of 1700 as the end of his career. His health, indeed, had never been robust and his appointment to the position of Secretary to the Island of Jamaica in 1714 relieved him of any pressing financial reasons for returning to the stage. Collier's attacks on Restoration drama probably do signal a shift in public attitudes as does the formation of such pressure groups as the Society for the Reformation of Manners. One or more of these facts may have exerted their influence on him but perhaps all such speculation is in the end fruitless and it is best simply to be grateful for what we have.

Eric S. Rump
October, 1984

ACKNOWLEDGEMENTS

I am deeply indebted to the many editors of Congreve, both to those who have provided far more detailed editions of single plays, such as those in the New Mermaids and Regents Restoration series, and to those who have produced collected editions of his plays, such as Montague Summers, Herbert Davis and, most recently, Anthony Henderson. To all, my thanks. I would like to thank, too, for their kindness and cooperation, the staff of the British Library and the librarians both at York University, Toronto, and the University of Toronto. I would like to express my gratitude to my own college, Glendon College, York University, for the financial support that has been provided.

A NOTE ON THE TEXT

For each of the plays I have based my text on the first quartos located in the British Library as these bring us closer to the original acting texts than the revised versions to be found in the collected *Works* of 1710. The spelling has been modernized but I have conserved as much of the original punctuation as seemed compatible with modern usage.

FURTHER READING

Virginia Ogden Birdsall, *Wild Civility: The English Comic Spirit on the Restoration Stage* (Bloomington, Indiana, 1970).

John C. Hodges, *William Congreve the Man: A Biography from New Sources* (London, 1941).

John C. Hodges, *William Congreve: Letters and Documents* (London, 1964).

Norman N. Holland, *The First Modern Comedies* (Harvard, 1959).

Peter Holland, *The Ornament of Action* (Cambridge, 1979).

Robert D. Hume, *The Development of English Drama in the Late Seventeenth Century* (Oxford, 1976).

Harold Love, *Congreve* (Oxford, 1974).

Maximillian E. Novak, *William Congreve* (New York, 1971).

W. H. Van Voris, *The Cultivated Stance: The Designs of Congreve's Plays* (London, 1965).

Aubrey L. Williams, *An Approach to Congreve* (Yale, 1979).

The
Old Bachelor

TO THE RIGHT HONOURABLE CHARLES,
LORD CLIFFORD OF LANESBOROUGH[1]

My Lord,

It is with a great deal of pleasure that I lay hold on this first occasion, which the accidents of my life have given me of writing to your Lordship: for since at the same time I write to all the world, it will be a means of publishing (what I would have everybody know) the respect and duty which I owe and pay to you. I have so much inclination to be yours, that I need no other engagement. But the particular ties, by which I am bound to your Lordship and family, have put it out of my power to make you any compliment, since all offers of myself, will amount to no more than an honest acknowledgment, and only show a willingness in me to be grateful.

I am very near wishing that it were not so much my interest to be your Lordship's servant, that it might be more my merit; not that I would avoid being obliged to you, but I would have my own choice to run me into the debt, that I might have it to boast I had distinguished a man, to whom I would be glad to be obliged, even without the hopes of having it in my power ever to make him a return.

It is impossible for me to come near your Lordship in any kind, and not to receive some favour; and while in appearance I am only making an acknowledgment (with the usual underhand dealing of the world), I am at the same time insinuating my own interest. I cannot give your Lordship your due, without tacking a bill of my own privileges. 'Tis true, if a man never committed a folly, he would never stand in need of a protection. But then power would have nothing to do, and good nature no occasion to show itself; and where those virtues are, 'tis pity they should want objects to shine

1. *Lord Clifford*: son of Richard Boyle, Earl of Burlington and Cork. Congreve's father was in charge of part of the Earl's estates.

upon. I must confess this is no reason why a man should do an idle thing, nor indeed any good excuse for it, when done; yet it reconciles the uses of such authority and goodness to the necessities of our follies, and is a sort of poetical logic, which at this time I would make use of, to argue your Lordship into a protection of this play. It is the first offence I have committed in this kind, or indeed in any kind of poetry, though not the first made public;[2] and, therefore, I hope will the more easily be pardoned. But had it been acted when it was first written, more might have been said in its behalf; ignorance of the town and stage would then have been excuses in a young writer, which now almost four years experience will scarce allow of. Yet I must declare myself sensible of the good nature of the town, in receiving this play so kindly, with all its faults, which I must own were for the most part very industriously covered by the care of the players; for, I think, scarce a character but received all the advantage it would admit of from the justness of action.

As for the critics, my Lord, I have nothing to say to, or against, any of them of any kind; from those who make just exceptions, to those who find fault in the wrong place. I will only make this general answer in behalf of my play (an answer, which Epictetus advises every man to make for himself to his censurers) viz. *That if they who find some faults in it were as intimate with it as I am, they would find a great many more.* This is a confession which I need not to have made; but, however, I can draw this use from it to my own advantage, that I think there are no faults in it but what I do know; which, as I take it, is the first step to an amendment.

Thus I may live in hopes (sometime or other) of making the town amends; but you, my Lord, I never can, though I am ever

Your Lordship's most obedient and most humble servant,

WILL. CONGREVE.

---

2. In addition to some verse, Congreve had also published a prose work, *Incognita*, in 1692.

PROLOGUE

Spoken by Mrs Bracegirdle[1]

How this vile world is changed! In former days,
Prologues were serious speeches before plays;
Grave solemn things, as graces are to feasts;
Where poets begged a blessing from their guests.
But now, no more like suppliants, we come;
A play makes war, and prologue is the drum:
Armed with keen satire, and with pointed wit,
We threaten you who do for judges sit,
To save our plays, or else we'll damn your pit.
But for your comfort, it falls out today,
We've a young author and his first-born play;
So, standing only on his good behaviour,
He's very civil, and entreats your favour.
Not but the man has malice, would he show it,
But on my conscience he's a bashful poet;
You think that strange – no matter, he'll outgrow it.
Well, I'm his advocate – by me he prays you,
(I don't know whether I shall speak to please you)
He prays – O bless me! what shall I do now!
Hang me if I know what he prays, or how!
And 'twas the prettiest prologue, as he wrote it!
Well, the deuce take me, if I han't forgot it.
O Lord, for heaven's sake excuse the play,
Because, you know, if it be damned today,
I shall be hanged for wanting what to say.
For my sake then – but I'm in such confusion,
I cannot stay to hear your resolution.
> [*Runs off.*]

1. *Anne Bracegirdle*: she played the part of Araminta.

DRAMATIS PERSONAE

MEN

HEARTWELL, *a surly old bachelor, pretending to slight women; secretly in love with* SILVIA

BELLMOUR, *in love with* BELINDA

VAINLOVE, *capricious in his love; in love with* ARAMINTA

SHARPER

SIR JOSEPH WITTOLL

CAPT. BLUFFE

FONDLEWIFE, *a banker*

SETTER, *a pimp*

SERVANT, *to* FONDLEWIFE

WOMEN

ARAMINTA, *in love with* VAINLOVE

BELINDA, *her cousin, an affected lady, in love with* BELLMOUR

LAETITIA, *wife to* FONDLEWIFE

SILVIA, VAINLOVE'S *forsaken mistress*

LUCY, *her maid*

BETTY

Boy and Footmen.

The scene,
LONDON.

ACT ONE

SCENE ONE

The street.

[BELLMOUR *and* VAINLOVE *meeting.*]

BELLMOUR: Vainlove! and abroad so early! good morrow; I
thought a contemplative lover could no more have parted with his
bed in a morning, than a' could have slept in't.

VAINLOVE: Bellmour, good morrow. Why, truth on't is, these
early sallies are not usual to me; but business as you see sir –
[*showing letters.*] And business must be followed, or be lost.

BELLMOUR: Pox o' business. – And so must time, my friend, be
close pursued, or lost. Business is the rub of life, perverts our aim,
casts off the bias, and leaves us wide and short of the intended
mark.[1]

VAINLOVE: Pleasure, I guess you mean.

BELLMOUR: Ay, what else has meaning?

VAINLOVE: Oh, the wise will tell you –

BELLMOUR: More than they believe – or understand.

VAINLOVE: How how, Ned, a wise man say more than he understands?

BELLMOUR: Ay, ay, pox, wisdom's nothing but a pretending to
know and believe more than really we do. You read of but one
wise man,[2] and all that he knew was, that he knew nothing. Come
come, leave business to idlers, and wisdom to fools; they have
need of 'em. Wit be my faculty, and pleasure my occupation and

1. *rub . . . aim . . . bias . . . mark*: all terms taken from the game of bowls.
2. *one wise man*: Socrates.

let Father Time shake his glass. Let low and earthy souls grovel till they have worked themselves six foot deep into a grave. Business is not my element; I roll in a higher orb and dwell –

VAINLOVE: In castles i'th'air of thy own building: that's thy element, Ned. Well as high as a flyer as you are, I have a lure may make you stoop. [*Flings a letter.*]

BELLMOUR: Ay, marry sir, I have a hawk's eye at a woman's hand. There's more elegancy in the false spelling of this superscription [*takes up the letter*] than in all Cicero. Let me see. [*Reads.*] How now! Dear, perfidious Vainlove!

VAINLOVE: Hold, hold, 'slife that's the wrong –

BELLMOUR: Nay let's see the name – Silvia! How canst thou be ungrateful to that creature? She's extremely pretty and loves thee entirely. I have heard her breathe such raptures about thee –

VAINLOVE: Ay, or anybody that she's about.

BELLMOUR: No, faith, Frank, you wrong her. She has been just to you.

VAINLOVE: That's pleasant, by my troth from thee, who hast enjoyed her.

BELLMOUR: Never her affections, 'tis true by heaven, she owned it to my face, and blushing like the virgin morn when it disclosed the cheat, which that trusty bawd of nature, night, had hid, confessed her soul was true to you, though I by treachery had stolen the bliss.

VAINLOVE: So was true as turtle[3] – in imagination Ned, ha? Preach this doctrine to husbands, and the married women will adore thee.

BELLMOUR: Why, faith, I think it will do well enough, if the husband be out of the way, for the wife to shew her fondness and impatience of his absence, by choosing a lover as like him as she can, and what is unlike she may help out with her own fancy.

VAINLOVE: But is it not an abuse to the lover to be made a blind of? For she only stalks under him to take aim at her husband.

BELLMOUR: As you say, the abuse is to the lover, not the husband:

3. *turtle*: turtledove.

for 'tis an argument of her great zeal towards him, that she will enjoy him in effigy.

VAINLOVE: It must be a very superstitious country, where such zeal passes for true devotion. I doubt it will be damned by all our Protestant husbands for flat idolatry. – But if you can make Alderman Fondlewife of your persuasion, this letter will be needless.

BELLMOUR: What, the old banker with the handsome wife?

VAINLOVE: Ay.

BELLMOUR: Let me see – Laetitia! Oh 'tis a delicious morsel. Dear Frank, thou art the truest friend in the world!

VAINLOVE: Ay, am I not? To be continually starting of hares for you to course. We were certainly cut out for one another; for my temper quits an amour, just where thine takes it up. – But read that. It is an appointment for me, this evening, when Fondlewife will be gone out of town, to meet the master of a ship about the return of a venture which he's in danger of losing. Read, read.

BELLMOUR [reads]: Hum, Hum – *Out of town this evening, and talks of sending for Mr Spintext to keep me company; but I'll take care he shall not be at home.* Good! Spintext? Oh, the fanatic,[4] one-eyed parson!

VAINLOVE: Ay.

BELLMOUR [reads]: Hum, hum – *That your conversation will be much more agreeable, if you can counterfeit his habit to blind the servants.* Very good! Then I must be disguised – with all my heart. It adds a gusto to an amour; gives it the greater resemblance of theft; and among us lewd mortals, the deeper the sin the sweeter. Frank, I'm amazed at thy good nature.

VAINLOVE: Faith, I hate love when 'tis forced upon a man, as I do wine. And this business is none of my seeking; I only happened to be once or twice where Laetitia was the handsomest woman in company, so consequently applied myself to her – and it seems she has taken me at my word. Had you been there or anybody, 't had been the same.

BELLMOUR: I wish I may succeed as the same.

VAINLOVE: Never doubt it; for if the spirit of cuckoldom be once

---

4. *fanatic*: hostile or derisive epithet for Protestant non-conformists.

raised up in a woman, the devil can't lay it, till she has done't.

BELLMOUR: Prithee, what sort of fellow is Fondlewife?

VAINLOVE: A kind of mongrel zealot, sometimes very precise and peevish. But I have seen him pleasant enough in his way; much addicted to jealousy, but more to fondness; so that as he is often jealous without a cause, he's as often satisfied without reason.

BELLMOUR: A very even temper and fit for my purpose. I must get your man Setter to provide my disguise.

VAINLOVE: Ay, you may take him for good-and-all if you will, for you have made him fit for nobody else. Well –

BELLMOUR: You're going to visit in return of Silvia's letter? Poor rogue. Any hour of the day or night will serve her. But do you know nothing of a new rival there?

VAINLOVE: Yes, Heartwell, that surly, old, pretended woman-hater thinks her virtuous; that's one reason why I fail her. I would have her fret herself out of conceit with me, that she may entertain some thoughts of him. I know he visits her every day.

BELLMOUR: Yet rails on still, and thinks his love unknown to us. A little time will swell him so, he must be forced to give it birth, and the discovery must needs be very pleasant from himself, to see what pains he will take, and how he will strain to be delivered of a secret, when he has miscarried on't already.

VAINLOVE: Well good morrow. Let's dine together, I'll meet at the old place.

BELLMOUR: With all my heart; it lies convenient for us, to pay our afternoon service to our mistresses. I find I am damnably in love; I'm so uneasy for not seeing Belinda yesterday.

VAINLOVE: But I saw my Araminta, yet am as impatient.
     [Exit.]

BELLMOUR: Why, what a cormorant in love am I! Who, not contented with the slavery of honourable love in one place, and the pleasure of enjoying some half a score mistresses of my own acquiring, must yet take Vainlove's business upon my hands, because it lay too heavy upon his; so am not only forced to lie with other men's wives for 'em, but must also undertake the harder task, of obliging their mistresses. – I must take up, or I shall never hold out; flesh and blood cannot bear it always.

[*Enter* SHARPER.]

SHARPER: I'm sorry to see this, Ned. Once a man comes to his soliloquies, I give him for gone.

BELLMOUR: Sharper, I'm glad to see thee.

SHARPER: What, is Belinda cruel, that you are so thoughtful?

BELLMOUR: No faith, not for that. – But there's a business of consequence fallen out today that requires some consideration.

SHARPER: Prithee, what mighty business of consequence canst thou have?

BELLMOUR: Why, you must know, 'tis a piece of work toward the finishing of an alderman; it seems I must put the last hand to it and dub him cuckold, that he may be of equal dignity with the rest of his brethren. So I must beg Belinda's pardon –

SHARPER: Faith, e'en give her over for good-and-all; you can have no hopes of getting her for a mistress, and she is too proud, too inconstant, too affected, and too witty, and too handsome for a wife.

BELLMOUR: But she can't have too much money. – There's twelve thousand pound, Tom. – 'Tis true she is excessively foppish and affected, but in my conscience I believe the baggage loves me, for she never speaks well of me herself, nor suffers anybody else to rail at me. Then, as I told you, there's twelve thousand pound – hum – why, faith, upon second thoughts, she does not appear to be so very affected neither. Give her her due, I think the woman's a woman, and that's all. As such I'm sure I shall like her; for the devil take me if I don't love all the sex.

SHARPER: And here comes one who swears as heartily he hates all the sex.

[*Enter* HEARTWELL.]

BELLMOUR: Who, Heartwell? Ay, but he knows better things. – How now, George, where hast thou been snarling odious truths, and entertaining company like a physician, with discourse of their diseases and infirmities? What fine lady hast thou been putting out of conceit with herself, and persuading that the face she had been making all the morning was none of her own? For I know thou art as unmannerly and as unwelcome to a woman, as a looking-glass after the small-pox.

HEARTWELL: I confess I have not been sneering fulsome lies and nauseous flattery, fawning upon a little tawdry whore, that will fawn upon me again, and entertain any puppy that comes, like a tumbler with the same tricks over and over. For such I guess may have been your late employment.

BELLMOUR: Would thou had'st come a little sooner. Vainlove would have wrought thy conversion and been a champion for the cause.

HEARTWELL: What, has he been here? That's one of love's April-fools, is always upon some errand that's to no purpose, ever embarking in adventures, yet never comes to harbour.

SHARPER: That's because he always sets out in foul weather, loves to buffet with the winds, meet the tide, and sail in the teeth of opposition.

HEARTWELL: What, has he not dropped anchor at Araminta?

BELLMOUR: Truth on't is she fits his temper best, is a kind of floating island; sometimes seems in reach, then vanishes and keeps him busied in the search.

SHARPER: She had need have a good share of sense, to manage so capricious a lover.

BELLMOUR: Faith, I don't know, he's of a temper the most easy to himself in the world; he takes as much always of an amour as he cares for, and quits it when it grows stale or unpleasant.

SHARPER: An argument of very little passion, very good understanding, and very ill nature.

HEARTWELL: And proves that Vainlove plays the fool with discretion.

SHARPER: You, Bellmour, are bound in gratitude to stickle for him;[5] you with pleasure reap that fruit which he takes pains to sow. He does the drudgery in the mine, and you stamp your image on the gold.

BELLMOUR: He's of another opinion, and says I do the drudgery in the mine. Well, we have each our share of sport, and each that which he likes best; 'tis his diversion to set, 'tis mine to cover the partridge.

5. *stickle for him*: take his part.

HEARTWELL: And it should be mine to let 'em go again.

SHARPER: Not till you had mouthed a little, George, I think that's all thou art fit for now.

HEARTWELL: Good Mr Young-fellow, you're mistaken; as able as yourself and as nimble too, though I mayn't have so much mercury[6] in my limbs. 'Tis true indeed, I don't force appetite, but wait the natural call of my lust, and think it time enough to be lewd after I have had the temptation.

BELLMOUR: Time enough! Ay, too soon, I should rather have expected, from a person of your gravity.

HEARTWELL: Yet it is oftentimes too late with some of you young, termagant flashy sinners – you have all the guilt of the intention, and none of the pleasure of the practice. 'Tis true you are so eager in pursuit of the temptation that you save the devil the trouble of leading you into it. Nor is it out of discretion that you don't swallow that very hook yourselves have baited, but you are cloyed with the preparative, and what you mean for a whet, turns the edge of your puny stomachs. Your love is like your courage, which you show for the first year or two upon all occasions; till in a little time, being disabled or disarmed, you abate of your vigour; and that daring blade which was so often drawn, is bound to the peace for ever after.

BELLMOUR: Thou art an old fornicator of a singular good principle, indeed! And art for encouraging youth, that they may be as wicked as thou art at thy years.

HEARTWELL: I am for having everybody be what they pretend to be; a whoremaster be a whoremaster, and not, like Vainlove, kiss a lap-dog with passion, when it would disgust him from the lady's own lips.

BELLMOUR: That only happens sometimes, where the dog has the sweeter breath, for the more cleanly conveyance. But George, you must not quarrel with little gallantries of this nature; women are often won by 'em. Who would refuse to kiss a lap-dog, if it were preliminary to the lips of his lady?

SHARPER: Or omit playing with her fan, and cooling her if she were

6. *mercury*: used in treating venereal disease.

hot, when it might entitle him to the office of warming her when she should be cold?

BELLMOUR: What is it to read a play in a rainy day, when it may be the means of getting into a fair lady's books? Though you should be now and then interrupted in a witty scene, and she perhaps preserve her laughter till the jest were over, even this may be born with, considering the reward in prospect.

HEARTWELL: I confess you that are women's asses bear greater burdens, are forced to undergo dressing, dancing, singing, sighing, whining, rhyming, flattering, lying, grinning, cringing, and the drudgery of loving to boot.

BELLMOUR: O brute, the drudgery of loving!

HEARTWELL: Ay, why to come to love through all these encumbrances is like coming to an estate overcharged with debts which, by the time you have paid, yields no further profit than what the bare tillage and manuring of the land will produce at the expense of your own sweat.

BELLMOUR: Prithee, how dost thou love?

SHARPER: He! He hates the sex.

HEARTWELL: So I hate physic[7] too – yet I may love to take it for my health.

BELLMOUR: Well, come off, George, if at any time you should be taken straying.

SHARPER: He has need of such an excuse, considering the present state of his body.

HEARTWELL: How d'ye mean?

SHARPER: Why, if whoring be purging (as you call it), then I may say marriage is entering into a course of physic.

BELLMOUR: How George, does the wind blow there?

HEARTWELL: It will as soon blow North and by South – marry quotha! I hope in heaven I have a greater portion of grace, and I think I have baited too many of those traps, to be caught in one myself.

BELLMOUR: Who the devil would have thee? Unless 'twere an

7. *physic*: medicine.

oyster-woman, to propagate young fry for Billingsgate[8] – thy talent will never recommend thee to anything of better quality.

HEARTWELL: My talent is chiefly that of speaking truth, which I don't expect should ever recommend me to people of quality. I thank heaven, I have very honestly purchased the hatred of all the great families in town.

SHARPER: And you in return of spleen hate them. But could you hope to be received into the alliance of a noble family –

HEARTWELL: No, I hope I shall never merit that affliction – to be punished with a wife of birth – be a stag of the first head[9] and bear my horns aloft, like one of the supporters of my wife's coat.[10] 'S'death, I would not be a cuckold to e'er an illustrious whore in England.

BELLMOUR: What, not to make your family, man! and provide for your children!

SHARPER: For her children, you mean.

HEARTWELL: Ay, there you've nicked it – there's the devil upon devil. Oh, the pride and joy of heart 'twould be to me, to have my son and heir resemble such a Duke – to have a fleering coxcomb scoff and cry, mister, your son's mighty like his Grace, has just his smile and air of's face. Then replies another – methink he has more of the Marquess of such a place, about his nose and eyes; though a' has my Lord what d'ye-call's mouth to a tittle. Then I to put it off as unconcerned, come chuck the infant under the chin, force a smile and cry, ay, the boy takes after his mother's relations – when the devil and she knows 'tis a little compound of the whole body of nobility.

BELLMOUR:
SHARPER: } Ha, ha, ha!

BELLMOUR: Well, but George, I have one question to ask you –

HEARTWELL [*looking on his watch*]: Pox, I have prattled away my

8. *Billingsgate*: fish market in London.
9. *stag of the first head*: a deer when its antlers are first developed; here, figuratively, a cuckold.
10. *coat*: coat of arms.

time – I hope you are in no haste for an answer, for I shan't stay now.

BELLMOUR: Nay, prithee, George –

HEARTWELL: No, besides my business, I see a fool coming this way. Adieu.

    [*Exit.*]

BELLMOUR: What does he mean? Oh, here he comes – stand close; let 'em pass.

    [SIR JOSEPH WITTOLL *and* CAPT. BLUFFE *cross the stage.*]

SHARPER: What in the name of wonder is it?

BELLMOUR: Why, a fool.

SHARPER: 'Tis a tawdry outside.

BELLMOUR: And a very beggarly lining – yet he may be worth your acquaintance. A little of thy chemistry, Tom, may extract gold from that dirt.

SHARPER: Say you so? faith, I am as poor as a chemist[11] and would be as industrious. But what was he that followed him, is not he a dragon that watches those golden pippins?[12]

BELLMOUR: Hang him, no, he a dragon! If he be, 'tis a very peaceful one. I can ensure his anger dormant; or should he seem to rouse, 'tis but well lashing him, and he will sleep like a top.

SHARPER: Ay, is he of that kidney?

BELLMOUR: Yet is adored by that bigot, Sir Joseph Wittoll, as the image of valour. He calls him his Back, and indeed they are never asunder. Yet last night, I know not by what mischance, the knight was alone, and had fallen into the hands of some nightwalkers, who I suppose would have pillaged him. But I chanced to come by and rescued him, though I believe he was heartily frightened; for as soon as ever he was loose, he ran away without staying to see who helped him.

SHARPER: Is that bully of his in the army?

BELLMOUR: No, but is a pretender, and wears the habit of a soldier, which nowadays as often cloaks cowardice, as a black gown does atheism. You must know he has been abroad – went purely to run

---

11. *chemist*: alchemist.
12. *golden pippins*: golden apples of the Hesperides.

away from a campaign; enriched himself with the plunder of a few
oaths – and here vents 'em against the general, who slighting men
of merit, and preferring only those of interest, has made him quit
the service.

SHARPER: Wherein, no doubt, he magnifies his own performance.

BELLMOUR: Speaks miracles, is the drum to his own praise – the
only implement of a soldier he resembles; like that, being full of
blustering noise and emptiness.

SHARPER: And like that, of no use but to be beaten.

BELLMOUR: Right, but then the comparison breaks, for he will take
a drubbing with as little noise as a pulpit cushion.

SHARPER: His name, and I have done.

BELLMOUR: Why that, to pass it current too, he has gilded with a
title; he is called, Captain Bluffe.

SHARPER: Well, I'll endeavour his acquaintance. You steer another
course, are bound

For love's island; I, for the golden coast.
May each succeed in what he wishes most.

[*Exeunt.*]

ACT TWO

SCENE ONE

[SIR JOSEPH WITTOLL, SHARPER *following*.]

SHARPER: Sure that's he, and alone.

SIR JOSEPH: Um. – Ay, this, this is the very damned place; the inhuman cannibals, the bloody-minded villains would have butchered me last night. No doubt, they would have flayed me alive, have sold my skin, and devoured my members.

SHARPER: How's this!

SIR JOSEPH: An it hadn't been for a civil gentleman as came by and frightened 'em away – but, agad, I durst not stay to give him thanks.

SHARPER: This must be Bellmour he means – ha! I have a thought –

SIR JOSEPH: Zooks, would the Captain would come; the very remembrance makes me quake; agad, I shall never be reconciled to this place heartily.

SHARPER: 'Tis but trying, and being where I am at worst. Now, luck! [*Aloud.*] Cursed fortune! this must be the place, this damned unlucky place –

SIR JOSEPH: Agad, and so 'tis – why, here has been more mischief done I perceive.

SHARPER: No, 'tis gone, 'tis lost – ten thousand devils on that chance which drew me hither; ay here, just here, this spot to me is hell; nothing to be found but the despair of what I've lost.

[*Looking about as in search.*]

SIR JOSEPH: Poor gentleman – by the Lord Harry I'll stay no longer, for I have found too –

SHARPER: Ha! who's that has found? What have you found? Restore it quickly, or by –

SIR JOSEPH: Not I sir, not I, as I've a soul to be saved, I have found nothing but what has been to my loss, as I may say, and as you were saying, sir.

SHARPER: Oh your servant, sir; you are safe then it seems. 'Tis an ill wind that blows nobody good. Well, you may rejoice over my ill fortune, since it paid the price of your ransom.

SIR JOSEPH: I rejoice! agad, not I, sir; I'm sorry for your loss, with all my heart, blood and guts, sir; and if you did but know me, you'd ne'er say I were so ill-natured.

SHARPER: Know you! Why, can you be so ungrateful, to forget me?

SIR JOSEPH: O Lord, forget him! No, no, sir, I don't forget you – because I never saw your face before, agad. Ha, ha, ha!

SHARPER [angrily]: How?

SIR JOSEPH: Stay, stay sir, let me recollect – [aside] he's a damned angry fellow – I believe I had better remember him, till I can get out of his sight; but out o'sight out o'mind, agad.

SHARPER: Methought the service I did you last night sir, in preserving you from those ruffians, might have taken better root in your shallow memory.

SIR JOSEPH: Gads-daggers-belts-blades-and scabbards, this is the very gentleman! How shall I make him a return suitable to the greatness of his merit? I had a pretty thing to that purpose, if he hasn't frighted it out of my memory. Hem, hem! Sir, I must submissively implore your pardon for my transgression of ingratitude and omission; having my entire dependence, sir, upon the superfluity of your goodness, which, like an inundation will I hope totally immerge the recollection of my error, and leave me floating in your sight, upon the full-blown bladders of repentance – by the help of which I shall once more hope to swim into your favour.

[Bows.]

SHARPER: So—h, O sir, I am easily pacified. The acknowledgment of a gentleman –

SIR JOSEPH: Acknowledgment! Sir I am all over acknowledgment, and will not stick to show it in the greatest extremity, by night, or by day, in sickness, or in health, winter, or summer, all seasons and occasions shall testify the reality and gratitude of your superabundant humble servant Sir Joseph Wittoll, Knight. Hem! Hem!

SHARPER: Sir Joseph Wittoll!

SIR JOSEPH: The same, sir, of Wittoll-hall in Comitatu Bucks.[1]

SHARPER: Is it possible! Then I am happy to have obliged the mirror of knighthood and pink of courtesy in the age. Let me embrace you.

SIR JOSEPH: O Lord, sir!

SHARPER: My loss I esteem as a trifle repaid with interest, since it has purchased me the friendship and acquaintance of the person in the world whose character I admire.

SIR JOSEPH: You are only pleased to say so, sir. – But pray, if I may be so bold, what is that loss you mention?

SHARPER: O term it no longer so, sir. In the scuffle last night I only dropped a bill of a hundred pound, which I confess I came, half despairing, to recover; but thanks to my better fortune –

SIR JOSEPH: You have found it, sir, then it seems? I profess I'm heartily glad.

SHARPER: Sir, your humble servant – I don't question but you are, that you have so cheap an opportunity of expressing your gratitude and generosity; since the refunding so trivial a sum will wholly acquit you and doubly engage me.

SIR JOSEPH [aside]: What a dickens does he mean by a trivial sum? But ha'n't you found it, sir?

SHARPER: No otherwise, I vow to Gad, but in my hopes in you, sir.

SIR JOSEPH: Humph!

SHARPER: But that's sufficient. – 'Twere injustice to doubt the honour of Sir Joseph Wittoll.

SIR JOSEPH: O Lord, sir.

SHARPER: You are above (I'm sure) a thought so low, to suffer me to lose what was ventured in your service; nay, 'twas in a manner paid down for your deliverance; 'twas so much lent you. And you scorn, I'll say that for you –

SIR JOSEPH: Nay, I'll say that for myself (with your leave, sir), I do scorn a dirty thing. But agad! I'm a little out of pocket at present.

1. *Comitatu Bucks*: Buckinghamshire.

SHARPER: Pshaw! you can't want a hundred pound. Your word is sufficient anywhere. 'Tis but borrowing so much dirt; you have large acres and can soon repay it. Money is but dirt, Sir Joseph – mere dirt.

SIR JOSEPH: But, I profess, 'tis a dirt I have washed my hands of at present; I have laid it all out upon my Back.

SHARPER: Are you so extravagant in clothes, Sir Joseph?

SIR JOSEPH: Ha, ha, ha, a very good jest, I profess, ha, ha, ha, a very good jest, and I did not know that I had said it and that's a better jest than t'other. 'Tis a sign you and I ha'n't been long acquainted; you have lost a good jest for want of knowing me. – I only mean a friend of mine whom I call my Back; he sticks as close to me, and follows me through all dangers. He is indeed back, breast and headpiece as it were to me – agad, he's a brave fellow. Pauh, I am quite another thing when I am with him; I don't fear the devil (God bless us) almost if he be by. Ah – had he been with me last night –

SHARPER [angrily]: If he had sir, what then? He could have done no more, nor perhaps have suffered so much. Had he a hundred pound to lose?

SIR JOSEPH: O Lord, sir, by no means (but I might have saved a hundred pound). I meant innocently, as I hope to be saved, sir (a damned hot fellow); only, as I was saying, I let him have all my ready money to redeem his great sword from limbo.[2] – But sir, I have a letter of credit to Alderman Fondlewife, as far as two hundred pound, and this afternoon you shall see I am a person, such a one as you would wish to have met with.

SHARPER [aside]: That you are I'll be sworn. [Aloud.] Why, that's great and like yourself.

[Enter BLUFFE.]

SIR JOSEPH: Oh, here 'a comes. – Ah, my Hector of Troy, welcome my bully, my Back; agad, my heart has gone a-pit-pat for thee.

BLUFFE: How how, my young knight? Not for fear I hope; he that knows me must be a stranger to fear.

2. *from limbo*: out of pawn.

SIR JOSEPH: Nay, agad, I hate fear ever since I had like to have died of a fright. But –

BLUFFE: But? Look you here boy, here's your antidote, here's your Jesuit's powder[3] for a shaking fit. – But who hast thou got with thee, is he of mettle?

[*Laying his hand upon his sword.*]

SIR JOSEPH: Ay bully, a devilish smart fellow, a' will fight like a cock.

BLUFFE: Say you so? then I honour him. But has he been abroad? for every cock will fight upon his own dunghill.

SIR JOSEPH: I don't know, but I'll present you –

BLUFFE: I'll recommend myself. – Sir, I honour you; I understand you love fighting, I reverence a man that loves fighting. Sir, I kiss your hilts.

SHARPER: Sir, your servant. But you are misinformed, for unless it be to serve my particular friend, as Sir Joseph here, my country, or my religion, or in some very justifiable cause, I'm not for it.

BLUFFE: O Lord, I beg your pardon, sir, I find you are not of my palate; you can't relish a dish of fighting without sweet sauce. Now I think fighting for fighting sake's sufficient cause; fighting to me's religion and the laws.

SIR JOSEPH: Ah, well said my hero; was not that great, sir? By the Lord Harry he says true; fighting is meat, drink and cloth to him. But Back, this gentleman is one of the best friends I have in the world, and saved my life last night. – You know I told you.

BLUFFE: Ay! Then I honour him again. – Sir, may I crave your name?

SHARPER: Ay sir, my name's Sharper.

SIR JOSEPH: Pray, Mr Sharper, embrace my Back. – Very well. – By the Lord Harry, Mr Sharper, he's as brave a fellow as Cannibal, are not you bully – Back?

SHARPER: Hannibal I believe you mean, Sir Joseph.

BLUFFE: Undoubtedly he did, sir; faith, Hannibal was a very pretty fellow. But, Sir Joseph, comparisons are odious – Hannibal was a very pretty fellow in those days, it must be granted. But alas, sir,

3. *Jesuit's powder*: quinine; first brought to Europe from Peru by Jesuit missionaries.

were he alive now, he would be nothing, nothing in the earth.

SHARPER: How sir? I make a doubt if there be at this day a greater General breathing.

BLUFFE: Oh, excuse me, sir; have you served abroad, sir?

SHARPER: Not I really, sir.

BLUFFE: Oh, I thought so. Why then you can know nothing, sir; I'm afraid you scarce know the history of the late war in Flanders,[4] with all its particulars.

SHARPER: Not I, sir, no more than public letters or Gazettes tell us.

BLUFFE: Gazette! Why, there again now. – Why, sir, there are not three words of truth, the year round, put into the Gazette. I'll tell you a strange thing now as to that. – You must know, sir, I was resident in Flanders the last campaign, had a small post there; but no matter for that. Perhaps, sir, there was a scarce anything of moment done but an humble servant of yours, that shall be nameless, was an eye-witness of – I won't say had the greatest share in't. Though I might say that too, since I name nobody you know. – Well, Mr Sharper, would you think it? In all this time – as I hope for a truncheon[5] – this rascally Gazette-writer never so much as once mentioned me – Not once, by the wars. – Took no more notice than as if Noll Bluffe had not been in the land of the living.

SHARPER: Strange!

SIR JOSEPH: Yet, by the Lord Harry 'tis true, Mr Sharper, for I went every day to coffee-houses to read the Gazette myself.

BLUFFE: Ay, ay, no matter. – You see, Mr Sharper, after all I am content to retire. – Live a private person. – Scipio[6] and others have done it.

SHARPER [aside]: Impudent rogue.

SIR JOSEPH: Ay, this damned modesty of yours. – Agad, if he would put in for't he might be made General himself yet.

BLUFFE: Oh, fie, no Sir Joseph! You know I hate this.

SIR JOSEPH: Let me but tell Mr Sharper a little, how you ate fire

4. *late war in Flanders*: probably the indecisive campaign of 1691.

5. *truncheon*: a marshal's baton.

6. *Scipio*: Scipio Africanus, Roman general. He defeated Hannibal but later retired from public life because of personal and political rivalries.

once out of the mouth of a cannon – agad he did; those impenetrable whiskers of his have confronted flames –

BLUFFE: Death, what do you mean, Sir Joseph?

SIR JOSEPH: Look you now, I tell you he's so modest he'll own nothing.

BLUFFE [*angrily*]: Pish, you have put me out, I have forgot what I was about. Pray hold your tongue, and give me leave.

SIR JOSEPH: I am dumb.

BLUFFE: This sword I think I was telling you of, Mr Sharper – this sword I'll maintain to be the best divine, anatomist, lawyer or casuist in Europe; it shall decide a controversy or split a cause –

SIR JOSEPH: Nay, now I must speak; it will split a hair, by the Lord Harry, I have seen it.

BLUFFE: Zoons sir, it's a lie, you have not seen it, nor shan't see it; sir, I say you can't see; what d'ye say to that now?

SIR JOSEPH: I am blind.

BLUFFE: Death, had any other man interrupted me –

SIR JOSEPH: Good Mr Sharper, speak to him; I dare not look that way.

SHARPER: Captain, Sir Joseph's penitent.

BLUFFE: Oh I am calm sir, calm as a discharged culverin.[7] But 'twas indiscreet, when you know what will provoke me. – Nay, come Sir Joseph, you know my heat's soon over.

SIR JOSEPH: Well I am a fool sometimes – but I'm sorry.

BLUFFE: Enough.

SIR JOSEPH: Come, we'll go take a glass to drown animosities. Mr Sharper, will you partake?

SHARPER: I wait on you sir; nay, pray Captain – you are Sir Joseph's Back.

[*Exeunt.*]

7. *culverin*: a large cannon.

SCENE TWO

Scene changes to lodgings.

[*Enter* ARAMINTA, BELINDA.]

BELINDA: Ah! nay dear – prithee good, dear sweet cousin, no more. O gad, I swear you'd make one sick to hear you.

ARAMINTA: Bless me! What have I said to move you thus?

BELINDA: Oh, you have raved, talked idly, and all in commendation of that filthy, awkward, two legged creature, man. – You don't know what you said, your fever has transported you.

ARAMINTA: If love be the fever which you mean, kind heaven avert the cure. Let me have oil to feed that flame and never let it be extinct, till I myself am ashes.

BELINDA: There was a whine – O gad, I hate your horrid fancy. This love is the devil, and sure to be in love is to be possessed. – 'Tis in the head, the heart, the blood, the – all over. – O gad, you are quite spoiled. I shall loathe the sight of mankind for your sake.

ARAMINTA: Fie, this is gross affectation. – A little of Bellmour's company would change the scene.

BELINDA: Filthy fellow! I wonder cousin –

ARAMINTA: I wonder, cousin, you should imagine I don't perceive you love him.

BELINDA: Oh, I love your hideous fancy! Ha, ha, ha, love a man!

ARAMINTA: Love a man! yes – you would not love a beast.

BELINDA: Of all beasts not an ass – which is so like your Vainlove. – Lard, I have seen an ass look so chagrin, ha, ha, ha, (you must pardon me, I can't help laughing) that an absolute lover would have concluded the poor creature to have had darts, and flames, and altars, and all that in his breast. Araminta, come I'll talk seriously to you now; could you but see with my eyes the buffoonery of one scene of address – a lover, set out with all his equipage and appurtenances; O gad! sure you would. But you play the game, and consequently can't see the miscarriages obvious to every stander-by.

ARAMINTA: Yes, yes, I can see something near it when you and Bellmour meet. You don't know that you dreamt of Bellmour last night, and called him aloud in your sleep.

BELINDA: Pish, I can't help dreaming of the devil sometimes; would you from thence infer I love him?

ARAMINTA: But that's not all; you caught me in your arms when you named him, and pressed me to your bosom. – Sure if I had not pinched you till you waked, you had stifled me with kisses.

BELINDA: O barbarous aspersion!

ARAMINTA: No aspersion, cousin, we are alone. – Nay, I can tell you more.

BELINDA: I deny it all.

ARAMINTA: What, before you hear it?

BELINDA: My denial is premeditated like your malice. Lard, cousin, you talk oddly. – Whatever the matter is, O my Sol,[8] I'm afraid you'll follow evil courses.

ARAMINTA: Ha, ha, ha, this is pleasant.

BELINDA: You may laugh, but –

ARAMINTA: Ha, ha, ha!

BELINDA: You think the malicious grin becomes you. The devil take Bellmour! – Why do you tell me of him?

ARAMINTA: Oh, is it come out? Now you are angry, I am sure you love him. I tell nobody else, cousin – I have not betrayed you yet.

BELINDA: Prithee, tell it all the world, it's false. – [Calls.] Betty!

ARAMINTA: Come then, kiss and friends.

BELINDA: Pish.

ARAMINTA: Prithee don't be so peevish.

BELINDA: Prithee don't be so impertinent.

ARAMINTA: Ha, ha, ha!

[Enter BETTY.]

BETTY: Did your ladyship call, madam?

BELINDA: Get my hoods and tippet,[9] and bid the footman call a chair.[10]

8. Sol: Apollo, the sun.
9. tippet: a cape or short cloak, usually of fur or wool.
10. chair: sedan-chair.

[*Exit* BETTY.]

ARAMINTA: I hope you are not going out in dudgeon, cousin.

[*Enter* FOOTMAN.]

FOOTMAN: Madam, there are –

BELINDA: Is there a chair?

FOOTMAN: No, madam, there are Mr Bellmour and Mr Vainlove to wait upon your ladyship.

ARAMINTA: Are they below?

FOOTMAN: No, madam, they sent before, to know if you were at home.

BELINDA: The visit's to you, cousin. I suppose I am at my liberty.

ARAMINTA: Be ready to show 'em up.

[*Exit* FOOTMAN.]

I can't tell, cousin, I believe we are equally concerned. But if you continue your humour, it won't be very entertaining. [*Aside.*] I know she'd fain be persuaded to stay.

BELINDA: I shall oblige you, in leaving you to the full and free enjoyment of that conversation you admire.

[*Enter* BETTY, *with hoods and looking-glass.*]

BELINDA: Let me see; hold the glass. – Lard I look wretchedly today.

ARAMINTA [*putting on her hoods*]: Betty, why don't you help my cousin?

BELINDA: Hold off your fists, and see that he gets a chair with a high roof, or a very low seat. Stay, come back here you Mrs Fidget – you are so ready to go to the footman. – Here, take 'em all again, my mind's changed; I won't go.

[*Exit* BETTY *with the things.*]

ARAMINTA: So, this I expected. You won't oblige me then, cousin, and let me have all the company to myself?

BELINDA: No; upon deliberation, I have too much charity to trust you to yourself. The devil watches all opportunities, and in this favourable disposition of your mind, heaven knows how far you may be tempted. I am tender of your reputation.

ARAMINTA: I am obliged to you – but who's malicious now, Belinda?

BELINDA: Not I; witness my heart I stay out of pure affection.

ARAMINTA: In my conscience I believe you.

    [*Enter* BELLMOUR, VAINLOVE.]

BELLMOUR: So Fortune be praised! To find you both within, ladies, is –

ARAMINTA: No miracle, I hope.

BELLMOUR: Not o' your side, madam, I confess – but my tyrant there and I are two buckets that can never come together.

BELINDA: Nor are ever like – yet we often meet and clash.

BELLMOUR: How never like? marry, Hymen forbid. But this it is to run so extravagantly in debt; I have laid out such a world of love in your service that you think you can never able to pay me all, so shun me for the same reason that you would a dun.

BELINDA: Ay, on my conscience, and the most impertinent and troublesome of duns. – A dun for money will be quiet, when he sees his debtor has not wherewithal, but a dun for love is an eternal torment that never rests –

BELLMOUR: Till he has created love where there was none, and then gets it for his pains. For importunity in love, like importunity at court, first creates its own interest, and then pursues it for the favour.

ARAMINTA: Favours that are got by impudence and importunity are like discoveries from the rack, when the afflicted person, for his ease, sometimes confesses secrets his heart knows nothing of.

VAINLOVE: I should rather think favours, so gained, to be due rewards to indefatigable devotion. For as love is a deity, he must be served by prayer.

BELINDA: O gad, would you would all pray to love then, and let us alone.

VAINLOVE: You are the temples of love, and 'tis through you our devotion must be conveyed.

ARAMINTA: Rather poor silly idols of your own making, which upon the least displeasure you forsake, and set up new. – Every man now changes his mistress and his religion, as his humour varies or his interest.

VAINLOVE: O madam –

ARAMINTA: Nay come, I find we are growing serious, and then we are in great danger of being dull. If my music master be not gone,

I'll entertain you with a new song which comes pretty near my own opinion of love and your sex. [*Calls.*] Who's there?

[*Enter* FOOTMAN.]

Is Mr Gavot gone?

FOOTMAN: Only to the next door, madam; I'll call him.

[*Exit.*]

BELLMOUR: Why, you won't hear me with patience?

ARAMINTA: What's the matter, cousin?

BELLMOUR: Nothing, madam, only –

BELINDA: Prithee hold thy tongue. – Lard, he has so pestered me with flames and stuff, I think I shan't endure the sight of a fire this twelvemonth.

BELLMOUR: Yet all can't melt that cruel, frozen heart.

BELINDA: O gad, I hate your hideous fancy – you said that once before. – If you must talk impertinently, for heaven's sake let it be with variety; don't come always, like the devil, wrapped in flames. I'll not hear a sentence more, that begins with an 'I burn', or an 'I beseech you, madam'.

BELLMOUR: But tell me how you would be adored; I am very tractable.

BELINDA: Then know, I would be adored in silence.

BELLMOUR: Humph, I thought so, that you might have all the talk to yourself. You had better let me speak; for if my thoughts fly to any pitch, I shall make villainous signs.

BELINDA: What will you get by that? To make such signs as I won't understand.

BELLMOUR: Ay, but if I'm tongue-tied, I must have all my actions free to – quicken your apprehension. And, i'gad, let me tell you, my standing argument is depressed in dumb show.

[*Enter music master.*]

ARAMINTA: Oh, I am glad we shall have a song to divert the discourse. Pray oblige us with the last new song.

(*Song*[11])

I

Thus, to a ripe, consenting maid,
Poor, old, repenting Delia said,
Would you long preserve your lover?
Would you still his goddess reign?
Never let him all discover,
Never let him much obtain.

II

Men will admire, adore and die,
While wishing at your feet they lie:
But admitting their embraces,
Wakes 'em from the golden dream;
Nothing's new besides our faces,
Every woman is the same.

ARAMINTA: So, how d'ye like the song, gentlemen?

BELLMOUR: Oh, very well performed – but I don't much admire
the words.

ARAMINTA: I expected it; there's too much truth in 'em. If Mr
Gavot will walk with us in the garden, we'll have it once again. –
You may like it better at second hearing. You'll bring my cousin?

BELLMOUR: Faith, madam, I dare not speak to her, but I'll make
signs.

[*Addresses* BELINDA *in dumb show*.]

BELINDA: O foh, your dumb rhetoric is more ridiculous than your
talking impertinence, as an ape is a much more troublesome
animal than a parrot.

ARAMINTA: Ay, cousin, and 'tis a sign the creatures mimic nature
well, for there are few men but do more silly things than they say.

BELLMOUR: Well, I find my apishness has paid the ransom for my
speech, and set it at liberty – though, I confess, I could be well
enough pleased to drive on a love-bargain in that silent manner. –
'Twould save a man a world of lying and swearing at the year's
end. Besides, I have had a little experience, that brings to my
mind –

11. The music for the play was composed by Henry Purcell.

When wit and reason both have failed to move;
Kind looks and action (from success) do prove,
Even silence may be eloquent in love.

[*Exeunt omnes.*]

ACT THREE

SCENE ONE

The street.

[SILVIA *and* LUCY.]

SILVIA: Will a' not come then?

LUCY: Yes, yes, come, I warrant him, if you will go in and be ready to receive him.

SILVIA: Why did you not tell me? Whom mean you?

LUCY: Whom you should mean, Heartwell.

SILVIA: Senseless creature, I meant my Vainlove.

LUCY: You may as soon hope to recover your own maidenhead as his love. Therefore e'en set your heart at rest, and in the name of opportunity mind your own business. Strike Heartwell home, before the bait's worn off the hook. Age will come. He nibbled fairly yesterday, and no doubt will be eager enough today to swallow the temptation.

SILVIA: Well, since there's no remedy. Yet tell me – for I would know, though to the anguish of my soul; how did he refuse? Tell me – how did he receive my letter, in anger or in scorn?

LUCY: Neither; but what was ten times worse, with damned, senseless indifference. By this light I could have spit in his face. Receive it! Why he received it as I would one of your lovers that should come empty-handed; as a court lord does his mercer's bill, or a begging dedication; – a' received it, as if 't had been a letter from his wife.

SILVIA: What, did he not read it?

LUCY: Hummed it over, gave you his respects, and said he would take time to peruse it – but then he was in haste.

SILVIA: Respects, and peruse it! He's gone, and Araminta has bewitched him from me. – Oh, how the name of rival fires my blood! I could curse 'em both; eternal jealousy attend her love, and disappointment meet his lust. Oh that I could revenge the torment he has caused! Methinks I feel the woman strong within me, and vengeance itches in the room of love.

LUCY: I have that in my head may make mischief.

SILVIA: How, dear Lucy?

LUCY: You know Araminta's dissembled coyness has won, and keeps him hers –

SILVIA: Could we persuade him that she loves another –

LUCY: No, you're out; could we persuade him that she dotes on him himself, contrive a kind letter as from her, 'twould disgust his nicety, and take away his stomach.

SILVIA: Impossible, 'twill never take.

LUCY: Trouble not your head. Let me alone; I will inform myself of what passed between 'em today, and about it straight. – Hold, I'm mistaken, or that's Heartwell who stands talking at the corner – 'tis he. Go get you in madam, receive him pleasantly, dress up your face in innocence and smiles, and dissemble the very want of dissimulation. – You know what will take him.

SILVIA: 'Tis as hard to counterfeit love, as it is to conceal it, but I'll do my weak endeavour, though I fear I have not art.

LUCY: Hang art, madam, and trust to nature for dissembling.

> Man was by nature woman's cully made:
> We never are but by ourselves betrayed.

[*Exeunt.*]

[*Enter* HEARTWELL, VAINLOVE *and* BELLMOUR *following.*]

BELLMOUR: Hist, hist, is not that Heartwell going to Silvia?

VAINLOVE: He's talking to himself, I think; prithee let's try if we can hear him.

HEARTWELL: Why, whither in the devil's name am I going now? Hum – let me think – is not this Silvia's house, the cave of that enchantress and which consequently I ought to shun as I would infection? To enter here is to put on the envenomed shirt,[1] to run

---

1. *envenomed shirt*: the robe, soaked in the poisoned blood of the slain centaur Nessus, that Deianeira unwittingly sent to Hercules, thus causing him an agonizing death.

into the embraces of a fever, and in some raving fit, be led to plunge myself into that more consuming fire, a woman's arms. Ha! well recollected. I will recover my reason and be gone.

BELLMOUR: Now Venus forbid!

VAINLOVE: Hush –

HEARTWELL: Well, why do you not move? Feet, do your office. – Not one inch? No, foregod, I'm caught! There stands my north, and thither my needle points. – Now could I curse myself, yet cannot repent. O thou delicious, damned, dear, destructive woman! 'S'death how the young fellows will hoot me! I shall be the jest of the town. Nay, in two days, I expect to be chronicled in ditty, and sung in woeful ballad, to the tune of the superannuated maiden's comfort, or the bachelor's fall; and upon the third, I shall be hanged in effigy, pasted up for the exemplary ornament of necessary houses[2] and cobblers' stalls. – Death, I can't think on't – I'll run into the danger to lose the apprehension.

[*Goes in.*]

BELLMOUR: A very certain remedy, *probatum est* – Ha, ha, ha, poor George, thou art i'th'right, thou hast sold thyself to laughter; the ill-natured town will find the jest just where thou hast lost it. Ha, ha, how a' struggled, like an old lawyer between two fees.

VAINLOVE: Or a young wench, betwixt pleasure and reputation.

BELLMOUR: Or as you did today, when half afraid you snatched a kiss from Araminta.

VAINLOVE: She had made a quarrel on't.

BELLMOUR: Pauh, women are only angry at such offences, to have the pleasure of forgiving 'em.

VAINLOVE: And I love to have the pleasure of making my peace. I should not esteem a pardon if too easy won.

BELLMOUR: Thou dost not know what thou would'st be at; whether thou would'st have her angry or pleased. Could'st thou be content to marry Araminta?

VAINLOVE: Could you be content to go to heaven?

BELLMOUR: Hum, not immediately, in my conscience, not heart-

---

2. *necessary houses*: privies.

ily. I'd do a little more good in my generation first, in order to deserve it.

VAINLOVE: Nor I to marry Araminta till I merit her.

BELLMOUR: But how the devil dost thou expect to get her if she never yield?

VAINLOVE: That's true; but I would –

BELLMOUR: Marry her without her consent; thou'rt a riddle beyond woman!

[Enter SETTER.]

Trusty Setter, what tidings? How goes the project?

SETTER: As all lewd projects do sir, where the devil prevents our endeavours with success.

BELLMOUR: A good hearing, Setter.

VAINLOVE: Well, I'll leave you with your engineer.

[Exit.]

BELLMOUR: And hast thou provided necessaries?

SETTER: All, all sir; the large sanctified hat, and the little precise band, with a swinging long spiritual cloak, to cover carnal knavery – not forgetting the black patch, which Tribulation Spintext wears, as I'm informed, upon one eye, as a penal mourning for the ogling offences of his youth; and some say, with that eye, he first discovered the frailty of his wife.

BELLMOUR: Well, in this fanatic father's habit will I confess Laetitia.

SETTER: Rather prepare her for confession, sir, by helping her to sin.

BELLMOUR: Be at your master's lodging in the evening. – I shall use the robes.

[Exit BELLMOUR.]

SETTER: I shall sir. – I wonder to which of these two gentlemen I do most properly appertain. The one uses me as his attendant, the other (being the better acquainted with my parts) employs me as a pimp; why, that's much the more honourable employment – by all means – I follow one as my master, but the other follows me as his conductor.

[Enter LUCY.]

LUCY [aside]: There's the hang-dog his man. I had a power over him in the reign of my mistress; but he is too true a *valet-de-chambre* not to affect his master's faults, and consequently is revolted from his allegiance.

SETTER: Undoubtedly 'tis impossible to be a pimp and not a man of parts. That is, without being politic, diligent, secret, wary, and so forth – and to all this, valiant as Hercules; that is, passively valiant and actively obedient. Ah, Setter, what a treasure is here lost for want of being known.

LUCY: Here's some villainy afoot, he's so thoughtful. Maybe I may discover something in my mask. [*Puts on her mask.*] Worthy sir, a word with you.

SETTER: Why, if I were known, I might come to be a great man.

LUCY: Not to interrupt your meditation –

SETTER: And I should not be the first that has procured his greatness by pimping.

LUCY: Now poverty and the pox light upon thee, for a contemplative pimp.

SETTER: Ha! What art, who thus maliciously hast awakened me from my dream of glory? Speak thou vile disturber –

LUCY: Of thy most vile cogitations! Thou poor, conceited wretch, how, wert thou valuing thyself upon thy master's employment? For he's the head pimp to Mr Bellmour.

SETTER: Good words, damsel, or I shall – but how dost thou know my master or me?

LUCY: Yes, I know both master and man to be –

SETTER: To be men perhaps? Nay, faith, like enough. I often march in the rear of my master, and enter the breaches which he has made.

LUCY: Ay, the breach of faith, which he has begun, thou traitor to thy lawful princess.

SETTER: Why how now! Prithee who art? Lay by that worldly face and produce your natural vizor.

LUCY: No sirrah, I'll keep it on to abuse thee and leave thee without hopes of revenge.

SETTER: Oh, I begin to smoak[3] ye! Thou art some forsaken Abigail[4]

3. *smoak*: understand.
4. *Abigail*: waiting-woman, from the character so named in Beaumont and Fletcher's comedy *The Scornful Lady*.

we have dallied with heretofore, and art come to tickle thy imagination with remembrance of iniquity past.

LUCY: No, thou pitiful flatterer of thy master's imperfections, thou maukin[5] made up of the shreds and parings of his superfluous fopperies.

SETTER: Thou art thy mistress's foul self, composed of her sullied iniquities and clothing.

LUCY: Hang thee, beggar's cur. – Thy master is but a mumper[6] in love; lies canting[7] at the gate, but never dare presume to enter the house.

SETTER: Thou art the wicket to thy mistress's gate, to be opened for all comers. In fine, thou art the high road to thy mistress, as a clap is to the pox.

LUCY: Beast, filthy toad, I can hold no longer. Look and tremble.
   [Unmasks.]

SETTER: How, Mrs Lucy!

LUCY: I wonder thou hast the impudence to look me in the face.

SETTER: Adsbud, who's in fault, mistress mine? Who flung the first stone? Who undervalued my function? And who the devil could know you by instinct?

LUCY: You could know my office by instinct, and be hanged, which you have slandered most abominably. It vexes me not what you said of my person, but that my innocent calling should be exposed and scandalized – I cannot bear it.
   [Cries.]

SETTER: Nay, faith, Lucy I'm sorry; I'll own myself to blame, though we were both in fault as to our offices. Come, I'll make you any reparation.

LUCY: Swear.

SETTER: I do swear to the utmost of my power.

LUCY: To be brief then; what is the reason your master did not appear today according to the summons I brought him?

SETTER: To answer you as briefly – he has a cause to be tried in another court.

5. *maukin*: scarecrow.
6. *mumper*: beggar.
7. *canting*: whining.

LUCY: Come, tell me in plain terms, how forward he is with Araminta.

SETTER: Too forward to be turned back – though he's a little in disgrace at present about a kiss which he forced. You and I can kiss, Lucy, without all that.

LUCY: Stand off! – He's a precious jewel.

SETTER: And therefore you'd have him to set in your lady's locket.

LUCY: Where is he now?

SETTER: He'll be in the Piazza[8] presently.

LUCY: Remember today's behaviour. Let me see you with a penitent face.

SETTER: What, no token of amity, Lucy? You and I don't use to part with dry lips.

LUCY: No, no, avaunt – I'll not be slabbered and kissed now – I'm not i'th' humour.

[Exit.]

SETTER: I'll not quit you so – I'll follow and put you into the humour.

[Exit after her.]

[Enter SIR JOSEPH WITTOLL, BLUFFE.]

BLUFFE: And so out of your unwonted generosity –

SIR JOSEPH: And good nature, Back; I am good natured and I can't help it.

BLUFFE: You have given him a note upon Fondlewife for a hundred pound.

SIR JOSEPH: Ay, ay, poor fellow, he ventured fair for't.

BLUFFE: You have disobliged me in it, for I have occasion for the money, and if you would look me in the face again and live, go, and force him to redeliver you the note. Go – and bring it me hither. I'll stay here for you.

SIR JOSEPH: You may stay till the day of judgment then, by the Lord Harry. I know better things than to be run through the guts for a hundred pound. – Why, I gave that hundred pound for being saved, and d'ye think, an there were no danger, I'll be so ungrateful to take it from the gentleman again?

8. *Piazza*: fashionable promenade in Covent Garden.

BLUFFE: Well, go to him from me. – Tell him, I say he must refund – or bilbo's[9] the word, and slaughter will ensue. If he refuse, tell him – but whisper that – tell him – I'll pink his soul – but whisper that softly to him.

SIR JOSEPH: So softly that he shall never hear on't, I warrant you. – Why, what a devil's the matter, bully, are you mad? Or d'ye think I'm mad? Agad, for my part, I don't love to be the messenger of ill news; 'tis an ungrateful office – so tell him yourself.

BLUFFE: By these hilts I believe he frightened you into this composition; I believe you gave it him out of fear, pure paltry fear – confess.

SIR JOSEPH: No, no, hang't, I was not afraid neither – though I confess he did in a manner snap me up. Yet I can't say that it was altogether out of fear, but partly to prevent mischief, for he was a devilish choleric fellow. And if my choler had been up too, agad there would have been mischief done, that's flat. And yet I believe if you had been by, I would as soon have let him a' had a hundred of my teeth. Adsheart, if he should come just now when I'm angry, I'd tell him – [Enter SHARPER, BELLMOUR.] – mum.

BELLMOUR: Thou'rt a lucky rogue; there's your benefactor. You ought to return him thanks now you have received the favour.

SHARPER: Sir Joseph, – your note was accepted, and the money paid at sight; I'm come to return my thanks –

SIR JOSEPH: They won't be accepted so readily as the bill, sir.

BELLMOUR: I doubt the knight repents, Tom; he looks like the Knight of the Sorrowful Face.[10]

SHARPER: This is a double generosity. – Do me a kindness and refuse my thanks – but I hope you are not offended that I offered 'em.

SIR JOSEPH: Maybe I am, sir, maybe I am not, sir, maybe I am both, sir; what then? I hope I may be offended without any offence to you, sir.

SHARPER: Hey day! Captain, what's the matter? You can tell.

BLUFFE: Mr Sharper, the matter is plain – Sir Joseph has found out

9. *bilbo*: sword.
10. *Knight of the Sorrowful Face*: Don Quixote.

your trick, and does not care to be put upon, being a man of honour.

SHARPER: Trick, sir?

SIR JOSEPH: Ay, trick, sir, and won't be put upon, sir, being a man of honour, sir, and so, sir –

SHARPER: Hearkee, Sir Joseph, a word with ye. In consideration of some favours lately received, I would not have you draw yourself into a premunire[11] by trusting to that sign of a man there – that pot-gun[12] charged with wind.

SIR JOSEPH: O Lord, O Lord, Captain, come justify yourself – I'll give him the lie if you'll stand to it.

SHARPER: Nay then I'll be beforehand with you; take that – Oaf!
    [Cuffs him.]

SIR JOSEPH: Captain, will you see this? Won't you pink his soul?

BLUFFE: Husht, 'tis not so convenient now. – I shall find a time.

SHARPER: What, do you mutter about a time, rascal? You were the incendiary. [Kicks him.] There's to put you in mind of your time – a memorandum.

BLUFFE: Oh, this is your time, sir; you had best make use on't.

SHARPER: I' gad and so I will; there's again for you.
    [Kicks him.]

BLUFFE: You are obliging sir, but this is too public a place to thank you in. But in your ear, you are to be seen again.

SHARPER: Ay, thou inimitable coward, and to be felt – as for example.
    [Kicks him.]

BELLMOUR: Ha, ha, ha, prithee come away; 'tis scandalous to kick this puppy without a man were cold, and had no other way to get himself a heat.
    [Exit BELLMOUR, SHARPER.]

BLUFFE: Very well – very fine – but 'tis no matter. Is not this fine, Sir Joseph?

SIR JOSEPH: Indifferent, agad, in my opinion very indifferent. – I'd rather go plain all my life than wear such finery.

11. *premunire*: a difficult predicament.
12. *pot-gun*: child's pop-gun.

BLUFFE: Death and hell to be affronted thus! I'll die before I'll suffer it.

[*Draws.*]

SIR JOSEPH: O Lord, his anger was not raised before. – Nay, dear Captain, don't be in passion now he's gone. Put up, put up, dear Back, 'tis your Sir Joseph begs, come let me kiss thee, so so, put up, put up.

BLUFFE: By heaven, 'tis not to be put up.

SIR JOSEPH: What, bully?

BLUFFE: Th' affront.

SIR JOSEPH: No agad, no more 'tis, for that's put up already; thy sword I mean.

BLUFFE: Well, Sir Joseph, at your entreaty – but were not you, my friend, abused and cuffed and kicked?

[*Putting up his sword.*]

SIR JOSEPH: Ay, ay, so were you too; no matter, 'tis past.

BLUFFE: By the immortal thunder of great guns, 'tis false! He sucks not vital air who dares affirm it to this face!

[*Looks big.*]

SIR JOSEPH: To that face, I grant you Captain. – No, no, I grant you; – not to that face, by the Lord Harry. If you had put on your fighting face before, you had done his business; he durst as soon have kissed you as kicked you to your face. But a man can no more help what's done behind his back than what's said. Come, we'll think no more of what's past.

BLUFFE: I'll call a council of war within to consider of my revenge to come.

[*Exeunt.*]

SCENE TWO

Scene changes to Silvia's lodgings.

[*Enter* HEARTWELL, SILVIA.]

(*Song*)

I

As Amoret and Thyrsis lay
Melting the hours in gentle play;
Joining faces, mingling kisses,
And exchanging harmless blisses:
He trembling, cried with eager haste,
O let me feed as well as taste;
I die, if I'm not wholly blest.

II

The fearful Nymph replied – *Forbear;*
I cannot, dare not, must not hear.
Dearest Thyrsis, do not move me,
Do not – do not – if you love me.
O let me – still the shepherd said;
But while she fond resistance made,
The hasty joy, in struggling, fled.

III

Vexed at the pleasure she had missed,
She frowned and blushed, then sighed and kissed,
And seemed to moan, in sullen cooing,
The sad miscarriage of their wooing:
But vain, alas! were all her charms;
For Thyrsis deaf to Love's alarms,
Baffled and senseless, tired her arms.

[*After the song, a dance of antics.*][13]

SILVIA: Indeed it is very fine – I could look upon 'em all day.

13. *antics*: dancers fantastically dressed.

HEARTWELL: Well, has this prevailed for me, and will you look upon me?

SILVIA: If you could sing and dance so, I should love to look upon you too.

HEARTWELL: Why, 'twas I sung and danced; I gave music to the voice, and life to their measures. – Look you here Silvia, here are songs and dances, poetry and music – hark! [*pulling out a purse and chinking it*] how sweetly one guinea rhymes to another, and how they dance to the music of their own chink. This buys all the 'tother – and this thou shalt have; this, and all that I am worth for the purchase of thy love. Say, is it mine then, ha? Speak, siren. – Oons, why do I look on her! Yet I must. Speak dear angel, devil, saint, witch; do not rack me in suspense.

SILVIA: Nay, don't stare at me so – you make me blush – I cannot look.

HEARTWELL: Oh manhood, where art thou! What am I come to? A woman's toy at these years! Death, a bearded baby[14] for a girl to dandle. O dotage, dotage! That ever that noble passion, lust, should ebb to this degree. No reflux of vigorous blood, but milky love supplies the empty channels and prompts me to the softness of a child – a mere infant and would suck. Can you love me Silvia? Speak.

SILVIA: I dare not speak till I believe you, and indeed I'm afraid to believe you yet.

HEARTWELL: Pox, how her innocence torments and pleases me! Lying, child, is indeed the art of love; and men are generally masters in it. But I'm so newly entered, you cannot distrust me of any skill in the treacherous mystery. Now by my soul, I cannot lie, though it were to serve a friend or gain a mistress.

SILVIA: Must you lie then, if you say you love me?

HEARTWELL: No, no, dear ignorance, thou beauteous changeling – I tell thee I do love thee, and tell it for a truth, a naked truth, which I'm ashamed to discover.

SILVIA: But love, they say, is a tender thing that will smooth

14. *baby*: doll.

frowns, and make calm an angry face; will soften a rugged temper, and make ill-humoured people good: you look ready to fright one, and talk as if your passion were not love, but anger.

HEARTWELL: 'Tis both; for I am angry with myself, when I am pleased with you – and a pox upon me for loving thee so well! Yet I must on – 'tis a bearded[15] arrow, and will more easily be thrust forward than drawn back.

SILVIA: Indeed, if I were well assured you loved; but how can I be well assured?

HEARTWELL: Take the symptoms, and ask all the tyrants of thy sex, if their fools are not known by this parti-coloured livery: I am melancholy when thou art absent; look like an ass when thou art present; wake for you, when I should sleep, and even dream of you, when I am awake; sigh much, drink little, eat less, court solitude, am grown very entertaining to myself, and (as I am informed), very troublesome to everybody else. If this be not love, it is madness, and then it is pardonable. – Nay yet a more certain sign than all this; I give thee my money.

SILVIA: Ay, but that is no sign, for they say gentlemen will give money to any naughty woman to come to bed to them. – O Gemini, I hope you don't mean so – for I won't be a whore.

HEARTWELL [aside]: The more is the pity.

SILVIA: Nay, if you would marry me, you should not come to bed to me. You have such a beard and would so prickle one. But do you intend to marry me?

HEARTWELL [aside]: That a fool should ask such a malicious question! Death, I shall be drawn in before I know where I am. However, I find I am pretty sure of her consent, if I am put to it. [Aloud.] Marry you? no, no, I'll love you.

SILVIA: Nay, but if you love me, you must marry me; what, don't I know my father loved my mother, and was married to her?

HEARTWELL: Ay, ay, in old days people married where they loved; but that fashion is changed, child.

SILVIA: Never tell me that. I know it is not changed by myself; for I love you, and would marry you.

15. *bearded*: barbed.

HEARTWELL: I'll have my beard shaved, it shan't hurt thee, and we'll go to bed –

SILVIA: No, no, I'm not such a fool neither but I can keep myself – honest. Here, I won't keep anything that's yours. [*Throws the purse.*] I hate you now, and I'll never see you again, 'cause you'd have me naught.

　　[*Going.*]

HEARTWELL: Damn her, let her go, and a good riddance. Yet so much tenderness and beauty and honesty together is a jewel. – Stay, Silvia. – But then to marry. – Why, every man plays the fool once in his life, but to marry is playing the fool all one's life long.

SILVIA: What did you call me for?

HEARTWELL: I'll give thee all I have, and thou shalt live with me in every thing so like my wife, the world shall believe it; nay, thou shalt think so thyself – only let me not think so.

SILVIA: No, I'll die before I'll be your whore – as well as I love you.

HEARTWELL [*aside*]: A woman, and ignorant, may be honest, when 'tis out of obstinacy and contradiction – but 's'death, it is but a may be, and upon scurvy terms. – Well, farewell then. – If I can get out of her sight I may get the better of myself.

SILVIA: Well – good-bye.

　　[*Turns and weeps.*]

HEARTWELL: Ha! Nay come, we'll kiss at parting. [*Kisses her.*] By heaven, she kisses sweeter than liberty – I will marry thee. There, thou hast done't. All my resolve melted in that kiss – one more.

SILVIA: But when?

HEARTWELL: I'm impatient till it be done; I will not give myself liberty to think, lest I should cool – I will about a licence straight – in the evening expect me. One kiss more, to confirm me mad; so.

　　[*Exit.*]

SILVIA: Ha, ha, ha, an old fox trapped –

　　[*Enter* LUCY.]

Bless me! you frighted me. I thought he had been come again, and had heard me.

LUCY: Lord, madam, I met your lover in as much haste as if he had been going for a midwife.

SILVIA: He's going for a parson, girl, the forerunner of a midwife,

some nine months hence. Well, I find dissembling to our sex is as
natural as swimming to a negro; we may depend upon our skill to
save us at a plunge, though till then we never make the experiment. But how hast thou succeeded?

LUCY: As you would wish. Since there is no reclaiming Vainlove, I
have found out a pique she has taken at him, and have framed a
letter that makes her sue for reconciliation first. I know that will
do – walk in and I'll shew it you. Come madam, you're like to
have a happy time on't, both your love and anger satisfied! All
that can charm our sex conspire to please you.

> That woman sure enjoys a blessed night,
> Whom love and vengeance do at once delight.

[*Exeunt.*]

ACT FOUR

SCENE ONE

The street

[*Enter* BELLMOUR *in fanatic habit,* SETTER.]

BELLMOUR: 'Tis pretty near the hour —
    [*Looking on his watch.*]
    Well and how, Setter, ha, does my hypocrisy fit me, ha? Does it sit
    easy on me?

SETTER: O most religiously well, sir.

BELLMOUR: I wonder why all our young fellows should glory
    in an opinion of atheism, when they may be so much more
    conveniently lewd under the coverlet of religion.

SETTER: S'bud sir, away quickly, there's Fondlewife just turned the
    corner, and's coming this way.

BELLMOUR: Gads, so there he is, he must not see me.
    [*Exeunt.*]
    [*Enter* FONDLEWIFE *and* BARNABY.]

FONDLEWIFE: I say I will tarry at home.

BARNABY: But sir.

FONDLEWIFE: Good lack! I profess the spirit of contradiction hath
    possessed the lad. I say I will tarry at home, varlet.

BARNABY: I have done, sir, then farewell five hundred pound.

FONDLEWIFE: Ha, how's that? Stay stay, did you leave word, say
    you, with his wife? With Comfort herself.

BARNABY: I did; and Comfort will send Tribulation hither as soon
    as ever he comes home. — I could have brought young Mr Prig, to
    have kept my mistress company in the meantime, but you say —

FONDLEWIFE: How, how, say, varlet! I say let him not come near my doors. I say he is a wanton young Levite[1] and pampereth himself up with dainties, that he may look lovely in the eyes of women. Sincerely I am afraid he hath already defiled the tabernacle of our Sister Comfort, while her good husband is deluded by his godly appearance. I say, that even lust doth sparkle in his eyes, and glow upon his cheeks, and that I would as soon trust my wife with a lord's high-fed chaplain.

BARNABY: Sir, the hour draws nigh – and nothing will be done there till you come.

FONDLEWIFE: And nothing can be done here till I go – so that I'll tarry, d'ye see?

BARNABY: And run the hazard to lose your affair so!

FONDLEWIFE: Good lack, good lack – I profess it is a very sufficient vexation for a man to have a handsome wife.

BARNABY: Never sir, but when the man is an insufficient husband. 'Tis then indeed like the vanity of taking a fine house, and yet be forced to let lodgings to help pay the rent.

FONDLEWIFE: I profess a very apt comparison, varlet. Go in and bid my Cocky come out to me, I will give her some instructions, I will reason with her before I go.

[*Exit* BARNABY.]

And in the mean time, I will reason with myself. – Tell me Isaac, why art thee jealous? Why art thee distrustful of the wife of thy bosom? – Because she is young and vigorous, and I am old and impotent. – Then why didst thee marry Isaac? – Because she was beautiful and tempting, and because I was obstinate and doting; so that my inclination was (and is still) greater than my power. – And will not that which tempted thee, also tempt others, who will tempt her, Isaac? – I fear it much. – But does not thy wife love thee, nay dote upon thee? – Yes – why then! – Ay, but to say truth, she's fonder of me than she has reason to be; and in the way of trade, we still suspect the smoothest dealers of the deepest designs. – And that she has some designs deeper than thou canst reach, th' hast experimented, Isaac – but mum.

[*Enter* LAETITIA.]

1. *Levite*: contemptuous term for a clergyman or domestic chaplain.

LAETITIA: I hope my dearest jewel is not going to leave me – are you, Nykin?

FONDLEWIFE: Wife – have you thoroughly considered how detestable, how heinous, and how crying a sin, the sin of adultery is? Have you weighed it I say? For it is a very weighty sin; and although it may lie heavy upon thee, yet thy husband must also bear his part: for thy iniquity will fall upon his head.

LAETITIA: Bless me, what means my dear?

FONDLEWIFE [aside]: I profess she has an alluring eye; I am doubtful whether I shall trust her even with Tribulation himself. – Speak, I say. Have you considered what it is to cuckold your husband?

LAETITIA [aside]: I'm amazed; sure he has discovered nothing. [Aloud.] – Who has wronged me to my dearest? I hope my jewel does not think that ever I had any such thing in my head, or ever will have.

FONDLEWIFE: No, no, I tell you I shall have it in my head. – You will have it somewhere else.

LAETITIA [aside]: I know not what to think. But I'm resolved to find the meaning of it. – Unkind dear! Was it for this you sent to call me? Is it not affliction enough that you are to leave me, but you must study to increase it by unjust suspicions? [Crying.] Well – well – you know my fondness, and you love to tyrannize. – Go on, cruel man, do. Triumph over my poor heart while it holds, which cannot be long with this usage of yours; but that's what you want. – Well, you will have your ends soon – you will – you will. Yes, it will break to oblige you.
    [Sighs.]

FONDLEWIFE [aside]: Verily I fear I have carried the jest too far. – Nay, look you now if she does not weep – 'tis the fondest fool. – Nay, Cocky, Cocky, nay dear Cocky, don't cry, I was but in jest, I was not ifeck.[2]

LAETITIA [aside]: Oh then all's safe. I was terrible frighted. [Aloud.] My affliction is always your jest, barbarous man! Oh that I should love to this degree! yet –

FONDLEWIFE: Nay, Cocky.

2. *ifeck*: in earnest.

LAETITIA: No no, you are weary of me, that's it – that's all, you would get another wife – another fond fool, to break her heart. Well, be as cruel as you can to me, I'll pray for you; and when I am dead with grief, may you have one that will love you as well as I have done. I shall be contented to lie at peace in my cold grave, since it will please you.

[*Sighs.*]

FONDLEWIFE: Good lack, good lack, she would melt a heart of oak – I profess I can hold no longer. Nay dear Cocky – ifeck you'll break my heart – ifeck you will. See, you have made me weep – made poor Nykin weep. Nay, come kiss, buss poor Nykin, and I won't leave thee – I'll lose all first.

LAETITIA [*aside*]: How! Heaven forbid! that will be carrying the jest too far indeed.

FONDLEWIFE: Won't you kiss Nykin?

LAETITIA: Go, naughty Nykin, you don't love me.

FONDLEWIFE: Kiss, kiss, ifeck I do.

LAETITIA: No you don't.

[*She kisses him.*]

FONDLEWIFE: What, not love Cocky?

LAETITIA: No—h.

[*Sighs.*]

FONDLEWIFE: I profess I do love thee better than 500 pound – and so thou shalt say, for I'll leave it to stay with thee.

LAETITIA: No, you shan't neglect your business for me – no indeed you s'an't. Nykin, if you don't go, I'll think you been dealous of me still.

FONDLEWIFE: He, he, he, wilt thou, poor fool? Then I will go, I won't be dealous. – Poor Cocky, kiss Nykin, kiss Nykin, ee, ee, ee. Here will be the good man anon, to talk to Cocky and teach her how a wife ought to behave herself.

LAETITIA [*aside*]: I hope to have one that will shew me how a husband ought to behave himself. [*Aloud.*] I shall be glad to learn, to please my jewel.

[*Kiss.*]

FONDLEWIFE: That's my good dear. Come, kiss Nykin once more, and then get you in – so. Get you in, get you in. Bye, bye.

LAETITIA: Bye, Nykin.

FONDLEWIFE: Bye, Cocky.

LAETITIA: Bye, Nykin.

[*She goes in.*]

FONDLEWIFE: Bye, Cocky, bye, bye.

[*Exit.*]

[*Enter* VAINLOVE, SHARPER.]

SHARPER: How! Araminta lost!

VAINLOVE: To confirm what I have said, read this.

[*Gives a letter.*]

SHARPER [*reads*]: Hum hum – *And what then appeared a fault, upon reflection, seems only an effect of a too powerful passion. I'm afraid I give too great a proof of my own at this time – I am in disorder for what I have written. But something, I know not what, forced me. I only beg a favourable censure[3] of this and your*

Araminta.

SHARPER: Lost! Pray heaven thou hast not lost thy wits. Here, here, she's thy own, man, signed and sealed too. – To her, man! – A delicious melon, pure and consenting ripe, and only waits thy cutting up. She has been breeding love to thee all this while, and just now she is delivered of it.

VAINLOVE: 'Tis an untimely fruit, and she has miscarried of her love.

SHARPER: Never leave this damned ill-natured whimsy, Frank? Thou hast a sickly peevish appetite; only chew love and cannot digest it.

VAINLOVE: Yes, when I feed myself. But I hate to be crammed. – By heaven, there's not a woman will give a man the pleasure of a chase: my sport is always balked or cut short – I stumble o'er the game I would pursue. 'Tis dull and unnatural to have a hare run full in the hounds' mouth, and would distaste the keenest hunter. I would have overtaken, not have met my game.

SHARPER: However, I hope you don't mean to forsake it; that will be but a kind of a mongrel cur's trick. Well, are you for the Mall?

---

3. *censure*: opinion.

VAINLOVE: No, she will be there this evening. – Yes, I will go too, and she shall see her error in –

SHARPER: In her choice i'gad – but thou canst not be so great a brute as to slight her.

VAINLOVE: I should disappoint her if I did not. By her management I should think she expects it.

> All naturally fly what does pursue;
> 'Tis fit men should be coy, when women woo.

[*Exeunt.*]

SCENE TWO

Scene changes to a chamber in FONDLEWIFE'S *house.*

[*A servant introducing* BELLMOUR *in fanatic habit, with a patch upon one eye, and a book in his hand.*]

SERVANT: Here's a chair, sir, if you please to repose yourself. I'll call my mistress.

[*Exit* SERVANT.]

BELLMOUR: Secure in my disguise, I have out-faced suspicion, and even dared discovery; this cloak my sanctity, and trusty Scarron's novels my prayer-book. – Methinks I am the very picture of Montufar in *The Hypocrites*.[4] – Oh! she comes.

[*Enter* LAETITIA.]

> *So breaks aurora through the veil of night;*
> *Thus fly the clouds, divided by her light,*
> *And ev'ry eye receives a new-born sight.*

[*Throwing off his cloak, patch, etc.*]

LAETITIA: *Thus strew'd with blushes, like –*

[*discovering him, starts.*]

Ah, heaven defend me! Who's this?

BELLMOUR: Your lover.

---

4. *Scarron*: Paul Scarron (1610–60), French writer. In his novella *Les Hypocrites*, the rogue, Montufar, successfully disguises himself as a holy friar.

LAETITIA [*aside*]: Vainlove's friend! I know his face, and he has betrayed me to him.

BELLMOUR: You are surprised. Did you not expect a lover, madam? Those eyes shone kindly on my first appearance, though now they are o'er-cast.

LAETITIA: I may well be surprised at your person and impudence; they are both new to me. – You are not what your first appearance promised: the piety of your habit was welcome, but not the hypocrisy.

BELLMOUR [*aside*]: Rather the hypocrisy was welcome, but not the hypocrite.

LAETITIA: Who are you, sir? You have mistaken the house, sure.

BELLMOUR: I have directions in my pocket, which agree with everything but your unkindness.

[*Pulls out the letter.*]

LAETITIA [*aside*]: My letter! Base Vainlove! Then 'tis too late to dissemble. [*Aloud.*] 'Tis plain then you have mistaken the person.

[*Going.*]

BELLMOUR [*aside*]: If we part so I'm mistaken. [*Aloud.*] Hold, hold, madam; – I confess I have run into an error: – I beg your pardon a thousand times. – What an eternal block-head am I! Can you forgive me the disorder I have put you into – but it is a mistake which anybody might have made.

LAETITIA [*aside*]: What can this mean! 'Tis impossible he should be mistaken after all this. – A handsome fellow if he had not surprised me: methinks, now I look on him again, I would not have him mistaken.

[*Aloud.*]

We are all liable to mistakes, sir: if you own it to be so, there needs no further apology.

BELLMOUR: Nay, faith, madam, 'tis a pleasant one, and worth your hearing. Expecting a friend last night at his lodgings till 'twas late, my intimacy with him gave me the freedom of his bed. He not coming home all night, a letter was delivered to me by a servant in the morning. Upon the perusal I found the contents so charming, that I could think of nothing all day but putting 'em in practice – 'till just now, (the first time I ever looked upon the superscription), I am the most surprised in the world to find it directed to Mr Vainlove. Gad, madam, I ask you a million of pardons, and will make you any satisfaction.

LAETITIA [aside]: I am discovered: – and either Vainlove is not guilty, or he has handsomely excused him.

BELLMOUR: You appear concerned, madam.

LAETITIA: I hope you are a gentleman, and since you are privy to a weak woman's failing, won't turn it to the prejudice of her reputation. You look as if you had more honour –

BELLMOUR: And more love, or my face is a false witness and deserves to be pilloried. – No, by heaven, I swear –

LAETITIA: Nay, don't swear if you'd have me believe you; but promise –

BELLMOUR: Well, I promise. – A promise is so cold. – Give me leave to swear – by those eyes, those killing eyes; by those healing lips. – Oh! press the soft charm close to mine, and seal 'em up for ever.

[He kisses her.]

LAETITIA: Upon that condition.

BELLMOUR: Eternity was in that moment. – One more, upon any condition.

LAETITIA: Nay, now. [Aside.] I never saw anything so agreeably impudent. [Aloud.] Won't you censure me for this, now; – but 'tis to buy your silence.

[Kiss.]

Oh, but what am I doing!

BELLMOUR: Doing! No tongue can express it, – not thy own; nor anything but thy lips. I am faint with the excess of bliss. – Oh, for love-sake, lead me any whither, where I may lie down – quickly, for I'm afraid I shall have a fit.

LAETITIA: Bless me! What fit?

BELLMOUR: Oh, a convulsion. – I feel the symptoms.

LAETITIA: Does it hold you long? I'm afraid to carry you into my chamber.

BELLMOUR: Oh, no: let me lie down upon the bed; the fit will be soon over.

[Exeunt.]

SCENE THREE

Scene changes to St James's Park.

[ARAMINTA *and* BELINDA *meeting.*]

BELINDA: Lard, my dear! I am glad I have met you. I have been at the Exchange[5] since, and am so tired –

ARAMINTA: Why, what's the matter?

BELINDA: Oh, the most inhuman, barbarous hackney-coach! I am jolted to a jelly. – Am I not horridly touzed?[6]

[*Pulls out a pocket-glass.*]

ARAMINTA: Your head's a little out of order.

BELINDA: A little! O frightful! What a furious fiz I have! O most rueful! Ha, ha, ha! O gad, I hope nobody will come this way till I put myself a little in repair. – Ah, my dear – I have seen such unhewn creatures since, ha, ha, ha! I can't for my soul help thinking that I look just like one of 'em. Good dear, pin this, and I'll tell you. – Very well. – So, thank you, my dear. – But as I was telling you – pish, this is the untoward'st lock. – So, as I was telling you – how d'ye like me now? Hideous, ha? Frightful still? Oh how?

ARAMINTA: No, no; you're very well as can be.

BELINDA: And so – but where did I leave off, my dear? I was telling you –

ARAMINTA: You were about to tell me something, child, but you left off before you began.

BELINDA: Oh, a most comical sight! A country squire, with the equipage of a wife and two daughters, came to Mrs Snipwel's shop while I was there. – But, oh gad, two such unlicked cubs!

ARAMINTA: I warrant, plump, cherry-cheeked country girls.

BELINDA: Ay, o' my conscience; fat as barn-door fowl; but so bedecked you would have taken 'em for Friezland-hens, with their feathers growing the wrong way. – O such outlandish

---

5. *Exchange*: shops on the south side of the Strand.
6. *touzed*: dishevelled.

creatures! Such Tramontanae,[7] and foreigners to the fashion, or any thing in practice! I had not patience to behold. – I undertook the modelling of one of their fronts, the more modern structure.

ARAMINTA: Bless me, cousin! Why would you affront anybody so? They might be gentlewomen of a very good family –

BELINDA: Of a very ancient one, I dare swear, by their dress. – Affront! Pshaw, how you're mistaken! The poor creature, I warrant, was as full of courtesies as if I had been her godmother. The truth on't is, I did endeavour to make her look like a Christian – and she was sensible of it, for she thanked me, and gave me two apples, piping hot, out of her under-petticoat pocket, ha, ha, ha. And t'other did so stare and gape – I fancied her like the front of her father's hall; her eyes were the two jut-windows, and her mouth the great door, most hospitably kept open for the entertainment of travelling flies.

ARAMINTA: So then; you have been diverted. What did they buy?

BELINDA: Why, the father bought a powder-horn, and an almanac, and a comb-case; the mother, a great fruz-tour,[8] and a fat amber necklace; the daughters only tore two pair of kid gloves with trying 'em on – Oh gad, here comes the fool that dined at my Lady Freelove's t'other day.

  [Enter SIR JOSEPH and BLUFFE.]

ARAMINTA: Maybe he may not know us again.

BELINDA: We'll put on our masks to secure his ignorance.

  [They put on their masks.]

SIR JOSEPH: Nay, gad, I'll pick up; I'm resolved to make a night on't. – I'll go to Alderman Fondlewife by-and-by, and get fifty pieces more from him. Adslidikins, bully, we'll wallow in wine and women. Why, this same Madeira-wine has made me as light as a grasshopper. – Hist, hist, bully, dost thou see those tearers?[9] [Sings.] Look you what here is, – Look you what here is: – Toll-loll-dera-toll-loll. – Agad, t'other glass of Madeira, and I durst have attacked 'em in my own proper person, without your help.

7. Tramontanae: dwelling or situated beyond the mountains; here: uncouth, unpolished.
8. fruz-tour: high, curled frontlet of false hair.
9. tearers: swaggerers.

BLUFFE: Come on then, knight. – But d'ye know what to say to 'em?

SIR JOSEPH: Say! Pooh, pox, I've enough to say, never fear it; – that is, if I can but think on't. Truth is, I have but a treacherous memory.

BELINDA: O frightful! Cousin, what shall we do? These things come toward us.

ARAMINTA: No matter, I see Vainlove coming this way, and, to confess my failing, I am willing to give him an opportunity of making his peace with me; and to rid me of these coxcombs, when I seem oppressed with 'em, will be a fair one.

BLUFFE: Ladies, by these hilts you are well met.

ARAMINTA: We are afraid not.

BLUFFE [To BELINDA]: What says my pretty little knapsack-carrier?[10]

BELINDA: O monstrous filthy fellow! Good slovenly Captain Huffe, Bluffe (what's your hideous name?) be gone: you stink of brandy and tobacco, most soldier-like, foh!
    [Spits.]

SIR JOSEPH [aside]: Now am I slap-dash down in the mouth, and have not one word to say.

ARAMINTA [aside]: I hope my fool has not confidence enough to be troublesome.

SIR JOSEPH: Hem! Pray madam, which way's the wind?

ARAMINTA: A pithy question. Have you sent your wits for a venture, sir, that you enquire?

SIR JOSEPH [aside]: Nay, now I'm in, I can prattle like a magpie.
    [Enter SHARPER and VAINLOVE, at a distance.]

BELINDA: Dear Araminta, I'm tired.

ARAMINTA: 'Tis but pulling off our masks and obliging Vainlove to know us. I'll be rid of my fool by fair means. – Well, Sir Joseph, you shall see my face. But, be gone immediately; I see one that will be jealous to find me in discourse with you. – Be discreet. – No reply, but away.
    [Unmasks.]

10. *knapsack-carrier*: soldier.

SIR JOSEPH [*aside*]: The great fortune, that dined at my Lady Free-love's! Sir Joseph, thou are a made man! Agad, I'm in love, up to the ears. But I'll be discreet, and hushed.

BLUFFE: Nay, by the world, I'll see your face.

BELINDA: You shall.

[*Unmasks.*]

SHARPER: Ladies, your humble servant. — We were afraid you would not have given us leave to know you.

ARAMINTA: We thought to have been private, but we find fools have the same advantage over a face in a mask that a coward has, while the sword is in the scabbard; so were forced to draw in our own defence.

BLUFFE [*to* SIR JOSEPH]: My blood rises at that fellow; I can't stay where he is, and I must not draw in the park.[11]

SIR JOSEPH: I wish I durst stay to let her know my lodging. —

[*Exeunt* SIR JOSEPH *and* BLUFFE.]

SHARPER: There is in true beauty, as in courage, somewhat which narrow souls cannot dare to admire. — And see; the owls are fled, as at the break of day.

BELINDA: Very courtly. I believe Mr Vainlove has not rubbed his eyes since break of day neither, he looks as if he durst not approach. — Nay, come cousin, be friends with him. I swear, he looks so very simply, ha, ha, ha! Well, a lover in the state of separation from his mistress is like a body without a soul. Mr Vainlove, shall I be bound for your good behaviour for the future?

VAINLOVE [*aside*]: Now must I pretend ignorance equal to hers of what she knows as well as I. [*Aloud.*] Men are apt to offend ('tis true) where they find most goodness to forgive. But, madam, I hope I shall prove of a temper not to abuse mercy, by committing new offences.

ARAMINTA [*aside*]: So cold!

BELINDA: I have broke the ice for you, Mr Vainlove, and so I leave you. Come, Mr Sharper, you and I will take a turn, and laugh at the vulgar; both the great vulgar and the small.[12] — Oh gad! I have

11. *draw in the park*: duelling was forbidden in St James's Park.
12. *both the great vulgar and the small*: the second line of Cowley's imitation of Horace *Odes*, III i.

a great passion for Cowley. Don't you admire him?

SHARPER: Oh madam, he was our English Horace!

BELINDA: Ah, so fine! So extremely fine! So every thing in the world that I like. – Oh Lord, walk this way; I see a couple, I'll give you their history.

[*Exeunt* BELINDA *and* SHARPER.]

VAINLOVE: I find, madam, the formality of the law must be observed, though the penalty of it be dispensed with; and an offender must plead to his arraignment, though he have his pardon in his pocket.

ARAMINTA: I'm amazed! This insolence exceeds the t'other. Who-ever has encouraged you to this assurance, presuming upon the easiness of my temper, has much deceived you, and so you shall find.

VAINLOVE [*aside*]: Hey-day! Which way now? Here's fine doubl-ing.

ARAMINTA: Base man! Was it not enough to affront me with your saucy passion?

VAINLOVE: You have given that passion a much kinder epithet than saucy, in another place.

ARAMINTA: Another place! Some villainous design to blast my honour. But though thou hadst all the treachery and malice of thy sex, thou canst not lay a blemish on my fame. – No, I have not erred in one favourable thought of mankind. How time might have deceived me in you, I know not; my opinion was but young, and your early baseness has prevented its growing to a wrong belief. – Unworthy, and ungrateful! Be gone, and never see me more.

VAINLOVE: Did I dream? Or do I dream? Shall I believe my eyes, or ears? The vision is here still. – Your passion, madam, will admit of no farther reasoning, but here is a silent witness of your acquaintance. –

[*Takes out the letter, and offers it: she snatches it, and throws it away.*]

ARAMINTA: There's poison in every thing you touch. Blisters will follow –

VAINLOVE: That tongue, which denies what the hands have done.

ARAMINTA: Still mystically senseless and impudent! I find I must leave the place.

VAINLOVE: No, madam, I'm gone. – She knows her name's to it, which she will be unwilling to expose to the censure of the first finder.

ARAMINTA: Woman's obstinacy made me blind to what woman's curiosity now tempts me to see.

[*Takes up the letter, and exit.*]

[*Enter* BELINDA, SHARPER.]

BELINDA: Nay, we have spared nobody, I swear. Mr Sharper, you're a pure man; where did you get this excellent talent of railing?

SHARPER: Faith, madam, the talent was born with me. – I confess, I have taken care to improve it, to qualify me for the society of ladies.

BELINDA: Nay, sure, railing is the best qualification in a woman's man.

SHARPER: The second-best, indeed I think.

[*Enter* FOOTMAN.]

BELINDA: How now, Pace? Where's my cousin?

FOOTMAN: She's not very well, madam, and has sent to know if your ladyship would have the coach come again for you?

BELINDA: O Lord, no, I'll go along with her. Come, Mr Sharper.

[*Exeunt.*]

SCENE FOUR

Scene changes to a chamber in Fondlewife's house.

[*Enter* LAETITIA *and* BELLMOUR, *his cloak, hat, etc. lying loose about the chamber.*]

BELLMOUR: Here's nobody, nor no noise; 'twas nothing but your fears.

LAETITIA: I durst have sworn I had heard my monster's voice. I swear, I was heartily frightened. – Feel how my heart beats.

BELLMOUR: 'Tis an alarm to love. Come in again, and let us –

FONDLEWIFE [*without*]: Cocky, Cocky, where are you, Cocky? I'm come home.

LAETITIA: Ah! There he is. Make haste, gather up your things.

FONDLEWIFE: Cocky, Cocky, open the door.

BELLMOUR: Pox choke him, would his horns were in his throat. My patch, my patch.

[*Looking about, and gathering up his things.*]

LAETITIA: My jewel, art thou there? No matter for your patch. – You s'an't tum in, Nykin. – Run into my chamber, quickly, quickly. You s'an't tum in.

[BELLMOUR *goes in.*]

FONDLEWIFE: Nay, prithee, dear, ifeck I'm in haste.

LAETITIA: Then I'll let you in.

[*Opens the door.*]

[*Enter* FONDLEWIFE, *and* SIR JOSEPH.]

FONDLEWIFE: Kiss, dear. – I met the master of the ship by the way, and I must have my papers of accounts out of your cabinet.

LAETITIA [*aside*]: Oh, I'm undone!

SIR JOSEPH: Pray, first let me have fifty pounds, good Alderman, for I'm in haste.

FONDLEWIFE: A hundred has already been paid, by your order. Fifty? I have the sum ready in gold, in my closet.

[*Goes into his closet.*]

SIR JOSEPH: Agad, it's a curious, fine, pretty rogue; I'll speak to her. – Pray, madam, what news d'ye hear?

LAETITIA: Sir, I seldom stir abroad.

[*Walks about in disorder.*]

SIR JOSEPH: I wonder at that, madam, for 'tis most curious fine weather.

LAETITIA: Methinks, 't has been very ill weather.

SIR JOSEPH: As you say, madam, 'tis pretty bad weather, and has been so a great while.

[*Enter* FONDLEWIFE.]

FONDLEWIFE: Here are fifty pieces in this purse, Sir Joseph. If you will tarry a moment, till I fetch my papers, I'll wait upon you downstairs.

LAETITIA [*aside*]: Ruined past redemption! What shall I do? – Ha!

This fool may be of use. [*As* FONDLEWIFE *is going into the chamber, she runs to* SIR JOSEPH, *almost pushes him down, and cries out.*] Stand off, rude ruffian! Help me, my dear – O bless me! Why will you leave me alone with such a satyr?

FONDLEWIFE: Bless us! What's the matter? What's the matter?

LAETITIA: Your back was no sooner turned, but like a lion he came open-mouthed upon me, and would have ravished a kiss from me by main force.

SIR JOSEPH: O Lord! Oh, terrible! Ha, ha, ha, is your wife mad, Alderman?

LAETITIA: Oh! I am sick with the fright; won't you take him out of my sight?

FONDLEWIFE: Oh traitor! I'm astonished. Oh bloody-minded traitor!

SIR JOSEPH: Hey day! traitor yourself. By the Lord Harry, I was in most danger of being ravished, if you go to that.

FONDLEWIFE: Oh, how the blasphemous wretch swears! Out of my house, thou son of the Whore of Babylon; offspring of Bell and the Dragon.[13] – Bless us! Ravish my wife! My Dinah! Oh Schechemite![14] Begone, I say.

SIR JOSEPH: Why, the devil's in the people, I think.
    [*Exit.*]

LAETITIA: Oh! Won't you follow and see him out of doors, my dear?

FONDLEWIFE: I'll shut this door, to secure him from coming back. – Give me the key of your cabinet, Cocky. – Ravish my wife before my face! I warrant he's a Papist in his heart, at least, if not a Frenchman.

LAETITIA [*aside*]: What can I do now! [*Aloud.*] Oh! my dear, I have been in such a fright that I forgot to tell you; poor Mr Spintext has a sad fit of the cholic and is forced to lie down upon our bed. – You'll disturb him; I can tread softlier.

13. *Bell and the Dragon*: two Babylonian idols destroyed by Daniel; see the Apocrypha.
14. *Dinah . . . Schechemite*: Shechem ravished Dinah, the daughter of Jacob and Leah; see Genesis 34.

FONDLEWIFE: Alack, poor man. – No, no, you don't know the papers. – I won't disturb him; give me the key.

[*She gives him the key, goes to the chamber-door, and speaks aloud.*]

LAETITIA: 'Tis nobody but Mr Fondlewife, Mr Spintext, lie still on your stomach; lying on your stomach will ease you of the cholic.

FONDLEWIFE: Ay, ay, lie still, lie still; don't let me disturb you.

[*Goes in.*]

LAETITIA: Sure, when he does not see his face, he won't discover him. Dear Fortune, help me but this once, and I'll never run in thy debt again. But this opportunity is the devil.

[FONDLEWIFE *returns with papers.*]

FONDLEWIFE: Good lack! Good lack! I profess, the poor man is in great torment, he lies as flat – dear, you should heat a trencher, or a napkin. – Where's Deborah? Let her clap a warm thing to his stomach, or chafe it with a warm hand, rather than fail. What book's this?

[*Sees the book that* BELLMOUR *forgot.*]

LAETITIA: Mr Spintext's prayer-book, dear. [*Aside.*] Pray heaven it be a prayer-book.

FONDLEWIFE: Good man! I warrant he dropped it on purpose, that you might take it up and read some of the pious ejaculations.

[*Taking up the book.*]

O bless me! O monstrous! A prayer-book? Ay, this is the devil's *Pater-noster.* Hold, let me see: *The Innocent Adultery.*[15]

LAETITIA [*aside*]: Misfortune! Now all's ruined again.

BELLMOUR [*peeping*]: Damned chance! If I had gone a-whoring with *The Practice of Piety*[16] in my pocket, I had never been discovered.

FONDLEWIFE: Adultery, and innocent! O Lord! Here's doctrine! Ay, here's discipline!

LAETITIA: Dear husband, I'm amazed. – Sure it's a good book, and only tends to the speculation of sin.

FONDLEWIFE: Speculation! No, no; something went farther than

15. *The Innocent Adultery*: another novella by Paul Scarron which in part relates the attempted adultery of a young wife married to an older husband.
16. *The Practice of Piety*: a popular religious manual.

speculation when I was not to be let in. – Where is this apocryphal Elder? I'll ferret him.

LAETITIA [aside]: I'm so distracted, I can't think of a lie.

[FONDLEWIFE haling out BELLMOUR.]

FONDLEWIFE: Come out here, thou Ananias incarnate. – Who, how now! Who have we here?

LAETITIA [shrieks, as surprised]: Ha!

FONDLEWIFE: Oh, thou salacious woman! Am I then brutified? Ay, I feel it here; I sprout, I bud, I blossom, I am ripe-horn-mad. But who, in the devil's name, are you? Mercy on me for swearing, but –

LAETITIA: Oh, goodness keep us! Who's this? Who are you? What are you?

BELLMOUR: Soh.

LAETITIA: In the name of the – Oh! Good, my dear, don't come near it, I'm afraid 'tis the devil; indeed it has hoofs, dear.

FONDLEWIFE: Indeed, and I have horns, dear. The devil, no. I'm afraid 'tis the flesh, thou harlot, dear, with the pox. Come siren, speak, confess, who is this reverend, brawny pastor?

LAETITIA: Indeed and indeed, now my dear Nykin – I never saw this wicked man before.

FONDLEWIFE: Oh, it is a man then, it seems.

LAETITIA: Rather, sure it is a wolf in the clothing of a sheep.

FONDLEWIFE: Thou art a devil in his proper clothing, woman's flesh. What, you know nothing of him but his fleece here! – You don't love mutton, you Magdalen unconverted?

BELLMOUR [aside]: Well, now I know my cue. – That is, very honourably to excuse her, and very impudently accuse myself.

LAETITIA: Why then, I wish I may never enter into the heaven of your embraces again, my dear, if ever I saw his face before.

FONDLEWIFE: O Lord! O strange! I am in admiration of your impudence. Look at him a little better; he is more modest, I warrant you, than to deny it. Come, were you two never face-to-face before? Speak.

BELLMOUR: Since all artifice is vain – and I think myself obliged to speak the truth in justice to your wife – no.

FONDLEWIFE: Humph!

LAETITIA: No, indeed dear.

FONDLEWIFE: Nay, I find you are both in a story; that, I must confess. But, what – not to be cured of the cholic? Don't you know your patient, Mrs Quack? Oh, lie upon your stomach; lying upon your stomach will cure you of the cholic. Ah! I wish he has lain upon nobody's stomach but his own. Answer me that, Jezebel!

LAETITIA: Let the wicked man answer for himself. Does he think that I have nothing to do but excuse him; 'tis enough, if I can clear my own innocence to my own dear.

BELLMOUR: By my troth, and so 'tis. [Aside.] I have been a little too backward, that's the truth on't.

FONDLEWIFE: Come, sir, who are you, in the first place? And what are you?

BELLEMOUR: A whoremaster.

FONDLEWIFE: Very concise.

LAETITIA: O beastly, impudent creature!

FONDLEWIFE: Well, sir, and what came you hither for?

BELLMOUR: To lie with your wife.

FONDLEWIFE: Good again. A very civil person this, and I believe speaks truth.

LAETITIA: Oh, insupportable impudence!

FONDLEWIFE: Well, sir. – Pray be covered – and you have – heh! You have finished the matter, heh? And I am, as I should be, a sort of a civil perquisite to a whoremaster, called a cuckold, heh. Is it not so? Come, I'm inclining to believe every word you say.

BELLMOUR: Why, faith, I must confess, so I designed you. But you were a little unlucky in coming so soon, and hindered the making of your own fortune.

FONDLEWIFE: Humph. Nay, if you mince the matter once, and go back of your word, you are not the person I took you for. Come, come, go on boldly. What, don't be ashamed of your profession. – Confess, confess, I shall love thee the better for't, I shall, ifeck. What, dost think I don't know how to behave myself in the employment of a cuckold, and have been three years' apprentice to matrimony? Come, come, plain-dealing is a jewel.

BELLMOUR: Well, since I see thou art a good honest fellow, I'll confess the whole matter to thee.

FONDLEWIFE: Oh, I am a very honest fellow. – You never lay with an honester man's wife in your life.

LAETITIA [aside]: How my heart aches! All my comfort lies in his impudence, and, heaven be praised, he has a considerable portion.

BELLMOUR: In short then, I was informed of the opportunity of your absence by my spy (for faith, honest Isaac, I have a long time designed thee this favour). I knew Spintext was to come by your direction, but I laid a trap for him, and procured his habit, in which I passed upon your servants and was conducted hither. I pretended a fit of the cholic to excuse my lying down upon your bed, hoping that when she heard of it her good nature would bring her to administer remedies for my distemper. – You know what might have followed, but like an uncivil person, you knocked at the door before your wife was come to me.

FONDLEWIFE: Ha! This is apocryphal; I may choose whether I will believe it or no.

BELLMOUR: That you may, faith, and I hope you won't believe a word on't. But I can't help telling the truth, for my life

FONDLEWIFE: How! Would not you have me believe you, say you?

BELLMOUR: No, for then you must of consequence part with your wife, and there will be some hopes of having her upon the public; then the encouragement of a separate maintenance –

FONDLEWIFE: No, no, for that matter, when she and I part, she'll carry her separate maintenance about her.

LAETITIA: Ah cruel dear, how can you be so barbarous? You'll break my heart if you talk of parting.

[Cries.]

FONDLEWIFE: Ah, dissembling vermin!

BELLMOUR: How canst thou be so cruel, Isaac? Thou hast the heart of a mountain tiger. By the faith of a sincere sinner, she's innocent for me. Go to him, madam; fling your snowy arms about his stubborn neck; bathe his relentless face in your salt trickling tears. – So, a few soft words, and a kiss, and the good man melts. See, how kind nature works and boils over in him.

[*She goes and hangs upon his neck, and kisses him.* BELLMOUR *kisses her hand, behind* FONDLEWIFE's *back.*]

LAETITIA: Indeed, my dear, I was but just coming downstairs, when you knocked at the door, and the maid told me Mr Spintext was ill of the cholic, upon our bed. And won't you speak to me, cruel Nykin? Indeed, I'll die if you don't.

FONDLEWIFE: Ah! No, no, I cannot speak; my heart's so full – I have been a tender husband, a tender yoke-fellow; you know I have. But thou hast been a faithless Delilah, and the Philistines have been upon thee. Heh! Art thou not vile and unclean, heh? Speak.

LAETITIA [*weeping and sighing*]: No-o.

FONDLEWIFE: Oh, that I could believe thee!

LAETITIA: Oh, my heart will break!

[*Seeming to faint.*]

FONDLEWIFE: Heh. – How? No, stay, stay, I will believe thee, I will. – Pray, bend her forward, sir.

LAETITIA: Oh! Oh! Where is my dear?

FONDLEWIFE: Here, here, I do believe thee. – I won't believe my own eyes.

BELLMOUR: For my part, I am so charmed with the love of your turtle to you that I'll go and solicit matrimony with all my might and main.

FONDLEWIFE: Well, well, sir, as long as I believe it, 'tis well enough. No thanks to you sir, for her virtue. – But, I'll show you the way out of my house, if you please. Come, my dear. Nay, I will believe thee, I do, ifeck.

BELLMOUR: See the great blessing of any easy faith; opinion cannot err:

No husband, by his wife, can be deceived:
She still is virtuous, if she's so believed.

[*Exeunt.*]

ACT FIVE

SCENE ONE

The street

[*Enter* BELLMOUR *in fanatic habit, and* SETTER.]

BELLMOUR: Setter! Well encountered.

SETTER: Joy of your return, sir. Have you made a good voyage? Or have you brought your own lading back?

BELLMOUR: No, I have brought nothing but ballast back. Made a delicious voyage, Setter, and might have rode at anchor in the port till this time, but the enemy surprised us. I would unrig.

SETTER: I attend you, sir.

[HEARTWELL *and* LUCY *appear at* SILVIA'S *door.*]

BELLMOUR: Ha! Is not that Heartwell at Silvia's door; be gone quickly, I'll follow you; – I would not be known. [*Exit* SETTER.] Pox take 'em, they stand just in my way.

HEARTWELL: I'm impatient till it be done.

LUCY: That may be, without troubling yourself to go again for your brother's chaplain. Don't you see that stalking form of godliness?

HEARTWELL: O pox; he's a fanatic.

LUCY: An executioner qualified to do your business. He has been lawfully ordained.

HEARTWELL: I'll pay him well, if you'll break the matter to him.

LUCY: I warrant you – do you go and prepare your bride.

[*Exit* HEARTWELL.]

BELLMOUR: Humph, sits the wind there? What a lucky rogue am I! Oh, what sport will be here, if I can persuade this wench to secrecy!

LUCY: Sir, reverend sir.

BELLMOUR: Madam.

[*Discovers himself.*]

LUCY: Now, goodness have mercy upon me! Mr Bellmour! Is it you?

BELLMOUR: Even I. What dost think?

LUCY: Think? That I should not believe my eyes, and that you are not what you seem to be.

BELLMOUR: True. But to convince thee who I am, thou know'st my own token.

[*Kisses her.*]

LUCY: Nay, Mr Bellmour. O Lard! I believe you are a parson in good earnest, you kiss so devoutly.

BELLMOUR: Well, your business with me, Lucy?

LUCY: I had none, but through mistake.

BELLMOUR: Which mistake you must go through with, Lucy. Come, I know the intrigue between Heartwell and your mistress; and you mistook me for Tribulation Spintext, to marry 'em – ha? Are not matters in this posture? Confess. – Come, I'll be faithful; I will, i'faith. – What, diffide in[1] me Lucy?

LUCY: Alas-a-day! You and Mr Vainlove between you have ruined my poor mistress. You have made a gap in her reputation, and can you blame her if she stop it up with a husband?

BELLMOUR: Well, it is as I say?

LUCY: Well, it is then. But you'll be secret?

BELLMOUR: Phuh, secret, ay. – And to be out of thy debt, I'll trust thee with another secret. Your mistress must not marry Heartwell, Lucy.

LUCY: How! O Lord! –

BELLMOUR: Nay, don't be in passion, Lucy; I'll provide a fitter husband for her. Come, here's earnest of my good intentions for thee too. Let this mollify. [*Gives her money.*] Look you, Heartwell is my friend; and though he be blind, I must not see him fall into the snare and unwittingly marry a whore.

LUCY: Whore! I'd have you know my mistress scorns –

BELLMOUR: Nay, nay; look you, Lucy, there are whores of as good

1. *diffide in*: distrust.

quality. – But to the purpose, if you will give me leave to acquaint you with it. Do you carry on the mistake of me: I'll marry 'em. – Nay, don't pause: if you do, I'll spoil all. I have some private reasons for what I do, which I'll tell you within. In the mean time, I promise – and rely upon me to help your mistress to a husband. Nay, and thee too, Lucy. – Here's my hand I will, with a fresh assurance.

[*Gives her more money.*]

LUCY: Ah, the devil is not so cunning. You know my easy nature. – Well, for once I'll venture to serve you; but if you do deceive me, the curse of all kind, tender-hearted women light upon you.

BELLMOUR: That's as much as to say, the pox take me. – Well, lead on.

[*Exeunt.*]

[*Enter* VAINLOVE, SHARPER *and* SETTER.]

SHARPER: Just now, say you, gone in with Lucy?

SETTER: I saw him, sir; and stood at the corner where you found me, and overheard all they said. Mr Bellmour is to marry 'em.

SHARPER: Ha, ha! 'Twill be a pleasant cheat. I'll plague Heartwell when I see him. Prithee, Frank, let's tease him; make him fret till he foam at the mouth, and disgorge his matrimonial oath with interest. Come, thou'rt so musty –

SETTER [*to* SHARPER]: Sir, a word with you.

[*Whispers him.*]

VAINLOVE: Sharper swears she has forsworn the letter. I'm sure he tells me truth – but I am not sure she told him truth. Yet she was unaffectedly concerned, he says, and often blushed with anger and surprise. – And so I remember in the park. She had reason, if I wrong her. – I begin to doubt.

SHARPER: Say'st thou so!

SETTER: This afternoon, sir, about an hour before my master received the letter.

SHARPER: In my conscience, like enough.

SETTER: Ay, I know her, sir; at least, I'm sure I can fish it out of her. She's the very sluice to her lady's secrets; 'tis but setting her mill a-going, and I can drain her of 'em all.

SHARPER: Here, Frank; your blood-hound has made out the fault.

This letter that so sticks in thy maw is counterfeit; only a trick of Silvia in revenge, contrived by Lucy.

VAINLOVE: Ha! It has a colour.[2] – But how do you know it, sirrah?

SETTER: I do suspect as much – because why, sir? She was pumping me about how your worship's affairs stood towards Madam Araminta. As, when you had seen her last; when you were to see her next; and, where you were to be found at that time; and such like.

VAINLOVE: And where did you tell her?

SETTER: In the Piazza.

VAINLOVE: There I received the letter; it must be so. And why did you not find me out to tell me this before, sot?

SETTER: Sir, I was pimping for Mr Bellmour.

SHARPER: You were well employed – I think there is no objection to the excuse.

VAINLOVE: Pox o' my saucy credulity! If I have lost her, I deserve it. But if confession and repentance be of force, I'll win her, or weary her into a forgiveness.

[Exit.]

SHARPER: Methinks I long to see Bellmour come forth.

[Enter BELLMOUR.]

SETTER: Talk of the devil! – See where he comes.

SHARPER: Hugging himself in his prosperous mischief. No real fanatic can look better pleased after a successful sermon of sedition.

BELLMOUR: Sharper, fortify thy spleen! Such a jest! Speak when thou art ready.

SHARPER: Now, were I ill-natured, would I utterly disappoint thy mirth: hear thee tell thy mighty jest with as much gravity as a bishop hears venereal causes in the Spiritual Court. Not so much as wrinkle my face with one smile, but let thee look simply, and laugh by thyself.

BELLMOUR: Pshaw, no; I have a better opinion of thy wit. – Gad, I defy thee.

SHARPER: Were it not loss of time, you should make the experi-

2. *It has a colour*: it seems plausible.

ment. But honest Setter here overheard you with Lucy, and has told me all.

BELLMOUR: Nay, then I thank thee for not putting me out of countenance. But, to tell you something you don't know – I got an opportunity (after I had married 'em), of discovering the cheat to Silvia. She took it at first as another woman would the like disappointment, but my promise to make her amends quickly with another husband, somewhat pacified her.

SHARPER: But how the devil do you think to acquit yourself of your promise? Will you marry her yourself?

BELLMOUR: I have no such intentions at present. – Prithee, wilt thou think a little for me? I am sure the ingenious Mr Setter will assist –

SETTER: O Lord, sir!

BELLMOUR: I'll leave him with you, and go shift my habit.[3]

[*Exit.*]

[*Enter* SIR JOSEPH *and* BLUFFE.]

SHARPER: Heh! Sure, fortune has sent this fool hither on purpose. Setter, stand close. Seem not to observe 'em, and hark ye.

[*Whispers.*]

BLUFFE: Fear him not – I am prepared for him now; and he shall find he might have safer roused a sleeping lion.

SIR JOSEPH: Hush, hush! Don't you see him?

BLUFFE: Show him to me. Where is he?

SIR JOSEPH: Nay, don't speak so loud. – I don't jest, as I did a little while ago. – Look yonder. – Agad, if he should hear the lion roar, he'd cudgel him into an ass, and his primitive braying. Don't you remember the story in Aesop's *Fables*, bully? Agad there are good morals to be picked out of Aesop's *Fables*, let me tell you that, and *Reynard the Fox* too.

BLUFFE: Damn your morals.

SIR JOSEPH: Prithee, don't speak so loud.

BLUFFE [*in a low voice*]: Damn your morals; I must revenge th' affront done to my honour.

SIR JOSEPH [*stealing away upon his tip-toes*]: Ay; do, do, Captain, if

3. *shift my habit*: change clothes.

you think fit. – You may dispose of your own flesh as you think fitting, d'ye see. But, by the Lord Harry, I'll leave you.

BLUFFE [*almost whispering, and treading softly after him*]: Prodigious! What, will you forsake your friend in his extremity! You can't, in honour, refuse to carry him a challenge.

SIR JOSEPH: Prithee, what do you see in my face that looks as if I would carry a challenge? Honour is your province, Captain; take it – all the world know me to be a knight, and a man of worship.

SETTER: I warrant you, sir, I'm instructed.

SHARPER [*aloud*]: Impossible! Araminta take a liking to a fool!

SETTER: Her head runs on nothing else, nor she can talk of nothing else.

SHARPER: I know she commended him all the while we were in the park; but I thought it had been only to make Vainlove jealous.

SIR JOSEPH: How's this! Good bully, hold your breath, and let's hearken. Agad, this must be I.

SHARPER: Death, it can't be – an oaf, an idiot, a wittol.

SIR JOSEPH: Ay, now it's out; 'tis I, my own individual person.

SHARPER: A wretch, that has flown for shelter to the lowest shrub of mankind, and seeks protection from a blasted coward.

SIR JOSEPH: That's you, bully Back.

[BLUFFE *frowns upon* SIR JOSEPH.]

SHARPER [*to* SETTER]: She has given Vainlove her promise to marry him before tomorrow morning, has she not?

SETTER: She has, sir; and I have it in charge to attend her all this evening, in order to conduct her to the place appointed.

SHARPER: Well, I'll go and inform your master; and do you press her to make all the haste imaginable.

[*Exit.*]

SETTER: Were I a rogue now, what a noble prize could I dispose of! A goodly pinnace,[4] richly laden, and to launch forth under my auspicious convoy. Twelve thousand pounds, and all her rigging, besides what lies concealed under hatches. – Ha! All this committed to my care! Avaunt, temptation! – Setter, show thyself a person of worth; be true to thy trust, and be reputed honest.

4. *pinnace*: small, light vessel; figuratively, a mistress.

Reputed honest? Hum; is that all? Ay, for to be honest is nothing; the reputation of it is all. Reputation! What have such poor rogues as I to do with reputation? 'Tis above us. – And, for men of quality, they are above it. So that reputation is e'en as foolish as honesty. – And, for my part, if I meet Sir Joseph with a purse of gold in his hand, I'll dispose of mine to the best advantage.

SIR JOSEPH: Heh, heh, heh. Here, 'tis for you i'faith, Mr Setter. Nay, I'll take you at your word.

[*Chinking a purse.*]

SETTER: Sir Joseph, and the Captain too! Undone, undone! I'm undone, my master's undone, my lady's undone, and all the business is undone.

SIR JOSEPH: No, no, never fear, man, the lady's business shall be done. What – come, Mr Setter, I have overheard all, and to speak is but loss of time; but if there be occasion, let these worthy gentlemen intercede for me.

[*Gives him gold.*]

SETTER: O Lord, sir, what d'ye mean? Corrupt my honesty? They have indeed, very persuading faces. But –

SIR JOSEPH: 'Tis too little, there's more, man. There, take all. Now –

SETTER: Well, Sir Joseph, you have such a winning way with you.

SIR JOSEPH: And how, and how, good Setter, did the little rogue look when she talked of Sir Joseph? Did not her eyes twinkle, and her mouth water? Did not she pull up her little bubbies?[5] And – agad I'm so over-joyed. – And stroke down her belly, and then step aside to tie her garter, when she was thinking of her love. Heh, Setter?

SETTER: Oh yes, sir.

SIR JOSEPH: How now, bully? What, melancholy because I'm in the lady's favours? – No matter, I'll make your peace. – I know, they were a little smart upon you, but I warrant I'll bring you into the lady's good graces.

BLUFFE: Pshaw, I have petitions to show from other guess-toys[6]

5. *bubbies*: breasts.
6. *guess-toys*: mistresses.

than she. Look here: these were sent me this morning – there, read. [*Shows letters.*] That – that's a scrawl of quality. Here, here's from a countess too. Hum – no, hold – that's from a knight's wife, she sent it me by her husband. But here, both these are from persons of great quality.

SIR JOSEPH: They are either from persons of great quality, or no quality at all, 'tis such a damned ugly hand.

[*While* SIR JOSEPH *reads,* BLUFFE *whispers to* SETTER.]

SETTER: Captain, I would do anything to serve you; but this is so difficult –

BLUFFE: Not at all. Don't I know him?

SETTER: You'll remember the conditions?

BLUFFE: I'll give't you under my hand. In the mean time, here's earnest. [*Gives him money*.] Come, knight; I'm capitulating with Mr Setter for you.

SIR JOSEPH: Ah, honest Setter. – Sirrah, I'll give thee anything but a night's lodging.

[*Exeunt.*]

[*Enter* SHARPER, *tugging in* HEARTWELL.]

SHARPER: Nay, prithee, leave railing, and come along with me: maybe she mayn't be within. 'Tis but to yond' corner-house.

HEARTWELL: Whither? Whither? Which corner-house?

SHARPER: Why, there; the two white posts.

HEARTWELL: And who would you visit there, say you? O'ons, how my heart aches.

SHARPER: Pshaw, thou'rt so troublesome and inquisitive. Why, I'll tell you; 'tis a young creature that Vainlove debauched, and has forsaken. Did you never hear Bellmour chide him about Silvia.

HEARTWELL [*aside*]: Death, and hell, and marriage! My wife!

SHARPER: Why, thou art as musty as a new-married man, that had found his wife knowing the first night.

HEARTWELL [*aside*]: Hell, and the devil! Does he know it? But hold – if he should not, I were a fool to discover it. I'll dissemble, and try him. Ha, ha, ha! Why Tom, is that such an occasion of melancholy? Is it such an uncommon mischief?

SHARPER: No, faith; I believe not. – Few women but have their year of probation, before they are cloistered in the narrow joys of wedlock. But prithee come along with me, or I'll go and have the lady to myself. B'w'y' George.

[*Going.*]

HEARTWELL: O torture! How he racks and tears me! Death! Shall I own my shame, or wittingly let him go and whore my wife? No, that's insupportable. – Oh, Sharper.

SHARPER: How now?

HEARTWELL: Oh, I am – married.

SHARPER: Now hold, spleen! Married?

HEARTWELL: Certainly, irrecoverably married.

SHARPER: Heaven forbid, man. How long?

HEARTWELL: Oh, an age, an age; I have been married these two hours.

SHARPER: My old bachelor married! That were a jest. Ha, ha, ha!

HEARTWELL: Death! D'ye mock me? Hark ye. If either you esteem my friendship, or your own safety, come not near that house, that corner-house – that hot brothel. Ask no questions.

[*Exit.*]

SHARPER: Mad, by this light.

Thus grief still treads upon the heels of pleasure:
Married in haste, we may repent at leisure.

[SETTER *entering.*]

SETTER: Some by experience find those words misplaced: at leisure married, they repent in haste. As, I suppose, my master, Heartwell.

SHARPER: Here again, my Mercury!

SETTER: Sublimate, if you please, sir: I think my achievements do deserve the epithet. – Mercury was a pimp too;[7] but, though I blush to own it at this time, I must confess I am somewhat fallen from the dignity of my function, and do condescend to be scandalously employed in the promotion of vulgar matrimony.

SHARPER: As how, dear dexterous pimp?

SETTER: Why, to be brief, for I have weighty affairs depending: our stratagem succeeding as you intended, Bluffe turns errant traitor;

7. Congreve is probably thinking of Mercury's role in Dryden's play, *Amphitryon* (1690).

bribes me to make a private conveyance of the lady to him, and put a sham settlement upon Sir Joseph.

SHARPER: O rogue! Well, but I hope –

SETTER: No, no; never fear me, sir. – I privately informed the knight of the treachery, who has agreed seemingly to be cheated, that the Captain may be so in reality.

SHARPER: Where's the bride?

SETTER: Shifting clothes for the purpose at a friend's house of mine. Here's company coming. If you'll walk this way, sir, I'll tell you. [*Exeunt.*]

[*Enter* BELLMOUR, BELINDA, ARAMINTA *and* VAINLOVE.]

VAINLOVE [*to* ARAMINTA]: Oh, 'twas frenzy all: cannot you forgive it? Men in madness have a title to your pity.

ARAMINTA: Which they forfeit when they are restored to their senses.

VAINLOVE: I am not presuming beyond a pardon.

ARAMINTA: You who could reproach me with one counterfeit, how insolent would a real pardon make you? But there's no need to forgive what is not worth my anger.

BELINDA [*to* BELLMOUR]: O', my conscience. I could find in my heart to marry thee, purely to be rid of thee. – At least thou art so troublesome a lover, there's hopes thou'lt make a more than ordinary quiet husband.

BELLMOUR: Say you so? – Is that a maxim among ye?

BELINDA: Yes! You flattering men of the mode have made marriage a mere French dish.

BELLMOUR [*aside*]: I hope there's no French sauce.[8]

BELINDA: You are so curious in the preparation, that is, your courtship, one would think you meant a noble entertainment. – But when we come to feed, 'tis all froth, and poor, but in show. Nay, often, only remains which have been, I know not how many times, warmed for other company, and at last served up cold to the wife.

BELLMOUR: That were a miserable wretch indeed, who could not afford one warm dish for the wife of his bosom. – But you

8. *French sauce*: the pox.

timorous virgins form a dreadful chimera of a husband, as of a creature contrary to that soft, humble, pliant, easy thing, a lover; so guess at plagues in matrimony in opposition to the pleasures of courtship. Alas! courtship to marriage is but as the music in the play-house till the curtain's drawn; but that once up, then opens the scene of pleasure.

BELINDA: Oh, foh, no; rather, courtship to marriage, as a very witty prologue to a very dull play.

[*Enter* SHARPER.]

SHARPER: Hist, Bellmour! If you'll bring the ladies, make haste to Silvia's lodgings, before Heartwell has fretted himself out of breath. – I'm in haste now, but I'll come in at the catastrophe.

[*Exit.*]

BELLMOUR [*to* BELINDA]: You have an opportunity now, madam, to revenge yourself upon Heartwell for affronting your squirrel.

BELINDA: Oh, the filthy rude beast!

ARAMINTA: 'Tis a lasting quarrel; I think he has never been at our house since.

BELLMOUR: But give yourselves the trouble to walk to that corner-house, and I'll tell you by the way what may divert and surprise you.

[*Exeunt.*]

SCENE TWO

Scene changes to Silvia's lodgings.

[*Enter* HEARTWELL *and* BOY.]

HEARTWELL: Gone forth, say you, with her maid!

BOY: There was a man too that fetched 'em out; Setter, I think they called him.

HEARTWELL: So-h, that precious pimp too! Damned, damned strumpet! Could she not contain herself on her wedding-day! Not hold out till night! Leave me.

[*Exit* BOY.]

O cursed state! How wide we err, when apprehensive of the load
of life! We hope to find
> That help which nature meant in woman-kind
> To man that supplemental self designed;
> But proves a burning caustic when applied.
> And Adam, sure, could with more ease abide
> The bone when broken, than when made a bride.

[*Enter* BELLMOUR, BELINDA, VAINLOVE, ARAMINTA.]

BELLMOUR: Now, George. What, rhyming! I thought the chimes
of verse were past when once the doleful marriage-knell was
rung.

HEARTWELL: Shame and confusion! I am exposed.

[VAINLOVE *and* ARAMINTA *talk apart.*]

BELINDA: Joy, joy Mr Bridegroom; I give you joy, sir.

HEARTWELL: 'Tis not in thy nature to give me joy. A woman can as
soon give immortality.

BELINDA: Ha, ha, ha. O gad, men grow such clowns when they are
married.

BELLMOUR: That they are fit for no company but their wives.

BELINDA: Nor for them neither, in a little time. I swear, at the
month's end, you shall hardly find a married man that will do a
civil thing to his wife, or say a civil thing to anybody else. Jesus!
how he looks already. Ha, ha, ha.

BELLMOUR: Ha, ha, ha.

HEARTWELL: Death, am I made your laughing-stock? For you, sir,
I shall find a time; but take off your wasp here, or the clown may
grow boisterous. I have a fly-flap.

BELINDA: You have occasion for't; your wife has been blown
upon.

BELLMOUR: That's home.

HEARTWELL: Not fiends or furies could have added to my vexation,
or anything, but another woman. You've wracked my patience;
begone, or by –

BELLMOUR: Hold, hold. What the devil, thou wilt not draw upon a
woman?

VAINLOVE: What's the matter?

ARAMINTA: Bless me! What have you done to him?

BELINDA: Only touched a galled beast till he winced.

VAINLOVE: Bellmour, give it over; you vex him too much; 'tis all serious to him.

BELINDA: Nay, I swear, I begin to pity him myself.

HEARTWELL: Damn your pity! But let me be calm a little. – How have I deserved this of you? Any of ye? Sir, have I impaired the honour of your house, promised your sister marriage, and whored her? Wherein have I injured you? Did I bring a physician to your father when he lay expiring, and endeavour to prolong his life, and you one-and-twenty? Madam, have I had an opportunity with you and balked it? Did you ever offer me the favour that I refused it? Or –

BELINDA: Oh foh! What does the filthy fellow mean? Lard, let me be gone.

ARAMINTA: Hang me, if I pity you; you are right enough served.

BELLMOUR: This is a little scurrilous though.

VAINLOVE: Nay, 'tis a sore of your own scratching. Well George –

HEARTWELL: You are the principal cause of all present ills. If Silvia had not been your whore, my wife might have been honest.

VAINLOVE: And if Silvia had not been your wife, my whore might have been just. – There, we are even. – But have a good heart; I heard of your misfortune, and come to your relief.

HEARTWELL: When execution's over, you offer a reprieve.

VAINLOVE: What would you give?

HEARTWELL: Oh! anything, everything, a leg or two, or an arm; nay, I would be divorced from my virility, to be divorced from my wife.

[Enter SHARPER.]

VAINLOVE: Faith, that's a sure way. – But here's one can sell you freedom better cheap.

SHARPER: Vainlove, I have been a kind of a godfather to you, yonder. I have promised and vowed some things in your name, which I think you are bound to perform.

VAINLOVE: No signing to a blank, friend.

SHARPER: No, I'll deal fairly with you. 'Tis a full and free discharge to Sir Joseph Wittoll and Captain Bluffe for all injuries whatsoever, done unto you by them, until the present date hereof. – How say you?

VAINLOVE: Agreed.

SHARPER: Then, let me beg these ladies to wear their masks a moment.

    [*Exit.*]

HEARTWELL: What the devil's all this to me?

VAINLOVE: Patience.

    [*Re-enter* SHARPER, *with* SIR JOSEPH, BLUFFE, SILVIA, LUCY, SETTER.]

BLUFFE: All injuries whatsoever, Mr Sharper.

SIR JOSEPH: Ay, ay, whatsoever, Captain, stick to that; whatsoever.

SHARPER: 'Tis done; those gentlemen are witnesses to the general release.

VAINLOVE: Ay, ay, to this instant moment. – I have passed an act of oblivion.

BLUFFE: 'Tis very generous, sir, since I needs must own –

SIR JOSEPH: No, no, Captain, you need not own, heh, heh, heh. 'Tis I must own –

BLUFFE: That you are over-reached too, ha, ha, ha; only a little art military used – only undermined, or so, as shall appear by the fair Araminta, my wife's permission. [LUCY *unmasks.*] Oh the devil, cheated at last!

SIR JOSEPH: Only a little art-military trick, Captain, only countermined, or so. Mr Vainlove, I suppose you know whom I have got – now; but all's forgiven.

VAINLOVE: I know whom you have not got; pray ladies, convince him.

    [ARAMINTA *and* BELINDA *unmask.*]

SIR JOSEPH: Ah! O Lord, my heart aches. – Ah! Setter, a rogue of all sides.

SHARPER: Sir Joseph, you had better have pre-engaged this gentleman's pardon; for though Vainlove be so generous to forgive the loss of his mistress, I know not how Heartwell may take the loss of his wife.

    [SILVIA *unmasks.*]

HEARTWELL: My wife! By this light 'tis she, the very cockatrice — Oh Sharper! Let me embrace thee. — But art thou sure she is really married to him?

SETTER: Really and lawfully married; I am witness.

SHARPER: Bellmour will unriddle to you.

[HEARTWELL *goes to* BELLMOUR.]

SIR JOSEPH: Pray, madam, who are you? For I find you and I are like to be better acquainted.

SILVIA: The worst of me is, that I am your wife.

SHARPER: Come, Sir Joseph, your fortune is not so bad as you fear. — A fine lady, and a lady of very good quality.

SIR JOSEPH: Thanks to my knighthood, she's a lady —

VAINLOVE: That deserves a fool with a better title. Pray use her as my relation, or you shall hear on't.

BLUFFE: What, are you a woman of quality too, spouse?

SETTER: And my relation; pray let her be respected accordingly. — Well, honest Lucy, fare thee well. I think you and I have been play-fellows off-and-on, any time this seven years.

LUCY: Hold your prating; I'm thinking what vocation I shall follow, while my spouse is planting laurels in the wars.

BLUFFE: No more wars, spouse, no more wars. While I plant laurels for my head abroad, I may find the branches sprout at home.

HEARTWELL: Bellmour, I approve thy mirth, and thank thee. And I cannot in gratitude (for I see which way thou art going) see thee fall into the same snare out of which thou hast delivered me.

BELLMOUR: I thank thee, George, for thy good intention. — But there is a fatality in marriage, for I find I'm resolute.

HEARTWELL: Then good counsel will be thrown away upon you. For my part, I have once escaped. And when I wed again, may she be — ugly as an old bawd. —

VAINLOVE: Ill-natured as an old maid —

BELLMOUR: Wanton as a young widow —

SHARPER: And jealous as a barren wife.

HEARTWELL: Agreed.

BELLMOUR: Well, 'midst of these dreadful denunciations, and notwithstanding the warning and example before me, I commit myself to lasting durance.

BELINDA: Prisoner, make much of your fetters.

[*Giving her hand.*]

BELLMOUR: Frank, will you keep us in countenance.

VAINLOVE [*to* ARAMINTA]: May I presume to hope so great a blessing?

ARAMINTA: We had better take the advantage of a little of our friends' experience first.

BELLMOUR [*aside*]: O' my conscience she dares not consent, for fear he should recant. [*Aloud.*] Well, we shall have your company to church in the morning? Maybe it may get you an appetite to see us fall to before ye. Setter, did not you tell me –

SETTER: They're at the door: I'll call 'em in.

[*A dance.*]

BELLMOUR: Now set we forward on a journey for life. Come, take your fellow-travellers. Old George, I'm sorry to see thee still plod on alone.

HEARTWELL:

> With gaudy plumes and jingling bells made proud,
> The youthful beast sets forth, and neighs aloud.
> A morning sun his tinselled harness gilds,
> And the first stage a downhill greensward yields.
> But, oh, –
> What rugged ways attend the noon of life!
> (Our sun declines), and with what anxious strife,
> What pain we tug that galling load, a wife.
> All coursers the first heat with vigour run;
> But 'tis with whip and spur the race is won.

[*Exeunt omnes.*]

EPILOGUE,

Spoken by Mrs Barry.[1]

As a rash girl, who will all hazards run,
And be enjoyed, though sure to be undone;
Soon as her curiosity is over,
Would give the world she could her toy recover:
So fares it with our poet; and I'm sent
To tell you, he already does repent:
Would you were all as forward, to keep Lent.
Now the deed's done, the giddy-thing has leisure
To think o'th' sting, that's in the tail of pleasure.
Methinks I hear him in consideration!
What will the world say? Where's my reputation?
Now that's at stake – No fool, 'tis out o'fashion.
If loss of that should follow want of wit,
How many undone men were in the pit!
Why that's some comfort to an author's fears,
If he's an ass, he will be tried by's peers.
But hold – I am exceeding my commission;
My business here, was humbly to petition:
But we're so used to rail on these occasions,
I could not help one trial of your patience:
For 'tis our way (you know) for fear o'th' worst,
To be before-hand still, and cry fool first.
How say you, sparks? How do you stand affected?
I swear, young Bays[2] within, is so dejected,
'Twould grieve your hearts to see him; shall I call him?
But then you cruel critics would so maul him!
Yet, may be, you'll encourage a beginner;
But how? – Just as the devil does a sinner.

---

1. Elizabeth Barry played the part of Laetitia.
2. The name given to Dryden in the burlesque of his plays in *The Rehearsal* (1671).

Women and wits are used e'en much at one;
You gain your end, and damn 'em when you've done.

FINIS.

The
Double Dealer

Sir,

I heartily wish this play were as perfect as I intended it, that it might be more worthy your acceptance, and that my dedication of it to you might be more becoming that honour and esteem which I, with everybody who are so fortunate as to know you, have for you. It had your countenance when yet unknown; and now it is made public, it wants your protection.

And give me leave, without any flattery to you or vanity in myself, to tell my illiterate critics, as an answer to their impotent objections, that they have found fault with that which has been pleasing to you. This play, in relation to my concern for its reputation, succeeded before it was acted, for through your early patronage it had an audience of several persons of the first rank both in wit and quality; and their allowance of it was a consequence of your approbation. Therefore, if I really wish it might have had a more popular reception, it is not at all in consideration of myself, but because I wish well, and would gladly contribute to the benefit of the stage, and diversion of the town. They were (not long since) so kind to a very imperfect comedy of mine, that I thought myself justly indebted to them all my endeavours for an entertainment that might merit some little of that applause, which they were so lavish of, when I thought I had no title to it. But I find they are to be treated cheaply, and I have been at an unnecessary expense.

I would not have anybody imagine that I think this play without its faults, for I am conscious of several (and ready to own 'em; but it shall be to those who are able to find 'em out). I confess I designed (whatever vanity or ambition occasioned that design) to have writ-

1. Whig politician and literary patron.

ten a true and regular comedy, but I found it an undertaking which put me in mind of – *sudet multum, frustraque laboret ausus idem.*[2] And now to make amends for the vanity of such a design, I do confess both the attempt, and the imperfect performance. Yet I must take the boldness to say, I have not miscarried in the whole; for the mechanical part of it is perfect. That, I may say with as little vanity as a builder may say he has built a house according to the model laid down before him, or a gardener that he has set his flowers in a knot of such or such a figure. I designed the moral first, and to that moral I invented the fable, and do not know that I have borrowed one hint of it anywhere. I made the plot as strong as I could, because it was single, and I made it single, because I would avoid confusion, and was resolved to preserve the three unities of the drama, which I have visibly done to the utmost severity. This is what I ought not to observe upon myself; but the ignorance and malice of the greater part of the audience is such that they would make a man turn herald to his own play, and blazon every character. However, sir, this discourse is very impertinent to you, whose judgment much better can discern the faults, than I can excuse them; and whose good nature, like that of a lover, will find out those hidden beauties (if there are any such) which it would be great immodesty in me to discover. I think I don't speak improperly when I call you a lover of poetry; for it is very well known she has been a kind mistress to you; she has not denied you the last favour; you have enjoyed her, and she has been fruitful in a most beautiful issue – if I break off abruptly here, I hope everybody will understand that it is to avoid a commendation, which, as it is your due, would be most easy for me to pay, and too troublesome for you to receive.

I have, since the acting of this play, hearkened after the objections which have been made to it; for I was conscious where a true critic might have put me upon my defence. I was prepared for their attack; and am pretty confident I could have vindicated some parts, and excused others; and where there were any plain miscarriages, I would most ingenuously have confessed 'em. But I have not heard

---

2. *sudet . . . idem*: yet in the attempt he shall sweat and strain without success (Horace, *Ars Poetica*, ll. 241–2).

anything said sufficient to provoke an answer. Some little snarling and barking there has been, but I don't know one well-mouthed cur that has opened at all. That which looks most like an objection, does not relate in particular to this play, but to all or most that ever have been written; and that is, soliloquy. Therefore I will answer it, not only for my own sake, but to save others the trouble, to whom it may hereafter be objected.

I grant, that for a man to talk to himself appears absurd and unnatural; and indeed it is so in most cases; but the circumstances which may attend the occasion, make great alteration. It oftentimes happens to a man to have designs which require him to himself, and in their nature, cannot admit of a confidant. Such, for certain, is all villainy; and other less mischievous intentions may be very improper to be communicated to a second person. In such a case therefore the audience must observe, whether the person upon the stage takes any notice of them at all, or no. For if he supposes anyone to be by when he talks to himself, it is monstrous and ridiculous to the last degree. Nay, not only in this case, but in any part of a play, if there is expressed any knowledge of an audience, it is insufferable. But otherwise when a man in soliloquy reasons with himself, and pros and cons, and weighs all his designs, we ought not to imagine that this man either talks to us, or to himself; he is only thinking, and thinking such matter as were inexcusable folly in him to speak. But because we are concealed spectators of the plot in agitation, and the poet finds it necessary to let us know the whole mystery of his contrivance, he is willing to inform us of this person's thoughts; and to that end is forced to make use of the expedient of speech, no other better way being yet invented for the communication of thought.

Another very wrong objection has been made by some who have not taken leisure to distinguish the characters. The hero of the play, as they are pleased to call him, (meaning Mellefont) is a gull, and made a fool and cheated. Is every man a gull and a fool that is deceived? At that rate I'm afraid the two classes of men will be reduced to one, and the knaves themselves be at a loss to justify their title: but if an open-hearted honest man, who has an entire confidence in one whom he takes to be his friend, and whom he has obliged to be so; and who (to confirm him in his opinion) in all appearance, and upon several trials has been so: if this man be deceived by the treachery of the other, must he of necessity commence fool immediately, only because the other has proved a villain? Ay, but there was caution given to Mellefont in the first act by his friend Careless. Of what nature was that caution? Only to give the audience some light into the character of Maskwell, before his appearance; and not to convince Mellefont of his treachery; for that was more than Careless was then able to do: he never knew Maskwell guilty of any villainy; he was only a sort of man which he did not like. As for his suspecting his familiarity with my Lady Touchwood: let 'em examine the answer that Mellefont makes him, and compare it with the conduct of Maskwell's character through the play.

I would have 'em again look into the character of Maskwell, before they accuse anybody of weakness for being deceived by him. For upon summing up the enquiry into this objection, [I] find they have only mistaken cunning in one character, for folly in another.

But there is one thing at which I am more concerned than all the false criticisms that are made upon me; and that is, some of the ladies are offended. I am heartily sorry for it, for I declare I would rather disoblige all the critics in the world, than one of the fair sex. They are concerned that I have represented some women vicious and affected: how can I help it? It is the business of a comic poet to paint the vices and follies of humankind; and there are but two sexes that I know, *viz.* men and women, which have a title to humanity: and if I leave one half of them out, the work will be imperfect. I should be very glad of an opportunity to make my compliment to those ladies who are offended: but they can no more expect it in a comedy, than to be tickled by a surgeon when he's letting 'em blood. They who are virtuous or discreet, I'm sure cannot be offended, for such characters as these distinguish them, and make their beauties more shining and observed: and they who are of the other kind, may nevertheless pass for such, by seeming not to be displeased, or touched with the satire of this comedy. Thus have they also wrongfully accused me of doing them a prejudice, when I have in reality done them a service.

I have heard some whispering, as if they intended to accuse this play of smuttiness and bawdy: but I declare I took a particular care to avoid it, and if they find any in it, it is of their own making, for I did not design it to be so understood. But to avoid my saying anything upon a subject which has been so admirably handled before, and for their better instruction, I earnestly recommend to their perusual the Epistle Dedicatory before the *Plain-Dealer*.[3]

You will pardon me, sir, for the freedom I take of making answers to other people, in an epistle which ought wholly to be sacred to you: but since I intend the play to be so too, I hope I may take the more liberty of justifying it, where it is in the right. I hear a great many of the fools are angry at me, and I am glad of it; for I writ at them, not to 'em. This is a bold confession, and yet I don't think I shall disoblige one person by it; for nobody can take it to himself, without owning the character.

I must now, sir, declare to the world, how kind you have been to my endeavours; for in regard of what was well meant, you have excused what was ill performed. I beg you would continue the same method in your acceptance of this dedication. I know no other way of making a return to that charity you showed, in protecting an infant, but by enrolling it in your service, now that it is of age and come into the world. Therefore be pleased to accept of this as an acknowledgment of the favour you have shown me, and an earnest of the real service and gratitude of,

SIR

Your Most Obliged Humble Servant

WILLIAM CONGREVE.

3. William Wycherley's final play, first performed in 1676.

PROLOGUE

Spoken by Mrs Bracegirdle[1]

Moors have this way (as story tells) to know
Whether their brats are truly got, or no;
Into the sea, the new-born babe is thrown,
There, as instinct directs, to swim, or drown.
A barbarous device, to try if spouse
Have kept religiously her nuptial vows!
    Such are the trials poets make of plays:
Only they trust to more inconstant seas;
So does our author this his child commit
To the tempestuous mercy of the pit,
To know if it be truly born of wit.
    Critics avaunt; for you are fish of prey,
And feed, like sharks, upon an infant play.
Be ev'ry monster of the deep away;
Let's have a fair trial, and a clear sea.
    Let Nature work, and do not damn too soon,
For life will struggle long, 'ere it sink down:
Let it at least rise thrice,[2] before it drown.
Let us consider, had it been our fate,
Thus hardly to be proved legitimate!
I will not say, we'd all in danger been,
Were each to suffer for his mother's sin:
But, by my troth, I cannot avoid thinking
How nearly some good men might have scaped sinking.
But heaven be praised, this custom is confined
Alone to the offspring of the Muses' kind:

---

1. Anne Bracegirdle played the part of Cynthia.
2. Playwrights only received payment if the play ran for at least three days.

Our Christian cuckolds are more bent to pity;
I know not one Moor-husband in the City.
In th' good man's arms the chopping[3] bastard thrives,
For he thinks all his own, that is his wife's.
  Whatever fate is for this play designed,
The poet's sure he shall some comfort find:
For if his Muse has played him false, the worst
That can befall him is to be divorced;
You husbands judge, if that be to be cursed.

3. *chopping*: healthy, strong.

DRAMATIS PERSONAE

MEN

MASKWELL, *a villain; pretended friend to* MELLEFONT, *gallant to* LADY TOUCHWOOD, *and in love with* CYNTHIA

LORD TOUCHWOOD, *uncle to* MELLEFONT

MELLEFONT, *promised to, and in love with* CYNTHIA

CARELESS, *his friend*

LORD FROTH, *a solemn coxcomb*

BRISK, *a pert coxcomb*

SIR PAUL PLYANT, *an uxorius, foolish, old knight; brother to* LADY TOUCHWOOD, *and father to* CYNTHIA

WOMEN

LADY TOUCHWOOD, *in love with* MELLEFONT

CYNTHIA, *daughter to* SIR PAUL *by a former wife, promised to* MELLEFONT

LADY FROTH, *a great coquette; pretender to poetry, wit, and learning*

LADY PLYANT, *insolent to her husband, and easy to any pretender*

Chaplain, Boy, Footmen, and Attendants.

The scene, a gallery in the Lord Touchwood's house

The time
from five o'clock to eight in the evening.

ACT ONE

SCENE ONE

A gallery in the Lord Touchwood's *house,*
with chambers adjoining

[*Enter* CARELESS, *crossing the stage, with his hat, gloves, and sword in his hands, as just risen from table;* MELLEFONT *following him.*]

MELLEFONT: Ned, Ned, whither so fast? What, turned flincher! Why, you wo' not leave us?

CARELESS: Where are the women? Pox, I'm weary of guzzling, and begin to think them the better company.

MELLEFONT: Then thy reason staggers, and thou'rt almost drunk.

CARELESS: No faith, but your fools grow noisy – and if a man must endure the noise of words without sense, I think the women have the more musical voices, and become nonsense better.

MELLEFONT: Why, they are at that end of the gallery; retired to their tea, and scandal, according to their ancient custom after dinner. – But I made a pretence of following you, because I had something to say to you in private, and I am not like to have many opportunities this evening.

CARELESS: And here's this cox-comb most critically come to interrupt you.

[*Enter* BRISK.]

BRISK: Boys, boys, lads, where are you? What, do you give ground? Mortgage for a bottle, ha? Careless, this is your trick; you're always spoiling company by leaving it.

CARELESS: And thou art always spoiling company by coming into't.

BRISK: Pooh, ha, ha, ha, I know you envy me. Spite, proud spite, by the gods! and burning envy. – I'll be judged by Mellefont here, who gives and takes raillery better, you or I. Pox, man, when I say you spoil company by leaving it, I mean you leave nobody for the company to laugh at. I think there I was with you, ha? Mellefont?

MELLEFONT: O' my word, Brisk, that was a home thrust; you have silenced him.

BRISK: Oh, my dear Mellefont, let me perish, if thou art not the soul of conversation, the very essence of wit, and spirit of wine! The deuce take me if there were three good things said, or one understood, since thy amputation from the body of our society. – He, I think that's pretty and metaphorical enough: i'gad I could not have said it out of thy company. – Careless, ha?

CARELESS: Hum, ay, what is't?

BRISK: O, mon cœur! What is't! nay gad, I'll punish you for want of apprehension: the deuce take me if I tell you.

MELLEFONT: No, no, hang him, he has no taste. – But, dear Brisk, excuse me, I have a little business.

CARELESS: Prithee get thee gone; thou seest we are serious.

MELLEFONT: We'll come immediately, if you'll but go in, and keep up good humour and sense in the company: prithee do, they'll fall asleep else.

BRISK: I'gad so they will. – Well I will, I will, gad, you shall command me from the zenith to the nadir. – But the deuce take me if I say a good thing till you come. – But prithee, dear rogue, make haste, prithee make haste, I shall burst else. – And yonder your uncle, my Lord Touchwood, swears he'll disinherit you, and Sir Paul Plyant threatens to disclaim you for a son-in-law, and my Lord Froth won't dance at your wedding tomorrow; nor the deuce take me, I won't write your epithalamium – and see what a condition you're like to be brought to.

MELLEFONT: Well, I'll speak but three words, and follow you.

BRISK: Enough, enough; Careless, bring your apprehension along with you.

[Exit.]

CARELESS: Pert cox-comb!

MELLEFONT: Faith, 'tis a good natured cox-comb, and has very entertaining follies – you must be more humane to him; at this juncture it will do me service. I'll tell you, I would have mirth continued this day at any rate; though patience purchase folly, and attention be paid with noise: there are times when sense may be unseasonable, as well as truth. Prithee do thou wear none today; but allow Brisk to have wit, that thou may'st seem a fool.

CARELESS: Why, how now, why this extravagant proposition?

MELLEFONT: Oh, I would have no room for serious design, for I am jealous of a plot. I would have noise and impertinence keep my Lady Touchwood's head from working; for hell is not more busy than her brain, nor contains more devils than that imaginations.[1]

CARELESS: I thought your fear of her had been over. Is not tomorrow appointed for your marriage with Cynthia; and her father, Sir Paul Plyant, come to settle the writings this day, on purpose?

MELLEFONT: True; but you shall judge whether I have not reason to be alarmed. None besides you and Maskwell are acquainted with the secret of my aunt Touchwood's violent passion for me. Since my first refusal of her addresses, she has endeavoured to do me all ill offices with my uncle; yet has managed 'em with that subtlety, that to him they have borne the face of kindness; while her malice, like a dark lanthorn, only shone upon me where it was directed. Still, it gave me less perplexity to prevent the success of her displeasure, than to avoid the importunities of her love; and of two evils, I thought myself favoured in her aversion. But whether urged by her despair and the short prospect of time she saw to accomplish her designs; whether the hopes of her revenge, or of her love, terminated in the view of this my marriage with Cynthia, I know not; but this morning she surprised me in my bed –

CARELESS: Was there ever such a fury! 'Tis well nature has not put it into her sex's power to ravish. – Well, bless us! Proceed. What followed?

MELLEFONT: What at first amazed me; for I looked to have seen her in all the transports of a slighted and revengeful woman. But when I expected thunder from her voice, and lightning in her eyes, I saw her melted into tears, and hushed into a sigh. It was long before

1. *imaginations*: plots, fancies.

either of us spoke; passion had tied her tongue, and amazement mine. – In short, the consequence was thus, she omitted nothing that the most violent love could urge, or tender words express; which when she saw had no effect, but still I pleaded honour and nearness of blood to my uncle, then came the storm I feared at first. For, starting from my bedside like a fury, she flew to my sword, and with much ado I prevented her doing me or herself a mischief. Having disarmed her, in a gust of passion she left me, and in a resolution, confirmed by a thousand curses, not to close her eyes till she had seen my ruin.

CARELESS: Exquisite woman! But what the devil, does she think thou hast no more sense than to get an heir upon her body to disinherit thyself: for as I take it, this settlement upon you is with a proviso that your uncle have no children.

MELLEFONT: It is so. Well, the service that you are to do me, will be a pleasure to yourself; I must get you to engage my Lady Plyant all this evening, that my pious aunt may not work her to her interest. And if you chance to secure her to yourself, you may incline her to mine. She's handsome, and knows it; is very silly, and thinks she has sense, and has an old fond husband.

CARELESS: I confess a very fair foundation for a lover to build upon.

MELLEFONT: For my Lord Froth, he and his wife will be sufficiently taken up with admiring one another, and Brisk's gallantry, as they call it. I'll observe my uncle myself; and Jack Maskwell has promised me to watch my aunt narrowly, and give me notice upon any suspicion. As for Sir Paul, my wise father-in-law that is to be, my dear Cynthia has such a share in his fatherly fondness, he would scarce make her a moment uneasy to have her happy hereafter.

CARELESS: So, you have manned your works. But I wish you may not have the weakest guard where the enemy is strongest.

MELLEFONT: Maskwell, you mean; prithee, why should you suspect him?

CARELESS: Faith, I cannot help it, you know I never liked him. I am a little superstitious in physiognomy.

MELLEFONT: He has obligations of gratitude to bind him to me; his dependence upon my uncle is through my means.

CARELESS: Upon your aunt, you mean.

MELLEFONT: My aunt!

CARELESS: I'm mistaken if there be not a familiarity between them you do not suspect, for all her passion for you.

MELLEFONT: Pooh, pooh, nothing in the world but his design to do me service; and he endeavours to be well in her esteem, that he may be able to effect it.

CARELESS: Well, I shall be glad to be mistaken; but your aunt's aversion in her revenge cannot be any way so effectually shown, as in bringing forth a child to disinherit you. She is handsome and cunning, and naturally wanton. Maskwell is flesh and blood at best, and opportunities between them are frequent. His affection to you, you have confessed, is grounded upon his interest; that, you have transplanted; and should it take root in my lady, I don't see what you can expect from the fruit.

MELLEFONT: I confess the consequence is visible, were your suspicions just. – But see, the company is broke up; let's meet 'em.

[Enter LORD TOUCHWOOD, LORD FROTH, SIR PAUL PLYANT, and BRISK.]

LORD TOUCHWOOD: Out upon't, nephew. – Leave your father-in-law and me to maintain our ground against young people.

MELLEFONT: I beg your lordship's pardon – we were just returning.

SIR PAUL: Were you, son? Gadsbud, much better as it is – good, strange! I swear I'm almost tipsy – t'other bottle would have been too powerful for me – as sure as can be it would. – We wanted your company, but Mr Brisk – where is he? I swear and vow, he's a most facetious person – and the best company. – And, my Lord Froth, your lordship is so merry a man, he, he, he.

LORD FROTH: Oh foy, Sir Paul, what do you mean? Merry! Oh barbarous! I'd as lieve you called me fool.

SIR PAUL: Nay, I protest and vow now, 'tis true; when Mr Brisk jokes, your lordship's laugh does so become you, he, he, he.

LORD FROTH: Ridiculous! Sir Paul, you're strangely mistaken, I find champagne is powerful. I assure you, Sir Paul, I laugh at nobody's jest but my own or a lady's; I assure you, Sir Paul.

BRISK: How? how, my lord? What, affront my wit! Let me perish, do I never say anything worthy to be laughed at?

LORD FROTH: Oh foy, don't misapprehend me, I don't say so, for I often smile at your conceptions. But there is nothing more unbecoming a man of quality than to laugh; Jesu, 'tis such a vulgar expression of the passion! Everybody can laugh. Then especially to laugh at the jest of an inferior person, or when anybody else of the same quality does not laugh with one. Ridiculous! To be pleased with what pleases the crowd! Now, when I laugh, I always laugh alone.

BRISK: I suppose that's because you laugh at your own jests, i'gad, ha, ha, ha.

LORD FROTH: He, he, I swear though, your raillery provokes me to a smile.

BRISK: Ay, my lord, it's a sign I hit you in the teeth, if you show 'em.

LORD FROTH: He, he, he, I swear that's so very pretty, I can't forbear.

CARELESS: I find a quibble[2] bears more sway in your lordship's face than a jest.

LORD TOUCHWOOD: Sir Paul, if you please, we'll retire to the ladies, and drink a dish of tea to settle our heads.

SIR PAUL: With all my heart. – Mr Brisk, you'll come to us, or call me when you're going to joke; I'll be ready to laugh incontinently.

[Exit LORD TOUCHWOOD and SIR PAUL.]

MELLEFONT: But does your lordship never see comedies?

LORD FROTH: Oh yes, sometimes – but I never laugh.

MELLEFONT: No?

LORD FROTH: Oh no – never laugh indeed, sir.

CARELESS: No, why, what d'ye go there for?

LORD FROTH: To distinguish myself from the commonalty, and mortify the poets: the fellows grow so conceited when any of their foolish wit prevails upon the side boxes, I swear, he, he, he, I have often constrained my inclinations to laugh, he, he, he, to avoid giving them encouragement.

2. *quibble*: pun.

MELLEFONT: You are cruel to yourself, my lord, as well as malicious to them.

LORD FROTH: I confess I did myself some violence at first, but now I
think I have conquered it.

BRISK: Let me perish, my lord, but there is something very particular and novel in the humour; 'tis true, it makes against wit, and
I'm sorry for some friends of mine that write, but, i'gad, I love to
be malicious. – Nay, deuce take me, there's wit in't too – and wit
must be foiled by wit; cut a diamond with a diamond; no other
way, i'gad.

LORD FROTH: Oh, I thought you would not be long before you
found out the wit.

CARELESS: Wit! In what? Where the devil's the wit in not laughing
when a man has a mind to't.

BRISK: O Lord, why, can't you find it out? – Why, there 'tis, in the
not laughing; don't you apprehend me? – My lord, Careless is a
very honest fellow, but harkee, – you understand me, somewhat
heavy, a little shallow, or so. – Why, I'll tell you now. Suppose
now you come up to me – nay, prithee Careless, be instructed.
Suppose, as I was saying, you come up to me, holding your sides,
and laughing as if you would bepiss yourself. I look grave, and ask
the cause of this immoderate mirth. – You laugh on still, and are
not able to tell me. – Still I look grave, not so much as smile. –

CARELESS: Smile, no, what the devil should you smile at, when you
suppose I can't tell you?

BRISK: Pshaw, pshaw, prithee don't interrupt me. – But I tell you,
you shall tell me – at last – but it shall be a great while first.

CARELESS: Well, but prithee don't let it be a great while, because I
long to have it over.

BRISK: Well then, you tell me some good jest, or very witty thing,
laughing all the while as if you were ready to die – and I hear it,
and look thus. – Would not you be disappointed?

CARELESS: No; for if it were a witty thing, I should not expect you
to understand it.

LORD FROTH: Oh foy, Mr Careless, all the world allows Mr Brisk
to have wit; my wife says he has a great deal. I hope you think her
a judge?

BRISK: Pooh, my lord, his voice goes for nothing. – I can't tell how to make him apprehend. [*To* Careless.] Take it t'other way. Suppose I say a witty thing to you?

CARELESS: Then I shall be disappointed indeed.

MELLEFONT: Let him alone, Brisk; he is obstinately bent not to be instructed.

BRISK: I'm sorry for him, deuce take me!

MELLEFONT: Shall we go to the ladies, my lord?

LORD FROTH: With all my heart, methinks we are a solitude without 'em.

MELLEFONT: Or what say you to another bottle of champagne?

LORD FROTH: Oh, for the universe, not a drop more I beseech you!
[*Takes out a pocket-glass, and looks in it.*]
O intemperate! I have a flushing in my face already.

BRISK: Let me see, let me see, my lord, I broke my glass that was in the lid of my snuff-box. [*Takes the glass and looks.*] Hum! Deuce take me, I have encouraged a pimple here too.

LORD FROTH: Then you must mortify him with a patch; my wife shall supply you. Come, gentlemen, *allons*.
[*Exeunt.*]
[*Enter* LADY TOUCHWOOD, *and* MASKWELL.]

LADY TOUCHWOOD: I'll hear no more! – Y'are false and ungrateful; come, I know you false.

MASKWELL: I have been frail, I confess, madam, for your ladyship's service.

LADY TOUCHWOOD: That I should trust a man whom I had known betray his friend!

MASKWELL: What friend have I betrayed? Or to whom?

LADY TOUCHWOOD: Your fond friend Mellefont, and to me; can you deny it?

MASKWELL: I do not.

LADY TOUCHWOOD: Have you not wronged my lord, who has been a father to you in your wants, and given you being? Have you not wronged him in the highest manner, in his bed?

MASKWELL: With your ladyship's help, and for your service, as I told you before. I can't deny that neither. – Anything more, madam?

LADY TOUCHWOOD: More! Audacious villain. Oh, what's more is most my shame – have you not dishonoured me?

MASKWELL: No, that I deny; for I never told in all my life: so that accusation's answered; on to the next.

LADY TOUCHWOOD: Death, do you dally with my passion? Insolent devil! But have a care, provoke me not; for, by the eternal fire, you shall not scape my vengeance. – Calm villain! How unconcerned he stands, confessing treachery and ingratitude! Is there vice more black! – O I have excuses, thousands, for my faults! Fire in my temper, passions in my soul, apt to every provocation; oppressed at once with love and with despair. But a sedate, a thinking villain, whose black blood runs temperately bad, what excuse can clear? One who is no more moved with the reflection of his crimes than of his face, but walks unstartled from the mirror, and straight forgets the hideous form.

[*She walks about disordered.*]

MASKWELL: Will you be in temper, madam? I would not talk not to be heard. I have been a very great rogue for your sake, and you reproach me with it; I am ready to be a rogue still, to do you service; and you are flinging conscience and honour in my face, to rebate my inclinations. How am I to behave myself? You know I am your creature, my life and fortune in your power; to disoblige you brings me certain ruin. Allow it, I would betray you, I would not be a traitor to myself: I don't pretend to honesty, because you know I am a rascal, but I would convince you from the necessity of my being firm to you.

LADY TOUCHWOOD: Necessity, impudence! Can no gratitude incline you, no obligations touch you? Have not my fortune, and my person, been subjected to your pleasure? Were you not in the nature of a servant, and have not I in effect made you lord of all, of me, and of my lord? Where is that humble love, the languishing, that adoration, which once was paid me, and everlastingly engaged?

MASKWELL: Fixed, rooted in my heart, whence nothing can remove 'em, yet you –

LADY TOUCHWOOD: Yet, what yet?

MASKWELL: Nay, misconceive me not, madam, when I say I have

had a generous and a faithful passion, which you had never favoured, but through revenge and policy.

LADY TOUCHWOOD: Ha!

MASKWELL: Look you, madam, we are alone – pray contain yourself, and hear me. You know you loved your nephew, when I first sighed for you; I quickly found it an argument that I loved, for with that art you veiled your passion; 'twas imperceptible to all but jealous eyes. This discovery made me bold, I confess it; for by it I thought you in my power. Your nephew's scorn of you added to my hopes; I watched the occasion, and took you, just repulsed by him, warm at once with love and indignation; your disposition, my arguments, and happy opportunity, accomplished my design; I pressed the yielding minute and was blest. How I have loved you since, words have not shown, then how should words express?

LADY TOUCHWOOD: Well, mollifying devil. – And have I not met your love with forward fire?

MASKWELL: Your zeal I grant was ardent, but misplaced; there was revenge in view; that woman's idol had defiled the temple of the god, and love was made a mock worship, – a son and heir would have edged young Mellefont upon the brink of ruin, and left him nought but you to catch at for prevention.

LADY TOUCHWOOD: Again, provoke me! Do you wind me like a larum, only to rouse my own stilled soul for your diversion? Confusion!

MASKWELL: Nay, madam, I'm gone, if you relapse. – What needs this? I say nothing but what yourself, in open hours of love, have told me. Why should you deny it? Nay, how can you? Is not all this present heat owing to the same fire? Do you not love him still? How have I this day offended you, but in not breaking off his match with Cynthia? Which ere tomorrow shall be done – had you but patience.

LADY TOUCHWOOD: How, what said you Maskwell, another caprice to unwind my temper?

MASKWELL: By heaven, no; I am your slave, the slave of all your pleasures; and will not rest till I have given you peace, would you suffer me.

LADY TOUCHWOOD: O Maskwell, in vain I do disguise me from thee; thou know'st me, know'st the very inmost windings and recesses of my soul. – O Mellefont! I burn; married tomorrow! Despair strikes me. Yet my soul knows I hate him too. Let him but once be mine, and next immediate ruin seize him.

MASKWELL: Compose yourself, you shall enjoy and ruin him too. – Will that please you?

LADY TOUCHWOOD: How, how? Thou dear, thou precious villain, how?

MASKWELL: You have already been tampering with my Lady Plyant?

LADY TOUCHWOOD: I have; she is ready for any impression I think fit.

MASKWELL: She must be thoroughly persuaded that Mellefont loves her.

LADY TOUCHWOOD: She is so credulous that way naturally, and likes him so well, that she will believe it faster than I can persuade her. But I don't see what you can propose from such a trifling design, for her first conversing with Mellefont will convince her of the contrary.

MASKWELL: I know it. – I don't depend upon it. – But it will prepare something else, and gain us leisure to lay a stronger plot. If I gain a little time, I shall not want contrivance.

> One minute gives invention to destroy,
> What, to rebuild, will a whole age employ.

[*Exeunt.*]

ACT TWO

SCENE ONE

[*Enter* LADY FROTH *and* CYNTHIA.]

CYNTHIA: Indeed, madam! Is it possible your ladyship could have been so much in love?

LADY FROTH: I could not sleep; I did not sleep one wink for three weeks together.

CYNTHIA: Prodigious! I wonder want of sleep, and so much love, and so much wit as your ladyship has, did not turn your brain.

LADY FROTH: O my dear Cynthia, you must not rally your friend. – But really, as you say, I wonder too; but then I had a way. – For between you and I, I had whimsies and vapours, but I gave them vent.

CYNTHIA: How pray, madam?

LADY FROTH: O I writ, writ abundantly – do you never write?

CYNTHIA: Write what?

LADY FROTH: Songs, elegies, satires, encomiums, panegyrics, lampoons, plays, or heroic poems.

CYNTHIA: O Lord, not I, madam; I'm content to be a courteous reader.

LADY FROTH: O inconsistent! In love, and not write! If my lord and I had been both of your temper, we had never come together. – O bless me! What a sad thing would that have been, if my lord and I should never have met!

CYNTHIA: Then neither my lord nor you would ever have met with your match, on my conscience.

LADY FROTH: O' my conscience, no more we should; thou say'st right – for sure my Lord Froth is as fine a gentleman, and as much a man of quality! Ah! Nothing at all of the common air. – I think I may say he wants nothing but a blue ribbon and a star[1] to make him shine the very phosphorus of our hemisphere. Do you understand those two hard words? If you don't, I'll explain 'em to you.

CYNTHIA: Yes, yes, madam, I'm not so ignorant. [*Aside.*] At least I won't own it, to be troubled with your instructions.

LADY FROTH: Nay, I beg your pardon; but being derived from the Greek, I thought you might have escaped the etymology. – But I'm the more amazed to find you a woman of letters, and not write! Bless me! how can Mellefont believe you love him?

CYNTHIA: Why faith, madam, he that won't take my word shall never have it under my hand.

LADY FROTH: I vow Mellefont's a pretty gentleman, but methinks he wants a manner.

CYNTHIA: A manner! What's that, madam?

LADY FROTH: Some distinguishing quality, as for example, the *belle air* or *brillant* of Mr Brisk; the solemnity, yet complaisance of my lord, or something of his own that should look a little *Je-ne-scay quoysh*; he is too much a mediocrity, in mind.

CYNTHIA: He does not indeed affect either pertness or formality; for which I like him. Here he comes.

LADY FROTH: And my lord with him; pray observe the difference.

[*Enter* LORD FROTH, MELLEFONT, BRISK.]

CYNTHIA [*aside*]: Impertinent creature, I could almost be angry with her now.

LADY FROTH: My lord, I have been telling my dear Cynthia how much I have been in love with you; I swear I have; I'm not ashamed to own it now; ah! it makes my heart leap, I vow I sigh when I think on't. My dear lord, ha, ha, ha, do you remember, my lord?

[*Squeezes him by the hand, looks kindly on him, sighs, and then laughs out.*]

LORD FROTH: Pleasant creature! perfectly well, ah! that look, ay, there it is; who could resist! 'Twas so my heart was made a captive first, and ever since 't has been in love with happy slavery.

---

1. *a blue ribbon and a star*: insignia of the Order of the Garter.

LADY FROTH: O that tongue, that dear deceitful tongue! That charming softness in your mien and your expression, and then your bow! Good my lord, bow as you did when I gave you my picture; here, suppose this is my picture –

[*Gives him a pocket-glass.*]

Pray mind, my lord; ah! he bows charmingly; nay my lord, you shan't kiss it so much; I shall grow jealous, I vow now.

[*He bows profoundly low, then kisses the glass.*]

LORD FROTH: I saw myself there, and kissed it for your sake.

LADY FROTH: Ah! gallantry to the last degree. – Mr Brisk, you're a judge; was ever anything so well-bred as my lord?

BRISK: Never anything but your ladyship, let me perish.

LADY FROTH: O prettily turned again; let me die, but you have a great deal of wit. Mr Mellefont, don't you think Mr Brisk has a world of wit?

MELLEFONT: O yes, madam.

BRISK: O Lord, madam –

LADY FROTH: An infinite deal!

BRISK: O Jesu, madam –

LADY FROTH: More wit than anybody.

BRISK: I'm everlastingly your humble servant, deuce take me, madam.

LORD FROTH: Don't you think us a happy couple?

CYNTHIA: I vow, my lord, I think you the happiest couple in the world, for you are not only happy in one another, and when you are together, but happy in yourselves and by yourselves.

LORD FROTH: I hope Mellefont will make a good husband too.

CYNTHIA: 'Tis my interest to believe he will, my lord.

LORD FROTH: D'ye think he'll love you as well as I do my wife? I'm afraid not.

CYNTHIA: I believe he'll love me better.

LORD FROTH: Heavens! that can never be; but why do you think so?

CYNTHIA: Because he has not so much reason to be fond of himself.

LORD FROTH: Oh, your humble servant for that, dear madam; well, Mellefont, you'll be a happy creature.

MELLEFONT: Ay, my lord, I shall have the same reason for my happiness that your lordship has; I shall think myself happy.

LORD FROTH: Ah, that's all.

BRISK [*to* LADY FROTH]: Your ladyship is in the right; but, i'gad, I'm wholly turned into satire. I confess I write but seldom, but when I do – keen iambics, i'gad. But my lord was telling me, your ladyship has made an essay toward an heroic poem.

LADY FROTH: Did my lord tell you? Yes I vow, and the subject is my lord's love to me. And what do you think I call it? I dare swear you won't guess – *The Sillibub*, ha, ha, ha.

BRISK: Because my lord's title's Froth, i'gad, ha, ha, ha. Deuce take me very apropos and surprising, ha, ha, ha.

LADY FROTH: He, ay, is not it? – and then I call my lord *Spumoso*; and myself, what d'ye think I call myself?

BRISK: *Lactilla* maybe – 'gad, I cannot tell.

LADY FROTH: *Biddy*, that's all; just my own name.

BRISK: *Biddy!* I'gad, very pretty! Deuce take me if your ladyship has not the art of surprising the most naturally in the world. – I hope you'll make me happy in communicating the poem.

LADY FROTH: Oh, you must be my confidant; I must ask your advice.

BRISK: I'm your humble servant, let me perish. I presume your ladyship has read Bossu?[2]

LADY FROTH: O yes, and Rapine,[3] and Dacier[4] upon Aristotle and Horace. – My lord, you must not be jealous, I'm communicating all to Mr Brisk.

LORD FROTH: No, no, I'll allow Mr Brisk; have you nothing about you to show him, my dear?

LADY FROTH: Yes, I believe I have. – Mr Brisk, come, will you go into the next room and there I'll shew you all I have.

[*Exit* LADY FROTH *and* BRISK.]

LORD FROTH: I'll walk a turn in the garden, and come to you.
    [*Exit.*]

MELLEFONT: You're thoughtful, Cynthia?

CYNTHIA: I'm thinking, that though marriage makes man and wife

---

2. *Bossu*: René le Bossu (1631–80), French critic.

3. *Rapine*: René Rapin (1621–87), French critic.

4. *Dacier*: André Dacier (1651–1722), French translator and commentator on both Aristotle and Horace.

one flesh, it leaves 'em still two fools; and they become more conspicuous by setting off one another.

MELLEFONT: That's only when two fools meet, and their follies are opposed.

CYNTHIA: Nay, I have known two wits meet, and by the opposition of their wits, render themselves as ridiculous as fools. 'Tis an odd game we're going to play at; what think you of drawing stakes, and giving over in time?

MELLEFONT: No, hang't, that's not endeavouring to win, because it's possible we may lose; since we have shuffled and cut, let's e'en turn up trump now.

CYNTHIA: Then I find it's like cards: if either of us have a good hand, it is an accident of fortune.

MELLEFONT: No, marriage is rather like a game at bowls; fortune indeed makes the match, and the two nearest, and sometimes the two farthest are together, but the game depends entirely upon judgment.

CYNTHIA: Still it is a game, and consequently one of us must be a loser.

MELLEFONT: Not at all; only a friendly trial of skill, and the winnings to be shared between us. –

[Musicians crossing the stage.]

What's here, the music? – Oh, my lord has promised the company a new song; we'll get 'em to give it us by the way. Pray let us have the favour of you to practise the song before the company hear it.

(Song[5])

I

Cynthia frowns whene'r I woo her,
Yet she's vexed if I give over;
Much she fears I should undo her,
But much more, to lose her lover:
Thus, in doubting, she refuses;
And not winning, thus she loses.

5. *Song*: music by Henry Purcell.

II

> Prithee, Cynthia, look behind you,
> Age and wrinkles will o'ertake you;
> Then too late, desire will find you,
> When the power does forsake you:
> Think, O think, o'th' sad condition,
> To be past, yet wish fruition.

MELLEFONT: You shall have my thanks below.

[*To the music, they go out.*]

[*Enter* SIR PAUL PLYANT *and* LADY PLYANT.]

SIR PAUL: Gadsbud! I am provoked into a fermentation, as my Lady Froth says; was ever the like read of in story?

LADY PLYANT: Sir Paul have patience; let me alone to rattle him up.

SIR PAUL: Pray, your ladyship, give me leave to be angry – I'll rattle him up, I warrant you; I'll firk[6] him with a *certiorari*.[7]

LADY PLYANT: You firk him, I'll firk him myself; pray, Sir Paul, hold you contented.

CYNTHIA: Bless me, what makes my father in such a passion! I never saw him thus before.

SIR PAUL: Hold yourself contented, my Lady Plyant. – I find passion coming upon me by inspiration, and I cannot submit as formerly, therefore give way.

LADY PLYANT: How now! will you be pleased to retire, and –

SIR PAUL: No, marry, will I not be pleased; I am pleased to be angry, that's my pleasure at this time.

MELLEFONT: What can this mean?

LADY PLYANT: Gad's my life, the man's distracted; why how now, who are you? What am I? 'Slidikins, can't I govern you? What did I marry you for? Am I not to be absolute and uncontrollable? Is it fit a woman of my spirit and conduct should be contradicted in a matter of this concern?

SIR PAUL: It concerns me, and only me; besides, I'm not to be governed at all times. When I am in tranquillity, my Lady Plyant shall command Sir Paul; but when I am provoked to fury, I cannot incorporate with patience and reason. As soon may tigers match

6. *firk*: beat, whip, lash.
7. *certiorari*: legal writ.

with tigers, lambs with lambs, and every creature couple with its foe, as the poet says.

LADY PLYANT: He's hot-headed still! 'Tis in vain to talk to you; but remember I have a curtain-lecture[8] for you, you disobedient, headstrong brute.

SIR PAUL: No, 'tis because I won't be headstrong, because I won't be a brute, and have my head fortified, that I am thus exasperated. – But I will protect my honour, and yonder is the violator of my fame.

LADY PLYANT: 'Tis my honour that is concerned, and the violation was intended to me. Your honour! You have none but what is in my keeping, and I can dispose of it when I please – therefore don't provoke me.

SIR PAUL: Hum, gadsbud, she says true. – Well, my lady, march on, I will fight under you then; I am convinced, as far as passion will permit.

[LADY PLYANT *and* SIR PAUL *come up to* MELLEFONT.]

LADY PLYANT: Inhuman and treacherous.

SIR PAUL: Thou serpent and first tempter of womankind. –

CYNTHIA: Bless me! Sir; madam; what mean you?

SIR PAUL: Thy, Thy, come away Thy, touch him not, come hither girl, go not near him, there's nothing but deceit about him; snakes are in his peruke, and the crocodile of Nilus in his belly, he will eat thee up alive.

LADY PLYANT: Dishonourable, impudent creature!

MELLEFONT: For heaven's sake, madam, to whom do you direct this language?

LADY PLYANT: Have I behaved myself with all the decorum and nicety befitting the person of Sir Paul's wife? Have I preserved my honour as it were in a snow-house for this three year past? Have I been white and unsullied even by Sir Paul himself?

SIR PAUL: Nay, she has been an impenetrable wife, even to me, that's the truth on't.

LADY PLYANT: Have I, I say, preserved myself, like a fair sheet of paper, for you to make a blot upon –

8. *curtain-lecture*: reproof given in bed.

SIR PAUL: And she shall make a simile with any woman in England.

MELLEFONT: I am so amazed, I know not what to speak.

SIR PAUL: Do you think my daughter, this pretty creature – gadsbud, she's a wife for a cherubin! – do you think her fit for nothing but to be a stalking-horse, to stand before you while you take aim at my wife? Gadsbud, I was never angry before in my life, and I'll never be appeased again.

MELLEFONT [aside]: Hell and damnation! This is my aunt; such malice can be engendered nowhere else.

LADY PLYANT: Sir Paul, take Cynthia from his sight; leave me to strike him with the remorse of his intended crime.

CYNTHIA: Pray, sir, stay, hear him, I dare affirm he's innocent.

SIR PAUL: Innocent! Why heark'ee, come hither Thy, heark'ee, I had it from his aunt, my sister Touchwood. – Gadsbud, he does not care a farthing for anything of thee but thy portion. Why, he's in love with my wife; he would have tantalized thee, and made a cuckold of thy poor father – and that would certainly have broke my heart. – I'm sure if ever I should have horns, they would kill me; they would never come kindly, I should die of 'em, like any child that were cutting his teeth – I should, indeed, Thy. – Therefore come away; but Providence has prevented all, therefore come away when I bid you.

CYNTHIA: I must obey.

[Exit SIR PAUL and CYNTHIA.]

LADY PLYANT: Oh, such a thing! The impiety of it startles me – to wrong so good, so fair a creature, and one that loved you tenderly – 'tis a barbarity of barbarities, and nothing could be guilty of it –

MELLEFONT: But the greatest villain imagination can form, I grant it; and, next to the villainy of such a fact, is the villainy of aspersing me with the guilt. How? Which way was I to wrong her, for yet I understand you not.

LADY PLYANT: Why, gads my life, cousin Mellefont, you cannot be so peremptory as to deny it, when I tax you with it to your face; for now Sir Paul's gone, you are *corum nobus*.[9]

9. *corum nobus*: for *coram nobis*, in our presence.

MELLEFONT: By heaven, I love her more than life, or –

LADY PLYANT: Fiddle, faddle, don't tell me of this and that, and everything in the world, but give me mathemacular demonstration, answer me directly. – But I have not patience. – Oh, the impiety of it, as I was saying, and the unparalleled wickedness! O merciful Father! how could you think to reverse nature so, to make the daughter the means of procuring the mother?

MELLEFONT: The daughter procure the mother!

LADY PLYANT: Ay, for though I am not Cynthia's own mother, I am her father's wife, and that's near enough to make it incest.

MELLEFONT [aside]: Incest! Oh, my precious aunt and the devil in conjunction.

LADY PLYANT: Oh, reflect upon the horror of that, and then the guilt of deceiving everybody! Marrying the daughter, only to make a cuckold of the father; and then seducing me, debauching my purity, and perverting me from the road of virtue, in which I have trod thus long, and never made one trip, not one *faux pas*. O consider it, what would you have to answer for, if you should provoke me to frailty? Alas! Humanity is feeble, heaven knows, very feeble, and unable to support itself.

MELLEFONT: Where am I? sure, is it day, and am I awake? Madam –

LADY PLYANT: And nobody knows how circumstances may happen together. – To my thinking, now I could resist the strongest temptation. – But yet I know, 'tis impossible for me to know whether I could or no, there is no certainty in the things of this life.

MELLEFONT: Madam, pray give me leave to ask you one question –

LADY PLYANT: O Lord, ask me the question, I'll swear I'll refuse it; I swear I'll deny it – therefore don't ask me. Nay you shan't ask me, I swear I'll deny it. O Gemini, you have brought all the blood into my face; I warrant I am as red as a turkey-cock; O fie, cousin Mellefont!

MELLEFONT: Nay, madam, hear me; I mean –

LADY PLYANT: Hear you, no, no; I'll deny you first, and hear you afterwards. For one does not know how one's mind may change upon hearing – hearing is one of the senses, and all the senses are fallible; I won't trust my honour, I assure you; my honour is infallible and uncomatible.

MELLEFONT: For heaven's sake, madam –

LADY PLYANT: O name it no more – bless me, how can you talk of heaven, and have so much wickedness in your heart? Maybe you don't think it a sin – they say some of you gentlemen don't think it a sin, – maybe it is no sin to them that don't think it so; – indeed, if I did not think it a sin – but still my honour, if it were no sin, – but then, to marry my daughter, for the conveniency of frequent opportunities – I'll never consent to that, as sure as can be, I'll break the match.

MELLEFONT: Death and amazement! Madam, upon my knees –

LADY PLYANT: Nay, nay, rise up; come, you shall see my good nature. I know love is powerful, and nobody can help his passion: 'tis not your fault; nor, I swear, it is not mine. How can I help it, if I have charms? And how can you help it, if you are made a captive? I swear it's pity it should be a fault – but my honour – well, but your honour too – but the sin! – well, but the necessity – O Lord, here's somebody coming, I dare not stay. Well, you must consider of your crime, and strive as much as can be against it. Strive, be sure – but don't be melancholy, don't despair, – but never think that I'll grant you anything; O Lord, no, – but be sure you lay aside all thoughts of the marriage, for though I know you don't love Cynthia, only as a blind for your passion to me, yet it will make me jealous, – O Lord, what did I say? Jealous! no, no, I can't be jealous, for I must not love you; therefore don't hope – but don't despair neither. – Oh, they're coming, I must fly.

[*Exit.*]

MELLEFONT [*after a pause*]: So then, spite of my care and foresight, I am caught in my security. – Yet this was but a shallow artifice, unworthy of my Machiavellian aunt. There must be more behind, this is but the first flash, the priming of her engine; destruction follows hard, if not most presently prevented.

[*Enter* MASKWELL.]

Maskwell, welcome, thy presence is a view of land, appearing to my shipwracked hopes. The witch has raised the storm, and her ministers have done their work; you see the vessels are parted.

MASKWELL: I know it; I met Sir Paul towing away Cynthia. Come, trouble not your head, I'll join you together ere tomorrow morning, or drown between you in the attempt.

MELLEFONT: There's comfort in a hand stretched out to one that's sinking, though ne'er so far off.

MASKWELL: No sinking, nor no danger. – Come, cheer up; why, you don't know that while I plead for you, your aunt has given me a retaining fee; nay, I am your greatest enemy, and she does but journey-work[10] under me.

MELLEFONT: Ha! how's this?

MASKWELL: What d'ye think of my being employed in the execution of all her plots? Ha, ha, ha, by heaven it's true: I have undertaken to break the match; I have undertaken to make your uncle disinherit you; to get you turned out of doors, and to – ha, ha, ha, I can't tell you for laughing. Oh, she has opened her heart to me, – I am to turn you a-grazing, and to – ha, ha, ha, marry Cynthia myself. There's a plot for you.

MELLEFONT: Ha! Oh I see, I see my rising sun! Light breaks through clouds upon me, and I shall live in day. O my Maskwell! how shall I thank or praise thee; thou hast outwitted woman. – But tell me, how could'st thou thus get into her confidence, ha? How? But was it her contrivance to persuade my Lady Plyant to this extravagant belief?

MASKWELL: It was, and to tell you the truth, I encouraged it for your diversion. Though it made you a little uneasy for the present, yet the reflection of it must needs be entertaining. – I warrant she was very violent at first.

MELLEFONT: Ha, ha, ha, ay, a very fury; but I was most afraid of her violence at last. If you had not come as you did, I don't know what she might have attempted.

MASKWELL: Ha, ha, ha, I know her temper. – Well, you must know then, that all my contrivances were but bubbles,[11] till at last I pretended to have been long secretly in love with Cynthia; that did my business; that convinced your aunt I might be trusted,

10. *journey-work*: work which is paid for by the day.
11. *bubbles*: deceptions, shams.

since it was as much my interest as hers to break the match. Then she thought my jealousy might qualify me to assist her in her revenge. And, in short, in that belief, told me the secrets of her heart. At length we made this agreement, if I accomplish her designs (as I told you before) she has engaged to put Cynthia with all her fortune into my power.

MELLEFONT: She is most gracious in her favour. – Well, and dear Jack, how hast thou contrived?

MASKWELL: I would not have you stay to hear it now, for I don't know but she may come this way. I am to meet her anon, after that I'll tell you the whole matter. Be here in this gallery an hour hence; by that time I imagine our consultation may be over.

MELLEFONT: I will; till then, success attend thee.

    [*Exit.*]

MASKWELL: Till then, success will attend me; for when I meet you, I meet the only obstacle to my fortune. Cynthia, let thy beauty gild my crimes; and whatsoever I commit of treachery or deceit shall be imputed to me as a merit. – Treachery? What treachery? Love cancels all the bonds of friendship, and sets men right upon their first foundations.

    Duty to kings, piety to parents, gratitude to benefactors, and fidelity to friends, are different and particular ties: but the name of rival cuts 'em all asunder, and is a general acquittance. Rival is equal, and love like death an universal leveller of mankind. Ha! But is there not such a thing as honesty? Yes, and whosoever has it about him, bears an enemy in his breast. For your honest man, as I take it, is that nice, scrupulous, conscientious person, who will cheat nobody but himself; such another coxcomb as your wise man, who is too hard for all the world, and will be made a fool of by nobody, but himself; ha, ha, ha. Well, for wisdom and honesty, give me cunning and hypocrisy; oh, 'tis such a pleasure to angle for fair-faced fools! Then that hungry gudgeon credulity will bite at anything. – Why, let me see, I have the same face, the same words and accents, when I speak what I do think, and when I speak what I do not think – the very same – and dear dissimulation is the only art not to be known from nature.

Why will mankind be fools, and be deceived?
And why are friends' and lovers' oaths believed;
When each, who searches strictly his own mind,
May so much fraud and power of baseness find?

ACT THREE

SCENE ONE

[*Enter* LORD TOUCHWOOD *and* LADY TOUCHWOOD.]

LADY TOUCHWOOD: My lord, can you blame my brother Plyant if he refuse his daughter upon this provocation? The contract's void by this unheard-of impiety.

LORD TOUCHWOOD: I don't believe it true; he has better principles – foh, 'tis nonsense. Come, come, I know my Lady Plyant has a large eye, and would centre everything in her own circle; 'tis not the first time she has mistaken respect for love, and made Sir Paul jealous of the civility of an undesigning person, the better to bespeak his security in her unfeigned pleasures.

LADY TOUCHWOOD: You censure hardly, my lord; my sister's honour is very well known.

LORD TOUCHWOOD: Yes, I believe I know some that have been familiarly acquainted with it. This is a little trick wrought by some pitiful contriver, envious of my nephew's merit.

LADY TOUCHWOOD: Nay, my lord, it may be so, and I hope it will be found so; but that will require some time, for in such a case as this, demonstration is necessary.

LORD TOUCHWOOD: There should have been demonstration of the contrary too, before it had been believed –

LADY TOUCHWOOD: So I suppose there was.

LORD TOUCHWOOD: How! Where? When?

LADY TOUCHWOOD: That I can't tell; nay, I don't say there was. – I am willing to believe as favourably of my nephew as I can.

LORD TOUCHWOOD [*half aside*]: I don't know that.

LADY TOUCHWOOD: How? Don't you believe that, say you, my lord?

LORD TOUCHWOOD: No, I don't say so. – I confess I am troubled to find you so cold in his defence.

LADY TOUCHWOOD: His defence! Bless me, would you have me defend an ill thing?

LORD TOUCHWOOD: You believe it then?

LADY TOUCHWOOD: I don't know; I am very unwilling to speak my thoughts in anything that may be to my cousin's disadvantage; besides, I find, my lord, you are prepared to receive an ill impression from any opinion of mine which is not consenting with your own. But since I am like to be suspected in the end, and 'tis a pain any longer to dissemble, I own it to you; in short, I do believe it, nay, and can believe anything worse if it were laid to his charge. – Don't ask me my reasons, my lord, for they are not fit to be told you.

LORD TOUCHWOOD [aside]: I'm amazed; here must be something more than ordinary in this. – [Aloud.] Not fit to be told me, madam? You can have no interests wherein I am not concerned, and consequently the same reasons ought to be convincing to me, which create your satisfaction or disquiet.

LADY TOUCHWOOD: But those which cause my disquiet, I am willing to have remote from your hearing. Good my lord, don't press me.

LORD TOUCHWOOD: Don't oblige me to press you.

LADY TOUCHWOOD: Whatever it was, 'tis past. And that is better to be unknown which cannot be prevented; therefore let me beg you rest satisfied –

LORD TOUCHWOOD: When you have told me, I will.

LADY TOUCHWOOD: You won't.

LORD TOUCHWOOD: By my life, my dear, I will.

LADY TOUCHWOOD: What if you can't?

LORD TOUCHWOOD: How? Then I must know; nay I will. No more trifling – I charge you tell me – by all our mutual peace to come; upon your duty –

LADY TOUCHWOOD: Nay, my lord, you need say no more to make me lay my heart before you, but don't be thus transported; compose yourself; it is not of concern to make you lose one minute's temper. 'Tis not indeed, my dear. Nay, by this kiss you

shan't be angry. O Lord, I wish I had not told you anything, –
Indeed, my lord, you have frighted me. Nay, look pleased, I'll tell
you.

LORD TOUCHWOOD: Well, well.

LADY TOUCHWOOD: Nay, but will you be calm? – indeed, it's
nothing but –

LORD TOUCHWOOD: But what?

LADY TOUCHWOOD: But will you promise me not to be angry –
nay, you must – not to be angry with Mellefont? I dare swear he's
sorry – and were it to do again, would not –

LORD TOUCHWOOD: Sorry, for what? 'Death, you rack me with
delay.

LADY TOUCHWOOD: Nay, no great matter, only – well, I have
your promise – foh, why nothing, only your nephew had a mind
to amuse himself sometimes with a little gallantry towards me.
Nay, I can't think he meant anything seriously, but methought it
looked oddly.

LORD TOUCHWOOD: Confusion and hell, what do I hear!

LADY TOUCHWOOD: Or, maybe, he thought he was not enough
akin to me, upon your account, and had a mind to create a nearer
relation on his own; a lover you know, my lord – ha, ha, ha. Well,
but that's all – now you have it. Well, remember your promise,
my lord, and don't take any notice of it to him.

LORD TOUCHWOOD: No, no, no – damnation!

LADY TOUCHWOOD: Nay, I swear you must not – a little harmless
mirth – only misplaced, that's all – but if it were more, 'tis over
now, and all well. For my part I have forgot it, and so has he,
I hope – for I have not heard anything from him these two
days.

LORD TOUCHWOOD: These two days! Is it so fresh? Unnatural
villain! 'Death, I'll have him stripped and turned naked out of
my doors this moment, and let him rot and perish, incestuous
brute!

LADY TOUCHWOOD: O for heaven's sake, my lord, you'll ruin me
if you take such public notice of it, it will be a town-talk. Consider
your own and my honour – nay, I told you you would not be
satisfied when you knew it.

LORD TOUCHWOOD: Before I've done, I will be satisfied. Ungrateful monster, how long? –

LADY TOUCHWOOD: Lord, I don't know; I wish my lips had grown together when I told you. – Almost a twelve-month – nay, I won't tell you any more till you are yourself. Pray, my lord, don't let the company see you in this disorder. Yet, I confess, I can't blame you; for I think I was never so surprised in my life. Who would have thought my nephew could have so misconstrued my kindness? But will you go into your closet, and recover your temper? I'll make an excuse of sudden business to the company, and come to you. Pray, good dear my lord, let me beg you do now. I'll come immediately and tell you all; will you, my lord?

LORD TOUCHWOOD: I will. – I am mute with wonder.

LADY TOUCHWOOD: Well but go now, here's somebody coming.

LORD TOUCHWOOD: Well I go – you won't stay, for I would hear more of this.

[*Exit* LORD TOUCHWOOD.]

LADY TOUCHWOOD: I follow instantly. – So.

[*Enter* MASKWELL.]

MASKWELL: This was a masterpiece, and did not need my help – though I stood ready for a cue to come in and confirm all, had there been occasion.

LADY TOUCHWOOD: Have you seen Mellefont?

MASKWELL: I have, and am to meet him here about this time.

LADY TOUCHWOOD: How does he bear his disappointment?

MASKWELL: Secure in my assistance, he seemed not much afflicted, but rather laughed at the shallow artifice, which so little time must of necessity discover. Yet he is apprehensive of some farther design of yours, and has engaged me to watch you. I believe he will hardly be able to prevent your plot, yet I would have you use caution and expedition.

LADY TOUCHWOOD: Expedition indeed; for all we do must be performed in the remaining part of this evening, and before the company break up, lest my lord should cool and have an opportunity to talk with him privately. – My lord must not see him again.

MASKWELL: By no means; therefore you must aggravate my lord's displeasure to a degree that will admit of no conference with him. – What think you of mentioning me?

LADY TOUCHWOOD: How?

MASKWELL: To my lord, as having been privy to Mellefont's design upon you, but still using my utmost endeavours to dissuade him, though my friendship and love to him has made me conceal it. Yet you may say I threatened the next time he attempted anything of that kind, to discover it to my lord.

LADY TOUCHWOOD: To what end is this?

MASKWELL: It will confirm my lord's opinion of my honour and honesty, and create in him a new confidence in me, which (should this design miscarry) will be necessary to the forming of another plot that I have in my head – [aside] to cheat you, as well as the rest.

LADY TOUCHWOOD: I'll do it. – I'll tell him you hindered him once from forcing me.

MASKWELL: Excellent! your ladyship has a most improving fancy. You had best go to my lord, keep him as long as you can in his closet, and I doubt not but you will mould him to what you please; your guests are so engaged in their own follies and intrigues, they'll miss neither of you.

LADY TOUCHWOOD: When shall we meet? – At eight this evening in my chamber; there rejoice at our success, and toy away an hour in mirth.

MASKWELL: I will not fail.

[Exit LADY TOUCHWOOD.]

I know what she means by toying away an hour well enough. Pox, I have lost all appetite to her; yet she's a fine woman, and I loved her once. But I don't know, since I have been in a great measure kept by her, the case is altered; what was my pleasure is become my duty, and I have as little stomach to her now as if I were her husband. Should she smoke my design upon Cynthia, I were in a fine pickle. She has a damned penetrating head, and knows how to interpret a coldness the right way; therefore I must dissemble ardour and ecstasy; that's resolved. How easily and pleasantly is that dissembled before fruition! Pox on't that a man can't drink without quenching his thirst. Ha! yonder comes

Mellefont thoughtful. Let me think: meet her at eight – hum – ha! By heaven I have it, if I can speak to my lord before. – Was it my brain or Providence? No matter which – I will deceive 'em all, and yet secure myself. 'Twas a lucky thought! Well, this double-dealing is a jewel. Here he comes, now for me –

[*Enter* MELLEFONT *musing;* MASKWELL, *pretending not to see him, walks by him, and speaks as it were to himself.*]

Mercy on us, what will the wickedness of this world come to?

MELLEFONT: How now, Jack? What, so full of contemplation that you run over!

MASKWELL: I'm glad you're come, for I could not contain myself any longer, and was just going to give vent to a secret which nobody but you ought to drink down. Your aunt's just gone from hence.

MELLEFONT: And having trusted thee with the secrets of her soul, thou art villainously bent to discover all to me, ha?

MASKWELL: I'm afraid my frailty leans that way – but I don't know whether I can in honour discover all.

MELLEFONT: All, all, man; what, you may in honour betray her as far as she betrays herself. No tragical design upon my person, I hope?

MASKWELL: No, but it's a comical design upon mine.

MELLEFONT: What dost thou mean?

MASKWELL: Listen and be dumb; we have been bargaining about the rate of your ruin –

MELLEFONT: Like any two guardians to an orphan heiress – well?

MASKWELL: And whereas pleasure is generally paid with mischief, what mischief I shall do is to be paid with pleasure.

MELLEFONT: So when you've swallow'd the potion, you sweeten your mouth with a plum.

MASKWELL: You are merry, sir, but I shall probe your constitution. In short, the price of your banishment is to be paid with the person of –

MELLEFONT: Of Cynthia, and her fortune. Why, you forget you told me this before.

MASKWELL: No, no. – So far you are right, and I am, as an earnest of that bargain, to have full and free possession of the person of – your aunt.

MELLEFONT: Ha! – Foh, you trifle.

MASKWELL: By this light, I'm serious; all raillery apart. – I knew 'twould stun you: this evening at eight she will receive me in her bed-chamber.

MELLEFONT: Hell and the devil, is she abandoned of all grace? Why, the woman is possessed!

MASKWELL: Well, will you go in my stead?

MELLEFONT: By heaven, into a hot furnace sooner.

MASKWELL: No, you would not – it would not be so convenient, as I can order matters.

MELLEFONT: What d'ye mean?

MASKWELL: Mean? Not to disappoint the lady, I assure you. Ha, ha, ha, how gravely he looks. – Come, come, I won't perplex you. 'Tis the only thing that Providence could have contrived to make me capable of serving you, either to my inclination or your own necessity.

MELLEFONT: How, how, for heaven's sake, dear Maskwell?

MASKWELL: Why thus – I'll go according to appointment; you shall have notice at the critical minute to come and surprise your aunt and me together: counterfeit a rage against me, and I'll make my escape through the private passage from her chamber, which I'll take care to leave open: 'twill be hard if then you can't bring her to any conditions. For this discovery will disarm her of all defence, and leave her entirely at your mercy: nay, she must ever after be in awe of you.

MELLEFONT: Let me adore thee, my better genius! By heaven I think it is not in the power of Fate to disappoint my hopes – my hopes, my certainty!

MASKWELL: Well, I'll meet you here, within a quarter of eight, and give you notice.

    [*Exit.*]

MELLEFONT: Good fortune ever go along with thee.

    [*Enter to him* CARELESS.]

CARELESS: Mellefont, get out o'th' way, my Lady Plyant's coming, and I shall never succeed while thou art in sight – though she begins to tack about; but I made love a great while to no purpose.

MELLEFONT: Why, what's the matter? She's convinced that I don't care for her.

CARELESS: 'Pox, I can't get an answer from her that does not begin with her honour, or her virtue, her religion, or some such cant. Then, she has told me the whole history of Sir Paul's nine years' courtship; how he has lain for whole nights together upon the stairs before her chamber door; and that the first favour he received from her, was a piece of an old scarlet petticoat for a stomacher,[1] which, since the day of his marriage, he has, out of a piece of gallantry, converted into a night-cap, and wears it still with much solemnity on his anniversary wedding-night.

MELLEFONT: That I have seen, with the ceremony thereunto belonging – for on that night he creeps in at the bed's feet like a gulled bassa that has married a relation of the Grand Signior's,[2] and that night he has his arms at liberty. Did not she tell you at what a distance she keeps him? He has confessed to me that but at some certain times, that is I suppose when she apprehends being with child, he never has the privilege of using the familiarity of a husband with his wife. He was once given to scrambling with his hands and sprawling in his sleep, and ever since she has him swaddled up in blankets, and his hands and feet swathed down, and so put to bed; and there he lies with a great beard, like a Russian bear upon a drift of snow. You are very great with him; I wonder he never told you his grievances. He will, I warrant you.

CARELESS: Excessively foolish. – But that which gives me most hopes of her, is her telling me of the many temptations she has resisted.

MELLEFONT: Nay, then you have her; for a woman's bragging to a man that she has overcome temptations, is an argument that they were weakly offered, and a challenge to him to engage her more irresistibly. 'Tis only an enhancing the price of the commodity, by telling you how many customers have underbid her.

1. *stomacher*: waistcoat.
2. Congreve owned an edition of Sir Paul Rycaut's *History of the Present State of the Ottoman Empire* in which an account appears of just such an obsequious approach by a pasha to his highborn bride.

CARELESS: Nay, I don't despair. — But still she has a grudging[3] to you. I talked to her t'other night at my Lord Froth's masquerade, when I'm satisfied she knew me, and I had no reason to complain of my reception; but I find women are not the same bare-faced and in masks, and a vizor disguises their inclinations as much as their faces.

MELLEFONT: 'Tis a mistake, for women may most properly be said to be unmasked when they wear vizors; for that secures them from blushing, and being out of countenance, and next to being in the dark, or alone, they are most truly themselves in a vizor mask. Here they come, I'll leave you. Ply her close, and by and by clap a *billet doux* into her hand. For a woman never thinks a man truly in love with her, till he has been fool enough to think of her out of her sight, and to lose so much time as to write to her.

   [*Exit.*]

   [*Enter* SIR PAUL *and* LADY PLYANT.]

SIR PAUL: Shan't we disturb your meditation, Mr Careless? You would be private?

CARELESS: You bring that along with you, Sir Paul, that shall be always welcome to my privacy.

SIR PAUL: O, sweet sir, you load your humble servants, both me and my wife, with continual favours.

LADY PLYANT: Jesu, Sir Paul, what a phrase was there? You will be making answers, and taking that upon you which ought to lie upon me. That you should have so little breeding to think Mr Careless did not apply himself to me. Pray, what have you about you to entertain anybody's privacy? I swear and declare in the face of the world, I'm ready to blush for your ignorance.

SIR PAUL [*aside to her*]: I acquiesce, my lady; but don't snub so loud.

LADY PLYANT: Mr Careless, if a person that is wholly illiterate might be supposed to be capable of being qualified to make a suitable return to those obligations which you are pleased to confer upon one that is wholly incapable of being qualified in all those circumstances, I'm sure I should rather attempt it than anything in the world, [*curtsies*] for I'm sure there's nothing in the

3. *grudging*: secret longing.

world that I would rather. [*Curtsies.*] But I know Mr Careless is so great a critic and so fine a gentleman, that it is impossible for me –

CARELESS: O heavens! Madam, you confound me.

SIR PAUL: Gadsbud, she's a fine person –

LADY PLYANT: O Lord! Sir, pardon me, we women have not those advantages: I know my own imperfections – but at the same time you must give me leave to declare in the face of the world that nobody is more sensible of favours and things; for with the reserve of my honour, I assure you, Mr Careless, I don't know anything in the world I would refuse to a person so meritorious – you'll pardon my want of expression.

CARELESS: Oh, your ladyship is abounding in all excellence, particularly that of phrase.

LADY PLYANT: You are so obliging, sir.

CARELESS: Your ladyship is so charming.

SIR PAUL: So, now, now; now, my lady.

LADY PLYANT: So well bred.

CARELESS: So surprising.

LADY PLYANT: So well dressed, so boon mein,[4] so eloquent, so unaffected, so easy, so free, so particular, so agreeable –

SIR PAUL: Ay, so, so, there.

CARELESS: O Lord, I beseech you, madam, don't –

LADY PLYANT: So gay, so graceful, so good teeth, so fine shape, so fine limbs, so fine linen, and I don't doubt but you have a very good skin, sir.

CARELESS: For heaven's sake, madam – I'm quite out of countenance.

SIR PAUL: And my lady's quite out of breath; or else you should hear – gadsbud, you may talk of my Lady Froth.

CARELESS: O fie, fie, not to be named of a day. My Lady Froth is very well in her accomplishments – but it is when my Lady Plyant is not thought of – if that can ever be.

LADY PLYANT: Oh, you overcome me – that is so excessive –

SIR PAUL: Nay, I swear and vow, that was pretty.

CARELESS: Oh, Sir Paul, you are the happiest man alive. Such a

4. *boon mein*: for *bonne mine*, prepossessing in appearance.

lady! that is the envy of her own sex, and the admiration of ours.

SIR PAUL: Your humble servant, I am, I thank heaven, in a fine way of living, as I may say, peacefully and happily, and I think need not envy any of my neighbours, blessed be Providence. Ay, truly, Mr Careless, my lady is a great blessing, a fine, discreet, well-spoken woman as you shall see – if it becomes me to say so; and we live very comfortably together; she's a little hasty sometimes, and so am I; but mine's soon over, and then I'm so sorry. – Oh, Mr Careless, if it were not for one thing –

[Enter BOY with a letter, carries it to SIR PAUL.]

LADY PLYANT: How often have you been told of that, you jack-a-napes?

SIR PAUL: Gadso, gadsbud – Tim, carry it to my lady, you should have carried it to my lady first.

BOY: 'Tis directed to your worship.

SIR PAUL: Well, well, my lady reads all letters first. – Child, do so no more; d'ye hear, Tim?

BOY: No, an please you.

[Carries the letter to LADY PLYANT, and exit.]

SIR PAUL: A humour of my wife's, you know women have little fancies. But as I was telling you, Mr Careless, if it were not for one thing, I should think myself the happiest man in the world; indeed, that touches me near, very near.

CARELESS: What can that be, Sir Paul?

SIR PAUL: Why, I have, I thank heaven, a very plentiful fortune, a good estate in the country, some houses in town, and some money, a pretty tolerable personal estate; and it is a great grief to me, indeed it is Mr Careless, that I have not a son to inherit this. – 'Tis true I have a daughter, and a fine dutiful child she is, though I say it, blessed be Providence I may say; for indeed, Mr Careless, I am mightily beholding to Providence – a poor unworthy sinner. – But if I had a son, ah, that's my affliction, and my only affliction; indeed I cannot refrain tears when it comes in my mind.

[Cries.]

CARELESS: Why, methinks that might be easily remedied – my lady's a fine likely woman –

SIR PAUL: Oh, a fine likely woman as you shall see in a summer's day – indeed she is, Mr Careless, in all respects.

CARELESS: And I should not have taken you to have been so old –

SIR PAUL: Alas, that's not it, Mr Careless; ah! that's not it; no, no, you shoot wide of the mark a mile; indeed you do, that's not it, Mr Careless; no, no, that's not it.

CARELESS: No? What can be the matter then?

SIR PAUL: You'll scarcely believe me, when I shall tell you – my lady is so nice – it's very strange, but it's true, too true – she's so very nice, that I don't believe she would touch a man for the world – at least not above once a year; I'm sure I have found it so; and alas, what's once a year to an old man, who would do good in his generation? Indeed it's true, Mr Careless, it breaks my heart. – I am her husband, as I may say, though far unworthy of that honour, yet I am her husband; but alas-a-day, I have no more familiarity with her person – as to that matter – than with my own mother – no indeed.

CARELESS: Alas-a-day, this is a lamentable story; my lady must be told on't; she must i'faith, Sir Paul; 'tis an injury to the world.

SIR PAUL: Ah! would to heaven you would, Mr Careless; you are mightily in her favour.

CARELESS: I warrant you. What, we must have a son some way or other.

SIR PAUL: Indeed, I should be mighty bound to you if you could bring it about, Mr Careless.

LADY PLYANT: Here, Sir Paul, it's from your steward. Here's a return of six hundred pounds; you may take fifty of it for your next half year.

[Gives him the letter.]

[Enter LORD FROTH, CYNTHIA.]

SIR PAUL: How does my girl? Come hither to thy father, poor lamb, thou'rt melancholy.

LORD FROTH: Heaven Sir Paul, you amaze me, of all things in the world – you are never pleased but when we are all upon the broad grin; all laugh and no company; ah, then 'tis such a sight to see some teeth. Sure you're a great admirer of my Lady Whifler, Mr Sneer, and Sir Laurence Loud, and that gang.

SIR PAUL: I vow and swear she's a very merry woman, but I think she laughs a little too much.

LORD FROTH: Merry! O Lord, what a character that is of a woman of quality. You have been at my Lady Whifler's upon her day, madam?

CYNTHIA: Yes, my lord. [*Aside*.] I must humour this fool.

LORD FROTH: Well and how? hee! What is your sense of the conversation there?

CYNTHIA: Oh, most ridiculous – a perpetual consort of laughing without any harmony; for sure, my lord, to laugh out of time is as disagreeable as to sing out of time or out of tune.

LORD FROTH: Hee, hee, hee, right; and then my Lady Whifler is so ready – she always comes in three bars too soon – and then, what do they laugh at? For you know laughing without a jest is as impertinent, hee! as, as –

CYNTHIA: As dancing without a fiddle.

LORD FROTH: Just, i'faith. That was at my tongue's end.

CYNTHIA: But that cannot be properly said of them, for I think they are all in good nature with the world, and only laugh at one another; and you must allow they have all jests in their persons, though they have none in their conversation.

LORD FROTH: True, as I'm a person of honour – for heaven's sake let us sacrifice 'em to mirth a little.

[*Enter* BOY *and whispers* SIR PAUL.]

SIR PAUL: 'Gads so – wife, wife, my Lady Plyant, I have a word.

LADY PLYANT: I'm busy, Sir Paul; I wonder at your impertinence.

CARELESS: Sir Paul, harkee, I'm reasoning the matter you know; madam, – if your ladyship please, we'll discourse of this in the next room.

[*Exit* CARELESS *and* LADY PLYANT.]

SIR PAUL: O ho, I wish you good success, I wish you good success. Boy, tell my lady, when she has done, I would speak with her below.

[*Exit* SIR PAUL.]

[*Enter* LADY FROTH *and* BRISK.]

LADY FROTH: Then you think that episode between Susan, the

dairymaid, and our coachman is not amiss; you know, I may suppose the dairy in town, as well as in the country.

BRISK: Incomparable, let me perish – but then being an heroic poem, had not you better call him a charioteer? Charioteer sounds great; besides your ladyship's coachman having a red face, and you comparing him to the sun – and you know the sun is called heaven's charioteer.

LADY FROTH: Oh, infinitely better; I'm extremely beholding to you for the hint. Stay, we'll read over those half a score lines again. [*Pulls out a paper.*] Let me see here, you know what goes before – the comparison, you know.

[*Reads.*]

> For as the sun shines every day,
> So of our coach-man I may say –

BRISK: I'm afraid that simile won't do in wet weather – because you say the sun shines every day.

LADY FROTH: No, for the sun it won't, but it will do for the coachman, for you know there's most occasion for a coach in wet weather.

BRISK: Right, right, that saves all.

LADY FROTH: Then I don't say the sun shines all the day, but that he peeps now and then, yet he does shine all the day too, you know, though we don't see him.

BRISK: Right, but the vulgar will never comprehend that.

LADY FROTH: Well, you shall hear – let me see.

[*Reads.*]

> For as the sun shines every day,
> So, of our coachman I may say,
> He shows his drunken fiery face
> Just as the sun does, more or less.

BRISK: That's right, all's well, all's well.

LADY FROTH [*reads*]:

> And when at night his labour's done,
> Then too like heaven's charioteer, the sun:

Ay, charioteer does better.

> Into the dairy he descends.
> And there his whipping and his driving ends;
> There he's secure from danger of a bilk,
> His fare is paid him, and he sets in milk.

For Susan, you know, is Thetis,[5] and so –

BRISK: Incomparable well and proper, i'gad – but I have one exception to make. – Don't you think *bilk* (I know it's good rhyme), but don't you think *bilk* and *fare* are too like a hackney coachman?

LADY FROTH: I swear and vow I'm afraid so. – And yet our Jehu was a hackney coachman when my lord took him.

BRISK: Was he? Then I'm answered, if Jehu was a hackney coachman. You may put that into the marginal notes, though, to prevent criticisms – only mark it with a small asterisk, and say, Jehu was formerly a hackney coachman.

LADY FROTH: I will; you'd oblige me extremely to write notes to the whole poem.

BRISK: With all my heart and soul, and proud of the vast honour, let me perish.

LORD FROTH: Hee, hee, hee, my dear, have you done? Won't you join with us, we were laughing at my Lady Whifler, and Mr Sneer.

LADY FROTH: Ay, my dear – were you? Oh filthy Mr Sneer; he's a nauseous figure, a most fulsamic[6] fop, foh! He spent two days together in going about Covent Garden to suit the lining of his coach with his complexion.

LORD FROTH: O silly! yet his aunt is as fond of him as if she had brought the ape into the world herself.

BRISK: Who, my Lady Toothless? Oh, she's a mortifying spectacle; she's always chewing the cud like an old ewe.

CYNTHIA: Fie, Mr Brisk; 'tis eringos[7] for her cough.

---

5. *Thetis*: sea-nymph, mother of Achilles.
6. *fulsamic*: fulsome.
7. *eringos*: 'the candied root of the Sea Holly . . . formerly used as a sweetmeat, and regarded as an aphrodisiac' (*OED*).

LADY FROTH: I have seen her take 'em half chewed out of her mouth, to laugh, and then put 'em in again – foh.

LORD FROTH: Foh.

LADY FROTH: Then she's always ready to laugh when Sneer offers to speak, and sits in expectation of his no jest, with her gums bare, and her mouth open –

BRISK: Like an oyster at low ebb, i'gad – ha, ha, ha.

CYNTHIA [aside]: Well, I find there are no fools so inconsiderable in themselves, but they can render other people contemptible in exposing their infirmities.

LADY FROTH: Then that t'other great strapping lady – I can't hit of her name; the old fat fool that paints so exorbitantly.

BRISK: I know whom you mean – but deuce take me, I can't hit of her name neither. Paints, d'ye say? Why she lays it on with a trowel. Then she has a great beard that bristles through it, and makes her look as if she were plastered with lime and hair, let me perish.

LADY FROTH: Oh, you made a song upon her, Mr Brisk.

BRISK: He? I'gad, so I did. – My lord can sing it.

CYNTHIA: O good my lord, let's hear it.

BRISK: 'Tis not a song neither – it's a sort of an epigram, or rather an epigrammatic sonnet; I don't know what to call it, but it's satire. Sing it, my lord.

(Song[8])

LORD FROTH [sings].

> Ancient Phillis has young graces,
> 'Tis a strange thing, but a true one;
> Shall I tell you how?
> She herself makes her own faces,
> And each morning wears a new one;
> Where's the wonder now?

BRISK: Short, but there's salt in't, my way of writing, i'gad.
    [Enter FOOTMAN.]

---

8. Song: John Bowman, who played Lord Froth, composed the music.

LADY FROTH: How now?

FOOTMAN: Your ladyship's chair is come.

LADY FROTH: Is nurse and the child in it?

FOOTMAN: Yes, madam.

LADY FROTH: O the dear creature! Let's go see it.

LORD FROTH: I swear, my dear, you'll spoil that child, with sending it to and again so often; this is the seventh time the chair has gone for her today.

LADY FROTH: O law, I swear it's but the sixth, – and I han't seen her these two hours. – The poor dear creature – I swear, my lord, you don't love poor little Sapho.[9] – Come my dear Cynthia, Mr Brisk, we'll go see Sapho, though my lord won't.

CYNTHIA: I'll wait upon your ladyship.

BRISK: Pray, madam, how old is Lady Sapho?

LADY FROTH: Three quarters, but I swear she has a world of wit, and can sing a tune already. My lord, won't you go? Won't you? What, not to see Saph? Pray, my lord, come see little Saph. I knew you could not stay.

[Exeunt.]

CYNTHIA: 'Tis not so hard to counterfeit joy in the depth of affliction, as to dissemble mirth in company of fools. – Why should I call 'em fools? The world thinks better of 'em; for these have quality and education, wit and fine conversation, are received and admired by the world. – If not, they like and admire themselves. – And why is not that true wisdom, for 'tis happiness. And for aught I know, we have misapplied the name all this while, and mistaken the thing; since

> If happiness in self-content is placed,
> The wise are wretched, and fools only blessed.

[Exit.]

9. *Sapho*: Sappho of Lesbos was a famous Greek poetess.

ACT FOUR

SCENE ONE

[*Enter* MELLEFONT *and* CYNTHIA.]

CYNTHIA: I heard him loud as I came by the closet-door, and my lady with him, but she seemed to moderate his passion.

MELLEFONT: Ay, hell thank her, as gentle breezes moderate a fire; but I shall counter-work her spells, and ride the witch in her own bridle.

CYNTHIA: It's impossible; she'll cast beyond you still. I'll lay my life it will never be a match.

MELLEFONT: What?

CYNTHIA: Between you and me.

MELLEFONT: Why so?

CYNTHIA: My mind gives me it won't – because we are both so willing; we each of us strive to reach the goal, and hinder one another in the race; I swear it never does well when the parties are so agreed. For when people walk hand in hand, there's neither overtaking nor meeting: we hunt in couples where we both pursue the same game, but forget one another; and 'tis because we are so near that we don't think of coming together.

MELLEFONT: Hum, 'gad I believe there's something in't; – marriage is the game that we hunt, and while we think that we only have it in view, I don't see but we have it in our power.

CYNTHIA: Within reach; for example, give me your hand; why have you looked through the wrong end of the perspective[1] all this while; for nothing has been between us but our fears.

MELLEFONT: I don't know why we should not steal out of the house

1. *perspective*: telescope.

this moment and marry one another, without consideration or the fear of repentance. Pox o'fortune, portion, settlements and jointures.

CYNTHIA: Ay, ay, what have we to do with 'em? You know we marry for love.

MELLEFONT: Love, love, downright, very villainous love.

CYNTHIA: And he that can't live upon love, deserves to die in a ditch. – Here then, I give you my promise, in spite of duty, any temptation of wealth, your inconstancy, or my own inclination to change –

MELLEFONT: To run most wilfully and unreasonably away with me this moment and be married.

CYNTHIA: Hold! – Never to marry anybody else.

MELLEFONT: That's but a kind of negative consent. – Why, you won't balk the frolic?

CYNTHIA: If you had not been so assured of your own conduct I would not. But 'tis but reasonable that since I consent to like a man without the vile consideration of money, he should give me a very evident demonstration of his wit: therefore let me see you undermine my Lady Touchwood, as you boasted, and force her to give her consent, and then –

MELLEFONT: I'll do't.

CYNTHIA: And I'll do't.

MELLEFONT: This very next ensuing hour of eight o'clock is the last minute of her reign, unless the devil assist her *in propria persona*.[2]

CYNTHIA: Well, if the devil should assist her, and your plot miscarry –

MELLEFONT: Ay, what am I to trust to then?

CYNTHIA: Why, if you give me very clear demonstration that it was the devil, I'll allow for irresistible odds. But if I find it to be only chance, or destiny, or unlucky stars, or anything but the very devil, I'm inexorable; only still I'll keep my word, and live a maid for your sake.

MELLEFONT: And you won't die one, for your own, so still there's hope.

2. *in propria persona*: in his own person.

CYNTHIA: Here's my mother-in-law[3] and your friend Careless. I would not have 'em see us together yet.

[*Exeunt.*]

[*Enter* CARELESS *and* LADY PLYANT.]

LADY PLYANT: I swear, Mr Careless, you are very alluring, and say so many fine things, and nothing is so moving to me as a fine thing. Well, I must do you this justice, and declare in the face of the world, never anybody gained so far upon me as yourself; with blushes I must own it, you have shaken, as I may say, the very foundation of my honour. – Well, sure if I escape your importunities, I shall value myself as long as I live, I swear.

CARELESS [*sighing*]: And despise me.

LADY PLYANT: The last of any man in the world, by my purity; now you make me swear. – O gratitude forbid that I should ever be wanting in a respectful acknowledgment of an entire resignation of all my best wishes, for the person and parts of so accomplished a person, whose merit challenges much more, I'm sure, than my illiterate praises can description.

CARELESS [*in a whining tone*]: Ah heavens, madam, you ruin me with kindness; your charming tongue pursues the victory of your eyes, while at your feet your poor adorer dies.

LADY PLYANT: Ah! Very fine.

CARELESS [*still whining*]: Ah, why are you so fair, so bewitching fair? O let me grow to the ground here, and feast upon that hand; O let me press it to my heart, my aching trembling heart! The nimble movement shall instruct your pulse, and teach it to alarm desire. [*Aside.*] Zoons! I'm almost at the end of my cant if she does not yield quickly.

LADY PLYANT: Oh, that's so passionate and fine, I cannot hear it – I am not safe if I stay, and must leave you.

CARELESS: And must you leave me! Rather let me languish out a wretched life, and breath my soul beneath your feet. [*Aside.*] I must say the same thing over again, and can't help it.

3. *mother-in-law*: step-mother.

LADY PLYANT: I swear I am ready to languish too. – O my honour! Whither is it going? I protest you have given me the palpitation of the heart.

CARELESS: Can you be so cruel –

LADY PLYANT: O rise, I beseech you, say no more till you rise. – Why did you kneel so long? I swear I was so transported, I did not see it. – Well, to show you how far you have gained upon me, I assure you if Sir Paul should die, of all mankind there's none I'd sooner make my second choice.

CARELESS: O heaven! I can't outlive this night without your favour. – I feel my spirits faint, a general dampness overspreads my face, a cold, deadly dew already vents through all my pores, and will tomorrow wash me forever from your sight, and drown me in my tomb.

LADY PLYANT: Oh, you have conquered, sweet, melting, moving sir, you have conquered. What heart of marble can refrain to weep and yield to such sad sayings?

    [*Cries.*]

CARELESS: I thank heaven, they are the saddest that I ever said – Oh! [*Aside.*] I shall never contain laughter.

LADY PLYANT: Oh, I yield myself all up to your uncontrollable embraces. Say, thou dear, dying man, when, where and how – Ah, there's Sir Paul.

    [*Enter* SIR PAUL *and* CYNTHIA.]

CARELESS: 'Slife, yonder's Sir Paul, but if he were not come, I'm so transported I cannot speak. – This note will inform you. [*Gives her a note.*]

    [*Exit.*]

SIR PAUL: Thou art my tender lambkin, and shalt do what thou wilt – but endeavour to forget this Mellefont.

CYNTHIA: I would obey you to my power, sir; but if I have not him, I have sworn never to marry.

SIR PAUL: Never to marry! Heaven forbid; must I neither have sons nor grandsons? Must the family of the Plyants be utterly extinct for want of issue male. Oh impiety! But did you swear, did that sweet creature swear! ha? How durst you swear without my consent, ha? Gadsbud, who am I?

CYNTHIA: Pray don't be angry, sir; when I swore, I had your consent, and therefore I swore.

SIR PAUL: Why then the revoking my consent does annul, or make of none effect your oath: so you may unswear it again. – The law will allow it.

CYNTHIA: Ay, but my conscience never will.

SIR PAUL: Gadsbud, no matter for that, conscience and law never go together; you must not expect that.

LADY PLYANT: Ay, but Sir Paul, I conceive if she has sworn, d'ye mark me, if she has once sworn, it is most unchristian, inhumane, and obscene that she should break it. [*Aside.*] I'll make up this match again, because Mr Careless said it would oblige him.

SIR PAUL: Does your ladyship conceive so? Why, I was of that opinion once too. Nay, if your ladyship conceives so, I'm of that opinion again; but I can neither find my lord nor my lady to know what they intend.

LADY PLYANT: I'm satisfied that my cousin Mellefont has been much wronged.

CYNTHIA [*aside*]: I'm amazed to find her of our side, for I'm sure she loved him.

LADY PLYANT: I know my Lady Touchwood has no kindness for him; and besides, I have been informed by Mr Careless that Mellefont had never anything more than a profound respect. – That he has owned himself to be my admirer 'tis true, but he never was so presumptuous to entertain any dishonourable notions of things; so that if this be made plain, I don't see how my daughter can in conscience, or honour, or anything in the world –

SIR PAUL: Indeed, if this be made plain, as my lady your mother says, child –

LADY PLYANT: Plain! I was informed of it by Mr Careless. – And I assure you Mr Careless is a person – that has a most extraordinary respect and honour for you, Sir Paul.

CYNTHIA [*aside*]: And for your ladyship too, I believe, or else you had not changed sides so soon; now I begin to find it.

SIR PAUL: I am much obliged to Mr Careless; really, he is a person that I have a great value for, not only for that, but because he has a great veneration for your ladyship.

LADY PLYANT: O las, no indeed, Sir Paul, 'tis upon your account.

SIR PAUL: No, I protest and vow, I have no title to his esteem, but in having the honour to appertain in some measure to your ladyship, that's all.

LADY PLYANT: O law now, I swear and declare it shan't be so, you're too modest, Sir Paul.

SIR PAUL: It becomes me, when there is any comparison made between –

LADY PLYANT: O fy, fy, Sir Paul, you'll put me out of countenance. Your very obedient and affectionate wife, that's all, and highly honoured in that title.

SIR PAUL: Gadsbud, I am transported! Give me leave to kiss your ladyship's hand.

CYNTHIA [aside]: That my poor father should be so very silly.

LADY PLYANT: My lip indeed, Sir Paul, I swear you shall.

[He kisses her, and bows very low.]

SIR PAUL: I humbly thank your ladyship. – I don't know whether I fly on ground, or walk in air. Gadsbud, she was never thus before. – Well, I must own myself the most beholden to Mr Careless. – As sure as can be this is all his doing; something that he has said. Well, 'tis a rare thing to have an ingenious friend. Well, your ladyship is of opinion that the match may go forward.

LADY PLYANT: By all means; Mr Careless has satisfied me of the matter.

SIR PAUL: Well, why then, lamb, you may keep your oath, but have a care of making rash vows. Come hither to me, and kiss papa.

LADY PLYANT: I swear and declare, I am in such a twitter to read Mr Careless his letter that I can't forbear any longer. – But though I may read all letters first by prerogative, yet I'll be sure to be unsuspected this time. – Sir Paul.

SIR PAUL: Did your ladyship call?

LADY PLYANT: Nay, not to interrupt you, my dear – only lend me your letter, which you had from your steward today; I would look upon the account again, and maybe increase your allowance.

SIR PAUL: There it is, madam. Do you want a pen and ink?

[Bows and gives the letter.]

LADY PLYANT: No, no, nothing else, I thank you, Sir Paul. [*Aside.*] So now I can read my own letter under the cover of his.

SIR PAUL: He? And wilt thou bring a grandson at nine months' end – he? A brave chopping boy. – I'll settle a thousand pounds a year upon the rogue as soon as ever he looks me in the face, I will gadsbud. I'm overjoyed to think I have any of my family that will bring children into the world. For I would fain have some resemblance of myself in my posterity, he, Thy? Can't you contrive that affair, girl? Do gadsbud, think on thy old father, heh? Make the young rogue as like as you can.

CYNTHIA: I'm glad to see you so merry, sir.

SIR PAUL: Merry! Gadsbud, I'm serious, I'll give thee five hundred pound for every inch of him that resembles me; ah this eye, this left eye! A thousand pound for this left eye. This has done execution in its time, girl; why thou hast my leer, hussy, just thy father's leer. – Let it be transmitted to the young rogue by the help of imagination; why, 'tis the mark of our family, Thy; our house is distinguished by a languishing eye, as the house of Austria is by a thick lip. – Ah! when I was of your age, hussy, I would have held fifty to one I could have drawn my own picture – gadsbud I could have done – not so much as you, neither, but – nay, don't blush –

CYNTHIA: I don't blush, sir, for I vow I don't understand –

SIR PAUL: Pshaw, pshaw, you fib, you baggage; you do understand, and you shall understand; come, don't be so nice, gadsbud, don't learn after your mother-in-law my lady here. Marry, heaven forbid that you should follow her example, that would spoil all indeed. Bless us, if you should take a vagary and make a rash resolution on your wedding night to die a maid, as she did, all were ruined, all my hopes lost. – My heart would break, and my estate would be left to the wide world, he? I hope you are a better Christian than to think of being a nun, he? Answer me.

CYNTHIA: I'm all obedience, sir, to your commands.

LADY PLYANT [*having read the letter*]: O dear Mr Careless, I swear he writes charmingly, and he talks charmingly, and he looks charmingly, and he has charmed me, as much as I have charmed him; and so I'll tell him in the wardrobe when 'tis dark. O crimine![4] I

4. *crimine*: variant of the oath, 'Gemini'.

hope Sir Paul has not seen both letters. [*Puts the wrong letter hastily up, and gives him her own.*] Sir Paul, here's your letter; tomorrow morning I'll settle the accounts to your advantage.

    [*Enter* BRISK.]

BRISK: Sir Paul, gadsbud you're an uncivil person, let me tell you, and all that; and I did not think it had been in you.

SIR PAUL: O law, what's the matter now? I hope you are not angry, Mr Brisk.

BRISK: Deuce take me, I believe you intend to marry your daughter yourself; you're always brooding over her like an old hen, as if she were not well hatched, i'gad, he?

SIR PAUL: Good, strange! Mr Brisk is such a merry, facetious person, he, he, he. No, no, I have done with her, I have done with her now.

BRISK: The fiddles have stayed this hour in the hall, and my Lord Froth wants a partner, we can never begin without her.

SIR PAUL: Go, go child, go, go get you gone and dance and be merry, I'll come and look at you by and by. Where's my son Mellefont?

    [*Exit* CYNTHIA.]

LADY PLYANT: I'll send him to them, I know where he is.

    [*Exit.*]

BRISK: Sir Paul, will you send Careless into the hall if you meet him.

SIR PAUL: I will, I will, I'll go and look for him on purpose.

    [*Exit.*]

BRISK: So now they are all gone, and I have an opportunity to practice. – Ah! My dear Lady Froth! She's a most engaging creature, if she were not so fond of that damned coxcombly lord of hers; and yet I am forced to allow him wit too, to keep in with him. – No matter, she's a woman of parts, and, i'gad, parts will carry her. She said she would follow me into the gallery. – Now to make my approaches. – Hem, hem! [*Bows.*] Ah madam! – Pox on't, why should I disparage my parts by thinking what to say? None but dull rogues *think*; witty men, like rich fellows, are always ready for all expenses; while your blockheads, like poor needy scoundrels, are forced to examine their stock, and forecast the charges of the day. Here she comes; I'll seem not to see her, and try to win her with a new airy invention of my own, hem!

[*Enter* LADY FROTH.]

BRISK [*sings*]: *I'm sick with love*, ha ha ha, *prithee come cure me.*

I'm sick with, etc.

O ye powers! O my Lady Froth, my Lady Froth! My Lady Froth! Heigho! Break heart; gods, I thank you.

[*Stands musing with his arms across.*]

LADY FROTH: O heavens, Mr Brisk! What's the matter?

BRISK: My Lady Froth! Your ladyship's most humble servant. – The matter, madam? Nothing, madam, nothing at all, i'gad. I was fallen into the most agreeable amusement in the whole province of contemplation, that's all. [*Aside.*] I'll seem to conceal my passion, and that will look like respect.

LADY FROTH: Bless me, why did you call out upon me so loud?

BRISK: O Lord, I, madam? I beseech your ladyship, when?

LADY FROTH: Just now as I came in, bless me. Why, don't you know it?

BRISK: Not I, let me perish. – But did I? Strange! I confess your ladyship was in my thoughts; and I was in a sort of dream that did in a manner represent a very pleasing object to my imagination, but – but did I indeed? – to see how love and murder will out. But did I really name my Lady Froth?

LADY FROTH: Three times aloud, as I love letters. – But did you talk of love? O Parnassus! Who would have thought Mr Brisk could have been in love, ha ha ha. O heavens, I thought you could have no mistress but the nine Muses.

BRISK: No more I have, i'gad, for I adore 'em all in your ladyship. – Let me perish, I don't know whether to be splenetic, or airy upon't; the deuce take me if I can tell whether I am glad or sorry that your ladyship has made the discovery.

LADY FROTH: O be merry by all means. – Prince Volscius[5] in love! Ha ha ha.

BRISK: O barbarous, to turn me into ridicule! Yet, ha ha ha, the

5. *Prince Volscius*: a character in Buckingham's *The Rehearsal* (1671).

deuce take me, I can't help laughing myself neither, ha ha ha; yet by heavens, I have a violent passion for your ladyship, seriously.

LADY FROTH: Seriously? Ha ha ha.

BRISK: Seriously, ha ha ha. Gad, I have, for all I laugh.

LADY FROTH: Ha ha ha! What d'ye think I laugh at? Ha ha ha.

BRISK: Me i'gad, ha, ha.

LADY FROTH: No, the deuce take me if I don't laugh at myself; for hang me if I have not a violent passion for Mr Brisk, ha ha ha.

BRISK: Seriously?

LADY FROTH: Seriously, ha ha ha.

BRISK: That's well enough; let me perish, ha ha ha. Oh miraculous, what a happy discovery! Ah, my dear charming Lady Froth!

LADY FROTH: Oh my adored Mr Brisk!

[*Embrace.*]

[*Enter* LORD FROTH.]

LORD FROTH: The company are all ready. — How now!

BRISK [*softly to her*]: Zoons, madam, there's my lord.

LADY FROTH [*aside to* BRISK]: Take no notice — but observe me. [*Aloud.*] Now cast off, and meet me at the lower end of the room, and then join hands again; I could teach my lord this dance purely, but I vow, Mr Brisk, I can't tell how to come so near any other man. [*They pretend to practice part of a country dance.*] Oh, here's my lord; now you shall see me do it with him.

LORD FROTH [*aside*]: Oh, I see there's no harm yet. — But I don't like this familiarity.

LADY FROTH: Shall you and I do our close dance to show Mr Brisk?

LORD FROTH: No, my dear, do it with him.

LADY FROTH: I'll do it with him, my lord, when you are out of the way.

BRISK [*aside*]: That's good i'gad, that's good. Deuce take me, I can hardly hold laughing in his face.

LORD FROTH: Any other time, my dear, or we'll dance it below.

LADY FROTH: With all my heart.

BRISK: Come my lord, I'll wait on you. [*To her.*] My charming witty angel!

LADY FROTH: We shall have whispering time enough, you know, since we are partners.

[*Exeunt.*]

[*Enter* LADY PLYANT, *and* CARELESS.]

LADY PLYANT: O Mr Careless, Mr Careless, I'm ruined, I'm undone.

CARELESS: What's the matter, madam?

LADY PLYANT: Oh the unluckiest accident, I'm afraid I shan't live to tell it you.

CARELESS: Heaven forbid! What is it?

LADY PLYANT: I'm in such a fright; the strangest quandary and premunire!⁶ I'm all over in a universal agitation, I dare swear every circumstance of me trembles. – O your letter, your letter! By an unfortunate mistake, I have given Sir Paul your letter instead of his own.

CARELESS: That was unlucky –

LADY PLYANT: Oh, yonder he comes reading of it; for heaven's sake step in here and advise me quickly, before he sees.

[*Exeunt.*]

[*Enter* SIR PAUL *with the letter.*]

SIR PAUL: O Providence, what a conspiracy have I discovered. – But let me see to make an end on't. [*Reads.*] Hum – *After supper in the wardrobe by the gallery. If Sir Paul should surprise us, I have a commission from him to treat with you about the very matter of fact.* – Matter of fact! Very pretty; it seems that I am conducting to my own cuckoldom. Why, this is the very traitorous position of taking up arms by my authority, against my person! Well, let me see – *Till then I languish in expectation of my adored charmer.*

Dying Ned Careless.

Gadsbud, would that were matter of fact too. Die and be damned for a Judas Maccabeus,⁷ and Iscariot both. O friendship! What art thou but a name! Henceforward, let no man make a friend that would not be a cuckold. For whomsoever he receives into his bosom will find the way to his bed, and there return his caresses with interest to his wife. Have I for this been pinioned night after night for three years past? Have I been swathed in blankets till I

6. *premunire*: difficulty, predicament.
7. *Judas Maccabeus*: The Jewish military leader who fell in battle in 160 BC

have even been deprived of motion, and rendered uncapable of
suing the common benefits of nature? Have I approached the
marriage bed with reverence as to a sacred shrine, and denied
myself the enjoyment of lawful domestic pleasures to preserve its
purity, and must I now find it polluted by foreign iniquity? O my
Lady Plyant, you were chaste as ice, but you are melted now, and
false as water. – But Providence has been constant to me in
discovering this conspiracy; still I am beholden to Providence. If it
were not for Providence, sure, poor Sir Paul, thy heart would
break.

   [*Enter* LADY PLYANT.]

LADY PLYANT: So, sir, I see you have read the letter. – Well now,
   Sir Paul, what do you think of your friend Careless? Has he been
   treacherous, or did you give his insolence a licence to make trial of
   your wife's suspected virtue? De'e see here? Look, read it.
   [*Snatches the letter as in anger.*] Gad's my life if I thought it were
   so, I would this moment renounce all communication with you.
   Ungrateful monster! He? Is it so? Ay, I see it, a plot upon my
   honour; your guilty cheeks confess it. Oh, where shall wronged
   virtue fly for reparation! I'll be divorced this instant.

SIR PAUL: Gadsbud, what shall I say? This is the strangest surprise!
   Why, I don't know anything at all, nor I don't know whether
   there be anything at all in the world, or no.

LADY PLYANT: I thought I should try you, false man. I that never
   dissembled in my life. Yet to make trial of you, pretended to like
   that monster of iniquity, Careless, and found out that contrivance
   to let you see this letter; which now I find was of your own
   inditing. – I do, heathen, I do. See my face no more; there has
   hardly been consummation between us, and I'll be divorced
   presently.

SIR PAUL: O strange, what will become of me? I'm so amazed, and
   so overjoyed, so afraid, and so sorry. – But did you give me this
   letter on purpose, he? Did you?

LADY PLYANT: Did I? Do you doubt me, Turk, Saracen? I have a
   cousin that's a proctor in the Commons,[8] I'll go to him instantly –

8. *proctor in the Commons*: lawyer for matrimonial cases who could plead in the courts
located in a group of buildings known as Doctors' Commons.

SIR PAUL: Hold, stay, I beseech your ladyship. – I'm so overjoyed, stay, I'll confess all.

LADY PLYANT: What will you confess, Jew?

SIR PAUL: Why, now, as I hope to be saved, I had no hand in this letter – nay, hear me, I beseech your ladyship. The devil take me now if he did not go beyond my commission. – If I desired him to do any more than speak a good word only just for me; gadsbud, only for poor Sir Paul, I'm an Anabaptist, or a Jew, or what you please to call me.

LADY PLYANT: Why, is not here matter of fact?

SIR PAUL: Ay, but by your own virtue and continency, that matter of fact is all his own doing. – I confess I had a great desire to have some honours conferred upon me, which lie all in your ladyship's breast, and he being a well-spoken man, I desired him to intercede for me.

LADY PLYANT: Did you so, Presumption! Well, remember for this, your right hand shall be swathed down again tonight – and I thought to have always allowed you that liberty –

SIR PAUL: Nay but madam, I shall offend again if you don't allow me that to reach –

LADY PLYANT: Drink the less you sot, and do't before you come to bed.

    [*Exit.*]

    [*Enter* CARELESS.]

CARELESS: Sir Paul, I'm glad I've met with you; gad, I have said all I could, but can't prevail. – Then my friendship to you has carried me a little farther in this matter –

SIR PAUL: Indeed – Well, sir – [*aside*] – I'll dissemble with him a little.

CARELESS: Why, faith, I have in my time known honest gentlemen abused by a pretended coyness in their wives, and I had a mind to try my lady's virtue. And when I could not prevail for you, 'gad, I pretended to be in love myself – but all in vain, she would not hear a word upon that subject. Then I writ a letter to her; I don't know what effects that will have, but I'll be sure to tell you when I do, though by this light I believe her virtue is impregnable.

SIR PAUL: O Providence! Providence! What discoveries are here made? Why, this is better and more miraculous than the rest.

CARELESS: What do you mean?

SIR PAUL: I can't tell you, I'm so overjoyed; come along with me to my lady. I can't contain myself; come my dear friend.

CARELESS [aside]: So, so, so, this difficulty's over.

[Exeunt.]

[Enter MELLEFONT and MASKWELL severally.]

MELLEFONT: Maskwell! I have been looking for you – 'tis within a quarter of eight.

MASKWELL: My lady is just gone down from my lord's closet; you had best steal into her chamber before she comes, and lie concealed there; otherwise she may lock the door when we are together, and you not easily get in to surprise us.

MELLEFONT: Ha! you say true.

MASKWELL: You had best make haste, for she's but gone to make some apology to the company for her own and my lord's absence all this while, and will to her chamber instantly.

MELLEFONT: I go this moment. Now, Fortune, I defy thee!

[Exit.]

MASKWELL: I confess you may be allowed to be secure in your own opinion; the appearance is very fair, but I have an after-game to play that shall turn the tables, and here comes the man that I must manage.

[Enter LORD TOUCHWOOD.]

LORD TOUCHWOOD: Maskwell, you are the man I wished to meet.

MASKWELL: I am happy to be in the way of your lordship's commands.

LORD TOUCHWOOD: I have always found you prudent and careful in anything that has concerned me or my family.

MASKWELL: I were a villain else. – I am bound by duty and gratitude, and my own inclination, to be ever your lordship's servant.

LORD TOUCHWOOD: Enough – you are my friend; I know it. Yet there has been a thing in your knowledge, which has concerned me nearly, that you have concealed from me.

MASKWELL: My lord!

LORD TOUCHWOOD: Nay, I excuse your friendship to my unnatural nephew thus far – but I know you have been privy to his impious designs upon my wife. This evening she has told me all. Her good nature concealed it as long as was possible, but he perseveres so in villainy, that she has told me even you were weary of dissuading him, though you have once actually hindered him from forcing her.

MASKWELL: I am sorry, my lord, I can make you no answer; this is an occasion in which I would not willingly be so silent.

LORD TOUCHWOOD: I know you would excuse him – and I know as well that you can't.

MASKWELL: Indeed I was in hopes 't had been a youthful heat that might have soon boiled over, but –

LORD TOUCHWOOD: Say on.

MASKWELL: I have nothing more to say, my lord – but to express my concern; for I think his frenzy increases daily.

LORD TOUCHWOOD: How! Give me but proof of it, ocular proof, that I may justify my dealing with him to the world, and share my fortunes.

MASKWELL: O my lord! Consider that is hard: besides, time may work upon him – then, for me to do it! I have professed an everlasting friendship to him.

LORD TOUCHWOOD: He is your friend, and what am I?

MASKWELL: I am answered.

LORD TOUCHWOOD: Fear not his displeasure; I will put you out of his, and fortune's power, and for that thou art scrupulously honest, I will secure thy fidelity to him, and give my honour never to own any discovery that you shall make me. Can you give me a demonstrative proof? Speak.

MASKWELL: I wish I could not. – To be plain, my lord, I intended this evening to have tried all arguments to dissuade him from a design which I suspect; and if I had not succeeded, to have informed your lordship of what I knew.

LORD TOUCHWOOD: I thank you. What is the villain's purpose?

MASKWELL: He has owned nothing to me of late, and what I mean now is only a bare suspicion of my own. If your lordship will meet me a quarter of an hour hence there, in that lobby by my lady's bedchamber, I shall be able to tell you more.

LORD TOUCHWOOD: I will.

MASKWELL: My duty to your lordship makes me do a severe piece of justice –

LORD TOUCHWOOD: I will be secret, and reward your honesty beyond your hopes.

[Exeunt, severally.]

SCENE TWO

Scene opening, shows Lady Touchwood's chamber

[MELLEFONT, *solus.*]

MELLEFONT: Pray heaven my aunt keep touch with her assignation. Oh that her lord were but sweating behind this hanging, with the expectation of what I shall see. – Hist, she comes. Little does she think what a mine is just ready to spring under her feet. But to my post.

[*Goes behind the hanging.*]

[*Enter* LADY TOUCHWOOD.]

LADY TOUCHWOOD: 'Tis eight o'clock: methinks I should have found him here. Who does not prevent[9] the hour of love outstays the time; for to be dully punctual is too slow. – I was accusing you of neglect.

[*Enter* MASKWELL.]

MASKWELL: I confess you do reproach me when I see you here before me; but 'tis fit I should be still behindhand, still to be more and more indebted to your goodness.

LADY TOUCHWOOD: You can excuse a fault too well, not to have been to blame – a ready answer shows you were prepared.

MASKWELL: Guilt is ever at a loss and confusion waits upon it; when innocence and bold truth are always ready for expression –

LADY TOUCHWOOD: Not in love; words are the weak support of cold indifference; love has no language to be heard.

MASKWELL: Excess of joy had made me stupid! Thus may my lips

9. *prevent*: arrive before.

be ever closed. [*Kisses her.*] And thus – oh, who would not lose his speech, upon condition to have joys above it?

LADY TOUCHWOOD: Hold, let me lock the door first.
  [*Goes to the door.*]

MASKWELL [*aside*]: That I believed; 'twas well I left the private passage open.

LADY TOUCHWOOD: So, that's safe.

MASKWELL: And so may all your pleasures be, and secret as this kiss –

MELLEFONT: And may all treachery be thus discovered.
  [*Leaps out.*]

LADY TOUCHWOOD: Ah! [*Shrieks.*]

MELLEFONT: Villain! [*Offers to draw.*]

MASKWELL: Nay then, there's but one way.
  [*Runs out.*]

MELLEFONT: Say you so, were you provided for an escape? Hold, madam, you have no more holes to your burrow. I'll stand between you and this sally-port.

LADY TOUCHWOOD: Thunder strike thee dead for this deceit, immediate lightning blast thee, me, and the whole world! Oh! I could rack myself, play the vulture to my own heart, and gnaw it piecemeal, for not boding to me this misfortune.

MELLEFONT: Be patient –

LADY TOUCHWOOD: Be damned!

MELLEFONT: Consider, I have you on the hook; you will but flounder yourself a-weary, and be nevertheless my prisoner.

LADY TOUCHWOOD: I'll hold my breath and die, but I'll be free!

MELLEFONT: O madam, have a care of dying unprepared. I doubt you have some unrepented sins that may hang heavy and retard your flight.

LADY TOUCHWOOD: Oh, what shall I do? Say? Whither shall I turn? Has hell no remedy?

MELLEFONT: None; hell has served you even as heaven has done, left you to yourself. – You're in a kind of Erasmus paradise;[10] yet

10. *Erasmus paradise*: between heaven and hell. Summers quotes Roger L'Estrange's introduction to his translation of Erasmus' *Colloquies* (1689): 'the Translator . . . is crushed betwixt two Extremes, as they hang up Erasmus himself, betwixt Heaven and Hell.'

if you please you may make it a purgatory, and with a little penance and my absolution, all this may turn to good account.

LADY TOUCHWOOD [aside]: Hold in my passion, and fall, fall a little, thou swelling heart. Let me have some intermission of this rage, and one minute's coolness to dissemble.

[She weeps.]

MELLEFONT: You have been to blame. I like those tears, and hope they are of the purest kind – penitential tears.

LADY TOUCHWOOD: Oh, the scene was shifted quick before me – I had not time to think – I was surprised to see a monster in the glass, [11] and now I find it is myself. Can you have mercy to forgive the faults I have imagined, but never put in practice? – O consider, consider, how fatal you have been to me. You have already killed the quiet of this life; the love of you was the first wandering fire that e'er misled my steps, and while I had only that in view, I was betrayed into unthought of ways of ruin.

MELLEFONT: May I believe this true?

LADY TOUCHWOOD: O be not cruelly incredulous. – How can you doubt these streaming eyes? Keep the severest eye o'er all my future conduct, and if I once relapse, let me not hope forgiveness; 'twill ever be in your power to ruin me. – My lord shall sign to your desires; I will myself create your happiness, and Cynthia shall be this night your bride. – Do but conceal my failings, and forgive.

MELLEFONT: Upon such terms I will be ever yours in every honest way.

[Enter LORD TOUCHWOOD, MASKWELL softly behind him.]

MASKWELL: I have kept my word, he's here, but I must not be seen.

[Exit.]

LORD TOUCHWOOD: Hell and amazement, she's in tears.

LADY TOUCHWOOD [kneeling]: Eternal blessings thank you. [Aside.] Ha! my lord listening! Oh, Fortune has o'erpaid me all, all! all's my own!

MELLEFONT: Nay, I beseech you rise.

LADY TOUCHWOOD [aloud]: Never, never! I'll grow to the

11. glass: mirror.

ground, be buried quick beneath it, e'er I'll be consenting to so damned a sin as incest, unnatural incest!

MELLEFONT: Ha!

LADY TOUCHWOOD: O cruel man, will you not let me go – I'll forgive all that's past. – O heaven, you will not ravish me!

MELLEFONT: Damnation!

LORD TOUCHWOOD: Monster! Dog! Your life shall answer this –

  [*Draws, and runs at* MELLEFONT, *is held by* LADY TOUCH-WOOD.]

LADY TOUCHWOOD: O heavens, my lord! hold, hold, for heaven's sake.

MELLEFONT: Confusion – my uncle! O the damned sorceress.

LADY TOUCHWOOD: Moderate your rage, good my lord! He's mad, alas he's mad – indeed he is, my lord, and knows not what he does – see how wild he looks.

MELLEFONT: By heaven, 'twere senseless not to be mad, and see such witchcraft.

LADY TOUCHWOOD: My lord, you hear him – he talks idly.

LORD TOUCHWOOD: Hence from my sight, thou living infamy to my name; when next I see that face, I'll write villain in't with my sword's point.

MELLEFONT: Now, by my soul, I will not go till I have made known my wrongs. – Nay, till I have made known yours, which (if possible) are greater – though she has all the host of hell her servants; though she can wear more shapes in shining day than fear shows cowards in the dark –

LADY TOUCHWOOD: Alas, he raves! talks very poetry! for heaven's sake away my lord; he'll either tempt you to extravagance, or commit some himself.

MELLEFONT: Death and furies, will you not hear me. [*As she is going she turns back and smiles at him.*] Why, by heaven she laughs, grins, points to your back; she forks out cuckoldom with her fingers, and you're running horn-mad after your fortune.

LORD TOUCHWOOD: I fear he's mad indeed. – Let's send Maskwell to him.

MELLEFONT: Send him to her.

LADY TOUCHWOOD: Come, come, good my lord, my heart aches so, I shall faint if I stay.

[*Exeunt.*]

MELLEFONT: Oh, I could curse my stars, fate, and chance; all causes and accidents of fortune in this life! But to what purpose? Yet, 'sdeath, for a man to have the fruit of all his industry grown full and ripe, ready to drop into his mouth, and just when he holds out his hand to gather it, to have a sudden whirlwind come, tear up tree and all, and bear away the very root and foundation of his hopes, what temper can contain? They talk of sending Maskwell to me; I never had more need of him. – But what can he do? Imagination cannot form a fairer and more plausible design than this of his which has miscarried. – O my precious aunt, I shall never thrive without I deal with the devil, or another woman.

> Women like flames have a destroying power,
> Ne'er to be quenched, till they themselves devour.

[*Exit.*]

ACT FIVE

SCENE ONE

[*Enter* LADY TOUCHWOOD *and* MASKWELL.]

LADY TOUCHWOOD: Was't not lucky?

MASKWELL: Lucky! Fortune is your own, and 'tis her interest so to
be. By heaven I believe you can control her power, and she fears
it; though chance brought my lord, 'twas your own art that
turned it to advantage.

LADY TOUCHWOOD: 'Tis true it might have been my ruin – but
yonder's my lord. I believe he's coming to find you; I'll not be
seen.

[*Exit.*]

MASKWELL: So; I durst not own my introducing my lord, though it
succeeded well for her, for she would have suspected a design
which I could have been puzzled to excuse. My lord is thoughtful
– I'll be so too; yet he shall know my thoughts, or think he does –

[*Enter* LORD TOUCHWOOD.]

MASKWELL: What have I done?

LORD TOUCHWOOD: Talking to himself!

MASKWELL: 'Twas honest – and shall I be rewarded for it? No,
'twas honest, therefore I shan't. – Nay, rather therefore I ought
not, for it rewards itself.

LORD TOUCHWOOD [*aside*]: Unequalled virtue!

MASKWELL: But should it be known! Then I have lost a friend! He
was an ill man, and I have gained; for half my self I lent him, and
that I have recalled; so I have served myself, and what is yet better,
I have served a worthy lord to whom I owe myself.

LORD TOUCHWOOD [*aside*]: Excellent man!

MASKWELL: Yet I am wretched. – Oh, there is a secret burns within this breast, which, should it once blaze forth, would ruin all, consume my honest character, and brand me with the name of villain.

LORD TOUCHWOOD: Ha!

MASKWELL: Why do I love! Yet heaven and my waking conscience are my witnesses, I never gave one working thought a vent which might discover that I loved, nor ever must; no, let it prey upon my heart; for I would rather die, than seem once, barely seem, dishonest. – Oh, should it once be known I love fair Cynthia, all this that I have done would look like rival's malice, false friendship to my lord, and base self-interest. Let me perish first, and from this hour avoid all sight and speech, and, if I can, all thought of that pernicious beauty. Ha! but what is my distraction doing? I am wildly talking to myself, and some ill chance might have directed malicious ears this way.

[*Seems to start, seeing* LORD TOUCHWOOD.]

LORD TOUCHWOOD: Start not – let guilty and dishonest souls start at the revelation of their thoughts, but be thou fixed, as is thy virtue.

MASKWELL: I am confounded, and beg your lordship's pardon for those free discourses which I have had with myself.

LORD TOUCHWOOD: Come, I beg your pardon that I overheard you, and yet it shall not need. – Honest Maskwell! thy and my good genius led me hither: mine, in that I have discovered so much manly virtue; thine, in that thou shalt have due reward of all thy worth. Give me thy hand – my nephew is the alone remaining branch of all our ancient family; him I thus blow away, and constitute thee in his room to be my heir –

MASKWELL: Now heaven forbid –

LORD TOUCHWOOD: No more – I have resolved. – The writings are ready drawn, and wanted nothing but to be signed, and have his name inserted – yours will fill the blank as well – I will have no reply. – Let me command this time; for 'tis the last in which I will assume authority. Hereafter, you shall rule where I have power.

MASKWELL: I humbly would petition –

[MASKWELL *pauses.*]

LORD TOUCHWOOD: Is't for yourself? – I'll hear of nought for anybody else.

MASKWELL: Then witness heaven for me, this wealth and honour was not of my seeking, nor would I build my fortune on another's ruin. I had but one desire –

LORD TOUCHWOOD: Thou shalt enjoy it. – If all I'm worth in wealth or interest can purchase Cynthia, she is thine. I'm sure Sir Paul's consent will follow fortune; I'll quickly show him which way that is going.

MASKWELL: You oppress me with bounty; my gratitude is weak, and shrinks beneath the weight, and cannot rise to thank you. – What, enjoy my love! Forgive the transports of a blessing so unexpected, so unhoped for, so unthought of!

LORD TOUCHWOOD: I will confirm it, and rejoice with thee.
    [*Exit.*]

MASKWELL: This is prosperous indeed. – Why, let him find me out a villain. Settled in possession of a fair estate and full fruition of my love, I'll bear the railings of a losing gamester. But should he find me out before! 'Tis dangerous to delay. – Let me think. – Should my lord proceed to treat openly of my marriage with Cynthia, all must be discovered, and Mellefont can be no longer blinded. – It must not be; nay, should my lady know it – ay, then were fine work indeed! Her fury would spare nothing, though she involved herself in ruin. No, it must be by stratagem. – I must deceive Mellefont once more, and get my lord to consent to my private management. He comes opportunely. Now will I, in my old way, discover the whole and real truth of the matter to him, that he may not suspect one word on't.

> No mask like open truth to cover lies,
> As to go naked is the best disguise.

[*Enter* MELLEFONT.]

MELLEFONT: O Maskwell, what hopes? I am confounded in a maze of thoughts, each leading into one another, and all ending in perplexity. My uncle will not see nor hear me.

MASKWELL: No matter, sir, don't trouble your head, all's in my power.

MELLEFONT: How, for heaven's sake?

MASKWELL: Little do you think that your aunt has kept her word. How the devil she wrought my lord into this dotage, I know not, but he's gone to Sir Paul about my marriage with Cynthia, and has appointed me his heir.

MELLEFONT: The devil he has! What's to be done?

MASKWELL: I have it! It must be by stratagem, for it's in vain to make application to him. I think I have that in my head that cannot fail. Where's Cynthia?

MELLEFONT: In the garden.

MASKWELL: Let us go and consult her. My life for yours, I cheat my lord.

    [*Exeunt.*]

    [*Enter* LORD TOUCHWOOD, LADY TOUCHWOOD.]

LADY TOUCHWOOD: Maskwell your heir, and marry Cynthia!

LORD TOUCHWOOD: I cannot do too much for so much merit.

LADY TOUCHWOOD: But this is a thing of too great moment to be so suddenly resolved. Why Cynthia? Why must he be married? Is there not reward enough in raising his low fortune, but he must mix his blood with mine, and wed my niece? How know you that my brother will consent, or she? Nay, he himself perhaps may have affections otherwise.

LORD TOUCHWOOD: No, I am convinced he loves her.

LADY TOUCHWOOD: Maskwell love Cynthia? Impossible!

LORD TOUCHWOOD: I told you, he confessed it to me.

LADY TOUCHWOOD [*aside*]: Confusion! How's this?

LORD TOUCHWOOD: His humility long stifled his passion, and his love of Mellefont would have made him still conceal it. But by encouragement, I wrung the secret from him, and know he's no way to be rewarded but in her. I'll defer my farther proceedings in it till you have considered it, but remember how we are both indebted to him.

    [*Exit.*]

LADY TOUCHWOOD: Both indebted to him! Yes, we are both indebted to him, if you knew all, damned villain! Oh, I am wild with this surprise of treachery: hell and fire, it is impossible, it cannot be, – he love Cynthia! What, have I been bawd to his designs, his property only, a baiting place to stay his stomach in the road to her? Now I see what made him false to Mellefont. – Shame and destruction! I cannot bear it; oh! what woman can bear to be a property? To be kindled to a flame, only to light him to another's arms! Oh, that I were fire indeed, that I might burn the vile traitor to a hell of torments, – but he's damnation proof, a devil already, and fire is his element. What shall I do? How shall I think? I cannot think, – all my designs are lost, my love unsated, my revenge unfinished, and fresh cause of fury from unthought-of plagues.

[*Enter* SIR PAUL.]

SIR PAUL: Madam, sister, my lady sister, did you see my lady my wife?

LADY TOUCHWOOD: Oh! Torture!

SIR PAUL: Gadsbud, I can't find her high nor low; where can she be, think you?

LADY TOUCHWOOD: Where she's serving you as all your sex ought to be served; making you a beast. Don't you know that you're a fool, brother?

SIR PAUL: A fool; he, he, he, you're merry – no, no, not I, I know no such matter.

LADY TOUCHWOOD: Why then you don't know half your happiness.

SIR PAUL: That's a jest with all my heart, faith and troth, – but hearkee, my lord told me something of a revolution of things; I don't know what to make on't. – Gadsbud, I must consult my wife. – He talks of disinheriting his nephew, and I don't know what. – Look you, sister, I must know what my girl has to trust to, or not a syllable of a wedding, gadsbud, to show you that I am not a fool.

LADY TOUCHWOOD: Hear me; consent to the breaking off this marriage, and the promoting any other without consulting me, and I'll renounce all blood, all relation and concern with you for ever, – nay, I'll be your enemy, and pursue you to destruction; I'll tear your eyes out, and tread you under my feet –

SIR PAUL: Why, what's the matter now? Good Lord, what's all this for? Pooh, here's a joke, indeed – why, where's my wife?

LADY TOUCHWOOD: With Careless in the close arbour; he may
  want you by this time, as much as you want her.
SIR PAUL: Oh, if she be with Mr Careless, 'tis well enough.
LADY TOUCHWOOD: Fool, sot, insensible ox! But remember what
  I said to you, or you had better eat your own horns, and pimp for
  your living; by this light you had.
  [Exit.]
SIR PAUL: She's a passionate woman, gadsbud, – but to say truth,
  all our family are choleric; I am the only peaceable person
  amongst 'em.
  [Exit.]
  [Enter MELLEFONT, MASKWELL, and CYNTHIA.]
MELLEFONT: I know no other way but this he has proposed, if you
  have love enough to run the venture.
CYNTHIA: I don't know whether I have love enough, but I find I
  have obstinacy enough to pursue whatever I have once resolved,
  and a true female courage to oppose anything that resists my will,
  though 'twere reason itself.
MASKWELL: That's right. – Well, I'll secure the writings and run the
  hazard along with you.
CYNTHIA: But how can the coach and six horses be got ready
  without suspicion?
MASKWELL: Leave it to my care; that shall be so far from being
  suspected, that it shall be got ready by my lord's own order.
MELLEFONT: How?
MASKWELL: Why, I intend to tell my lord the whole matter of our
  contrivance; that's my way.
MELLEFONT: I don't understand you.
MASKWELL: Why, I'll tell my lord I laid this plot with you on
  purpose to betray you; and that which put me upon it was the
  finding it impossible to gain the lady any other way, but in the
  hopes of her marrying you –
MELLEFONT: So –
MASKWELL: So, why so, while you are busied in making yourself
  ready, I'll wheedle her into the coach; and instead of you, borrow
  my lord's chaplain, and so run away with her myself.
MELLEFONT: Oh, I conceive you; you'll tell him so?

MASKWELL: Tell him so! Ay, why you don't think I mean to do so?

MELLEFONT: No, no; ha, ha, I dare swear thou wilt not.

MASKWELL [aside]: You may be deceived. – Therefore, for our farther security, I would have you disguised like a parson, that if my lord should have curiosity to peep, he may not discover you in the coach, but think the cheat is carried on as he would have it.

MELLEFONT: Excellent Maskwell, thou wert certainly meant for a statesman or a Jesuit, but that thou'rt too honest for one, and too pious for the other.

MASKWELL: Well, get yourselves ready, and meet me in half an hour, yonder in my lady's dressing-room; go by the back stairs, and so we may slip down without being observed. – I'll send the chaplain to you with his robes; I have made him my own, and ordered him to meet us tomorrow morning at St Albans; there we will sum up this account to all our satisfactions.

MELLEFONT: Should I begin to thank or praise thee, I should waste the little time we have.

[Exit.]

MASKWELL: Madam, you will be ready?

CYNTHIA: I will be punctual to the minute.

[Going.]

MASKWELL: Stay, I have a doubt. – Upon second thoughts, we had better meet in the chaplain's chamber here, the corner chamber at this end of the gallery; there is a back way into it, so that you need not come through this door, and a pair of private stairs leads down to the stables. – It will be more convenient.

CYNTHIA: I am guided by you, – but Mellefont will mistake.

MASKWELL: No, no, I'll after him immediately, and tell him.

CYNTHIA: I will not fail.

[Exit.]

MASKWELL: Why, qui vult decipi decipiatur.[1] – 'Tis no fault of mine; I have told 'em in plain terms how easy 'tis for me to cheat 'em, and if they will not hear the serpent's hiss, they must be stung into experience, and future caution. – Now to prepare my lord to

___

1. qui . . . decipiatur: may he who wishes to be deceived, be deceived.

consent to this. – But first I must instruct my little Levite; there is no plot, public or private, that can expect to prosper without one of 'em have a finger in't. He promised me to be within at this hour. – Mr Saygrace, Mr Saygrace.

[*Goes to the chamber door and knocks.*]

SAYGRACE [*looking out*]: Sweet sir, I will but pen the last line of an acrostic, and be with you in the twinkling of an ejaculation, in the pronouncing of an *Amen*, or before you can –

MASKWELL: Nay, good Mr Saygrace, do not prolong the time by describing to me the shortness of your stay; rather if you please, defer the finishing of your wit, and let us talk about our business. It shall be tithes in your way.

SAYGRACE [*enters*]: You shall prevail; I would break off in the middle of a sermon to do you pleasure.

MASKWELL: You could not do me a greater – except the business in hand. Have you provided a habit for Mellefont?

SAYGRACE: I have; they are ready in my chamber, together with a clean starched band and cuffs.

MASKWELL: Good, let them be carried to him. – Have you stitched the gown sleeve, that he may be puzzled, and waste time in putting it on?

SAYGRACE: I have; the gown will not be indued without perplexity.

MASKWELL: Meet me in half an hour, here in your own chamber. When Cynthia comes, let there be no light, and do not speak, that she may not distinguish you from Mellefont. I'll urge haste, to excuse your silence.

SAYGRACE: You have no more commands?

MASKWELL: None, your text is short.

SAYGRACE: But pithy, and I will handle it with discretion.

[*Exit.*]

MASKWELL: It will be the first you have so served.

[*Enter* LORD TOUCHWOOD.]

LORD TOUCHWOOD: Sure I was born to be controlled by those I should command. My very slaves will shortly give me rules how I shall govern them.

MASKWELL: I am concerned to see your lordship discomposed –

LORD TOUCHWOOD: Have you seen my wife lately, or disobliged her?

MASKWELL: No, my lord. [*Aside.*] What can this mean?

LORD TOUCHWOOD: Then Mellefont has urged somebody to incense her – something she has heard of you which carries her beyond the bounds of patience.

MASKWELL [*aside*]: This I feared. Did not your lordship tell her of the honours you designed me?

LORD TOUCHWOOD: Yes.

MASKWELL: 'Tis that; you know my lady has a high spirit, she thinks I am unworthy.

LORD TOUCHWOOD: Unworthy! 'tis an ignorant pride in her to think so. Honesty to me is true nobility. However, 'tis my will it should be so, and that should be convincing to her as much as reason – by heaven, I'll not be wife-ridden; were it possible it should be done this night.

MASKWELL [*aside*]: By heaven, he meets my wishes. [*To him.*] Few things are impossible to willing minds.

LORD TOUCHWOOD: Instruct me how this may be done; you shall see I want no inclination.

MASKWELL: I had laid a small design for tomorrow (as love will be inventing) which I thought to communicate to your lordship – but it may be as well done tonight.

LORD TOUCHWOOD: Here's company – come this way and tell me.

[*Exeunt.*]

[*Enter* CARELESS *and* CYNTHIA.]

CARELESS: Is not that he, now gone out with my lord?

CYNTHIA: Yes.

CARELESS: By heaven, there's treachery – the confusion that I saw your father in, my Lady Touchwood's passion, with what imperfectly I overheard between my lord and her, confirm me in my fears. Where's Mellefont?

CYNTHIA: Here he comes.

[*Enter* MELLEFONT.]

Did Maskwell tell you anything of the chaplain's chamber?

MELLEFONT: No; my dear, will you get ready – the things are all in my chamber; I want nothing but the habit.

CARELESS: You are betrayed, and Maskwell is the villain that I always thought him.

CYNTHIA: When you were gone, he said his mind was changed, and bid me meet him in the chaplain's room, pretending immediately to follow you and give you notice.

MELLEFONT: How!

CARELESS: There's Saygrace tripping by with a bundle under his arm. He cannot be ignorant that Maskwell means to use his chamber; let's follow and examine him.

MELLEFONT: 'Tis loss of time – I cannot think him false.

[*Exeunt* MELLEFONT *and* CARELESS.]

[*Enter* LORD TOUCHWOOD.]

CYNTHIA [*aside*]: My lord musing!

LORD TOUCHWOOD: He has a quick invention, if this were suddenly designed; yet he says he had prepared my chaplain already.

CYNTHIA: How's this? Now I fear indeed.

LORD TOUCHWOOD: Cynthia here. Alone, fair cousin, and melancholy?

CYNTHIA: Your lordship was thoughtful.

LORD TOUCHWOOD: My thoughts were on serious business, not worth your hearing.

CYNTHIA: Mine were on treachery concerning you, and may be worth your hearing.

LORD TOUCHWOOD: Treachery concerning me? Pray be plain – hark! what noise!

MASKWELL [*within*]: Will you not hear me?

LADY TOUCHWOOD [*within*]: No, monster! hellish traitor, no!

CYNTHIA: My lady and Maskwell! This may be lucky. – My lord, let me entreat you to stand behind this screen and listen; perhaps this chance may give you proof of what you ne'er could have believed from my suspicions.

[*They abscond.*]

[*Enter* LADY TOUCHWOOD *with a dagger,* MASKWELL.]

LADY TOUCHWOOD: You want but leisure to invent fresh falsehood, and soothe me to a fond belief of all your fictions; but I will stab the lie that's forming in your heart, and save a sin in pity to your soul.

MASKWELL: Strike then – since you will have it so.

LADY TOUCHWOOD: Ha! A steady villain to the last!

MASKWELL: Come, why do you dally with me thus?

LADY TOUCHWOOD: Thy stubborn temper shocks me, and you knew it would. – By heaven, this is cunning all, and not courage; no, I know thee well: but thou shalt miss thy aim.

MASKWELL: Ha, ha, ha.

LADY TOUCHWOOD: Ha! do you mock my rage? Then this shall punish your fond, rash contempt! Again smile! [*Goes to strike.*] And such a smile as speaks in ambiguity! Ten thousand meanings lurk in each corner of that various face. O that they were written in thy heart, that I, with this, might lay thee open to my sight! But then 'twill be too late to know. – Thou hast, thou hast found the only way to turn my rage. Too well thou knowest my jealous soul could never bear uncertainty. Speak then, and tell me. – Yet are you silent? Oh, I am wildered[2] in all passions! But thus my anger melts. [*Weeps.*] Here, take this poniard, for my very spirits faint, and I want strength to hold it; thou hast disarmed my soul.

[*Gives the dagger.*]

LORD TOUCHWOOD: Amazement shakes me – where will this end?

MASKWELL: So, 'tis well. – Let your wild fury have a vent, and when you have temper, tell me.

LADY TOUCHWOOD: Now, now, now I am calm, and can hear you.

MASKWELL [*aside*]: Thanks, my invention; and now I have it for you. [*Aloud.*] – First tell me what urged you to this violence? For your passion broke in such imperfect terms that yet I am to learn the cause.

LADY TOUCHWOOD: My lord himself surprised me with the news you were to marry Cynthia – that you had owned your love to him, and his indulgence would assist you to attain your ends.

CYNTHIA [*aside to* LORD TOUCHWOOD]: How, my lord!

LORD TOUCHWOOD [*aside to* CYNTHIA]: Pray forbear all resentments for a while, and let us hear the rest.

MASKWELL: I grant you in appearance all is true; I seemed consent-

2. *wildered*: perplexed, confused.

ing to my lord; nay, transported with the blessing – but could you think that I who had been happy in your loved embraces, could e'er be fond of an inferior slavery.

LORD TOUCHWOOD [*aside*]: Ha! O poison to my ears! What do I hear!

CYNTHIA [*aside*]: Nay, good my lord, forbear resentment, let us hear it out.

LORD TOUCHWOOD [*aside*]: Yes, I will contain, though I could burst.

MASKWELL: I that had wantoned in the wide circle of your world of love, could be confined within the puny province of a girl? No – yet though I dote on each last favour more than all the rest; though I would give a limb for every look you cheaply throw away on any other object of your love; yet so far I prize your pleasures o'er my own, that all this seeming plot that I have laid has been to gratify your taste and cheat the world, to prove a faithful rogue to you.

LADY TOUCHWOOD: If this were true – but how can it be?

MASKWELL: I have so contrived that Mellefont will presently, in the chaplain's habit, wait for Cynthia in your dressing-room: but I have put the change upon her that she may be otherwhere employed. – Do you procure her night-gown, and with your hoods tied over your face, meet him in her stead. You may go privately by the back stairs, and, unperceived, there you may propose to reinstate him in his uncle's favour, if he'll comply with your desires; his case is desperate, and I believe he'll yield to any conditions. If not, here, take this; you may employ it better than in the death of one who is nothing when not yours.

[*Gives the dagger.*]

LADY TOUCHWOOD: Thou canst deceive everybody, – nay, thou hast deceived me; but 'tis as I would wish, – trusty villain! I would worship thee.

MASKWELL: No more; there want but a few minutes of the time, and Mellefont's love will carry him there before his hour.

LADY TOUCHWOOD: I go, I fly, incomparable Maskwell!
    [*Exit.*]

MASKWELL: So, this was a pinch indeed; my invention was upon the rack, and made discovery of her last plot. I hope Cynthia and my chaplain will be ready; I'll prepare for the expedition.

[*Exit.*]

[CYNTHIA *and* LORD TOUCHWOOD *come forward.*]

CYNTHIA: Now, my lord?

LORD TOUCHWOOD: Astonishment binds up my rage! Villainy upon villainy! Heavens, what a long track of dark deceit has this discovered! I am confounded when I look back, and want a clue to guide me through the various mazes of unheard-of treachery. My wife! Damnation – my hell!

CYNTHIA: My lord, have patience, and be sensible how great our happiness is that this discovery was not made too late.

LORD TOUCHWOOD: I thank you, yet it may be still too late, if we don't presently prevent the execution of their plots. – Ha, I'll do't. Where's Mellefont, my poor injured nephew, – how shall I make him ample satisfaction?

CYNTHIA: I dare answer for him.

LORD TOUCHWOOD: I do him fresh wrong to question his forgiveness, for I know him to be all goodness. – Yet my wife! Damn her: she'll think to meet him in that dressing-room – was't not so? And Maskwell will expect you in the chaplain's chamber. – For once, I'll add my plot too, – let us haste to find out, and inform my nephew, and do you quickly as you can, bring all the company into this gallery. – I'll expose the strumpet, and the villain.

[*Exeunt.*]

[*Enter* LORD FROTH *and* SIR PAUL.]

LORD FROTH: By heavens, I have slept an age. – Sir Paul, what o'clock is't? Past eight, on my conscience; my lady's is the most inviting couch, and a slumber there is the prettiest amusement! But where's all the company?

SIR PAUL: The company, gadsbud, I don't know, my lord, but here's the strangest revolution; all turned topsy-turvy, as I hope for Providence.

LORD FROTH: O heavens, what's the matter? Where's my wife?

SIR PAUL: All turned topsy-turvy, as sure as a gun.

LORD FROTH: How do you mean? My wife!

SIR PAUL: The strangest posture of affairs!

LORD FROTH: What, my wife?

SIR PAUL: No, no, I mean the family. – Your lady's affairs may be in a very good posture; I saw her go into the garden with Mr Brisk.

LORD FROTH: How? Where, when, what to do?

SIR PAUL: I suppose they have been laying their heads together.

LORD FROTH: How?

SIR PAUL: Nay, only about poetry, I suppose, my lord; making couplets.

LORD FROTH: Couplets.

SIR PAUL: Oh, here they come.

[*Enter* LADY FROTH, BRISK.]

BRISK: My lord, your humble servant; Sir Paul, yours. – The finest night!

LADY FROTH: My dear, Mr Brisk and I have been star-gazing, I don't know how long.

SIR PAUL: Does it not tire your ladyship? Are not you weary with looking up?

LADY FROTH: Oh, no, I love it violently. – My dear, you're melancholy.

LORD FROTH: No, my dear; I'm but just awake.

LADY FROTH: Snuff some of my spirit of hartshorn.[3]

LORD FROTH: I've some of my own, thank you my dear.

LADY FROTH: Well, I swear, Mr Brisk, you understood astronomy like an old Egyptian.

BRISK: Not comparable to your ladyship; you are the very Cynthia of the skies, and queen of stars.

LADY FROTH: That's because I've no light but what's by reflection from you, who are the sun.

BRISK: O Jesu! Madam, you have eclipsed me quite, let me perish, – I can't answer that.

LADY FROTH: No matter. – Heark'ee, shall you and I make an almanac together?

3. *spirit of hartshorn*: aqueous solution of ammonia.

BRISK: With all my soul. – Your ladyship has made me the man in't already, I'm so full of the wounds which you have given.[4]

LADY FROTH: O finely taken! I swear now you are even with me. O Parnassus, you have an infinite deal of wit.

SIR PAUL: So he has, gadsbud, and so has your ladyship.

[*Enter* LADY PLYANT, CARELESS, CYNTHIA.]

LADY PLYANT: You tell me most surprising things; bless me, who would ever trust a man? Oh, my heart aches for fear they should be all deceitful alike.

CARELESS: You need not fear, madam; you have charms to fix inconstancy itself.

LADY PLYANT: Oh dear, you make me blush.

LORD FROTH: Come my dear, shall we take leave of my lord and lady?

CYNTHIA: They'll wait upon your lordship presently.

LORD FROTH: Mr Brisk, my coach shall set you down.

[*A great shriek from the corner of the stage.* LADY TOUCHWOOD *runs out affrighted,* LORD TOUCHWOOD *after her, like a parson.*]

ALL: What's the matter?

LADY TOUCHWOOD: Oh, I'm betrayed, – save me, help me.

LORD TOUCHWOOD: Now what evasion, strumpet?

LADY TOUCHWOOD: Stand off, let me go, and plagues and curses seize you all.

[*Runs out.*]

LORD TOUCHWOOD: Go, and thy own infamy pursue thee. – You stare as you were all amazed, – I don't wonder at it, – but too soon you'll know mine, and that woman's shame.

[*Enter* MELLEFONT *lugging in* MASKWELL *from the other side of the stage,* MELLEFONT *like a parson.*]

MELLEFONT: Nay, by heaven you shall be seen. – Careless, your hand; – do you hold down your head? Yes, I am your chaplain; look in the face of your injured friend, thou wonder of all falsehood.

LORD TOUCHWOOD: Are you silent, monster?

4. *almanac . . . given*: old almanacs often displayed a picture of a man surrounded by the signs of the Zodiac, with each sign next to the part of the body it affected.

MELLEFONT: Good heavens! How I believed and loved this man! – Take him hence, for he's a disease to my sight.

LORD TOUCHWOOD: Secure that manifold villain.

CARELESS: Miracle of ingratitude!

[*They carry out* MASKWELL, *who hangs down his head.*]

BRISK: This is all very surprising, let me perish.

LADY FROTH: You know I told you Saturn looked a little more angry than usual.

LORD TOUCHWOOD: We'll think of punishment at leisure but let me hasten to do justice in rewarding virtue and wronged innocence. – Nephew, I hope I have your pardon, and Cynthia's.

MELLEFONT: We are your lordship's creatures.

LORD TOUCHWOOD: And be each other's comfort. – Let me join your hands. – Unwearied nights, and wishing days attend you both; mutual love, lasting health, and circling joys, tread round each happy year of your long lives.

> Let secret villainy from hence be warned;
> Howe'er in private, mischiefs are conceived,
> Torture and shame attend their open birth;
> Like vipers in the womb, base treachery lies,
> Still gnawing that, whence first it did arise;
> No sooner born, but the vile parent dies.

[*Exeunt omnes.*]

FINIS

EPILOGUE

Spoken by Mrs Mountford.[1]

Could poets but forsee how plays would take,
Then they could tell what epilogues to make;
Whether to thank, or blame their audience most:
But that late knowledge, does much hazard cost:
Till dice are thrown, there's nothing won, nor lost.
So till the thief has stol'n, he cannot know
Whether he shall escape the law, or no.
But poets run much greater hazards far,
Than they who stand their trials at the Bar;
The law provides a curb for its own fury,
And suffers judges to direct the jury.
But in this court, what difference does appear!
For every one's both judge and jury here;
Nay, and what's worse, an executioner.
All have a right and title to some part,
Each choosing that in which he has most art.
The dreadful men of learning all confound,
Unless the fable's good, and moral sound.
The vizor-masks,[2] that are in pit and gallery,
Approve, or damn the repartee and raillery.
The lady critics, who are better read,
Enquire if characters are nicely bred;
If the soft things are penned and spoke with grace;
They judge of action too, and time, and place;
In which we do not doubt but they're discerning,
For that's a kind of assignation learning.[3]
Beaus judge of dress; the witlings judge of songs;

1. Susanna Mountfort – later Susanna Verbruggen – took the part of Lady Froth.
2. *vizor-masks*: masked women; also, prostitutes.
3. *assignation learning*: knowledge not of the 'time' and 'place' of the neo-classical unities (two lines above) but of a secret meeting or tryst.

The cuckoldom, of ancient right, to cits[4] belongs.
Thus poor poets the favour are denied
Even to make exceptions, when they're tried.
'Tis hard that they must every one admit;
Methinks I see some faces in the pit,
Which must of consequence be foes to wit.
You who can judge, to sentence may proceed;
But though he cannot write, let him be freed
At least from their contempt, who cannot read.

4. *cits*: citizens; a somewhat contemptuous way of referring to City tradesmen and merchants.

Love
for Love

TO THE RIGHT HONOURABLE CHARLES
EARL OF DORSET AND MIDDLESEX,[1]
Lord Chamberlain of His Majesty's Household,
and Knight of the Most Noble Order of the Garter, etc.

My Lord,
A young poet is liable to the same vanity and indiscretion with a young lover; and the great man that smiles upon one, and the fine woman that looks kindly upon t'other, are each of 'em in danger of having the favour published with the first opportunity.

But there may be a different motive, which will a little distinguish the offenders. For though one should have a vanity in ruining another's reputation, yet the other may only have an ambition to advance his own. And I beg leave, my Lord, that I may plead the latter, both as the cause and excuse of this dedication.

Whoever is King, is also the father of his country; and as nobody can dispute your Lordship's monarchy in poetry, so all that are concerned ought to acknowledge your universal patronage; and it is only presuming on the privilege of a loyal subject that I have ventured to make this my address of thanks to your Lordship; which at the same time, includes a prayer for your protection.

I am not ignorant of the common form of poetical dedications, which are generally made up of panegyrics, where the authors endeavour to distinguish their patrons, by the shining characters they give them, above other men. But that, my Lord, is not my business at this time, nor is your Lordship *now* to be distinguished. I am contented with the honour I do myself in this epistle, without the vanity of attempting to add to, or explain, your Lordship's character.

I confess it is not without some struggling that I behave myself in this case as I ought, for it is very hard to be pleased with a subject, and

---

1. *Charles . . . Middlesex*: Charles Sackville (1638–1706), poet and literary patron.

yet forbear it. But I choose rather to follow Pliny's precept than his example, when in his panegyric to the emperor Trajan, he says,

> *Nec minus considerabo quid aures ejus pati*
> *possint, Quam quid virtutibus debeatur.*[2]

I hope I may be excused the pedantry of a quotation when it is so justly applied. Here are some lines in the print (and which your Lordship read before this play was acted) that were omitted on the stage; and particularly one whole scene in the third act,[3] which not only helps the design forward with less precipitation, but also heightens the ridiculous character of Foresight, which indeed seems to be maimed without it. But I found myself in great danger of a long play, and was glad to help it where I could. Though notwithstanding my care, and the kind reception it had from the town, I could heartily wish it yet shorter, but the number of different characters represented in it would have been too much crowded in less room.

This reflection on prolixity (a fault for which scarce any one beauty will atone) warns me not to be tedious now, and detain your Lordship any longer with the trifles of,

MY LORD,
   your Lordship's most obedient and most humble servant,

                              WILL. CONGREVE.

---

2. *Nec . . . debeatur*: I shall consider what he can tolerate hearing no less than what may be due to his virtues.
3. *scene . . . act*: possibly the passage where Scandal and Foresight discuss the importance of astrology.

PROLOGUE

*Spoken at the opening of the new house,[1]
By Mr Betterton.[2]*

The husbandman in vain renews his toil,
To cultivate each year a hungry soil;
And fondly hopes for rich and generous fruit,
When what should feed the tree, devours the root:
Th' unladen boughs, he sees, bode certain dearth,
Unless transplanted to more kindly earth.
So, the poor husbands of the stage, who found
Their labours lost upon the ungrateful ground,
This last and only remedy have proved;
And hope new fruit from ancient stocks removed.
Well may they hope, when you so kindly aid,
And plant a soil which you so rich have made.
As Nature gave the world to man's first age,
So from your bounty, we receive this stage;
The freedom man was born to, you've restored,
And to our world, such plenty you afford,
It seems like Eden, fruitful of its own accord.
But since in Paradise frail flesh gave way,
And when but two were made, both went astray;
Forbear your wonder, and the fault forgive,
If in our larger family we grieve
One falling Adam, and one tempted Eve.[3]

1. *new house*: Lincoln's Inn Fields, which reopened as a theatre with this play in April 1695.
2. *Mr Betterton*: Thomas Betterton (1635–1710), the greatest English actor of his time, who, although 59, undertook the part of Valentine.
3. *Adam . . . Eve*: Joseph Williams and Susanna Mountfort, who had gone over to the rival company at Drury Lane.

We who remain, would gratefully repay
What our endeavours can, and bring this day,
The first-fruit offering of a virgin play.
We hope there's something that may please each taste,
And though of homely fare we make the feast,
Yet you will find variety at least.
There's humour, which for cheerful friends we got,
And for the thinking party there's a plot.
We've something too, to gratify ill nature
(If there be any here) and that is satire.
Though satire scarce dares grin, 'tis grown so mild;
Or only shows its teeth, as if it smiled.
As asses thistles, poets mumble wit,
And dare not bite, for fear of being bit.
They hold their pens, as swords are held by fools,
And are afraid to use their own edge-tools.
Since the *Plain-Dealer*'s scenes of manly rage,[4]
Not one has dared to lash this crying age.
This time the poet owns the bold essay,
Yet hopes there's no ill-manners in his play:
And he declares by me, he has designed
Affront to none, but frankly speaks his mind.
And should th' ensuing scenes not chance to hit,
He offers but this one excuse: 'twas writ
Before your late encouragement of wit.

4. *Plain-Dealer's . . . manly rage*: Manly is the central figure in Wycherley's final play, *The Plain Dealer* (1676).

DRAMATIS PERSONAE

MEN

SIR SAMPSON LEGEND, *father to* VALENTINE *and* BEN.

VALENTINE, *fallen under his father's displeasure by his expensive way of living, in love with* ANGELICA.

SCANDAL, *his friend, a free speaker.*

TATTLE, *a half-witted beau, vain of his amours, yet valuing himself for secrecy.*

BEN, SIR SAMPSON'S *younger son, half home-bred, and half sea-bred, designed to marry* MISS PRUE.

FORESIGHT, *an illiterate old fellow, peevish and positive, superstitious, and pretending to understand astrology, palmistry, physiognomy, omens, dreams, etc. Uncle to* ANGELICA.

JEREMY, *servant to* VALENTINE.

TRAPLAND, *a scrivener.*

BUCKRAM, *a lawyer.*

WOMEN

ANGELICA, *niece to* FORESIGHT, *of a considerable fortune in her own hands.*

MRS FORESIGHT, *second wife to* FORESIGHT.

MRS FRAIL, *sister to* MRS FORESIGHT, *a woman of the town.*

MISS PRUE, *daughter to* FORESIGHT *by a former wife, a silly, awkward, country girl.*

NURSE, *to* MISS PRUE.

JENNY, *maid to* ANGELICA.

A Steward, Officers, Sailors, and several servants.

The scene
in LONDON.

ACT ONE

SCENE ONE

[VALENTINE *in his chamber, reading.* JEREMY *waiting. Several books upon the table.*]

VALENTINE: Jeremy.

JEREMY: Sir.

VALENTINE: Here, take away; I'll walk a turn and digest what I have read –

JEREMY [*aside and taking away the books*]: You'll grow devilish fat upon this paper diet.

VALENTINE: And d'ye hear, go you to breakfast. – There's a page doubled down in Epictetus[1] that is a feast for an emperor.

JEREMY: Was Epictetus a real cook, or did he only write receipts?[2]

VALENTINE: Read, read, sirrah, and refine your appetite; learn to live upon instruction; feast your mind, and mortify your flesh; read, and take your nourishment in your eyes; shut up your mouth, and chew the cud of understanding. So Epictetus advises.

JEREMY: O Lord! I have heard much of him when I waited upon a gentleman at Cambridge: pray, what was that Epictetus?

VALENTINE: A very rich man. – Not worth a groat.

JEREMY: Humph, and so he has made a very fine feast, where there is nothing to be eaten.

VALENTINE: Yes.

JEREMY: Sir, you're a gentleman, and probably understand this fine feeding; but if you please, I had rather be at board-wages. Does your Epictetus, or your Seneca here, or any of these poor, rich

---

1. *Epictetus*: Greek Stoic philosopher, born *c*.60 AD.
2. *receipts*: recipes.

rogues, teach you how to pay your debts without money? Will they shut up the mouths of your creditors? Will Plato be bail for you? Or Diogenes, because he understands confinement and lived in a tub, go to prison for you? 'Slife, sir, what do you mean, to mew yourself up here with three or four musty books in commendation of starving and poverty?

VALENTINE: Why, sirrah, I have no money, you know it; and therefore resolve to rail at all that have: and in that I but follow the examples of the wisest and wittiest men in all ages; these poets and philosophers whom you naturally hate, for just such another reason: because they abound in sense, and you are a fool.

JEREMY: Ay, sir, I am a fool, I know it; and yet, heaven help me, I'm poor enough to be a wit. But I was always a fool when I told you what your expenses would bring you to; your coaches and your liveries; your treats and your balls; your being in love with a lady that did not care a farthing for you in your prosperity; and keeping company with wits that cared for nothing but your prosperity; and now when you are poor, hate you as much as they do one another.

VALENTINE: Well, and now I am poor, I have an opportunity to be revenged on 'em all; I'll pursue Angelica with more love than ever, and appear more notoriously her admirer in this restraint, than when I openly rivalled the rich fops that made court to her; so shall my poverty be a mortification to her pride, and perhaps make her compassionate that love which has principally reduced me to this lowness of fortune. And for the wits, I'm sure I'm in a condition to be even with them –

JEREMY: Nay, your condition is pretty even with theirs, that's the truth on't.

VALENTINE: I'll take some of their trade out of their hands.

JEREMY: Now heaven of mercy continue the tax upon paper; you don't mean to write!

VALENTINE: Yes, I do; I'll write a play.

JEREMY: Hem! – Sir, if you please to give me a small certificate of three lines – only to certify those whom it may concern: that the bearer hereof, Jeremy Fetch by name, has for the space of seven years truly and faithfully served Valentine Legend Esq.; and that

he is not now turned away for any misdemeanour; but does
voluntarily dismiss his master from any future authority over
him –

VALENTINE: No, sirrah, you shall live with me still.

JEREMY: Sir, it's impossible – I may die with you, starve with you,
or be damned with your works; but to live even three days, the life
of a play, I no more expect it than to be canonized for a muse after
my decease.

VALENTINE: You are witty, you rogue. I shall want your help; I'll
have you learn to make couplets, to tag the ends of acts, d'ye hear,
get the maids to crambo³ in an evening, and learn the knack of
rhyming: you may arrive at the height of a song, sent by an
unknown hand, or a chocolate-house lampoon.

JEREMY: But sir, is this the way to recover your father's favour?
Why, Sir Sampson will be irreconcilable. If your younger brother
should come from sea, he'd never look upon you again. You're
undone, sir; you're ruined; you won't have a friend left in the
world if you turn poet. – Ah, pox confound that Will's Coffee-
House,⁴ it has ruined more young men than the Royal Oak
lottery. Nothing thrives that belongs to't. The man of the house
would have been an alderman by this time with half the trade, if he
had set up in the City. For my part, I never sit at the door that I
don't get double the stomach that I do at a horse-race. The air
upon Banstead Downs is nothing to it for a whetter; yet I never
see it, but the spirit of famine appears to me; sometimes like a
decayed porter, worn out with pimping, and carrying *billet doux*
and songs; not like other porters for hire, but for the jest's sake;
now like a thin chairman, melted down to half his proportion
with carrying a poet upon tick to visit some great fortune; and his
fare to be paid him like the wages of sin, either at the day of
marriage, or the day of death.

VALENTINE: Very well, sir; can you proceed?

JEREMY: Sometimes like a bilked bookseller, with a meagre ter-

3. *crambo*: 'a game in which one player gives a word or line of verse to which each of
the others has to find a rime' (*OED*).
4. *Will's Coffee-House*: well-known coffee-house in Covent Garden that was fre-
quented by writers.

rified countenance, that looks as if he had written for himself, or were resolved to turn author and bring the rest of his brethren into the same condition. And lastly, in the form of a worn-out punk,[5] with verses in her hand, which her vanity had preferred to settlements, without a whole tatter to her tail, but as ragged as one of the Muses; or as if she were carrying her linen to the paper mill, to be converted into folio books, of warning to all young maids not to prefer poetry to good sense; or lying in the arms of a needy wit, before the embraces of a wealthy fool.

[*Enter* SCANDAL.]

SCANDAL: What, Jeremy holding forth?

VALENTINE: The rogue has (with all the wit he could muster up) been declaiming against wit.

SCANDAL: Ay? Why then I'm afraid Jeremy has wit; for wherever it is, it's always contriving its own ruin.

JEREMY: Why, so I have been telling my master, sir. Mr Scandal, for heaven's sake, sir, try if you can dissuade him from turning poet.

SCANDAL: Poet! He shall turn soldier first, and rather depend upon the outside of his head than the lining. Why, what the devil, has not your poverty made you enemies enough? Must you needs show your wit to get more?

JEREMY: Ay, more indeed; for who cares for anybody that has more wit than himself?

SCANDAL: Jeremy speaks like an oracle. Don't you see how worthless great men, and dull rich rogues, avoid a witty man of small fortune? Why, he looks like a writ of enquiry into their titles and estates; and seems commissioned by heaven to seize the better half.

VALENTINE: Therefore I would rail in my writings, and be revenged.

SCANDAL: Rail? At whom? The whole world? Impotent and vain! Who would die a martyr to sense in a country where the religion is folly? You may stand at bay for a while; but when the full cry is against you, you won't have fair play for your life. If you can't be

5. *punk*: prostitute.

fairly run down by the hounds, you will be treacherously shot by the huntsmen. – No, turn pimp, flatterer, quack, lawyer, parson, be chaplain to an atheist, or stallion to an old woman, anything but poet; a modern poet is worse, more servile, timorous, and fawning, than any I have named; without you could retrieve the ancient honours of the name, recall the stage of Athens, and be allowed the force of open honest satire.

VALENTINE: You are as inveterate against our poets, as if your character had been lately exposed upon the stage. – Nay, I am not violently bent upon the trade.

[*One knocks.*]

Jeremy, see who's there.

[*Exit* JEREMY.]

But tell me what you would have me do? – What do the world say of me, and of my forced confinement?

SCANDAL: The world behaves itself as it used to do on such occasions; some pity you, and condemn your father; others excuse him, and blame you; only the ladies are merciful and wish you well, since love and pleasurable expense have been your greatest faults.

[*Enter* JEREMY.]

VALENTINE: How now?

JEREMY: Nothing new, sir; I have dispatched some half a dozen duns[6] with as much dexterity as a hungry judge does causes at dinner time.

VALENTINE: What answer have you given 'em?

SCANDAL: Patience, I suppose, the old receipt.

JEREMY: No, faith, sir; I have put 'em off so long with patience and forbearance and other fair words, that I was forced now to tell 'em in plain downright English –

VALENTINE: What?

JEREMY: That they should be paid.

VALENTINE: When?

JEREMY: Tomorrow.

VALENTINE: And how the devil do you mean to keep your word?

6. *duns*: creditors or debt collectors.

JEREMY: Keep it? Not at all; it has been so very much stretched, that I reckon it will break of course by tomorrow, and nobody be surprised at the matter. [*Knocking.*] Again! Sir, if you don't like my negotiation, will you be pleased to answer these yourself.

VALENTINE: See who they are.

[*Exit* JEREMY.]

By this, Scandal, you may see what it is to be great; Secretaries of State, Presidents of the Council, and generals of an army lead just such a life as I do; have just such crowds of visitants in a morning, all soliciting of past promises; which are but a civiller sort of duns, that lay claim to voluntary debts.

SCANDAL: And you, like a true great man, having engaged their attendance, and promised more than ever you intend to perform, are more perplexed to find evasions than you would be to invent the honest means of keeping your word, and gratifying your creditors.

VALENTINE: Scandal, learn to spare your friends, and do not provoke your enemies; this liberty of your tongue will one day bring a confinement on your body, my friend.

[*Re-enter* JEREMY.]

JEREMY: O sir, there's Trapland the scrivener,[7] with two suspicious fellows like lawful pads[8] that would knock a man down with pocket-tipstaves[9] – and there's your father's steward, and the nurse with one of your children from Twitnam.[10]

VALENTINE: Pox on her, could she find no other time to fling my sins in my face? Here, give her this, [*gives money*] and bid her trouble me no more. A thoughtless two-handed whore, she knows my condition well enough and might have overlaid[11] the child a fortnight ago if she had had any forecast in her.

SCANDAL: What, is it bouncing Margery and my godson?

JEREMY: Yes, sir.

SCANDAL: My blessing to the boy, with this token [*gives money*] of

7. *scrivener*: money lender.
8. *pads*: footpads, robbers.
9. *tipstaves*: staffs with metal tips or caps.
10. *Twitnam*: Twickenham, in Middlesex.
11. *overlaid*: smothered.

my love. And d'ye hear, bid Margery put more flocks in her bed, shift twice a week, and not work so hard, that she may not smell so vigorously. – I shall take the air shortly.

VALENTINE: Scandal, don't spoil my boy's milk. – Bid Trapland come in.

[*Exit* JEREMY.]

If I can give that Cerberus a sop, I shall be at rest for one day.

[*Enter* TRAPLAND *and* JEREMY.]

O Mr Trapland! My old friend! Welcome. Jeremy, a chair quickly; a bottle of sack and a toast – fly – a chair first.

TRAPLAND: A good morning to you, Mr Valentine, and to you, Mr Scandal.

SCANDAL: The morning's a very good morning, if you don't spoil it.

VALENTINE: Come sit you down, you know his way.

TRAPLAND [*sits*]: There is a debt, Mr Valentine, of fifteen hundred pounds of pretty long standing –

VALENTINE: I cannot talk about business with a thirsty palate. – Sirrah, the sack. – [12]

TRAPLAND: And I desire to know what course you have taken for the payment?

VALENTINE: Faith and troth, I am heartily glad to see you – my service to you – fill, fill, to honest Mr Trapland, fuller.

TRAPLAND: Hold, sweetheart, this is not to our business – my service to you, Mr Scandal. [*Drinks.*] I have forborn as long –

VALENTINE: T'other glass, and then we'll talk. Fill, Jeremy.

TRAPLAND: No more, in truth. – I have forborn, I say –

VALENTINE: Sirrah, fill when I bid you. – And how does your handsome daughter? Come, a good husband to her.

[*Drinks.*]

TRAPLAND: Thank you. – I have been out of this money –

VALENTINE: Drink first. Scandal, why do you not drink?

[*They drink.*]

TRAPLAND: And in short, I can be put off no longer.

VALENTINE: I was much obliged to you for your supply: it did me

12. *sack*: Spanish wine.

signal service in my necessity. But you delight in doing good. –
Scandal, drink to me my friend Trapland's health. An honester
man lives not, nor one more ready to serve his friend in distress,
though I say it to his face. Come, fill each man his glass.

SCANDAL: What, I know Trapland has been a whoremaster, and
loves a wench still. You never knew a whoremaster that was not
an honest fellow.

TRAPLAND: Fie, Mr Scandal, you never knew –

SCANDAL: What don't I know? – I know the buxom black widow in
the Poultry[13] – eight hundred pounds a year jointure,[14] and
twenty thousand pounds in money. Ahah, old Trap!

VALENTINE: Say you so, i'faith. Come, we'll remember the
widow; I know whereabouts you are. Come, to the widow –

TRAPLAND: No more indeed.

VALENTINE: What, the widow's health; give it him – off with it.
   [*They drink.*]
A lovely girl, i'faith, black sparkling eyes, soft pouting ruby lips!
Better sealing there than a bond for a million, hah!

TRAPLAND: No, no, there's no such thing; we'd better mind our
business. – You're a wag.

VALENTINE: No, faith, we'll mind the widow's business. Fill again.
Pretty round heaving breasts, a Barbary shape,[15] and a jut with
her bum would stir an anchoret;[16] and the prettiest foot! Oh, if a
man could but fasten his eyes to her feet, as they steal in and out,
and play at bo-peep under her petticoats, ah, Mr Trapland?

TRAPLAND: Verily, give me a glass – you're a wag – and here's to
the widow.
   [*Drinks.*]

SCANDAL: He begins to chuckle; ply him close, or he'll relapse into
a dun.
   [*Enter* Officer.]

OFFICER: By your leave, gentlemen. – Mr Trapland, if we must do

13. *the Poultry*: a street to the east of Cheapside.
14. *jointure*: property settled on the wife at marriage as a provision for her in the event
of widowhood.
15. *Barbary shape*: elegantly shaped like an Arabian mare.
16. *anchoret*: anchorite.

our office, tell us. We have half a dozen gentlemen to arrest in Pall Mall and Covent Garden; and if we don't make haste, the chairmen will be abroad and block up the chocolate-houses, and then our labour's lost.

TRAPLAND: Udso, that's true. Mr Valentine, I love mirth, but business must be done. Are you ready to –

JEREMY: Sir, your father's steward says he comes to make proposals concerning your debts.

VALENTINE: Bid him come in. Mr Trapland, send away your officer. You shall have an answer presently.

TRAPLAND: Mr Snap, stay within call.

[*Exit* OFFICER.]

[*Enter* STEWARD *and whispers* VALENTINE.]

SCANDAL: Here's a dog now, a traitor in his wine. [*To Trapland.*] Sirrah, refund the sack: Jeremy, fetch him some warm water, or I'll rip up his stomach and go the shortest way to his conscience.

TRAPLAND: Mr Scandal, you are uncivil; I did not value your sack; but you cannot expect it again when I have drank it.

SCANDAL: And how do you expect to have your money again when a gentleman has spent it?

VALENTINE [*to* STEWARD]: You need say no more, I understand the conditions; they are very hard, but my necessity is very pressing, I agree to 'em. Take Mr Trapland with you, and let him draw the writing. – Mr Trapland, you know this man; he shall satisfy you.

TRAPLAND: Sincerely, I am loth to be thus pressing, but my necessity –

VALENTINE: No apology, good Mr Scrivener, you shall be paid.

TRAPLAND: I hope you forgive me, my business requires –

[*Exeunt* STEWARD, TRAPLAND *and* JEREMY.]

SCANDAL: He begs pardon like a hangman at an execution.

VALENTINE: But I have got a reprieve.

SCANDAL: I am surprised; what, does your father relent?

VALENTINE: No; he has sent me the hardest conditions in the world. You have heard of a booby brother of mine that was sent to sea three years ago? This brother, my father hears, is landed; whereupon he very affectionately sends me word, if I will make a deed of conveyance of my right to his estate after his death to my younger brother, he will immediately furnish me with four thousand pound to pay my debts, and make my fortune. This was once proposed before, and I refused it; but the present impatience of my creditors for their money, and my own impatience of confinement and absence from Angelica, force me to consent.

SCANDAL: A very desperate demonstration of your love to Angelica; and I think she has never given you any assurance of hers.

VALENTINE: You know her temper; she never gave me any great reason either for hope or despair.

SCANDAL: Women of her airy temper, as they seldom think before they act, so they rarely give us any light to guess at what they mean: but you have little reason to believe that a woman of this age, who has had an indifference for you in your prosperity, will fall in love with your ill fortune; besides, Angelica has a great fortune of her own; and great fortunes either expect another great fortune, or a fool.

[*Enter* JEREMY.]

JEREMY: More misfortunes, sir.

VALENTINE: What, another dun?

JEREMY: No sir, but Mr Tattle is come to wait upon you.

VALENTINE: Well, I can't help it, – you must bring him up; he knows I don't go abroad.

[*Exit* JEREMY.]

SCANDAL: Pox on him, I'll be gone.

VALENTINE: No, prithee stay: Tattle and you should never be asunder; you are light and shadow, and show one another; he is perfectly thy reverse both in humour and understanding; and as you set up for defamation, he is a mender of reputations.

SCANDAL: A mender of reputations! Ay, just as he is a keeper of secrets, another virtue that he sets up for in the same manner. For the rogue will speak aloud in the posture of a whisper, and deny a woman's name while he gives you the marks of her person. He will forswear receiving a letter from her, and at the same time show you her hand upon the superscription; and yet perhaps he has counterfeited the hand too, and sworn to a truth; but he hopes not to be believed, and refuses the reputation of a lady's favour, as a doctor says no to a bishopric, only that it may be granted him. In short, he is a public professor of secrecy, and makes proclamation that he holds private intelligence. – He's here.

[*Enter* TATTLE.]

TATTLE: Valentine, good morrow; Scandal I am yours – that is, when you speak well of me.

SCANDAL: That is, when I am yours; for while I am my own, or anybody's else, that will never happen.

TATTLE: How inhumane!

VALENTINE: Why Tattle, you need not be much concerned at anything that he says: for to converse with Scandal is to play at losing loadum;[17] you must lose a good name to him before you can win it for yourself.

TATTLE: But how barbarous that is, and how unfortunate for him, that the world shall think the better of any person for his calumniation! I thank heaven it has always been a part of my character to handle the reputation of others very tenderly.

SCANDAL: Ay, such rotten reputations as you have to deal with are to be handled tenderly indeed.

TATTLE: Nay, but why rotten? Why should you say rotten, when you know not the persons of whom you speak? How cruel that is.

SCANDAL: Not know 'em? Why, thou never hadst to do with anybody that did not stink to all the town.

TATTLE: Ha, ha, ha; nay, now you make a jest of it indeed. For there is nothing more known, than that nobody knows anything of that nature of me. As I hope to be saved, Valentine, I never exposed a woman since I knew what woman was.

VALENTINE: And yet you have conversed with several.

TATTLE: To be free with you, I have – I don't care if I own that. Nay more (I'm going to say a bold word now), I never could meddle with a woman that had to do with anybody else.

SCANDAL: How!

VALENTINE: Nay faith, I'm apt to believe him. – Except her husband, Tattle.

17. *losing loadum*: a card game in which the winner is the one who makes the fewest tricks.

TATTLE: Oh that –

SCANDAL: What think you of that noble commoner, Mrs Drab?

TATTLE: Pooh, I know Madam Drab has made her brags in three or four places that I said this and that, and writ to her, and did I know not what – but, upon my reputation, she did me wrong. – Well, well, that was malice – but I know the bottom of it. She was bribed to that by one that we all know – a man too – only to bring me into disgrace with a certain woman of quality –

SCANDAL: Whom we all know.

TATTLE: No matter for that. – Yes, yes, everybody knows – no doubt on't, everybody knows my secrets. But I soon satisfied the lady of my innocence; for I told her – madam, says I, there are some persons who make it their business to tell stories, and say this and that of one and t'other, and everything in the world; and, says I, if your Grace –

SCANDAL: Grace!

TATTLE: O Lord, what have I said? My unlucky tongue!

VALENTINE: Ha, ha, ha!

SCANDAL: Why, Tattle, thou hast more impudence than one can in reason expect: I shall have an esteem for thee. Well, and ha, ha, ha, well, go on, and what did you say to her Grace?

VALENTINE: I confess this is something extraordinary.

TATTLE: Not a word, as I hope to be saved; an errant *lapsus linguae*. Come, let's talk of something else.

VALENTINE: Well, but how did you acquit yourself?

TATTLE: Pooh, pooh, nothing at all, I only rallied with you. – A woman of ordinary rank was a little jealous of me, and I told her something or other, faith – I know not what. – Come, let's talk of something else.

[*Hums a song.*]

SCANDAL: Hang him, let him alone; he has a mind we should enquire.

TATTLE: Valentine, I supped last night with your mistress, and her uncle, old Foresight. I think your father lies at Foresight's?

VALENTINE: Yes.

TATTLE: Upon my soul, Angelica's a fine woman – and so is Mrs Foresight, and her sister Mrs Frail.

SCANDAL: Yes, Mrs Frail is a very fine woman; we all know her.

TATTLE: Oh, that is not fair.

SCANDAL: What?

TATTLE: To tell.

SCANDAL: To tell what? Why, what do you know of Mrs Frail?

TATTLE: Who, I? Upon honour I don't know whether she be man or woman but by the smoothness of her chin and roundness of her lips.

SCANDAL: No!

TATTLE: No.

SCANDAL: She says otherwise.

TATTLE: Impossible!

SCANDAL: Yes, faith. Ask Valentine else.

TATTLE: Why then, as I hope to be saved, I believe a woman only obliges a man to secrecy that she may have the pleasure of telling herself.

SCANDAL: No doubt on't. Well, but has she done you wrong, or no? You have had her? Ha?

TATTLE: Though I have more honour than to tell first, I have more manners than to contradict what a lady has declared.

SCANDAL: Well, you own it?

TATTLE: I am strangely surprised! Yes, yes, I can't deny't, if she taxes me with it.

SCANDAL: She'll be here by and by; she sees Valentine every morning.

TATTLE: How!

VALENTINE: She does me the favour – I mean of a visit sometimes. I did not think she had granted more to anybody.

SCANDAL: Nor I, faith – but Tattle does not use to belie a lady; it is contrary to his character. – How one may be deceived in a woman, Valentine!

TATTLE: Nay, what do you mean, gentlemen?

SCANDAL: I'm resolved I'll ask her.

TATTLE: O barbarous! Why did you not tell me –

SCANDAL: No, you told us.

TATTLE: And bid me ask Valentine.

VALENTINE: What did I say? I hope you won't bring me to confess an answer, when you never asked me the question.

TATTLE: But, gentlemen, this is the most inhumane proceeding –

VALENTINE: Nay, if you have known Scandal thus long, and cannot avoid such a palpable decoy as this was, the ladies have a fine time whose reputations are in your keeping.

[*Enter* JEREMY.]

JEREMY: Sir, Mrs Frail has sent to know if you are stirring.

VALENTINE: Show her up when she comes.

[*Exit* JEREMY.]

TATTLE: I'll be gone.

VALENTINE: You'll meet her.

TATTLE: Have you not a back way?

VALENTINE: If there were, you have more discretion than to give Scandal such an advantage; why, your running away will prove all that he can tell her.

TATTLE: Scandal, you will not be so ungenerous. – O, I shall lose my reputation of secrecy forever. – I shall never be received but upon public days, and my visits will never be admitted beyond a drawing room: I shall never see a bedchamber again, never be locked in a closet, nor run behind a screen, or under a table; never be distinguished among the waiting-women by the name of trusty Mr Tattle more. – You will not be so cruel.

VALENTINE: Scandal, have pity on him; he'll yield to any conditions.

TATTLE: Any, any terms.

SCANDAL: Come then, sacrifice half a dozen women of good reputation to me presently. Come, where are you familiar? – And see that they are women of quality too, the first quality.

TATTLE: 'Tis very hard. Won't a baronet's lady pass?

SCANDAL: No, nothing under a Right Honourable.

TATTLE: O inhumane! You don't expect their names.

SCANDAL: No, their titles shall serve.

TATTLE: Alas, that's the same thing. Pray spare me their titles; I'll describe their persons.

SCANDAL: Well, begin then; but take notice, if you are so ill a painter that I cannot know the person by your picture of her, you must be condemned, like other bad painters, to write the name at the bottom.

TATTLE: Well, first then –

[*Enter* MRS FRAIL.]

O unfortunate! She's come already; will you have patience till another time – I'll double the number.

SCANDAL: Well, on that condition. Take heed you don't fail me.

MRS FRAIL: Hey day! I shall get a fine reputation by coming to see fellows in a morning. Scandal, you devil, are you here too? Oh, Mr Tattle, everything is safe with you, we know.

SCANDAL: Tattle!

TATTLE: Mum. – Oh, madam, you do me too much honour.

VALENTINE: Well Lady Galloper, how does Angelica?

MRS FRAIL: Angelica? Manners!

VALENTINE: What, you will allow an absent lover –

MRS FRAIL: No, I'll allow a lover present with his mistress to be particular, but otherwise I think his passion ought to give place to his manners.

VALENTINE: But what if he have more passion than manners?

MRS FRAIL: Then let him marry and reform.

VALENTINE: Marriage indeed may qualify the fury of his passion, but it very rarely mends a man's manners.

MRS FRAIL: You are the most mistaken in the world; there is no creature perfectly civil but a husband. For in a little time he grows only rude to his wife, and that is the highest good breeding, for it begets his civility to other people. Well, I'll tell you news; but I suppose you hear your brother Benjamin is landed. And my brother Foresight's daughter is come out of the country. – I assure you, there's a match talked of by the old people. – Well, if he be but as great a sea-beast as she is a land-monster, we shall have a most amphibious breed. – The progeny will be all otters; he has been bred at sea, and she has never been out of the country.

VALENTINE: Pox take 'em, their conjunction bodes no good, I'm sure.

MRS FRAIL: Now you talk of conjunction, my brother Foresight has cast both their nativities, and prognosticates an admiral and an eminent justice of the peace to be the issue-male of their two bodies. 'Tis the most superstitious old fool! He would have persuaded me that this was an unlucky day and would not let me come abroad: but I invented a dream, and sent him to Artimedorus[18] for interpretation, and so stole out to see you. Well, and what will you give me now? Come, I must have something.

VALENTINE: Step into the next room – and I'll give you something.

SCANDAL: Ay, we'll all give you something.

MRS FRAIL: Well, what will you all give me?

VALENTINE: Mine's a secret.

MRS FRAIL: I thought you would give me something that would be a trouble to you to keep.

VALENTINE: And Scandal shall give you a good name.

MRS FRAIL: That's more than he has for himself. And what will you give me, Mr Tattle?

TATTLE: I? My soul, madam.

MRS FRAIL: Pooh, no, I thank you, I have enough to do to take care of my own. Well, but I'll come and see you one of these mornings: I hear you have a great many pictures.

TATTLE: I have a pretty good collection at your service, some originals.

SCANDAL: Hang him, he has nothing but the *Seasons* and the *Twelve Caesars*, paltry copies; and the *Five Senses*,[19] as ill represented as they are in himself. And he himself is the only original you will see there.

MRS FRAIL: Ay, but I hear he has a closet of beauties.

SCANDAL: Yes, all that have done him favours, if you will believe him.

MRS FRAIL: Ay, let me see those, Mr Tattle.

TATTLE: Oh madam, those are sacred to love and contemplation. No man but the painter and myself was ever blest with the sight.

MRS FRAIL: Well, but a woman –

18. *Artimedorus*: Greek soothsayer and interpreter of dreams; second century AD.
19. *Seasons . . . Senses*: popular prints.

TATTLE: Nor woman, till she consented to have her picture there too – for then she is obliged to keep the secret.

SCANDAL: No, no; come to me if you would see pictures.

MRS FRAIL: You?

SCANDAL: Yes, faith, I can show you your own picture, and most of your acquaintance to the life, and as like as at Kneller's.[20]

MRS FRAIL: O lying creature – Valentine, does not he lie? – I can't believe a word he says.

VALENTINE: No indeed, he speaks truth now: for as Tattle has pictures of all that have granted him favours, he has the pictures of all that have refused him; if satires, descriptions, characters, and lampoons are pictures.

SCANDAL: Yes, mine are most in black and white. – And yet there are some set out in their true colours, both men and women. I can show you pride, folly, affectation, wantonness, inconstancy, covetousness, dissimulation, malice, and ignorance, all in one piece. Then I can show you lying, foppery, vanity, cowardice, bragging, lechery, impotence, and ugliness in another piece; and yet one of these is a celebrated beauty, and t'other a professed beau. I have paintings too, some pleasant enough.

MRS FRAIL: Come, let's hear 'em.

SCANDAL: Why, I have a beau in a bagnio,[21] cupping[22] for a complexion, and sweating for a shape.

MRS FRAIL: So.

SCANDAL: Then I have a lady burning of brandy in a cellar with a hackney-coachman.

MRS FRAIL: O devil! Well, but that story is not true.

SCANDAL: I have some hieroglyphics too; I have a lawyer with a hundred hands, two heads, and but one face; a divine with two faces, and one head; and I have a soldier with his brains in his belly, and his heart where his head should be.

MRS FRAIL: And no head?

SCANDAL: No head.

MRS FRAIL: Pooh, this is all invention. Have you ne'er a poet?

20. *Kneller's*: Sir Godfrey Kneller (1646–1723), portrait painter.
21. *bagnio*: steam bath.
22. *cupping*: being bled.

SCANDAL: Yes, I have a poet weighing words, and selling praise for praise, and a critic picking his pocket. I have another large piece too, representing a school, where there are huge proportioned critics, with long wigs, laced coats, Steinkirk cravats,[23] and terrible faces; with catcalls[24] in their hands, and hornbooks[25] about their necks. I have many more of this kind, very well painted, as you shall see.

MRS FRAIL: Well, I'll come, if it be only to disprove you.

[*Enter* JEREMY.]

JEREMY: Sir, here's the steward again from your father.

VALENTINE: I'll come to him. – Will you give me leave, I'll wait on you again presently.

MRS FRAIL: No, I'll be gone. Come, who squires me to the Exchange?[26] I must call my sister Foresight there.

SCANDAL: I will; I have a mind to your sister.

MRS FRAIL: Civil!

TATTLE: I will; because I have a tender for your ladyship.

MRS FRAIL: That's somewhat the better reason, to my opinion.

SCANDAL: Well, if Tattle entertains you, I have the better opportunity to engage your sister.

VALENTINE: Tell Angelica, I am about making hard conditions to come abroad and be at liberty to see her.

SCANDAL: I'll give an account of you, and your proceedings. If indiscretion be a sign of love, you are the most a lover of anybody that I know: you fancy that parting with your estate will help you to your mistress. – In my mind he is a thoughtless adventurer,

> Who hopes to purchase wealth, by selling land;
> Or win a mistress, with a losing hand.

[*Exeunt.*]

23. *Steinkirk cravats*: casually tied neckcloths; so named, because at the battle of Steenkerke (1692), the French officers had not time to tie their cravats properly.
24. *catcalls*: squeaking instruments or whistles used in the theatre to express disapproval.
25. *hornbooks*: child's first spelling books.
26. *Exchange*: a kind of shopping plaza on the south side of the Strand.

ACT TWO

SCENE ONE

A room in Foresight's *house.*

[FORESIGHT *and* SERVANT.]

FORESIGHT: Hey day! What, are all the women of my family abroad? Is not my wife come home? Nor my sister, nor my daughter?

SERVANT: No, sir.

FORESIGHT: Mercy on us, what can be the meaning of it? Sure the moon is in all her fortitudes.[1] Is my niece Angelica at home?

SERVANT: Yes, sir.

FORESIGHT: I believe you lie, sir.

SERVANT: Sir?

FORESIGHT: I say you lie, sir. It is impossible that anything should be as I would have it; for I was born, sir, when the Crab was ascending, and all my affairs go backward.

SERVANT: I can't tell indeed, sir.

FORESIGHT: No, I know you can't, sir: but I can tell, sir, and foretell, sir.

[*Enter* NURSE.]

Nurse, where's your young mistress?

NURSE: Wee'st[2] heart, I know not; they're none of 'em come home yet: poor child, I warrant she's fond o'seeing the town – marry, pray heaven they ha' given her any dinner. – Good lack-a-day, ha, ha, ha, O strange; I'll vow and swear now, ha, ha, ha, marry, and did you ever see the like!

1. *moon . . . fortitudes*: the moon is exerting her fullest power.
2. *wee'st*: woe is my.

FORESIGHT: Why, how now, what's the matter?

NURSE: Pray heaven send your worship good luck, marry and amen with all my heart, for you have put on one stocking with the wrong side outward.

FORESIGHT: Ha, how? Faith and troth I'm glad of it, and so I have. That may be good luck in troth, in troth it may, very good luck. Nay, I have had some omens: I got out of bed backwards too this morning, without premeditation; pretty good that too; but then I stumbled coming downstairs, and met a weasel; bad omens those. Some bad, some good, our lives are chequered; mirth and sorrow, want and plenty, night and day, make up our time. – But in troth I am pleased at my stocking, very well pleased at my stocking. – Oh, here's my niece!

[*Enter* ANGELICA.]

Sirrah, go tell Sir Sampson Legend I'll wait on him, if he's at leisure. – 'Tis now three o'clock, a very good hour for business; Mercury governs this hour.

[*Exit* SERVANT.]

ANGELICA: Is not it a good hour for pleasure too? Uncle, pray lend me your coach; mine's out of order.

FORESIGHT: What, would you be gadding too? Sure all females are mad today. It is of evil portent, and bodes mischief to the master of a family. – I remember an old prophecy written by Messehalah[3] the Arabian, and thus translated by a reverend Buckinghamshire bard.[4]

> When housewifes all the house forsake,
> And leave good man to brew and bake,
> Withouten guile, then be it said,
> That house doth stond upon its head;
> And when the head is set in grond,
> Ne marl, if it be fruitful fond.

Fruitful, the head fruitful, that bodes horns; the fruit of the head is horns. – Dear niece, stay at home – for by the head of the

3. *Messehalah*: Jewish astrologer of the ninth century A D.
4. *Buckinghamshire bard*: usually identified as John Mason (d. 1694), poet and millenarian preacher.

house is meant the husband; the prophecy needs no explanation.

ANGELICA: Well, but I can neither make you a cuckold, uncle, by going abroad; nor secure you from being one by staying at home.

FORESIGHT: Yes, yes; while there's one woman left, the prophecy is not in full force.

ANGELICA: But my inclinations are in force; I have a mind to go abroad, and if you won't lend me your coach, I'll take a hackney or a chair[5] and leave you to erect a scheme and find who's in conjunction with your wife. Why don't you keep her at home, if you're jealous when she's abroad? You know my aunt is a little retrograde (as you call it) in her nature. Uncle, I'm afraid you are not lord of the ascendant, ha, ha, ha.

FORESIGHT: Well, jill-flirt, you are very pert – and always ridiculing that celestial science.

ANGELICA: Nay uncle, don't be angry. – If you are, I'll reap up all your false prophecies, ridiculous dreams, and idle divinations. I'll swear you are a nuisance to the neighbourhood. – What a bustle did you keep against the last invisible eclipse, laying in provision as 'twere for a siege? What a world of fire and candle, matches and tinderboxes did you purchase! One would have thought we were ever after to live under ground, or at least making a voyage to Greenland, to inhabit there all the dark season.

FORESIGHT: Why, you malapert slut –

ANGELICA: Will you lend me your coach, or I'll go on. – Nay, I'll declare how you prophesied popery was coming, only because the butler had mislaid some of the apostle's spoons, and thought they were lost. Away went religion and spoon-meat[6] together. Indeed, uncle, I'll indict you for a wizard.

FORESIGHT: How, hussy! Was there ever such a provoking minx?

NURSE: O merciful Father, how she talks!

ANGELICA: Yes, I can make oath of your unlawful midnight practices; you and the old nurse there –

NURSE: Marry, heaven defend! I at midnight practices! – O Lord, what's here to do? – I in unlawful doings with my master's

5. *chair*: sedan chair.
6. *spoon-meat*: soft, easily digested food.

worship? – Why, did you ever hear the like now? – Sir, did ever I
do anything of your midnight concerns but warm your bed, and
tuck you up, and set the candle, and your tobacco-box, and your
urinal by you, and now and then rub the soles of your feet? – O
Lord, I!

ANGELICA: Yes, I saw you together, through the key-hole of the
closet one night, like Saul and the witch of Endor,[7] turning the
sieve and shears,[8] and pricking thumbs, to write poor innocent
servants' names in blood, about a little nutmeg-grater which she
had forgot in the caudle-cup.[9] – Nay, I know something worse, if
I would speak of it –

FORESIGHT: I defy you, hussy! But I'll remember this, I'll be
revenged on you, cockatrice;[10] I'll hamper you. – You have your
fortune in your own hands, but I'll find a way to make your lover,
your prodigal spendthrift gallant, Valentine, pay for all, I will.

ANGELICA: Will you? I care not, but all shall out then. – Look to it,
nurse; I can bring witness that you have a great unnatural teat
under your left arm, and he another, and that you suckle a young
devil in the shape of a tabby-cat by turns, I can.

NURSE: A teat, a teat, I an unnatural teat! O the false slanderous
thing; feel, feel here, if I have any thing but like another Christian,
[crying] or any teats, but two that han't given suck this thirty
years.

FORESIGHT: I will have patience, since it is the will of the stars I
should be thus tormented. This is the effect of the malicious
conjunctions and oppositions in the third house of my nativity;
there the curse of kindred was foretold. – But I will have my doors
locked up – I'll punish you, not a man shall enter my house.

ANGELICA: Do, uncle, lock 'em up quickly before my aunt come
home. You'll have a letter for alimony tomorrow morning. – But
let me be gone first, and then let no mankind come near the house,
but converse with spirits and the celestial signs, the Bull, and the
Ram, and the Goat. Bless me! There are a great many horned

7. *Saul . . . Endor*: see I Samuel 28.
8. *sieve and shears*: a means of divination.
9. *caudle*: warm, spicy drink.
10. *cockatrice*: serpent able to kill by its mere glance.

beasts among the twelve signs, uncle. But cuckolds go to heaven.

FORESIGHT: But there's but one Virgin among the twelve signs, spitfire, but one Virgin.

ANGELICA: Nor there had not been that one, if she had had to do with anything but astrologers, uncle. That makes my aunt go abroad.

FORESIGHT: How? How? Is that the reason? Come, you know something; tell me, and I'll forgive you; do, good niece. – Come, you shall have my coach and horses – faith and troth you shall – does my wife complain? Come, I know women tell one another. She is young and sanguine, has a wanton hazel eye, and was born under Gemini, which may incline her to society; she has a mole upon her lip, with a moist palm, and an open liberality on the mount of Venus.

ANGELICA: Ha, ha, ha!

FORESIGHT: Do you laugh? Well, gentlewoman, I'll – but come, be a good girl, don't perplex your poor uncle, tell me – won't you speak? Odd, I'll –

[Enter SERVANT.]

SERVANT: Sir Sampson is coming down to wait upon you –

ANGELICA: Good-bye, uncle. [To SERVANT.] Call me a chair. I'll find out my aunt, and tell her she must not come home.

[Exit ANGELICA and SERVANT.]

FORESIGHT: I'm so perplexed and vexed, I am not fit to receive him; I shall scarce recover myself before the hour be past. Go, nurse, tell Sir Sampson I'm ready to wait on him.

NURSE: Yes, sir.

[Exit.]

FORESIGHT: Well – why, if I was born to be a cuckold, there's no more to be said –

[Enter SIR SAMPSON LEGEND with a paper.]

SIR SAMPSON: Nor no more to be done, old boy, that's plain. Here 'tis, I have it in my hand, old Ptolomee;[11] I'll make the ungracious prodigal know who begat him, I will, old Nostradamus.[12] What,

11. *Ptolomee*: Ptolemy of Alexandria, astronomer, second century AD.
12. *Nostradamus*: assumed name of Michel de Notredame (1503–66), French astrologer.

I warrant my son thought nothing belonged to a father but forgiveness and affection; no authority, no correction, no arbitrary power; nothing to be done but for him to offend and me to pardon. I warrant you, if he danced till doomsday, he thought I was to pay the piper. Well, but here it is under black and white, *signatum, sigillatum*, and *deliberatum*;[13] that as soon as my son Benjamin is arrived, he is to make over to him his right of inheritance. Where's my daughter that is to be? – Hah! old Merlin, body o' me, I'm so glad I'm revenged on this undutiful rogue.

FORESIGHT: Odso, let me see; let me see the paper. – Ay, faith and troth, here 'tis, if it will but hold. I wish things were done, and the conveyance made. – When was this signed, what hour? Odso, you should have consulted me for the time. Well, but we'll make haste –

SIR SAMPSON: Haste, ay, ay, haste enough. My son Ben will be in town tonight. I have ordered my lawyer to draw up writings of settlement and jointure. – All shall be done tonight. – No matter for the time. Prithee, brother Foresight, leave superstition. – Pox o'th 'time; there's no time but the time present, there's no more to be said of what's past, and all that is to come will happen. If the sun shine by day, and the stars by night, why, we shall know one another's faces without the help of a candle, and that's all the stars are good for.

FORESIGHT: How, how? Sir Sampson, that all? Give me leave to contradict you, and tell you you are ignorant.

SIR SAMPSON: I tell you I am wise, and *sapiens dominabitur astris*;[14] there's Latin for you to prove it, and an argument to confound your Ephemeris.[15] – Ignorant! – I tell you, I have travelled, old Fircu,[16] and know the globe. I have seen the Antipodes, where the sun rises at midnight and sets at noon-day.

FORESIGHT: But I tell you, I have travelled, and travelled in the celestial spheres, know the signs and the planets, and their

13. *signatum, sigillatum* and *deliberatum*: signed, sealed and delivered.
14. *sapiens . . . astris*: the wise man will be ruled by the stars.
15. *Ephemeris*: almanac.
16. *Fircu*: probably a name for a witch's familiar spirit.

houses: can judge of motions direct and retrograde, of Sextiles, Quadrates, Trines and Oppositions, Fiery Trigons and Aquatical Trigons;[17] know whether life shall be long or short, happy or unhappy; whether diseases are curable or incurable; if journeys shall be prosperous, undertakings successful, or goods stolen, recovered. I know –

SIR SAMPSON: I know the length of the emperor of China's foot, have kissed the Great Mogul's slipper, and rid a-hunting upon an elephant with the Cham of Tartary. – Body o' me, I have made a cuckold of a king, and the present majesty of Bantam[18] is the issue of these loins.

FORESIGHT: I know when travellers lie or speak truth, when they don't know it themselves.

SIR SAMPSON: I have known an astrologer made a cuckold in the twinkling of a star, and seen a conjurer that could not keep the devil out of his wife's circle.

FORESIGHT [aside]: What, does he twit me with my wife too? I must be better informed of this. – Do you mean my wife, Sir Sampson? Though you made a cuckold of the King of Bantam, yet by the body of the sun –

SIR SAMPSON: By the horns of the moon, you would say, brother Capricorn.

FORESIGHT: Capricorn in your teeth, thou modern Mandevil; Ferdinand Mandez Pinto[19] was but a type of thee, thou liar of the first magnitude. Take back your paper of inheritance; send your son to sea again. I'll wed my daughter to an Egyptian mummy, ere she shall incorporate with a contemner of sciences, and a defamer of virtue.

SIR SAMPSON [aside]: Body o' me, I have gone too far; I must not provoke honest Albumazar[20]. – An Egyptian mummy is an illustrious creature, my trusty hieroglyphic, and may have signifi-

17. *trigons*: a trigon is a set of three signs of the zodiac.
18. *Bantam*: western Java.
19. *Mandevil . . . Pinto*: unlike Sir John Mandeville's fourteenth-century account of travels in the Far East, Fernao Pinto's *Peregrinations* (1614) is, in fact, more closely based on his own travels.
20. *Albumazar*: Arabian astrologer of the ninth century.

cations of futurity about him; odsbud, I would my son were an Egyptian mummy for thy sake. What, thou art not angry for a jest, my good Haly?[21] I reverence the sun, moon and stars with all my heart. – What, I'll make thee a present of a mummy. Now I think on't, body o' me, I have a shoulder of an Egyptian king that I purloined from one of the pyramids, powdered with hieroglyphics; thou shalt have it sent home to thy house, and make an entertainment for all the philomaths[22] and students in physic and astrology in and about London.

FORESIGHT: But what do you know of my wife, Sir Sampson?

SIR SAMPSON: Thy wife is a constellation of virtues; she's the moon, and thou art the man in the moon. Nay, she is more illustrious than the moon, for she has her chastity without her inconstancy. 'Sbud, I was but in jest.

[Enter JEREMY.]

How now, who sent for you? Ha! what would you have?

FORESIGHT: Nay, if you were but in jest. – Who's that fellow? I don't like his physiognomy.

SIR SAMPSON: My son, sir; what son, sir? My son Benjamin, hoh?

JEREMY: No, sir, Mr Valentine, my master; 'tis the first time he has been abroad since his confinement, and he comes to pay his duty to you.

SIR SAMPSON: Well, sir.

[Enter VALENTINE.]

JEREMY: He is here, sir.

VALENTINE: Your blessing, sir.

SIR SAMPSON: You've had it already, sir: I think I sent it you today in a bill of four thousand pound. A great deal of money, brother Foresight.

FORESIGHT: Ay, indeed, Sir Sampson, a great deal of money for a young man; I wonder what he can do with it!

SIR SAMPSON: Body o' me, so do I. – Hark ye, Valentine, if there is too much, refund the superfluity; do'st hear, boy?

VALENTINE: Superfluity; sir, it will scarce pay my debts. I hope you

21. *Haly*: Arabian astrologer, ninth century.
22. *philomaths*: lovers of learning; savants.

will have more indulgence than to oblige me to those hard conditions which my necessity signed to.

SIR SAMPSON: Sir, how; I beseech you, what were you pleased to intimate concerning indulgence?

VALENTINE: Why, sir, that you would not go to the extremity of the conditions, but release me at least from some part –

SIR SAMPSON: Oh sir, I understand you, – that's all, ha?

VALENTINE: Yes, sir, all that I presume to ask. – But what you, out of fatherly fondness, will be pleased to add, shall be doubly welcome.

SIR SAMPSON: No doubt of it, sweet sir, but your filial piety and my fatherly fondness would fit like two tallies.[23] – Here's a rogue, brother Foresight, makes a bargain under hand and seal in the morning, and would be released from it in the afternoon. – Here's a rogue, dog, here's conscience and honesty; this is your wit now, this is the morality of your wits! You are a wit, and have been a beau, and may be a – why, sirrah, is it not here under hand and seal? Can you deny it?

VALENTINE: Sir, I don't deny it –

SIR SAMPSON: Sirrah, you'll be hanged; I shall live to see you go up Holborn Hill.[24] Has he not a rogue's face? – Speak, brother, you understand physiognomy; a hanging look to me; of all my boys the most unlike me; a' has a damned Tyburn face, without the benefit o' the clergy.[25]

FORESIGHT: Hum – truly I don't care to discourage a young man; he has a violent death in his face, but I hope no danger of hanging.

VALENTINE: Sir, is this usage for your son? For that old, weather-headed fool, I know how to laugh at him; but you, sir –

SIR SAMPSON: You, sir; and you, sir! – Why, who are you, sir?

VALENTINE: Your son, sir.

SIR SAMPSON: That's more than I know, sir, and I believe not.

VALENTINE: Faith, I hope not.

23. *two tallies*: the two halves of a stick which had been notched to represent the amount of a debt; the matching up of the two halves constituted legal proof of a debt.
24. *Holborn Hill*: on the way from Newgate prison to the gallows at Tyburn.
25. *benefit o' the clergy*: privilege of exemption from sentencing for certain first offences granted to those who could read.

SIR SAMPSON: What, would you have your mother a whore! Did you ever hear the like! Did you ever hear the like! Body o' me –

VALENTINE: I would have an excuse for your barbarity and unnatural usage.

SIR SAMPSON: Excuse! Impudence! Why, sirrah, mayn't I do what I please? Are not you my slave? Did not I beget you? And might not I have chosen whether I would have begot you or not? Oons, who are you? Whence came you? What brought you into the world? How came you here, sir? Here, to stand here, upon those two legs, and look erect with that audacious face, hah? Answer me that! Did you come a volunteer into the world? Or did I beat up for you with the lawful authority of a parent, and press you to service?

VALENTINE: I know no more why I came, than you do why you called me. But here I am, and if you don't mean to provide for me, I desire you would leave me as you found me.

SIR SAMPSON: With all my heart. Come, uncase, strip, and go naked out of the world as you came into't.

VALENTINE: My clothes are soon put off; but you must also deprive me of reason, thought, passions, inclinations, affections, appetites, senses, and the huge train of attendants that you begot along with me.

SIR SAMPSON: Body o' me, what a many-headed monster have I propagated!

VALENTINE: I am of myself a plain easy simple creature, and to be kept at small expense; but the retinue that you gave me are craving and invincible; they are so many devils that you have raised, and will have employment.

SIR SAMPSON: Oons, what had I to do to get children? Can't a private man be born without all these followers? Why, nothing under an emperor should be born with appetites. Why, at this rate a fellow that has but a groat in his pocket may have a stomach capable of a ten-shilling ordinary.[26]

JEREMY: Nay, that's as clear as the sun; I'll make oath of it before any justice in Middlesex.

26. *ordinary*: restaurant.

SIR SAMPSON: Here's a cormorant too. – 'S'heart, this fellow was not born with you? – I did not beget him, did I?

JEREMY: By the provision that's made for me, you might have begot me too: nay, and to tell your worship another truth, I believe you did, for I find I was born with those same whoreson appetites too, that my master speaks of.

SIR SAMPSON: Why look you there now. I'll maintain it, that by the rule of right reason, this fellow ought to have been born without a palate. – 'S'heart, what should he do with a distinguishing taste? – I warrant now he'd rather eat a pheasant than a piece of poor John;[27] and smell, now, why I warrant he can smell, and loves perfumes above a stink. – Why there's it; and music – don't you love music, scoundrel?

JEREMY: Yes, I have a reasonable good ear, sir, as to jigs and country dances and the like; I don't much matter[28] your solos or sonatas; they give me the spleen.

SIR SAMPSON: The spleen, ha, ha, ha, a pox confound you – solos and sonatas? Oons, whose son are you? How were you engendered, muckworm?

JEREMY: I am, by my father, the son of a chairman; my mother sold oysters in winter and cucumbers in summer; and I came up stairs into the world, for I was born in a cellar.

FORESIGHT: By your looks, you should go up stairs out of the world too, friend.

SIR SAMPSON: And if this rogue were anatomized now, and dissected, he has his vessels of digestion and concoction, and so forth, large enough for the inside of a cardinal, this son of a cucumber. These things are unaccountable and unreasonable. Body o' me, why was not I a bear, that my cubs might have lived upon sucking their paws? Nature has been provident only to bears and spiders; the one has its nutriment in his own hands, and t'other spins his habitation out of his entrails.

VALENTINE: Fortune was provident enough to supply all the necessities of my nature, if I had my right of inheritance.

27. *poor John*: dried, salted fish.
28. *matter*: care for.

SIR SAMPSON: Again! Oons, han't you four thousand pound? If I had it again, I would not give thee a groat. – What, wouldst thou have me turn pelican, and feed thee out of my own vitals?[29] 'S'heart, live by your wits. – You were always fond of the wits, now let's see if you have wit enough to keep yourself. Your brother will be in town tonight, or tomorrow morning, and then look you perform covenants, and so your friend and servant. – Come, brother Foresight.

[*Exeunt* SIR SAMPSON *and* FORESIGHT.]

JEREMY: I told you what your visit would come to.

VALENTINE: 'Tis as much as I expected – I did not come to see him: I came to Angelica; but since she was gone abroad, it was easily turned another way, and at least looked well on my side. – What's here? Mrs Foresight and Mrs Frail; they are earnest. – I'll avoid 'em. Come this way, and go and enquire when Angelica will return.

[*Exeunt.*]

[*Enter* MRS FORESIGHT *and* MRS FRAIL.]

MRS FRAIL: What have you to do to watch me? 'Slife, I'll do what I please.

MRS FORESIGHT: You will?

MRS FRAIL: Yes, marry will I. A great piece of business to go to Covent Garden Square in a hackney coach and take a turn with one's friend.

MRS FORESIGHT: Nay, two or three turns, I'll take my oath.

MRS FRAIL: Well, what if I took twenty? I warrant if you had been there, it had been only innocent recreation. – Lord, where's the comfort of this life, if we can't have the happiness of conversing where we like?

MRS FORESIGHT: But can't you converse at home? I own it, I think there's no happiness like conversing with an agreeable man; I don't quarrel at that, nor I don't think but your conversation was very innocent; but the place is public, and to be seen with a man in a hackney coach is scandalous. What if anybody else should have

29. *pelican* . . . *vitals*: pelicans were often portrayed as self-sacrificingly tearing their own breasts in order to feed their young.

seen you alight as I did? – How can anybody be happy, while they're in perpetual fear of being seen and censured? Besides, it would not only reflect upon you, sister, but me.

MRS FRAIL: Pooh, here's a clutter. Why should it reflect upon you? I don't doubt but you have thought yourself happy in a hackney coach before now. – If I had gone to Knightsbridge, or to Chelsea, or to Spring Garden, or Barn-Elms with a man alone, something might have been said.

MRS FORESIGHT: Why, was I ever in any of these places? What do you mean sister?

MRS FRAIL: Was I? What do you mean?

MRS FORESIGHT: You have been at a worst place.

MRS FRAIL: I at a worse place, and with a man!

MRS FORESIGHT: I suppose you would not go alone to the World's-End.[30]

MRS FRAIL: The world's end! What, do you mean to banter me?

MRS FORESIGHT: Poor innocent! You don't know that there's a place called the World's-End? I'll swear you can keep your countenance purely; you'd make an admirable player.

MRS FRAIL: I'll swear you have a great deal of impudence, and in my mind too much for the stage.

MRS FORESIGHT: Very well, that will appear who has most. You never were at the World's-End?

MRS FRAIL: No.

MRS FORESIGHT: You deny it positively to my face.

MRS FRAIL: Your face, what's your face?

MRS FORESIGHT: No matter for that; it's as good a face as yours.

MRS FRAIL: Not by a dozen year's wearing. – But I do deny it positively to your face then.

MRS FORESIGHT: I'll allow you now to find fault with my face; for I'll swear your impudence has put me out of countenance. But look you here now – where did you lose this gold bodkin? – O sister, sister!

MRS FRAIL: My bodkin!

---

30. *World's-End*: tavern in Chelsea. The other places mentioned were of an equally dubious reputation.

MRS FORESIGHT: Nay, 'tis yours, look at it.

MRS FRAIL: Well, if you go to that, where did you find this bodkin?
– O sister, sister! – Sister every way.

MRS FORESIGHT [aside]: O devil on't, that I could not discover her
without betraying myself!

MRS FRAIL: I have heard gentlemen say, sister, that one should take
great care when one makes a thrust in fencing, not to lie open
one's self.

MRS FORESIGHT: It's very true, sister. Well, since all's out, and as
you say, since we are both wounded, let us do that is often done in
duels, take care of one another, and grow better friends than
before.

MRS FRAIL: With all my heart; ours are but slight flesh wounds, and
if we keep 'em from air, not at all dangerous. Well, give me your
hand in token of sisterly secrecy and affection.

MRS FORESIGHT: Here 'tis with all my heart.

MRS FRAIL: Well, as an earnest of friendship and confidence, I'll
acquaint you with a design that I have. To tell truth, and speak
openly one to another, I'm afraid the world have observed us
more than we have observed one another. You have a rich
husband and are provided for; I am at a loss and have no great
stock either of fortune or reputation, and therefore must look
sharply about me. Sir Sampson has a son that is expected tonight,
and by the account I have heard of his education, can be no
conjurer; the estate, you know, is to be made over to him. – Now
if I could wheedle him, sister, ha? You understand me?

MRS FORESIGHT: I do; and will help you to the utmost of my
power. – And I can tell you one thing that falls out luckily enough:
my awkward daughter-in-law,[31] who you know is designed for
his wife, is grown fond of Mr Tattle; now if we can improve that,
and make her have an aversion for the booby, it may go a great
way towards his liking of you. Here they come together; and let
us contrive some way or other to leave 'em together.

[Enter TATTLE, and MISS PRUE.]

MISS PRUE: Mother, mother, mother, look you here.

31. *daughter-in-law*: step-daughter.

MRS FORESIGHT: Fie, fie, miss, how you bawl. Besides, I have told you, you must not call me mother.

MISS PRUE: What must I call you then? Are not you my father's wife?

MRS FORESIGHT: Madam; you must say madam. By my soul, I shall fancy myself old indeed, to have this great girl call me mother. – Well, but miss, what are you so overjoyed at?

MISS PRUE: Look you here, madam, then, what Mr Tattle has given me. – Look you here, cousin, here's a snuff-box; nay, there's snuff in't; – here, will you have any? – Oh good! How sweet it is. – Mr Tattle is all over sweet, his peruke is sweet and his gloves are sweet, and his handkerchief is sweet, pure sweet, sweeter than roses. – Smell him mother – madam, I mean. He gave me this ring for a kiss.

TATTLE: O fie, miss, you must not kiss and tell.

MISS PRUE: Yes; I may tell my mother. – And he says he'll give me something to make me smell so. Oh pray lend me your handkerchief. – Smell, cousin; he says he'll give me something that will make my smocks smell this way. Is not it pure? – It's better than lavender, mun. I'm resolved I won't let nurse put any more lavender among my smocks – ha, cousin?

MRS FRAIL: Fie, miss; amongst your linen, you must say. You must never say smock.

MISS PRUE: Why, it is not bawdy, is it, cousin?

TATTLE: Oh madam, you are too severe upon miss; you must not find fault with her pretty simplicity, it becomes her strangely. – Pretty miss, don't let 'em persuade you out of your innocency.

MRS FORESIGHT: Oh, demm you, toad – I wish you don't persuade her out of her innocency.

TATTLE: Who I, madam? O Lord, how can your ladyship have such a thought? Sure, you don't know me.

MRS FRAIL: Ah devil, sly devil. – He's as close, sister, as a confessor. He thinks we don't observe him.

MRS FORESIGHT: A cunning cur; how soon he could find out a fresh harmless creature, and left us, sister, presently.

TATTLE: Upon reputation –

MRS FORESIGHT: They're all so, sister, these men. – They love to have the spoiling of a young thing; they are as fond of it, as of being first in the fashion, or of seeing a new play the first day. – I warrant it would break Mr Tattle's heart to think that anybody else should be beforehand with him.

TATTLE: O Lord, I swear I would not for the world –

MRS FRAIL: O hang you; who'll believe you? You'd be hanged before you'd confess. – We know you. – She's very pretty! Lord, what pure red and white! She looks so wholesome; ne'er stir, I don't know, but I fancy, if I were a man –

MISS PRUE: How you love to jeer one, cousin.

MRS FORESIGHT: Heark'ee, sister, by my soul, the girl is spoiled already. D'ye think she'll ever endure a great lubberly tarpaulin? Gad, I warrant you, she won't let him come near her, after Mr Tattle.

MRS FRAIL: O' my soul, I'm afraid not. Eh! filthy creature, that smells all of pitch and tar. – Devil take you, you confounded toad – why did you see her before she was married?

MRS FORESIGHT: Nay, why did we let him? My husband will hang us. – He'll think we brought 'em acquainted.

MRS FRAIL: Come, faith, let us be gone. If my brother Foresight should find us with them, he'd think so, sure enough.

MRS FORESIGHT: So he would – but then, leaving 'em together is as bad. And he's such a sly devil, he'll never miss an opportunity.

MRS FRAIL: I don't care; I won't be seen in't.

MRS FORESIGHT: Well, if you should, Mr Tattle, you'll have a world to answer for. Remember I wash my hands of it; I'm thoroughly innocent.

[*Exeunt* MRS FORESIGHT *and* MRS FRAIL.]

MISS PRUE: What makes 'em go away, Mr Tattle? What do they mean, do you know?

TATTLE: Yes, my dear – I think I can guess. But hang me if I know the reason of it.

MISS PRUE: Come, must not we go too?

TATTLE: No, no, they don't mean that.

MISS PRUE: No! What then? What shall you and I do together?

TATTLE: I must make love to you, pretty miss; will you let me make love to you?

MISS PRUE: Yes, if you please.

TATTLE [*aside*]: Frank, egad, at least. What a pox does Mrs Foresight mean by this civility? Is it to make a fool of me? Or does she leave us together out of good morality, and do as she would be done by? Gad, I'll understand it so.

MISS PRUE: Well, and how will you make love to me? Come, I long to have you begin. Must I make love too? You must tell me how.

TATTLE: You must let me speak miss, you must not speak first; I must ask you questions, and you must answer.

MISS PRUE: What, is it like the catechism? – Come then, ask me.

TATTLE: D'ye think you can love me?

MISS PRUE: Yes.

TATTLE: Pooh, pox, you must not say yes already; I shan't care a farthing for you then in a twinkling.

MISS PRUE: What must I say then?

TATTLE: Why you must say no, or you believe not, or you can't tell –

MISS PRUE: Why, must I tell a lie then?

TATTLE: Yes, if you would be well-bred. All well-bred persons lie. – Besides, you are a woman, you must never speak what you think; your words must contradict your thoughts; but your actions may contradict your words. So, when I ask you if you can love me, you must say no, but you must love me too. If I tell you you are handsome, you must deny it, and say I flatter you. But you must think yourself more charming than I speak you, and like me for the beauty which I say you have as much as if I had it myself. If I ask you to kiss me, you must be angry, but you must not refuse me. If I ask you for more, you must be more angry – but more complying; and as soon as ever I make you say you'll cry out, you must be sure to hold your tongue.

MISS PRUE: O Lord, I swear this is pure. I like it better than our old-fashioned country way of speaking one's mind; – and must not you lie too?

TATTLE: Hum – yes – but you must believe I speak truth.

MISS PRUE: O Gemini! Well, I always had a great mind to tell lies – but they frighted me, and said it was a sin.

TATTLE: Well, my pretty creature; will you make me happy by giving me a kiss?

MISS PRUE: No, indeed; I'm angry at you.

[*Runs and kisses him.*]

TATTLE: Hold, hold, that's pretty well, but you should not have given it me, but have suffered me to take it.

MISS PRUE: Well, we'll do it again.

TATTLE: With all my heart. Now then, my little angel.

[*Kisses her.*]

MISS PRUE: Pish.

TATTLE: That's right. – Again, my charmer.

[*Kisses again.*]

MISS PRUE: O fie, nay, now I can't abide you.

TATTLE: Admirable! That was as well as if you had been born and bred in Covent Garden all the days of your life. And won't you show me, pretty miss, where your bed chamber is?

MISS PRUE: No, indeed won't I: but I'll run there, and hide myself from you behind the curtains.

TATTLE: I'll follow you.

MISS PRUE: Ah, but I'll hold the door with both hands, and be angry – and you shall push me down before you come in.

TATTLE: No, I'll come in first, and push you down afterwards.

MISS PRUE: Will you? Then I'll be more angry, and more complying.

TATTLE: Then I'll make you cry out.

MISS PRUE: Oh, but you shan't, for I'll hold my tongue. –

TATTLE: O my dear, apt scholar.

MISS PRUE: Well, now I'll run and make more haste than you.

[*Exit* MISS PRUE.]

TATTLE: You shall not fly so fast, as I'll pursue.

[*Exit after her.*]

ACT THREE

SCENE ONE

[*Enter* NURSE.]

NURSE: Miss, miss, Miss Prue. – Mercy on me, marry and amen:
why, what's become of the child? – Why miss, Miss Foresight.
Sure she has not locked herself up in her chamber and gone to
sleep, or to prayers. Miss, miss! I hear her. – Come to your father,
child; open the door. Open the door, miss. – I hear you cry husht.
O Lord, who's there? [*Peeps.*] What's here to do? – O the Father! a
man with her! Why, miss I say, God's my life, here's fine doings
towards. – O Lord, we're all undone. O you young harlotry.
[*Knocks.*] Od's my life, won't you open the door? I'll come in the
back way.

[*Exit.*]

[TATTLE *and* MISS PRUE *at the door.*]

MISS PRUE: O Lord, she's coming – and she'll tell my father. What
shall I do now?

TATTLE: Pox take her; if she had stayed two minutes longer, I
should have wished for her coming.

MISS PRUE: Oh dear, what shall I say? Tell me, Mr Tattle, tell me a
lie.

TATTLE: There's no occasion for a lie; I could never tell a lie to no
purpose. But since we have done nothing, we must say nothing,
I think. I hear her. I'll leave you together, and come off as you
can.

[*Thrusts her in, and shuts the door.*]

[*Enter* VALENTINE, SCANDAL, *and* ANGELICA.]

ANGELICA: You can't accuse me of inconstancy; I never told you
that I loved you.

VALENTINE: But I can accuse you of uncertainty, for not telling me whether you did or no.

ANGELICA: You mistake indifference for uncertainty; I never had concern enough to ask myself the question.

SCANDAL: Nor good nature enough to answer him that did ask you; I'll say that for you, madam.

ANGELICA: What, are you setting up for good nature?

SCANDAL: Only for the affectation of it, as the women do for ill nature.

ANGELICA: Persuade your friend that it is all affectation.

VALENTINE: I shall receive no benefit from the opinion: for I know no effectual difference between continued affectation and reality.

TATTLE [coming up. Aside to SCANDAL]: Scandal, are you in private discourse, anything of secrecy?

SCANDAL: Yes, but I dare trust you; we were talking of Angelica's love for Valentine. You won't speak of it?

TATTLE: No, no, not a syllable. I know that's a secret, for it's whispered everywhere.

SCANDAL: Ha, ha, ha.

ANGELICA: What is, Mr Tattle? I heard you say something was whispered everywhere.

SCANDAL: Your love of Valentine.

ANGELICA: How!

TATTLE: No, madam, his love for your ladyship. – Gad take me, I beg your pardon – for I never heard a word of your ladyship's passion till this instant.

ANGELICA: My passion! And who told you of my passion, pray, sir?

SCANDAL: Why, is the devil in you? Did not I tell it you for a secret?

TATTLE: Gadso; but I thought she might have been trusted with her own affairs.

SCANDAL: Is that your discretion? Trust a woman with herself?

TATTLE: You say true, I beg your pardon; I'll bring all off. – It was impossible, madam, for me to imagine that a person of your ladyship's wit and gallantry could have so long received the passionate addresses of the accomplished Valentine, and yet remain insensible; therefore, you will pardon me if from a just weight of his merit, with your ladyship's good judgment, I formed the balance of a reciprocal affection.

VALENTINE: O the devil, what damned costive poet has given thee this lesson of fustian to get by rote?

ANGELICA: I dare swear you wrong him; it is his own. – And Mr Tattle only judges of the success of others from the effects of his own merit. For certainly Mr Tattle was never denied anything in his life.

TATTLE: O Lord! Yes indeed, madam, several times.

ANGELICA: I swear I don't think 'tis possible.

TATTLE: Yes, I vow and swear I have: Lord, madam, I'm the most unfortunate man in the world, and the most cruelly used by the ladies.

ANGELICA: Nay, now you're ungrateful.

TATTLE: No, I hope not – 'tis as much ingratitude to own some favours, as to conceal others.

VALENTINE: There, now it's out.

ANGELICA: I don't understand you now. I thought you had never asked anything, but what a lady might modestly grant, and you confess.

SCANDAL: So faith, your business is done here; now you may go brag somewhere else.

TATTLE: Brag! O heavens! Why, did I name anybody?

ANGELICA: No; I suppose that is not in your power; but you would if you could, no doubt on't.

TATTLE: Not in my power, madam! What does your ladyship mean, that I have no woman's reputation in my power?

SCANDAL [aside]: Oons, why you won't own it, will you?

TATTLE: Faith, madam, you're in the right; no more I have, as I hope to be saved; I never had it in my power to say anything to a lady's prejudice in my life. For as I was telling you madam, I have been the most unsuccessful creature living in things of that nature, and never had the good fortune to be trusted once with a lady's secret, not once.

ANGELICA: No?

VALENTINE: Not once, I dare answer for him.

SCANDAL: And I'll answer for him; for I'm sure if he had, he would have told me. I find, madam, you don't know Mr Tattle.

TATTLE: No indeed, madam, you don't know me at all I find: for sure my intimate friends would have known –

ANGELICA: Then it seems you would have told, if you had been trusted.

TATTLE: O pox, Scandal, that was too far put. – Never have told particulars, madam. Perhaps I might have talked as of a third person, or have introduced an amour of my own in conversation by way of novel; but never have explained particulars.

ANGELICA: But whence comes the reputation of Mr Tattle's secrecy, if he was never trusted?

SCANDAL: Why thence it arises – the thing is proverbially spoken, but may be applied to him – as if we should say in general terms, he only is secret who never was trusted: a satirical proverb upon our sex. There's another upon yours – as she is chaste, who was never asked the question. That's all.

VALENTINE: A couple of very civil proverbs, truly: 'tis hard to tell whether the lady or Mr Tattle be the more obliged to you. For you found her virtue upon the backwardness of the men; and his secrecy, upon the mistrust of the women.

TATTLE: Gad, it's very true, madam; I think we are obliged to acquit ourselves. And for my part – but your ladyship is to speak first –

ANGELICA: Am I? Well, I freely confess I have resisted a great deal of temptation.

TATTLE: And I, gad, I have given some temptation that has not been resisted.

VALENTINE: Good.

ANGELICA: I cite Valentine here, to declare to the court how fruitless he has found his endeavours, and to confess all his solicitations and my denials.

VALENTINE: I am ready to plead, not guilty for you; and guilty for myself.

SCANDAL: So, why this is fair, here's demonstration with a witness.

TATTLE: Well, my witnesses are not present. But I confess I have had favours from persons – but as the favours are numberless, so the persons are nameless.

SCANDAL: Pooh, pox, this proves nothing.

TATTLE: No? I can show letters, lockets, pictures, and rings, and if
there be occasion for witnesses, I can summon the maids at the
chocolate-houses, all the porters of Pall Mall and Covent Garden,
the door-keepers at the play-house, the drawers at Locket's,
Pontack's, the Rummer, Spring Garden;[1] my own landlady and
valet de chambre; all who shall make oath that I receive more letters
than the Secretary's Office,[2] and that I have more vizor-masks to
enquire for me than ever went to see the hermaphrodite, or the
naked prince.[3] And it is notorious that in a country church, once,
an enquiry being made who I was, it was answered, I was the
famous Tattle, who had ruined so many women.

VALENTINE: It was there, I suppose, you got the nickname of the
Great Turk.

TATTLE: True; I was called Turk-Tattle all over the parish. The next
Sunday all the old women kept their daughters at home, and the
parson had not half his congregation. He would have brought me
into the spiritual court, but I was revenged upon him, for he had a
handsome daughter whom I initiated into the science. But I
repented it afterwards, for it was talked of in town – and a lady of
quality that shall be nameless, in a raging fit of jealousy, came
down in her coach and six horses, and exposed herself upon my
account; gad, I was sorry for it with all my heart. – You know
whom I mean – you know where we raffled –

SCANDAL: Mum, Tattle.

VALENTINE: 'S'death, are not you ashamed?

ANGELICA: O barbarous! I never heard so insolent a piece of vanity.
Fie, Mr Tattle, I'll swear I could not have believed it. – Is this your
secrecy?

TATTLE: Gadso, the heat of my story carried me beyond my
discretion, as the heat of the lady's passion hurried her beyond her
reputation. But I hope you don't know whom I mean, for there
were a great many ladies raffled. – Pox on't, now could I bite off
my tongue.

•SCANDAL: No don't; for then you'll tell us no more. [Goes to the

1. Locket's etc.: drinking and eating places of the day.
2. Secretary's Office: Secretary of State's Office.
3. hermaphrodite . . . naked prince: popular shows in the 1690s.

door.] Come, I'll recommend a song to you upon the hint of my two proverbs, and I see one in the next room that will sing it.

TATTLE: For heaven's sake, if you do guess, say nothing. Gad, I'm very unfortunate.

[*Re-enter* SCANDAL, *with one to sing*.]

SCANDAL: Pray sing the first song in the last new play.

(*Song*)

Set by Mr John Eccles.[4]

A nymph and a swain to Apollo once prayed,
The swain had been jilted, the nymph been betrayed;
Their intent was to try if his oracle knew
E'er a nymph that was chaste, or a swain that was true.

2

Apollo was mute, and had like t' have been posed,[5]
But sagely at length he this secret disclosed:
He alone won't betray in whom none will confide,
And the nymph may be chaste that has never been tried.

[*Enter* SIR SAMPSON, MRS FRAIL, MISS PRUE, *and* SERVANT.]

SIR SAMPSON: Is Ben come? Odso, my son Ben come? Odd, I'm glad on't. Where is he? I long to see him. Now, Mrs Frail, you shall see my son Ben. Body o' me, he's the hopes of my family. I han't seen him these three years – I warrant he's grown. Call him in, bid him make haste. – I'm ready to cry for joy.

[*Exit* SERVANT.]

MRS FRAIL: Now miss, you shall see your husband.

MISS PRUE [*aside to* MRS FRAIL]: Pish, he shall be none of my husband.

MRS FRAIL: Hush. Well he shan't, leave that to me. – I'll beckon Mr Tattle to us.

ANGELICA: Won't you stay and see your brother?

VALENTINE: We are the twin stars[6] and cannot shine in one sphere: when he rises I must set. Besides, if I should stay, I don't know but

---

4. *John Eccles*: wrote the music for many plays of the period.
5. *posed*: perplexed.
6. *twin stars*: Castor and Pollux.

my father in good nature may press me to the immediate signing
the deed of conveyance of my estate, and I'll defer it as long as I
can. Well, you'll come to a resolution.

ANGELICA: I can't. Resolution must come to me, or I shall never
have one.

SCANDAL: Come, Valentine, I'll go with you; I've something in my
head to communicate to you.

[*Exit* VALENTINE *and* SCANDAL.]

SIR SAMPSON: What, is my son Valentine gone? What, is he
sneaked off, and would not see his brother? There's an unnatural
whelp! There's an ill-natured dog! What, were you here too,
madam, and could not keep him! Could neither love, nor duty,
nor natural affection oblige him? Odsbud, madam, have no more
to say to him; he is not worth your consideration. The rogue has
not a dram of generous love about him: all interest, all interest;
he's an undone scoundrel, and courts your estate. Body o' me, he
does not care a doit[7] for your person.

ANGELICA: I'm pretty even with him, Sir Sampson; for if ever I
could have liked anything in him, it should have been his estate
too. But since that's gone, the bait's off, and the naked hook
appears.

SIR SAMPSON: Odsbud, well spoken, and you are a wiser woman
than I thought you were; for most young women now-a-days are
to be tempted with a naked hook.

ANGELICA: If I marry, Sir Sampson, I'm for a good estate with any
man, and for any man with a good estate. Therefore, if I were
obliged to make a choice, I declare I'd rather have you than your
son.

SIR SAMPSON: Faith and troth, you're a wise woman, and I'm glad
to hear you say so; I was afraid you were in love with the
reprobate. Odd, I was sorry for you with all my heart. Hang him,
mongrel, cast him off; you shall see the rogue show himself and
make love to some desponding Cadua[8] of four score for susten-
ance. Odd, I love to see a young spendthrift forced to cling to an

7. *doit*: small Dutch coin of very little value.
8. *Cadua*: wealthy older woman.

old woman for support, like ivy round a dead oak. Faith, I do; I
love to see 'em hug and cotton together, like down upon a thistle.

[*Enter* BEN LEGEND *and* SERVANT.]

BEN: Where's father?

SERVANT: There, sir, his back's toward you.

SIR SAMPSON: My son Ben! Bless thee, my dear boy; body o' me,
thou are heartily welcome.

BEN: Thank you father, and I'm glad to see you.

SIR SAMPSON: Odsbud, and I'm glad to see thee; kiss me boy, kiss
me again and again, dear Ben.

   [*Kisses him.*]

BEN: So, so, enough father. – Mess, I'd rather kiss these gentlewomen.

SIR SAMPSON: And so thou shalt. – Mrs Angelica, my son Ben.

BEN: Forsooth an you please. [*Salutes her.*] Nay mistress, I'm not for
dropping anchor here; about ship, i' faith –

   [*Kisses* MRS FRAIL.]

Nay, and you too, my little cock-boat[9] – so –

   [*Kisses* MISS PRUE.]

TATTLE: Sir, you're welcome ashore.

BEN: Thank you, thank you, friend.

SIR SAMPSON: Thou hast been many a weary league, Ben, since I
saw thee.

BEN: Ey, ey, been! Been far enough, an that be all. – Well father, and
how do all at home? How do's brother Dick, and brother Val?

SIR SAMPSON: Dick, body o' me, Dick has been dead these two
years; I writ you word when you were at Leghorn.

BEN: Mess, and that's true; marry I had forgot. Dick's dead as you
say – well, and how? I have a many questions to ask you. Well,
you ben't married again, father, be you?

SIR SAMPSON: No, I intend you shall marry, Ben; I would not
marry for thy sake.

BEN: Nay, what does that signify? An you marry again – why then,
I'll go to sea again, so there's one for t'other, an that be all. Pray
don't let me be your hindrance; e'en marry a God's name, an the

9. *cock-boat*: small ship's-boat.

wind sit that way. As for my part, mayhap I have no mind to marry.

MRS FRAIL: That would be pity, such a handsome young gentleman.

BEN: Handsome! he, he he, nay forsooth, an you be for joking, I'll joke with you, for I love my jest, an the ship were sinking, as we sayn at sea. But I'll tell you why I don't much stand towards matrimony. I love to roam about from port to port, and from land to land: I could never abide to be port-bound as we call it. Now a man that is married has, as it were, d'ye see, his feet in the bilboes,[10] and mayhap mayn't get 'em out again when he would.

SIR SAMPSON: Ben's a wag.

BEN: A man that is married, d'ye see, is no more like another man than a galley slave is like one of us free sailors; he is chained to an oar all his life, and mayhap forced to tug a leaky vessel into the bargain.

SIR SAMPSON: A very wag, Ben's a very wag; only a little rough, he wants a little polishing.

MRS FRAIL: Not at all; I like his humour mightily, it's plain and honest. I should like such a humour in a husband extremely.

BEN: Say'n you so, forsooth? Marry and I should like such a handsome gentlewoman for a bed fellow hugely. How say you mistress, would you like going to sea? Mess, you're a tight vessel and well rigged, an you were but as well manned.

MRS FRAIL: I should not doubt that, if you were master of me.

BEN: But I'll tell you one thing, an you come to sea in a high wind, or that lady, you mayn't carry so much sail o' your head – top and top-gallant, by the mess.

MRS FRAIL: No, why so?

BEN: Why, an you do, you may run the risk to be overset, and then you'll carry your keels above water, he, he, he.

ANGELICA: I swear, Mr Benjamin is the veriest wag in nature; an absolute sea-wit.

SIR SAMPSON: Nay, Ben has parts, but as I told you before, they want a little polishing: you must not take anything ill, madam.

10. *bilboes*: fetters.

BEN: No, I hope the gentlewoman is not angry; I mean all in good part: for if I give a jest, I'll take a jest. And so forsooth you may be as free with me.

ANGELICA: I thank you, sir, I am not at all offended; but methinks, Sir Sampson, you should leave him alone with his mistress. Mr Tattle, we must not hinder lovers.

TATTLE [*aside to* MISS PRUE]: Well miss, I have your promise.

SIR SAMPSON: Body o' me, madam, you say true. Look you Ben; this is your mistress. – Come miss, you must not be shame-faced; we'll leave you together.

MISS PRUE: I can't abide to be left alone. Mayn't my cousin stay with me?

SIR SAMPSON: No, no. Come, let's away.

BEN: Look you father, mayhap the young woman mayn't take a liking to me.

SIR SAMPSON: I warrant thee, boy. Come, come, we'll be gone; I'll venture that.

[*Exeunt all but* BEN *and* MISS PRUE.]

BEN: Come mistress, will you please to sit down, for an you stand a stern a that'n, we shall never grapple together. – Come, I'll haul a chair; there, an you please to sit, I'll sit by you.

MISS PRUE: You need not sit so near one; if you have anything to say, I can hear you farther off, I an't deaf.

BEN: Why, that's true, as you say, nor I an't dumb; I can be heard as far as another. – I'll heave off to please you.

[*Sits further off.*]

An we were a league asunder, I'd undertake to hold discourse with you, an 'twere not a main high wind indeed, and full in my teeth. Look you forsooth, I am, as it were, bound for the land of matrimony; 'tis a voyage d'ye see that was none of my seeking. I was commanded by father, and if you like of it, mayhap I may steer into your harbour. How say you, mistress? The short of the thing is this, that if you like me, and I like you, we may chance to swing in a hammock together.

MISS PRUE: I don't know what to say to you, nor I don't care to speak with you at all.

BEN: No? I'm sorry for that. But pray, why are you so scornful?

MISS PRUE: As long as one must not speak one's mind, one had better not speak at all, I think, and truly I won't tell a lie for the matter.

BEN: Nay, you say true in that, it's but a folly to lie. For to speak one thing, and to think just the contrary way is, as it were, to look one way, and to row another. Now, for my part, d'ye see, I'm for carrying things above board, I'm not for keeping anything under hatches; – so that if you ben't as willing as I, say so, a God's name, there's no harm done; mayhap you may be shame-faced; some maidens tho'f they love a man well enough, yet they don't care to tell'n so to's face. If that's the case, why, silence gives consent.

MISS PRUE: But I'm sure it is not so, for I'll speak sooner than you should believe that; and I'll speak truth, though one should always tell a lie to a man; and I don't care, let my father do what he will; I'm too big to be whipped, so I'll tell you plainly, I don't like you, nor love you at all, nor never will, that's more: so, there's your answer for you, and don't trouble me no more, you ugly thing.

BEN: Look you, young woman, you may learn to give good words, however. I spoke you fair, d'ye see, and civil. – As for your love or your liking, I don't value it of a rope's end; and mayhap I like you as little as you do me. What I said was in obedience to father; gad, I fear a whipping no more than you do. But I tell you one thing, if you should give such language at sea, you'd have a cat-o'-nine-tails laid cross your shoulders. Flesh! who are you? You heard t'other handsome young woman speak civilly to me, of her own accord. Whatever you think of yourself, gad, I don't think you are any more to compare to her than a can of small-beer to a bowl of punch.

MISS PRUE: Well, and there's a handsome gentleman, and a fine gentleman, and a sweet gentleman, that was here that loves me, and I love him; and if he sees you speak to me any more, he'll thrash your jacket for you, he will, you great sea-calf.

BEN: What, do you mean that fair-weather spark that was here just now? Will he thrash my jacket? – Let'n, let'n. – But an he comes near me, mayhap I may giv'n a salt eel[11] for's supper, for all that.

---

11. *salt eel*: rope's end; a flogging.

What do's father mean to leave me alone as soon as I come home with such a dirty dowdy. – Sea-calf? I an't calf enough to lick your chalked face, you cheese-curd you. – Marry thee! Oons, I'll marry a Lapland witch as soon, and live upon selling of contrary winds and wracked vessels.

MISS PRUE: I won't be called names, nor I won't abused thus, so I won't – if I were a man, [cries] you durst not talk at this rate – no you durst not, you stinking tar-barrel.

[Enter MRS FORESIGHT and MRS FRAIL.]

MRS FORESIGHT: They have quarrelled just as we could wish.

BEN: Tar-barrel? Let your sweet-heart there call me so, if he'll take your part, your Tom Essence,[12] and I'll say something to him; gad, I'll lace his musk-doublet for him, I'll make him stink; he shall smell more like a weasel than a civet-cat afore I ha' done with 'en.

MRS FORESIGHT: Bless me, what's the matter? Miss – what, does she cry? – Mr Benjamin, what have you done to her?

BEN: Let her cry: the more she cries, the less she'll – she has been gathering foul weather in her mouth, and now it rains out at her eyes.

MRS FORESIGHT: Come, miss, come along with me, and tell me, poor child.

MRS FRAIL: Lord, what shall we do? There's my brother Foresight and Sir Sampson coming. Sister, do you take miss down into the parlour, and I'll carry Mr Benjamin into my chamber, for they must not know that they are fallen out. Come, sir, will you venture yourself with me?

[Looks kindly on him.]

BEN: Venture, mess, and that I will, though 'twere to sea in a storm.

[Exeunt.]

[Enter SIR SAMPSON and FORESIGHT.]

SIR SAMPSON: I left 'em together here. What, are they gone? Ben's a brisk boy: he has got her into a corner, father's own son; faith, he'll tousle her and mousle her: the rogue's sharp set, coming

12. *Tom Essence*: character in Thomas Rawlins' *Tom Essence: or, The Modish Wife* (1676).

from sea. If he should not stay for saying grace, old Foresight, but fall too without the help of a parson, ha? Odd, if he should, I could not be angry with him; 'twould be but like me, a chip of the old block. Ha! thou'rt melancholy, old prognostication; as melancholy as if thou hadst spilt the salt, or pared thy nails of a Sunday. – Come, cheer up, look about thee. Look up, old star-gazer. Now is he poring upon the ground for a crooked pin, or an old horse-nail with the head towards him.

FORESIGHT: Sir Sampson, we'll have the wedding tomorrow morning.

SIR SAMPSON: With all my heart.

FORESIGHT: At ten o'clock, punctually at ten.

SIR SAMPSON: To a minute, to a second; thou shall set thy watch, and the bridegroom shall observe its motions; they shall be married to a minute, go to bed to a minute; and when the alarm strikes, they shall keep time like the figures of St Dunstan's clock, and *consummatum est* shall ring all over the parish.

   [*Enter* SCANDAL.]

SCANDAL: Sir Sampson, sad news.

FORESIGHT: Bless us!

SIR SAMPSON: Why, what's the matter?

SCANDAL: Can't you guess at what ought to afflict you and him, and all of us, more than anything else?

SIR SAMPSON: Body o' me, I don't know any universal grievance, but a new tax and the loss of the Canary fleet.[13] Without popery should be landed in the West, or the French fleet were at anchor at Blackwall.[14]

SCANDAL: No. Undoubtedly Mr Foresight knew all this, and might have prevented it.

FORESIGHT: 'Tis no earthquake!

SCANDAL: No, not yet; nor whirlwind. But we don't know what it may come to. But it has had a consequence already that touches us all.

SIR SAMPSON: Why, body o' me, out with't.

13. *Canary fleet*: the British fleet that was seeking an engagement with the French off the coast of Spain and Africa.
14. *Blackwall*: dockyards on the Thames.

SCANDAL: Something has appeared to your son Valentine. He's
gone to bed upon't, and very ill. He speaks little, yet says he has a
world to say. Asks for his father and the wise Foresight; talks of
Raymond Lully,[15] and the ghost of Lilly.[16] He has secrets to
impart, I suppose, to you two. I can get nothing out of him but
sighs. He desires he may see you in the morning, but would not be
disturbed tonight, because he has some business to do in a dream.

SIR SAMPSON: Hoity toity, what have I to do with his dreams or his
divination? Body o' me, this is a trick to defer signing the
conveyance. I warrant the devil will tell him in a dream that he
must not part with his estate: but I'll bring him a parson to tell him
that the devil's a liar. – Or if that won't do, I'll bring a lawyer that
shall out-lie the devil. And so I'll try whether my black-guard or
his shall get the better of the day.
  [Exit.]

SCANDAL: Alas, Mr Foresight, I'm afraid all is not right. – You are a
wise man, and a conscientious man; a searcher into obscurity and
futurity; and if you commit an error, it is with a great deal of
consideration, and discretion, and caution.

FORESIGHT: Ah, good Mr Scandal –

SCANDAL: Nay, nay, 'tis manifest; I do not flatter you. But Sir
Sampson is hasty, very hasty; I'm afraid he is not scrupulous
enough, Mr Foresight. He has been wicked, and heaven grant he
may mean well in his affair with you – but my mind misgives me,
these things cannot be wholly insignificant. You are wise, and
should not be over-reached, methinks you should not –

FORESIGHT: Alas Mr Scandal – *humanum est errare*.

SCANDAL: You say true, man will err; mere man will err – but you
are something more. There have been wise men; but they were
such as you: men who consulted the stars, and were observers of
omens. Solomon was wise, but how? – By his judgment in
astrology. So says Pineda[17] in his third book and eighth chapter –

FORESIGHT: You are learned, Mr Scandal.

15. *Raymond Lully*: the thirteenth-century philosopher and theologian.
16. *Lilly*: William Lilly, seventeenth-century English astrologer.
17. *Pineda*: Juan de Pineda (1558–1637). Spanish scholar who published a commentary on Solomon in 1609.

SCANDAL: A trifler – but a lover of art – and the wise men of the east
owed their instruction to a star, which is rightly observed by
Gregory the Great[18] in favour of astrology! And Albertus
Magnus[19] makes it the most valuable science, because, says he, it
teaches us to consider the causation of causes, in the causes of
things.

FORESIGHT: I protest I honour you, Mr Scandal – I did not think
you had read in these matters. Few young men are inclined –

SCANDAL: I thank my stars that have inclined me. But I fear this
marriage and making over this estate, this transferring of a
rightful inheritance, will bring judgments upon us. I prophesy it,
and I would not have the fate of Cassandra not to be believed.
Valentine is disturbed; what can be the cause of that? And Sir
Sampson is hurried on by an unusual violence. – I fear he does not
act wholly from himself; methinks he does not look as he used to
do.

FORESIGHT: He was always of an impetuous nature. But as to this
marriage, I have consulted the stars, and all appearances are
prosperous –

SCANDAL: Come, come, Mr Foresight, let not the prospect of
worldly lucre carry you beyond your judgment, nor against your
conscience. – You are not satisfied that you act justly.

FORESIGHT: How!

SCANDAL: You are not satisfied, I say. – I am loath to discourage
you, but it is palpable that you are not satisfied.

FORESIGHT: How does it appear, Mr Scandal? I think I am very well
satisfied.

SCANDAL: Either you suffer yourself to deceive yourself, or you do
not know yourself.

FORESIGHT: Pray explain yourself.

SCANDAL: Do you sleep well o'nights?

FORESIGHT: Very well.

SCANDAL: Are you certain? You do not look so.

FORESIGHT: I am in health, I think.

SCANDAL: So was Valentine this morning, and looked just so.

18. *Gregory the Great*: Pope, 590–604.
19. *Albertus Magnus*: scholastic philosopher of the thirteenth century.

FORESIGHT: How! Am I altered any way? I don't perceive it.

SCANDAL: That may be, but your beard is longer than it was two hours ago.

FORESIGHT: Indeed? Bless me!

[Enter MRS FORESIGHT.]

MRS FORESIGHT: Husband, will you go to bed? It's ten o'clock. Mr Scandal, your servant –

SCANDAL: Pox on her, she has interrupted my design. – But I must work her into the project. – You keep early hours, madam.

MRS FORESIGHT: Mr Foresight is punctual; we sit up after him.

FORESIGHT: My dear, pray lend me your glass, your little looking-glass.

SCANDAL: Pray lend it him, madam – I'll tell you the reason. [She gives him the glass; SCANDAL and she whisper.] My passion for you is grown so violent – that I am no longer master of myself. I was interrupted in the morning, when you had charity enough to give me your attention, and I had hopes of finding another opportunity of explaining myself to you, but was disappointed all this day; and the uneasiness that has attended me ever since brings me now hither at this unseasonable hour.

MRS FORESIGHT: Was there ever such impudence, to make love to me before my husband's face? I'll swear I'll tell him.

SCANDAL: Do; I'll die a martyr, rather than disclaim my passion. But come a little farther this way, and I'll tell you what project I had to get him out of the way, that I might have an opportunity of waiting upon you.

[Whisper.]

FORESIGHT [looking in the glass]: I do not see any revolution here. Methinks I look with a serene and benign aspect – pale, a little pale – but the roses of these cheeks have been gathered many years. Ha! I do not like that sudden flushing – gone already! – Hem, hem, hem! faintish. My heart is pretty good; yet it beats; and my pulses, ha! – I have none – mercy on me! – Hum – yes, here they are. Gallop, gallop, gallop, gallop, gallop, gallop, hey! Whither will they hurry me? – Now they're gone again. – And now I'm faint again; and pale again, and hem! and my hem! – breath, hem! – grows short; hem! hem! he, he, hem!

SCANDAL: It takes; pursue it in the name of love and pleasure.

MRS FORESIGHT: How do you do, Mr Foresight?

FORESIGHT: Hum, not so well as I thought I was. Lend me your hand.

SCANDAL: Look you there now. – Your lady says your sleep has been unquiet of late.

FORESIGHT: Very likely.

MRS FORESIGHT: Oh, mighty restless, but I was afraid to tell him so. He has been subject to talking and starting.

SCANDAL: And he did not use to be so.

MRS FORESIGHT: Never, never; till within these three nights, I cannot say that he has once broken my rest since we have been married.

FORESIGHT: I will go to bed.

SCANDAL: Do so, Mr Foresight, and say your prayers. He looks better than he did.

MRS FORESIGHT [calls]: Nurse, nurse!

FORESIGHT: Do you think so, Mr Scandal?

SCANDAL: Yes, yes, I hope this will be gone by morning, taking it in time.

FORESIGHT: I hope so.

[Enter NURSE.]

MRS FORESIGHT: Nurse, your master is not well; put him to bed.

SCANDAL: I hope you will be able to see Valentine in the morning. You had best take a little diacodion[20] and cowslip water, and lie upon your back; maybe you may dream.

FORESIGHT: I thank you, Mr Scandal, I will. – Nurse, let me have a watch-light, and lay the *Crumbs of Comfort*[21] by me.

NURSE: Yes, sir.

FORESIGHT: And – hem, hem! I am very faint.

SCANDAL: No, no, you look much better.

FORESIGHT: Do I? [*To* NURSE.] And d'ye hear – bring me, let me see – within a quarter of twelve – hem – he, hem! – just upon the turning of the tide, bring me the urinal; – and I hope neither the

20. *diacodion*: an opiate prepared from poppy heads.
21. *Crumbs of Comfort*: popular seventeenth-century work of devotion.

lord of my ascendant nor the moon will be combust,[22] and then I may do well.

SCANDAL: I hope so. Leave that to me; I will erect a scheme;[23] and I hope I shall find both Sol and Venus in the sixth house.

FORESIGHT: I thank you, Mr Scandal. Indeed, that would be a great comfort to me. Hem, hem! Good night.

[*Exit.*]

SCANDAL: Good night, good Mr Foresight; and I hope Mars and Venus will be in conjunction – while your wife and I are together.

MRS FORESIGHT: Well; and what use do you hope to make of this project? You don't think that you are ever like to succeed in your design upon me?

SCANDAL: Yes, faith I do; I have a better opinion both of you and myself than to despair.

MRS FORESIGHT: Did you ever hear such a toad? Heark'ee devil; do you think any woman honest?

SCANDAL: Yes, several, very honest; they'll cheat a little at cards, sometimes, but that's nothing.

MRS FORESIGHT: Pshaw! but virtuous, I mean.

SCANDAL: Yes, faith, I believe some women are virtuous too; but 'tis as I believe some men are valiant, through fear. – For why should a man court danger, or a woman shun pleasure?

MRS FORESIGHT: O monstrous! What are conscience and honour?

SCANDAL: Why, honour is a public enemy, and conscience a domestic thief; and he that would secure his pleasure, must pay a tribute to one, and go halves with the t'other. As for honour, that you have secured, for you have purchased a perpetual opportunity for pleasure.

MRS FORESIGHT: An opportunity for pleasure!

SCANDAL: Ay, your husband. A husband is an opportunity for pleasure, so you have taken care of honour, and 'tis the least I can do to take care of conscience.

MRS FORESIGHT: And so you think we are free for one another?

SCANDAL: Yes faith, I think so; I love to speak my mind.

22. *combust*: lacking in influence.
23. *erect a scheme*: cast a horoscope.

MRS FORESIGHT: Why then, I'll speak my mind. Now as to this affair between you and me. Here you make love to me; why, I'll confess it does not displease me. Your person is well enough, and your understanding is not amiss.

SCANDAL: I have no great opinion of myself; yet I think I'm neither deformed, nor a fool.

MRS FORESIGHT: But you have a villainous character; you are a libertine in speech as well as practice.

SCANDAL: Come, I know what you would say. You think it more dangerous to be seen in conversation with me, than to allow some other men the last favour. You mistake; the liberty I take in talking is purely affected for the service of your sex. He that first cries out stop thief, is often he that has stolen the treasure. I am a juggler that acts by confederacy; and if you please, we'll put a trick upon the world.

MRS FORESIGHT: Ay; but you are such an universal juggler – that I'm afraid you have a great many confederates.

SCANDAL: Faith, I'm sound.

MRS FORESIGHT: O, fie – I'll swear you're impudent.

SCANDAL: I'll swear you're handsome.

MRS FORESIGHT: Pish, you'd tell me so, though you did not think so.

SCANDAL: And you'd think so, though I should not tell you so: and now I think we know one another pretty well.

MRS FORESIGHT: O Lord, who's here?

[Enter MRS FRAIL, and BEN.]

BEN: Mess, I love to speak my mind. Father has nothing to do with me. – Nay, I can't say that neither; he has something to do with me. But what do's that signify? If so be that I ben't minded to be steered by him, 'tis as tho'f he should strive against wind and tide.

MRS FRAIL: Ay, but, my dear, we must keep it secret, till the estate be settled; for you know, marrying without an estate is like sailing in a ship without ballast.

BEN: He, he, he; why, that's true; just so for all the world it is indeed, as like as two cable ropes.

MRS FRAIL: And though I have a good portion, you know one would not venture all in one bottom.

BEN: Why that's true again; for mayhap one bottom may spring a leak. You have hit it indeed; mess, you've nicked the channel.

MRS FRAIL: Well, but if you should forsake me after all, you'd break my heart.

BEN: Break your heart? I'd rather the *Mary-gold* should break her cable in a storm, as well as I love her. Flesh, you don't think I'm false-hearted, like a landman? A sailor will be honest, tho'f mayhap he has never a penny of money in his pocket. Mayhap I may not have so fair a face as a citizen or a courtier, but for all that, I've as good blood in my veins, and a heart as sound as a biscuit.

MRS FRAIL: And will you love me always?

BEN: Nay, an I love once, I'll stick like pitch; I'll tell you that. Come, I'll sing you a song of a sailor.

MRS FRAIL: Hold, there's my sister; I'll call her to hear it.

MRS FORESIGHT: Well, I won't go to bed to my husband tonight, because I'll retire to my own chamber and think of what you have said.

SCANDAL: Well, you'll give me leave to wait upon you to your chamber-door, and leave you my last instructions?

MRS FORESIGHT: Hold, here's my sister coming toward us.

MRS FRAIL: If it won't interrupt you, I'll entertain you with a song.

BEN: The song was made upon one of our ship's crew's wife; our boatswain made the song; mayhap you may know her, sir. Before she was married, she was called buxom Joan of Deptford.

SCANDAL: I have heard of her.

[BEN *sings.*]

(*Ballad*)

Set by Mr John Eccles.

A soldier and a sailor,
A tinker, and a tailor,
Had once a doubtful strife, sir,
To make a maid a wife, sir,
   Whose name was buxom Joan.
For now the time was ended,
When she no more intended,

To lick her lips at men, sir,
And gnaw the sheets in vain, sir,
And lie o'nights alone.

2

The soldier swore like thunder,
He loved her more than plunder;
And showed her many a scar, sir,
That he had brought from far, sir,
 With fighting for her sake.
The tailor thought to please her,
With offering her his measure.
The tinker too with mettle,
Said he could mend her kettle,
And stop up ev'ry leak.

3

But while these three were prating,
The sailor slyly waiting,
Thought if it came about, sir,
That they should all fall out, sir;
 He then might play his part.
And just e'en as he meant, sir,
To loggerheads they went, sir,
And then he let fly at her,
A shot 'twixt wind and water,
 That won this fair maid's heart.

BEN: If some of our crew that came to see me are not gone, you shall
  see that we sailors can dance sometimes as well as other folks.
    [*Whistles.*]
  I warrant that brings 'em, an' they be within hearing.
    [*Enter* SEAMEN.]
  Oh, here they be – and fiddles along with 'em. Come my lads,
  let's have a round, and I'll make one.
    [*Dance.*]
  We're merry folk, we sailors; we han't much to care for. Thus we
  live at sea; eat biscuit and drink flip,[24] put on a clean shirt once a

24. *flip*: a warm, sweetened drink of beer and spirits.

quarter, come home and lie with our landladies once a year, get rid of a little money; and then put off with the next fair wind. How d'ye like us?

MRS FRAIL: Oh, you are the happiest, merriest men alive.

MRS FORESIGHT: We're beholding to Mr Benjamin for this entertainment. I believe it's late.

BEN: Why, forsooth, an you think so, you had best go to bed. For my part, I mean to toss a can and remember my sweet-heart a-fore I turn in; mayhap I may dream of her.

MRS FORESIGHT: Mr Scandal, you had best go to bed and dream too.

SCANDAL: Why faith, I have a good lively imagination, and can dream as much to the purpose as another, if I set about it. But dreaming is the poor retreat of a lazy, hopeless, and imperfect lover; 'tis the last glimpse of love to worn out sinners, and the faint dawning of a bliss to wishing girls and growing boys.

> There's nought but willing, waking love, that can
> Make blest the ripened maid, and finished man.

[*Exeunt.*]

ACT FOUR

SCENE ONE

Valentine's *lodging*.

[*Enter* SCANDAL *and* JEREMY.]

SCANDAL: Well, is your master ready? Does he look madly, and talk madly?

JEREMY: Yes, sir; you need make no great doubt of that; he that was so near turning poet yesterday morning can't be much to seek in playing the madman today.

SCANDAL: Would he have Angelica acquainted with the reason of his design?

JEREMY: No, sir, not yet. He has a mind to try whether his playing the madman won't make her play the fool, and fall in love with him; or at least own that she has loved him all this while and concealed it.

SCANDAL: I saw her take coach just now with her maid, and think I heard her bid the coachman drive hither.

JEREMY: Like enough, sir, for I told her maid this morning my master was run stark mad only for love of her mistress. I hear a coach stop; if it should be she, sir, I believe he would not see her till he hears how she takes it.

SCANDAL: Well, I'll try her. – 'Tis she, here she comes.

[*Enter* ANGELICA *with* JENNY.]

ANGELICA: Mr Scandal, I suppose you don't think it a novelty to see a woman visit a man at his own lodgings in a morning.

SCANDAL: Not upon a kind occasion, madam. But when a lady comes tyrannically to insult a ruined lover, and make manifest the cruel triumphs of her beauty, the barbarity of it something surprises me.

ANGELICA: I don't like raillery from a serious face. – Pray tell me what is the matter.

JEREMY: No strange matter, madam; my master's mad, that's all. I suppose your ladyship has thought him so a great while.

ANGELICA: How d'ye mean, mad?

JEREMY: Why faith, madam, he's mad for want of his wits, just as he was poor for want of money; his head is e'en as light as his pockets, and anybody that has a mind to a bad bargain can't do better than to beg him for his estate.

ANGELICA: If you speak truth, your endeavouring at wit is very unseasonable –

SCANDAL [aside]: She's concerned, and loves him.

ANGELICA: Mr Scandal, you can't think me guilty of so much inhumanity as not to be concerned for a man I must own myself obliged to – pray tell me truth.

SCANDAL: Faith, madam, I wish telling a lie would mend the matter. But this is no new effect of an unsuccessful passion.

ANGELICA [aside]: I know not what to think. – Yet I should be vexed to have a trick put upon me. [Aloud.] May I not see him?

SCANDAL: I'm afraid the physician is not willing you should see him yet. Jeremy, go in and enquire.

[Exit JEREMY.]

ANGELICA [aside]: Ha! I saw him wink and smile. I fancy 'tis a trick! I'll try. [Aloud.] – I would disguise to all the world a failing, which I must own to you. – I fear my happiness depends upon the recovery of Valentine. Therefore I conjure you, as you are his friend, and as you have compassion upon one fearful of affliction, to tell me what I am to hope for – I cannot speak. – But you may tell me; tell me, for you know what I would ask.

SCANDAL [aside]: So, this is pretty plain. [Aloud.] – Be not too much concerned, madam; I hope his condition is not desperate: an acknowledgment of love from you, perhaps, may work a cure, as the fear of your aversion occasioned his distemper.

ANGELICA [aside]: Say you so; nay, then I'm convinced: and if I don't play trick for trick, may I never taste the pleasure of revenge. [*Aloud.*] – Acknowledgment of love! I find you have mistaken my compassion, and think me guilty of a weakness I am a stranger to. But I have too much sincerity to deceive you, and too much charity to suffer him to be deluded with vain hopes. Good nature and humanity oblige me to be concerned for him; but to love is neither in my power nor inclination; and if he can't be cured without I suck the poison from his wounds, I'm afraid he won't recover his senses till I lose mine.

SCANDAL: Hey, brave woman, i' faith. – Won't you see him then, if he desire it?

ANGELICA: What signify a madman's desires? Besides, 'twould make me uneasy. If I don't see him, perhaps my concern for him may lessen. – If I forget him, 'tis no more than he has done by himself; and now the surprise is over, methinks I am not half so sorry for him as I was.

SCANDAL: So, faith, good nature works apace; you were confessing just now an obligation to his love.

ANGELICA: But I have considered that passions are unreasonable and involuntary; if he loves, he can't help it; and if I don't love, I can't help it; no more than he can help his being a man, or I my being a woman; or no more than I can help my want of inclination to stay longer here. – Come, Jenny.

[*Exit* ANGELICA *and* JENNY.]

SCANDAL: Humph! An admirable composition, faith, this same womankind.

[*Enter* JEREMY.]

JEREMY: What, is she gone, sir?

SCANDAL: Gone! Why, she was never here, nor anywhere else; nor I don't know her if I see her, nor you neither.

JEREMY: Good lack! What's the matter now? Are any more of us to be mad? Why, sir, my master longs to see her, and is almost mad in good earnest with the joyful news of her being here.

SCANDAL: We are all under a mistake. – Ask no questions, for I can't resolve you; but I'll inform your master. In the meantime, if our project succeed no better with his father than it does with his mistress, he may descend from his exaltation of madness into the road of common sense, and be content only to be made a fool with other reasonable people. I hear Sir Sampson; you know your cue. I'll to your master.

[*Exit.*]

[*Enter* SIR SAMPSON LEGEND *with* (BUCKRAM) *a lawyer.*]

SIR SAMPSON: D'ye see, Mr Buckram, here's the paper signed with his own hand.

BUCKRAM: Good, sir. And the conveyance is ready drawn in this box, if he be ready to sign and seal.

SIR SAMPSON: Ready, body o' me, he must be ready; his sham sickness shan't excuse him. – Oh, here's his scoundrel. Sirrah, where's your master?

JEREMY: Ah, sir, he's quite gone.

SIR SAMPSON: Gone! What, he is not dead?

JEREMY: No, sir, not dead.

SIR SAMPSON: What, is he gone out of town, run away, ha! Has he tricked me? Speak, varlet.

JEREMY: No, no, sir; he's safe enough, sir, an he were but as sound, poor gentleman. He is indeed here, sir, and not here, sir.

SIR SAMPSON: Hey day, rascal, do you banter me? Sirrah, d'ye banter me? Speak sirrah, where is he, for I will find him.

JEREMY: Would you could, sir, for he has lost himself. Indeed, sir, I have almost broke my heart about him. – I can't refrain tears when I think of him, sir; I'm as melancholy for him as a passing-bell, sir, or a horse in a pound.

SIR SAMPSON: A pox confound your similitudes, sir. – Speak to be understood, and tell me in plain terms what the matter is with him, or I'll crack your fool's skull.

JEREMY: Ah, you've hit it, sir; that's the matter with him, sir; his skull's cracked, poor gentleman; he's stark mad, sir.

SIR SAMPSON: Mad!

BUCKRAM: What, is he *non compos*?

JEREMY: Quite *non compos*, sir.

BUCKRAM: Why then all's obliterated, Sir Sampson. If he be *non compos mentis*, his act and deed will be of no effect; it is not good in law.

SIR SAMPSON: Oons, I won't believe it; let me see him, sir. – Mad! I'll make him find his senses.

JEREMY: Mr Scandal is with him, sir; I'll knock at the door.

> [*Goes to the scene, which opens and discovers* VALENTINE *upon a couch disorderly dressed,* SCANDAL *by him.*]

SIR SAMPSON: How now, what's here to do? –

VALENTINE [*starting*]: Ha! who's that?

SCANDAL: For heaven's sake softly, sir, and gently; don't provoke him.

VALENTINE: Answer me; who is that? and that?

SIR SAMPSON: Gads bobs, does he not know me? Is he mischievous? I'll speak gently. – Val, Val, dost thou not know me, boy? Not know thy own father, Val! I am thy own father, and this is honest Brief Buckram the lawyer.

VALENTINE: It may be so – I did not know you. – The world is full. – There are people that we do know, and people that we do not know; and yet the sun shines upon all alike. There are fathers that have many children, and there are children that have many fathers. – 'Tis strange! But I am Truth, and come to give the world the lie.

SIR SAMPSON: Body o' me, I know not what to say to him.

VALENTINE: Why does that lawyer wear black? Does he carry his conscience withoutside? Lawyer, what art thou? Dost thou know me?

BUCKRAM: O Lord, what must I say? – Yes, sir.

VALENTINE: Thou liest, for I am Truth. 'Tis hard I cannot get a livelihood amongst you. I have been sworn out of Westminster Hall[1] the first day of every term. – Let me see – no matter how long. – But I'll tell you one thing; it's a question that would puzzle an arithmetician if you should ask him: whether the Bible saves more souls in Westminster Abbey, or damns more in Westminster Hall. For my part, I am Truth, and can't tell; I have very few acquaintance.

SIR SAMPSON: Body o' me, he talks sensibly in his madness. – Has he no intervals?

JEREMY: Very short, sir.

BUCKRAM: Sir, I can do you no service while he's in this condition;

---

1. *Westminster Hall*: the principal law courts.

here's your paper, sir. – He may do me a mischief if I stay. – The conveyance is ready, sir, if he recover his senses.

[*Exit.*]

SIR SAMPSON: Hold, hold, don't you go yet.

SCANDAL: You'd better let him go, sir, and send for him if there be occasion, for I fancy his presence provokes him more.

VALENTINE: Is the lawyer gone? 'Tis well. Then we may drink about without going together by the ears[2] – heigh ho! What o'clock is't? My father here! Your blessing, sir?

SIR SAMPSON: He recovers. – Bless thee, Val – how dost thou do, boy?

VALENTINE: Thank you, sir, pretty well. – I have been a little out of order. Won't you please to sit, sir?

SIR SAMPSON: Aye, boy. – Come, thou shalt sit down by me.

VALENTINE: Sir, 'tis my duty to wait.

SIR SAMPSON: No, no, come, come, sit you down, honest Val. How dost thou do? Let me feel thy pulse – Oh, pretty well now, Val. Body o' me, I was sorry to see thee indisposed; but I'm glad thou'rt better, honest Val.

VALENTINE: I thank you, sir.

SCANDAL [*aside*]: Miracle! The monster grows loving.

SIR SAMPSON: Let me feel thy hand again, Val. It does not shake – I believe thou can'st write, Val: ha, boy? Thou canst write thy name, Val? [*In whisper to* JEREMY.] Jeremy, step and overtake Mr Buckram, bid him make haste back with the conveyance – quick – quick.

[*Exit* JEREMY.]

SCANDAL [*aside*]: That ever I should suspect such a heathen of any remorse!

SIR SAMPSON: Dost thou know this paper, Val? I know thou'rt honest and wilt perform articles.

[*Shows him the paper, but holds it out of his reach.*]

VALENTINE: Pray let me see it, sir. You hold it so far off that I can't tell whether I know it or no.

SIR SAMPSON: See it, boy? Ay, ay, why, thou dost see it – 'tis thy

2. *going together by the ears*: quarrelling.

own hand, Val. Why, let me see, I can read it as plain as can be: look you here. [*Reads.*] *The condition of this obligation* – look you, as plain as can be, so it begins. – And then at the bottom, *As witness my hand*, VALENTINE LEGEND, in great letters. Why, 'tis as plain as the nose in one's face. What, are my eyes better than thine? I believe I can read it farther off yet – let me see.

  [*Stretches his arm as far as he can.*]

VALENTINE: Will you please to let me hold it, sir?

SIR SAMPSON: Let thee hold it, say'st thou? Ay, with all my heart. – What matter is it who holds it? What need anybody hold it? – I'll put it up in my pocket, Val, and then nobody need hold it. [*Puts the paper in his pocket.*] There Val: it's safe enough, boy. – But thou shalt have it as soon as thou hast set thy hand to another paper, little Val.

  [*Re-enter* JEREMY *with* BUCKRAM.]

VALENTINE: What, is my bad genius here again! Oh no, 'tis the lawyer with an itching palm, and he's come to be scratched. – My nails are not long enough. – Let me have a pair of red-hot tongs quickly, quickly, and you shall see me act St Dunstan, and lead the devil by the nose.

BUCKRAM: O Lord, let me be gone; I'll not venture myself with a madman.

  [*Exit* BUCKRAM.]

VALENTINE: Ha, ha, ha, you need not run so fast; honesty will not overtake you. – Ha, ha, ha, the rogue found me out to be *in forma pauperis*[3] presently.

SIR SAMPSON: Oons! What a vexation is here! I know not what to do, or say, nor which way to go.

VALENTINE: Who's that, that's out of his way? – I am Truth, and can set him right. – Hearkee, friend, the straight road is the worst way you can go. – He that follows his nose always, will very often be led into a stink, *probatum est*. But what are you for? Religion or politics? There's a couple of topics for you, no more like one another than oil and vinegar; and yet those two beaten together by a state-cook make sauce for the whole nation.

3. *in forma pauperis*: not liable for legal costs because of poverty.

SIR SAMPSON: What the devil had I to do ever to beget sons? Why did I ever marry?

VALENTINE: Because thou wert a monster, old boy: the two greatest monsters in the world are a man and a woman. What's thy opinion?

SIR SAMPSON: Why, my opinion is that those two monsters joined together make yet a greater, that's a man and his wife.

VALENTINE: Aha! Old truepenny, say'st thou so? Thou hast nicked it – but it's wonderful strange, Jeremy.

JEREMY: What is, sir?

VALENTINE: That grey hairs should cover a green head – and I make a fool of my father.

[Enter FORESIGHT, MRS FORESIGHT, and MRS FRAIL.]

VALENTINE: What's here! Erra Pater?[4] or a bearded sybil? If Prophecy comes, Truth must give place.

[Exit with JEREMY.]

FORESIGHT: What says he? What, did he prophesy? Ha, Sir Sampson, bless us! How are we?

SIR SAMPSON: Are we? A pox o'your prognostication. Why, we are fools as we use to be. Oons, that you could not foresee that the moon would predominate, and my son be mad. – Where's your oppositions, your trines, and your quadrates? – What did your Cardan[5] and your Ptolemy tell you? Your Messahalah and your Longomontanus,[6] your harmony of chiromancy with astrology. Ah! pox on't, that I that know the world, and men and manners, that don't believe a syllable in the sky and stars, and sun and almanacs and trash, should be directed by a dreamer, an omen-hunter, and defer business in expectation of a lucky hour, when, body o' me, there never was a lucky hour after the first opportunity.

[Exit SIR SAMPSON.]

FORESIGHT: Ah, Sir Sampson, heaven help your head. – This is none of your lucky hour; nemo omnibus horis sapit.[7] What, is he

4. Erra Pater: term used for an astrologer.
5. Cardan: Girolamo Cardan (1501–76), Italian mathematician, astrologer and physician.
6. Longomontanus: Christian Longomontanus (1562–1647), Danish astronomer.
7. nemo . . . sapit: no one is wise at all times.

gone, and in contempt of science! Ill stars and unconverted ignorance attend him.

SCANDAL: You must excuse his passion, Mr Foresight, for he has been heartily vexed. His son is *non compos mentis*, and thereby incapable of making any conveyance in law; so that all his measures are disappointed.

FORESIGHT: Ha! say you so?

MRS FRAIL [*aside to* MRS FORESIGHT]: What, has my sea-lover lost his anchor of hope then?

MRS FORESIGHT: O sister, what will you do with him?

MRS FRAIL: Do with him? Send him to sea again in the next foul weather. – He's used to an inconstant element, and won't be surprised to see the tide turned.

FORESIGHT: Wherein was I mistaken, not to forsee this? [*Considers.*]

SCANDAL [*aside to* MRS FORESIGHT]: Madam, you and I can tell him something else that he did not foresee, and more particularly relating to his own fortune.

MRS FORESIGHT: What do you mean? I don't understand you.

SCANDAL: Hush, softly – the pleasures of last night, my dear, too considerable to be forgot so soon.

MRS FORESIGHT: Last night! And what would your impudence infer from last night? Last night was like the night before, I think.

SCANDAL: S'death, do you make no difference between me and your husband?

MRS FORESIGHT: Not much – he's superstitious, and you are mad, in my opinion.

SCANDAL: You make me mad. – You are not serious. – Pray recollect yourself.

MRS FORESIGHT: Oh yes, now I remember; you were very impertinent and impudent – and would have come to bed to me.

SCANDAL: And did not?

MRS FORESIGHT: Did not! With that face can you ask the question?

SCANDAL [*aside*]: This I have heard of before, but never believed. I have been told she had that admirable quality of forgetting to a man's face in the morning that she had lain with him all night, and denying favours with more impudence than she could

grant 'em. – Madam, I'm your humble servant, and honour you.
– You look pretty well, Mr Foresight. How did you rest last
night?

FORESIGHT: Truly Mr Scandal, I was so taken up with broken
dreams and distracted visions that I remember little.

SCANDAL: 'Twas a very forgetting night. – But would you not talk
with Valentine? Perhaps you may understand him; I'm apt to
believe there is something mysterious in his discourses, and
sometimes rather think him inspired than mad.

FORESIGHT: You speak with singular good judgment, Mr Scandal,
truly. – I am inclining to your Turkish opinion[8] in this matter, and
do reverence a man whom the vulgar think mad. Let us go in to
him.

MRS FRAIL: Sister, do you stay with them; I'll find out my lover and
give him his discharge, and come to you. O' my conscience, here
he comes.

[*Exeunt* FORESIGHT, MRS FORESIGHT *and* SCANDAL.]
[*Enter* BEN.]

BEN: All mad, I think. – Flesh, I believe all the calentures[9] of the sea
are come ashore, for my part.

MRS FRAIL: Mr Benjamin in choler!

BEN: No, I'm pleased well enough, now I have found you. – Mess,
I've had such a hurricane upon your account yonder.

MRS FRAIL: My account? Pray, what's the matter?

BEN: Why, father came and found me squabbling with yon chitty-
faced thing as he would have me marry – so he asked what was the
matter. – He asked in a surly sort of a way. (It seems brother Val is
gone mad, and so that put'n into a passion; but what did I know
that; what's that to me?) – So he asked in a surly manner, and gad I
answered as surlily. – What tho'f he be my father, I an't bound
prentice to en: so faith, I told 'n in plain terms, if I were minded to
marry, I'd marry to please myself, not him; and for the young
woman that he provided for me, I thought it more fitting for her
to learn her sampler, and make dirt-pies, than to look after a

8. *Turkish opinion*: mystical as opposed to scientific.
9. *calentures*: tropical fevers that can cause delirium.

husband; for my part I was none of her man. – I had another voyage to make, let him take it as he will.

MRS FRAIL: So then you intend to go to sea again?

BEN: Nay, nay, my mind run upon you, but I would not tell him so much. – So he said he'd make my heart ache, and if so be that he could get a woman to his mind, he'd marry himself. Gad, says I, an you play the fool and marry at these years, there's more danger of your head's aching than my heart. – He was woundy angry when I gav'n that wipe. – He had'nt a word to say, and so I left'n, and the green girl together. Mayhap the bee may bite, and he'll marry her himself, with all my heart.

MRS FRAIL: And were you this undutiful and graceless wretch to your father?

BEN: Then why was he graceless first? If I am undutiful and graceless, why did he beget me so? I did not get myself.

MRS FRAIL: O impiety! How have I been mistaken! What an inhuman merciless creature have I set my heart upon? Oh, I am happy to have discovered the shelves and quicksands that lurk beneath that faithless smiling face.

BEN: Hey toss! What's the matter now? Why, you ben't angry, be you?

MRS FRAIL: Oh, see me no more – for thou wert born amongst rocks, suckled by whales, cradled in a tempest, and whistled to by winds; and thou art come forth with fins and scales, and three rows of teeth, a most outrageous fish of prey.

BEN: O Lord, O Lord, she's mad, poor young woman! Love has turned her senses, her brain is quite overset. Well-a-day, how shall I do to set her to rights?

MRS FRAIL: No, no, I am not mad, monster; I am wise enough to find you out. – Had'st thou the impudence to aspire at being a husband with that stubborn and disobedient temper? – You that know not how to submit to a father, presume to have a sufficient stock of duty to undergo a wife? I should have been finely fobbed[10] indeed, very finely fobbed.

BEN: Hearkee forsooth; if so be that you are in your right senses,

10. *fobbed*: deceived.

d'ye see, for ought as I perceive I'm like to be finely fobbed – if I have got anger here upon your account, and you are tacked about already. What d'ye mean, after all your fair speeches, and stroking my cheeks, and kissing and hugging, what, would you sheer off so? Would you, and leave me aground?

MRS FRAIL: No, I'll leave you adrift, and go which way you will.

BEN: What, are you false-hearted then?

MRS FRAIL: Only the wind's changed.

BEN: More shame for you – the wind's changed? It's an ill wind blows nobody good. Mayhap I have good riddance on you, if these be your tricks. – What d'ye mean all this while, to make a fool of me?

MRS FRAIL: Any fool but a husband.

BEN: Husband! Gad, I would not be your husband if you would have me, now I know your mind, tho'f you had your weight in gold and jewels, and tho'f I loved you never so well.

MRS FRAIL: Why, canst thou love, porpoise?

BEN: No matter what I can do. Don't call names – I don't love you so well as to bear that, whatever I did. I'm glad you shew yourself, mistress: let them marry you as don't know you. – Gad, I know you too well, by sad experience; I believe he that marries you will go to sea in a hen-pecked frigate. – I believe that, young woman – and mayhap may come to an anchor at Cuckold's-point;[11] so there's a dash for you, take it as you will. Mayhap you may holla after me when I won't come to.

    [*Exit.*]

MRS FRAIL: Ha, ha, ha, no doubt on't. –

    [*Sings.*]

My true love is gone to sea. –

    [*Enter* MRS FORESIGHT.]

O sister, had you come a minute sooner, you would have seen the resolution of a lover. – Honest tar and I are parted; and with the same indifference that we met. O' my life, I am half vexed at the insensibility of a brute that I despised.

MRS FORESIGHT: What then, he bore it most heroically?

11. *Cuckold's-point*: on the Thames below Rotherhithe.

MRS FRAIL: Most tyranically, for you see he has got the start of me; and I, the poor forsaken maid, am left complaining on the shore. But I'll tell you a hint that he has given me: Sir Sampson is enraged, and talks desperately of commiting matrimony himself. – If he has a mind to throw himself away, he can't do it more effectually than upon me, if we could bring it about.

MRS FORESIGHT: Oh, hang him, old fox, he's too cunning; besides he hates both you and me. – But I have a project in my head for you, and I have gone a good way towards it. I have almost made a bargain with Jeremy, Valentine's man, to sell his master to us.

MRS FRAIL: Sell him, how?

MRS FORESIGHT: Valentine raves upon Angelica, and took me for her, and Jeremy says will take anybody for her that he imposes on him. – Now I have promised him mountains, if in one of his mad fits he will bring you to him in her stead, and get you married together, and put to bed together; and after consummation, girl, there's no revoking. And if he should recover his senses, he'll be glad at least to make you a good settlement. – Here they come. Stand aside a little, and tell me how you like the design.

[*Enter* VALENTINE, SCANDAL, FORESIGHT, *and* JEREMY.]

SCANDAL [*to* JEREMY]: And have you given your master a hint of their plot upon him?

JEREMY: Yes, sir; he says he'll favour it, and mistake her for Angelica.

SCANDAL: It may make sport.

FORESIGHT: Mercy on us!

VALENTINE: Husht – interrupt me not – I'll whisper prediction to thee, and thou shalt prophesy. – I am Truth, and can teach thy tongue a new trick. – I have told thee what's past, now I tell what's to come. Dost thou know what will happen tomorrow? – Answer me not, for I will tell thee. Tomorrow, knaves will thrive through craft, and fools through fortune; and honesty will go as it did, frost-nipped in a summer suit. Ask me questions concerning tomorrow.

SCANDAL: Ask him, Mr Foresight.

FORESIGHT: Pray, what will be done at court?

VALENTINE: Scandal will tell you; I am Truth, I never come there.

FORESIGHT: In the City?

VALENTINE: Oh, prayers will be said in empty churches at the usual hours. Yet you will see such zealous faces behind counters, as if religion were to be sold in every shop. Oh, things will go methodically in the City; the clocks will strike twelve at noon, and the horned herd buzz in the Exchange at two. Wives and husbands will drive distinct trades, and care and pleasure separately occupy the family. Coffee-houses will be full of smoke and stratagem. And the cropped 'prentice, that sweeps his master's shop in the morning, may, ten to one, dirty his sheets before night. But there are two things that you will see very strange; which are wanton wives, with their legs at liberty, and tame cuckolds, with chains about their necks. But hold, I must examine you before I go further; you look suspiciously. Are you a husband?

FORESIGHT: I am married.

VALENTINE: Poor creature! Is your wife of Covent Garden parish?

FORESIGHT: No; St Martin's in the Fields.

VALENTINE: Alas, poor man; his eyes are sunk, and his hands shrivelled; his legs dwindled, and his back bowed. Pray, pray, for a metamorphosis. – Change thy shape, and shake off age; get thee Medea's kettle[12] and be boiled a-new, come forth with labouring callous hands, a chine of steel, and Atlas' shoulders. Let Taliacotius[13] trim the calves of twenty chairmen, and make thee pedestals to stand erect upon, and look matrimony in the face. Ha, ha, ha! That a man should have a stomach to a wedding supper, when the pigeons ought rather to be laid to his feet,[14] ha, ha, ha.

FORESIGHT: His frenzy is very high now, Mr Scandal.

SCANDAL: I believe it is a spring tide.

FORESIGHT: Very likely truly; you understand these matters – Mr Scandal, I shall be very glad to confer with you about these things which he has uttered. – His sayings are very mysterious and hieroglyphical.

12. *Medea's kettle*: the cauldron in which Medea prepared the youth-restoring potion for Jason's father.
13. *Taliacotius*: Gasparo Tagliacozzi (1546–99), famous Italian surgeon.
14. *pigeons . . . feet*: so used as a cure for the plague.

VALENTINE: Oh, why would Angelica be absent from my eyes so long?

JEREMY: She's here, sir.

MRS FORESIGHT: Now, sister.

MRS FRAIL: O Lord, what must I say?

SCANDAL: Humour him, madam, by all means.

VALENTINE: Where is she? Oh, I see her. – She comes, like riches, health, and liberty at once, to a despairing, starving, and abandoned wretch. O welcome, welcome.

MRS FRAIL: How d'ye, sir? Can I serve you?

VALENTINE: Heark'ee, I have a secret to tell you – Endymion and the moon shall meet us upon Mount Latmos,[15] and we'll be married in the dead of night – but say not a word. Hymen shall put his torch into a dark lanthorn, that it may be secret; and Juno shall give her peacock poppy-water, that he may fold his ogling tail, and Argos's hundred eyes[16] be shut, ha? Nobody shall know but Jeremy.

MRS FRAIL: No, no, we'll keep it secret; it shall be done presently.

VALENTINE: The sooner the better. – Jeremy, come hither – closer – that none may overhear us. Jeremy, I can tell you news; Angelica is turned nun, and I am turning friar, and yet we'll marry one another in spite of the Pope. Get me a cowl and beads that I may play my part, for she'll meet me two hours hence in black and white, and a long veil to cover the project, and we won't see one another's faces till we have done something to be ashamed of; and then we'll blush once for all.

[Enter TATTLE, and ANGELICA.]

JEREMY: I'll take care, and –

VALENTINE: Whisper.

ANGELICA: Nay, Mr Tattle, if you make love to me, you spoil my design, for I intended to make you my confidant.

TATTLE: But, madam, to throw away your person, such a person! and such a fortune, on a madman!

15. Endymion . . . Latmos: Endymion was the shepherd with whom the moon fell in love while he was asleep on Mount Latmos.

16. Juno . . . eyes: Argos's hundred eyes were placed by Juno in the tail of the peacock.

ANGELICA: I never loved him till he was mad; but don't tell anybody so.

SCANDAL: How's this! Tattle making love to Angelica!

TATTLE: Tell, madam! Alas, you don't know me. I have much ado to tell your ladyship how long I have been in love with you – but encouraged by the impossibility of Valentine's making any more addresses to you, I have ventured to declare the very inmost passion of my heart. Oh, madam, look upon us both. There you see the ruins of a poor decayed creature; here, a complete and lively figure, with youth and health, and all his five senses in perfection, madam, and to all this, the most passionate lover –

ANGELICA: O fie, for shame, hold your tongue; a passionate lover, and five senses in perfection! When you are as mad as Valentine, I'll believe you love me, and the maddest shall take me.

VALENTINE: It is enough. Ha! Who's here?

MRS FRAIL [to JEREMY]: O Lord, her coming will spoil all.

JEREMY: No, no, madam, he won't know her. If he should, I can persuade him.

VALENTINE: Scandal, who are all these? Foreigners? If they are, I'll tell you what I think. [Whispers.] Get away all the company but Angelica, that I may discover my design to her.

SCANDAL: I will. – I have discovered something of Tattle that is of a piece with Mrs Frail. He courts Angelica. If we could contrive to couple 'em together. – Heark'ee –
    [Whisper.]

MRS FORESIGHT: He won't know you, cousin; he knows nobody.

FORESIGHT: But he knows more than anybody. O niece, he knows things past and to come, and all the profound secrets of time.

TATTLE: Look you, Mr Foresight, it is not my way to make many words of matters, and so I shan't say much – but in short, d'ye see, I will hold you a hundred pound now, that I know more secrets than he.

FORESIGHT: How! I cannot read that knowledge in your face, Mr Tattle. – Pray, what do you know?

TATTLE: Why d'ye think I'll tell you, sir! Read it in my face? No, sir, 'tis written in my heart. And safer there, sir, than letters writ in juice of lemon, for no fire can fetch it out. I am no blab, sir.

VALENTINE [*to* SCANDAL]: Acquaint Jeremy with it; he may easily
   bring it about. They are welcome, and I'll tell 'em so myself.
   [*Aloud.*] What, do you look strange upon me? – Then I must be
   plain. [*Coming up to them.*] I am Truth, and hate an old acquaintance with a new face.

   [SCANDAL *goes aside with* JEREMY.]

TATTLE: Do you know me, Valentine?

VALENTINE: You? Who are you? No, I hope not.

TATTLE: I am Jack Tattle, your friend.

VALENTINE: My friend, what to do? I am no married man, and thou
   can'st not lie with my wife; I am very poor, and thou can'st not
   borrow money of me; then what employment have I for a friend?

TATTLE: Hah! A good open speaker, and not to be trusted with a
   secret.

ANGELICA: Do you know me, Valentine?

VALENTINE: Oh, very well.

ANGELICA: Who am I?

VALENTINE: You're a woman – one to whom heaven gave beauty
   when it grafted roses on a briar. You are the reflection of heaven in
   a pond, and he that leaps at you is sunk. You are all white, a sheet
   of lovely spotless paper, when you first are born; but you are to be
   scrawled and blotted by every goose's quill. I know you; for I
   loved a woman, and loved her so long that I found out a strange
   thing: I found out what a woman was good for.

TATTLE: Aye, prithee, what's that?

VALENTINE: Why, to keep a secret.

TATTLE: O Lord!

VALENTINE: O exceeding good to keep a secret: for though she
   should tell, yet she is not to be believed.

TATTLE: Hah! good again, faith.

VALENTINE: I would have music – sing me the song that I like.

(Song)

Set by Mr Finger.[17]

I tell thee, Charmion, could I time retrieve,
And could again begin to love and live,
To you I should my earliest off'ring give;
  I know my eyes would lead my heart to you,
  And I should all my vows and oaths renew,
  But to be plain, I never would be true.

2

For by our weak and weary truth, I find,
Love hates to centre in a point assigned,
But runs with joy the circle of the mind.
  Then never let us chain what should be free,
  But for relief of either sex agree,
  Since women love to change, and so do we.

No more, for I am melancholy.

[*Walks musing.*]

JEREMY [*to* SCANDAL]: I'll do't, sir.

SCANDAL: Mr Foresight, we had best leave him. He may grow outrageous, and do mischief.

FORESIGHT: I will be directed by you.

JEREMY [*to* MRS FRAIL]: You'll meet, madam; I'll take care everything shall be ready.

MRS FRAIL: Thou shalt do what thou wilt, have what thou wilt; in short, I will deny thee nothing.

TATTLE [*to* ANGELICA]: Madam, shall I wait upon you?

ANGELICA: No, I'll stay with him – Mr Scandal will protect me. Aunt, Mr Tattle desires you would give him leave to wait on you.

TATTLE [*aside*]: Pox on't, there's no coming off, now she has said that. – Madam, will you do me the honour?

MRS FORESIGHT: Mr Tattle might have used less ceremony.

SCANDAL: Jeremy, follow Tattle.

17. *Mr Finger*: Gottfried Finger, a native of Moravia, settled in England around 1685.

[*Exeunt* FORESIGHT, MRS FORESIGHT, TATTLE, MRS FRAIL, *and* JEREMY.]

ANGELICA: Mr Scandal, I only stay till my maid comes, and because I had a mind to be rid of Mr Tattle.

SCANDAL: Madam, I am very glad that I overheard a better reason, which you gave to Mr Tattle; for his impertinence forced you to acknowledge a kindness for Valentine, which you denied to all his sufferings and my solicitations. So I'll leave him to make use of the discovery, and your ladyship to the free confession of your inclinations.

ANGELICA: Oh heavens! You won't leave me alone with a madman?

SCANDAL: No, madam; I only leave a madman to his remedy.
[*Exit* SCANDAL.]

VALENTINE: Madam, you need not be very much afraid, for I fancy I begin to come to myself.

ANGELICA [*aside*]: Ay, but if I don't fit[18] you, I'll be hanged.

VALENTINE: You see what disguises love makes us put on. Gods have been in counterfeited shapes for the same reason, and the divine part of me, my mind, has worn this mask of madness, and this motley livery, only as the slave of love, and menial creature of your beauty.

ANGELICA: Mercy on me, how he talks! Poor Valentine!

VALENTINE: Nay, faith, now let us understand one another, hypocrisy apart. – The comedy draws toward an end, and let us think of leaving acting and be ourselves; and since you have loved me, you must own I have at length deserved you should confess it.

ANGELICA [*sighs*]: I would I had loved you – for heaven knows I pity you; and could I have foreseen the sad effects, I would have striven; but that's too late.
[*Sighs.*]

VALENTINE: What sad effects? – What's too late? My seeming madness has deceived my father, and procured me time to think of means to reconcile me to him, and preserve the right of my inheritance to his estate, which otherwise by articles I must this

18. *fit*: punish.

morning have resigned: and this I had informed you of today, but you were gone before I knew you had been here.

ANGELICA: How! I thought your love of me had caused this transport in your soul, which, it seems, you only counterfeited for mercenary ends and sordid interest.

VALENTINE: Nay, now you do me wrong; for if any interest was considered, it was yours, since I thought I wanted more than love to make me worthy of you.

ANGELICA: Then you thought me mercenary. – But how am I deluded by this interval of sense, to reason with a madman?

VALENTINE: Oh, 'tis barbarous to misunderstand me longer.

[Enter JEREMY.]

ANGELICA: Oh, here's a reasonable creature. – Sure he will not have the impudence to persevere. – Come, Jeremy, acknowledge your trick, and confess your master's madness counterfeit.

JEREMY: Counterfeit, madam! I'll maintain him to be as absolutely and substantially mad, as any freeholder in Bethlehem;[19] nay, he's as mad as any projector, fanatic, chemist, lover, or poet in Europe.

VALENTINE: Sirrah, you lie; I am not mad.

ANGELICA: Ha, ha, ha, you see he denies it.

JEREMY: O Lord, madam, did you ever know any madman mad enough to own it?

VALENTINE: Sot, can't you apprehend?

ANGELICA: Why, he talked very sensibly just now.

JEREMY: Yes, madam, he has intervals: but you see he begins to look wild again now.

VALENTINE: Why you thick-skulled rascal, I tell you the farce is done, and I will be mad no longer.

[Beats him.]

ANGELICA: Ha, ha, ha, is he mad, or no, Jeremy?

JEREMY: Partly I think – for he does not know his mind two hours. – I'm sure I left him just now in a humour to be mad, and I think I have not found him very quiet at this present.

[One knocks.]

19. *Bethlehem*: the lunatic asylum of St Mary of Bethlehem or Bedlam.

Who's there?

VALENTINE: Go see, you sot. I'm very glad that I can move your mirth, though not your compassion.

[*Exit* JEREMY.]

ANGELICA: I did not think you had apprehension enough to be exceptious: but madmen show themselves most by over-pretending to a sound understanding, as drunken men do by over-acting sobriety. I was half inclining to believe you, till I accidentally touched upon your tender part; but now you have restored me to my former opinion and compassion.

[*Enter* JEREMY.]

JEREMY: Sir, your father has sent to know if you are any better yet. – Will you please to be mad, sir, or how?

VALENTINE: Stupidity! You know the penalty of all I'm worth must pay for the confession of my senses; I'm mad, and will be mad to everybody but this lady.

JEREMY: So, just the very backside of Truth. But lying is a figure in speech that interlards the greatest part of my conversation. – Madam, your ladyship's woman.

[*Goes to the door.*]

[*Enter* JENNY.]

ANGELICA: Well, have you been there? Come hither.

JENNY [*aside to* ANGELICA]: Yes, madam, Sir Sampson will wait upon you presently.

VALENTINE: You are not leaving me in this uncertainty?

ANGELICA: Would anything but a madman complain of uncertainty? Uncertainty and expectation are the joys of life. Security is an insipid thing, and the overtaking and possessing of a wish discovers the folly of the chase. Never let us know one another better, for the pleasure of a masquerade is done when we come to show faces. But I'll tell you two things before I leave you: I am not the fool you take me for; and you are mad and don't know it.

[*Exeunt* ANGELICA *and* JENNY.]

VALENTINE: From a riddle you can expect nothing but a riddle. There's my instruction, and the moral of my lesson.

[*Re-enter* JEREMY.]

JEREMY: What, is the lady gone again, sir? I hope you understood one another before she went.

VALENTINE: Understood! She is harder to be understood than a piece of Egyptian antiquity, or an Irish manuscript; you may pore till you spoil your eyes, and not improve your knowledge.

JEREMY: I have heard 'em say, sir, they read hard Hebrew books backwards; maybe you begin to read at the wrong end.

VALENTINE: They say so of a witch's prayer, and dreams and Dutch almanacs are to be understood by contraries. But there's regularity and method in that; she is a medal without a reverse or inscription, for indifference has both sides alike. Yet while she does not seem to hate me, I will pursue her, and know her if it be possible, in spite of the opinion of my satirical friend, Scandal, who says,

> That women are like tricks by sleight of hand,
> Which, to admire, we should not understand.

[*Exeunt.*]

ACT FIVE

SCENE ONE

A room in Foresight's *house.*

[*Enter* ANGELICA *and* JENNY.]

ANGELICA: Where is Sir Sampson? Did you not tell me he would be here before me?

JENNY: He's at the great glass in the dining room, madam, setting his cravat and wig.

ANGELICA: How! I'm glad on't. – If he has a mind I should like him, it's a sign he likes me; and that's more than half my design.

JENNY: I hear him, madam.

ANGELICA: Leave me, and d'ye hear, if Valentine should come, or send, I am not to be spoken with.

[*Exit* JENNY.]

[*Enter* SIR SAMPSON.]

SIR SAMPSON: I have not been honoured with the commands of a fair lady a great while – odd, madam, you have revived me – not since I was five and thirty.

ANGELICA: Why, you have no great reason to complain, Sir Sampson; that is not long ago.

SIR SAMPSON: Zooks, but it is, madam, a very great while, to a man that admires a fine woman as much as I do.

ANGELICA: You're an absolute courtier, Sir Sampson.

SIR SAMPSON: Not at all, madam; odsbud you wrong me; I am not so old, neither, to be a bare courtier, only a man of words. Odd, I have warm blood about me yet; I can serve a lady any way. – Come, come, let me tell you, you women think a man old too soon, faith and troth you do. – Come, don't despise fifty; odd, fifty, in a hale constitution, is no such contemptible age.

ANGELICA: Fifty a contemptible age! Not at all; a very fashionable age I think. – I assure you I know very considerable beaux that set a good face upon fifty. Fifty! I have seen fifty, in a side box by candle-light, out-blossom five and twenty.

SIR SAMPSON: O pox, outsides, outsides, a pize take 'em, mere outsides. Hang your side-box beaux; no, I'm none of those, none of your forced trees, that pretend to blossom in the fall, and bud when they should bring forth fruit. I am of a long-lived race, and inherit vigour; none of my family married till fifty, yet they begot sons and daughters till fourscore. I am of your patriarchs, I, a branch of one of your antideluvian families, fellows that the flood could not wash away. Well, madam, what are your commands? Has any young rogue affronted you, and shall I cut his throat? or –

ANGELICA: No, Sir Sampson, I have no quarrel upon my hands – I have more occasion for your conduct than your courage at this time. To tell you the truth, I'm weary of living single, and want a husband.

SIR SAMPSON: Odsbud, and 'tis pity you should. [Aside.] Odd, would she would like me, then I should hamper my young rogues; odd, would she would; faith and troth, she's devilish handsome. [Aloud.] Madam, you deserve a good husband, and 'twere pity you should be thrown away upon any of these young idle rogues about the town. Odd, there's ne'er a young fellow worth hanging – that is, a very young fellow. – Pize on 'em, they never think beforehand of anything; and if they commit matrimony, 'tis as they commit murder, out of a frolic; and are ready to hang themselves, or to be hanged by the law, the next morning. – Odso, have a care, madam.

ANGELICA: Therefore I ask your advice, Sir Sampson: I have fortune enough to make any man easy that I can like; if there were such a thing as a young, agreeable man, with a reasonable stock of good nature and sense – for I would neither have an absolute wit, nor a fool.

SIR SAMPSON: Odd, you are hard to please, madam; to find a young fellow that is neither a wit in his own eye, nor a fool in the eye of the world, is a very hard task. But, faith and troth, you speak very discreetly, for I hate both a wit and a fool.

ANGELICA: She that marries a fool, Sir Sampson, commits the reputation of her honesty or understanding to the censure of the world; and she that marries a very witty man, submits both to the severity and insolent conduct of her husband. I should like a man of wit for a lover, because I would have such an one in my power; but I would no more be his wife than his enemy. For his malice is not a more terrible consequence of his aversion, than his jealousy is of his love.

SIR SAMPSON: None of old Foresight's sibyls ever uttered such a truth. Odsbud, you have won my heart: I hate a wit; I had a son that was spoiled among 'em; a good hopeful lad, till he learned to be a wit – and might have risen in the state. – But, a pox on't, his wit run him out of his money, and now his poverty has run him out of his wits.

ANGELICA: Sir Sampson, as your friend, I must tell you, you are very much abused in that matter; he's no more mad than you are.

SIR SAMPSON: How, madam! Would I could prove it.

ANGELICA: I can tell you how that may be done. – But it is a thing that would make me appear to be too much concerned in your affairs.

SIR SAMPSON [aside]: Odsbud, I believe she likes me. [Aloud.] Ah, madam, all my affairs are scarce worthy to be laid at your feet; and I wish, madam, they stood in a better posture, that I might make a more becoming offer to a lady of your incomparable beauty and merit. – If I had Peru in one hand, and Mexico in t'other, and the Eastern empire under my feet, it would make me only a more glorious victim to be offered at the shrine of your beauty.

ANGELICA: Bless me, Sir Sampson, what's the matter?

SIR SAMPSON: Odd, madam, I love you – and if you would take my advice in a husband –

ANGELICA: Hold, hold, Sir Sampson. I asked your advice for a husband, and you are giving me your consent. – I was indeed thinking to propose something like it in a jest, to satisfy you about Valentine: for if a match were seemingly carried on between you and me, it would oblige him to throw off his disguise of madness in apprehension of losing me, for you know he has long pretended a passion for me.

SIR SAMPSON: Gadzooks, a most ingenious contrivance – if we were to go through with it. But why must the match only be seemingly carried on? Odd, let it be a real contract.

ANGELICA: O fie, Sir Sampson, what would the world say?

SIR SAMPSON: Say, they would say you were a wise woman, and I a happy man. Odd, madam, I'll love you as long as I live, and leave you a good jointure when I die.

ANGELICA: Ay, but that is not in your power, Sir Sampson; for when Valentine confesses himself in his senses, he must make over his inheritance to his younger brother.

SIR SAMPSON: Odd, you're cunning, a wary baggage! Faith and troth, I like you the better. But, I warrant you, I have a proviso in the obligation in favour of myself. – Body o' me, I have a trick to turn the settlement upon the issue male of our two bodies begotten. Odsbud, let us find children, and I'll find an estate.

ANGELICA: Will you? Well, do you find the estate, and leave the t'other to me –

SIR SAMPSON: O rogue! But I'll trust you. And will you consent? Is it a match then?

ANGELICA: Let me consult my lawyer concerning this obligation; and if I find what you propose practicable, I'll give you my answer.

SIR SAMPSON: With all my heart. – Come in with me, and I'll lend you the bond. – You shall consult your lawyer, and I'll consult a parson. Odzooks, I'm a young man; odzooks, I'm a young man, and I'll make it appear – odd, you're devilish handsome; faith and troth, you're very handsome, and I'm very young, and very lusty. – Odsbud, hussy, you know how to choose, and so do I. – Odd, I think we are very well met. – Give me your hand; odd, let me kiss it; 'tis as warm and as soft – as what? – odd, as t'other hand – give me t'other hand, and I'll mumble 'em, and kiss 'em till they melt in my mouth.

ANGELICA: Hold, Sir Sampson. – You're profuse of your vigour before your time. You'll spend your estate before you come to it.

SIR SAMPSON: No, no, only give you a rent-roll of my possessions – ah, baggage! – I warrant you, for little Sampson. Odd, Sampson's

a very good name for an able fellow; your Sampsons were strong
dogs from the beginning.

ANGELICA: Have a care, and don't overact your part. – If you
remember, the strongest Sampson of your name pulled an old
house over his head at last.

SIR SAMPSON: Say you so, hussy? Come, let's go then. Odd, I long
to be pulling down too, come away. – Odso, here's somebody
coming.

[*Exeunt.*]

[*Enter* TATTLE *and* JEREMY.]

TATTLE: Is not that she, gone out just now?

JEREMY: Ay, sir, she's just going to the place of appointment. Ah
sir, if you are not very faithful and close in this business, you'll
certainly be the death of a person that has a most extraordinary
passion for your honour's service.

TATTLE: Ay, who's that?

JEREMY: Even my unworthy self, sir. – Sir, I have had an appetite to
be fed with your commands a great while; and now, sir, my
former master, having much troubled the fountain of his understanding, it is a very plausible occasion for me to quench my thirst
at the spring of your bounty. – I thought I could not recommend
myself better to you, sir, than by the delivery of a great beauty and
fortune into your arms, whom I have heard you sigh for.

TATTLE: I'll make thy fortune; say no more. – Thou art a pretty
fellow, and canst carry a message to a lady in a pretty soft kind of
phrase, and with a good persuading accent.

JEREMY: Sir, I have the seeds of rhetoric and oratory in my head – I
have been at Cambridge.

TATTLE: Ay, 'tis well enough for a servant to be bred at an
university, but the education is a little too pedantic for a gentleman. I hope you are secret in your nature, private, close, ha?

JEREMY: O sir, for that, sir, 'tis my chief talent; I'm as secret as the
head of Nilus.[1]

TATTLE: Ay? Who's he, though? A Privy Counsellor?

JEREMY [*aside*]: O ignorance! [*Aloud.*] A cunning Egyptian, sir, that

_____

1. *head of Nilus*: the source of the Nile was then unknown.

with his arms would overrun the country, yet nobody could ever find out his head-quarters.

TATTLE: Close dog! A good whoremaster, I warrant him. – The time draws nigh, Jeremy. Angelica will be veiled like a nun, and I must be hooded like a friar, ha, Jeremy?

JEREMY: Ay, sir, hooded like a hawk, to seize at first sight upon the quarry. It is the whim of my master's madness to be so dressed; and she is so in love with him, she'll comply with anything to please him. Poor lady, I'm sure she'll have reason to pray for me, when she finds what a happy exchange she has made between a madman and so accomplished a gentleman.

TATTLE: Ay, faith, so she will, Jeremy; you're a good friend to her, poor creature. – I swear I do it hardly so much in consideration of myself, as compassion to her.

JEREMY: 'Tis an act of charity, sir, to save a fine woman with thirty thousand pound from throwing herself away.

TATTLE: So 'tis, faith. I might have saved several others in my time; but, i'gad, I could never find in my heart to marry anybody before.

JEREMY: Well, sir, I'll go and tell her my master's coming, and meet you in half a quarter of an hour, with your disguise, at your own lodgings. You must talk a little madly; she won't distinguish the tone of your voice.

TATTLE: No, no, let me alone for a counterfeit; I'll be ready for you.

[Enter MISS PRUE.]

MISS PRUE: O Mr Tattle, are you here! I'm glad I have found you; I have been looking up and down for you like anything, till I'm as tired as anything in the world.

TATTLE [aside]: O pox, how shall I get rid of this foolish girl?

MISS PRUE: Oh, I have pure news; I can tell you pure news. – I must not marry the seaman now – my father says so. Why won't you be my husband? You say you love me, and you won't be my husband. And I know you may be my husband now if you please.

TATTLE: O fie, miss; who told you so, child?

MISS PRUE: Why, my father – I told him that you loved me.

TATTLE: O fie, miss, why did you do so? And who told you so, child?

MISS PRUE: Who? Why you did; did not you?

TATTLE: O pox, that was yesterday, miss; that was a great while ago, child. I have been asleep since; slept a whole night, and did not so much as dream of the matter.

MISS PRUE: Pshaw! Oh, but I dreamt that it was so, though.

TATTLE: Ay, but your father will tell you that dreams come by contraries, child. – O fie; what, we must not love one another now; pshaw, that would be a foolish thing indeed. Fie, fie, you're a woman now, and must think of a new man every morning, and forget him every night. – No, no, to marry is to be a child again, and play with the same rattle always. O fie, marrying is a paw² thing.

MISS PRUE: Well, but don't you love me as well as you did last night, then?

TATTLE: No, no, child, you would not have me.

MISS PRUE: No? Yes, but I would, though.

TATTLE: Pshaw, but I tell you, you would not. – You forget you're a woman, and don't know your own mind.

MISS PRUE: But here's my father, and he knows my mind.

[Enter FORESIGHT.]

FORESIGHT: Oh, Mr Tattle, your servant. You are a close man, but methinks your love to my daughter was a secret I might have been trusted with – or had you a mind to try if I could discover it by my art – hum, ha? I think there is something in your physiognomy that has a resemblance of her; and the girl is like me.

TATTLE: And so you would infer that you and I are alike. [Aside.] What does the old prig mean? I'll banter him, and laugh at him, and leave him. [Aloud.] I fancy you have a wrong notion of faces.

FORESIGHT: How? What? A wrong notion! How so?

TATTLE: In the way of art. I have some taking features, not obvious to vulgar eyes, that are indications of a sudden turn of good fortune in the lottery of wives, and promise a great beauty and great fortune reserved alone for me, by a private intrigue of destiny, kept secret from the piercing eye of perspicuity, from all astrologers and the stars themselves.

2. *paw*: nasty, unbecoming.

FORESIGHT: How! I will make it appear that what you say is impossible.

TATTLE: Sir, I beg your pardon, I'm in haste —

FORESIGHT: For what?

TATTLE: To be married, sir, married.

FORESIGHT: Ay, but pray take me along with you, sir —

TATTLE: No, sir; 'tis to be done privately. – I never make confidants.

FORESIGHT: Well; but my consent, I mean. – You won't marry my daughter without my consent?

TATTLE: Who I, sir? I'm an absolute stranger to you and your daughter, sir.

FORESIGHT: Hey day! What time of the moon is this?

TATTLE: Very true, sir, and desire to continue so. I have no more love for your daughter than I have likeness of you; and I have a secret in my heart, which you would be glad to know, and shan't know; and yet you shall know it too, and be sorry for't afterwards. I'd have you to know, sir, that I am as knowing as the stars, and as secret as the night. – And I'm going to be married just now, yet did you know of it half an hour ago; and the lady stays for me, and does not know of it yet. – There's a mystery for you. – I know you love to untie difficulties. – Or, if you can't solve this, stay here a quarter of an hour, and I'll come and explain it to you.

[*Exit.*]

MISS PRUE: O father, why will you let him go? Won't you make him be my husband?

FORESIGHT: Mercy on us, what do these lunacies portend? Alas! he's mad, child, stark wild.

MISS PRUE: What, and must not I have e'er a husband then? What, must I go to bed to nurse again, and be a child as long as she's an old woman? Indeed, but I won't: for now my mind is set upon a man, I will have a man some way or other. Oh! methinks I'm sick when I think of a man; and if I can't have one, I would go to sleep all my life, for when I'm awake, it makes me wish and long, and I don't know for what – and I'd rather be always a-sleeping, than sick with thinking.

FORESIGHT: O fearful! I think the girl's influenced too. – Hussy, you shall have a rod.

MISS PRUE: A fiddle of a rod, I'll have a husband; and if you won't get me one, I'll get one for myself: I'll marry our Robin, the butler. He says he loves me, and he's a handsome man, and shall be my husband: I warrant he'll be my husband and thank me too, for he told me so.

[*Enter* SCANDAL, MRS FORESIGHT, *and* NURSE.]

FORESIGHT: Did he so? – I'll dispatch him for't presently. Rogue! – Oh, nurse, come hither.

NURSE: What is your worship's pleasure?

FORESIGHT: Here, take your young mistress, and lock her up presently, till farther orders from me. – Not a word hussy – do what I bid you; no reply, away. And bid Robin make ready to give an account of his plate and linen; d'ye hear, be gone when I bid you.

[*Exeunt* NURSE *and* MISS PRUE.]

MRS FORESIGHT: What's the matter, husband?

FORESIGHT: 'Tis not convenient to tell you now. – Mr Scandal, heaven keep us all in our senses; I fear there is a contagious frenzy abroad. How does Valentine?

SCANDAL: Oh, I hope he will do well again. I have a message from him to your niece Angelica.

FORESIGHT: I think she has not returned since she went abroad with Sir Sampson.

[*Enter* BEN.]

MRS FORESIGHT: Here's Mr Benjamin; he can tell us if his father be come home.

BEN: Who, father? Ay, he's come home with a vengeance.

MRS FORESIGHT: Why, what's the matter?

BEN: Matter! Why, he's mad.

FORESIGHT: Mercy on us, I was afraid of this.

BEN: And there's the handsome young woman, she, as they say, brother Val went mad for; she's mad too, I think.

FORESIGHT: O my poor niece, my poor niece, is she gone too? Well, I shall run mad next.

MRS FORESIGHT: Well, but how mad? How d'ye mean?

BEN: Nay, I'll give you leave to guess. – I'll undertake to make a voyage to Antegoa[3] – no, hold, I mayn't say so neither – but I'll sail as far as Ligorn[4] and back again, before you shall guess at the matter, and do nothing else; mess, you may take in all the points of the compass, and not hit right.

MRS FORESIGHT: Your experiment will take up a little too much time.

BEN: Why, then, I'll tell you: there's a new wedding upon the stocks, and they two are a-going to be married to rights.

SCANDAL: Who?

BEN: Why father and – the young woman. I can't hit of her name.

SCANDAL: Angelica?

BEN: Ay, the same.

MRS FORESIGHT: Sir Sampson and Angelica, impossible!

BEN: That may be – but I'm sure it is as I tell you.

SCANDAL: 'S'death it's a jest. I can't believe it.

BEN: Look you, friend, it's nothing to me, whether you believe it or no. What I say is true; d'ye see, they are married, or just going to be married, I know not which.

FORESIGHT: Well, but they are not mad, that is, not lunatic?

BEN: I don't know what you may call madness, but she's mad for a husband, and he's horn-mad, I think, or they'd ne'er make a match together. – Here they come.

[*Enter* SIR SAMPSON, ANGELICA, *with* BUCKRAM.]

SIR SAMPSON: Where is this old soothsayer, this uncle of mine elect? Aha, old Foresight, uncle Foresight, wish me joy, uncle Foresight, double joy, both as uncle and astrologer; here's a conjunction that was not foretold in all your Ephemeris.[5] The brightest star in the blue firmament – is shot from above, in a jelly of love,[6] and so forth, and I'm Lord of the Ascendant. Odd, you're an old fellow, Foresight; uncle I mean, a very old fellow,

3. *Antegoa*: Antigua.
4. *Ligorn*: Leghorn (Livorno, Italy).
5. *Ephemeris*: an astronomical almanac.
6. *is . . . love*: see act four of John Dryden's *Tyrannic Love*:
                              And drop from above
                              In a jelly of love!

uncle Foresight; and yet you shall live to dance at my wedding;
faith and troth you shall. Odd, we'll have the music of the spheres
for thee, old Lilly, that we will, and thou shalt lead up a dance in
Via Lactea.[7]

FORESIGHT: I'm thunderstruck! You are not married to my niece?

SIR SAMPSON: Not absolutely married, uncle, but very near it;
within a kiss of the matter, as you see.

  [Kisses ANGELICA.]

ANGELICA: 'Tis very true indeed, uncle; I hope you'll be my father,
and give me.

SIR SAMPSON: That he shall, or I'll burn his globes. Body o'me, he
shall be thy father, I'll make him thy father, and thou shalt make
me a father, and I'll make thee a mother, and we'll beget sons and
daughters enough to put the weekly bills out of countenance.

SCANDAL: Death and hell! Where's Valentine?

  [Exit SCANDAL.]

MRS FORESIGHT: This is so surprising –

SIR SAMPSON: How! What does my aunt say? Surprising, aunt?
Not at all, for a young couple to make a match in winter. Not at all
– it's a plot to undermine cold weather, and destroy that usurper
of a bed called a warming-pan.

MRS FORESIGHT: I'm glad to hear you have so much fire in you, Sir
Sampson.

BEN: Mess, I fear his fire's little better than tinder; mayhap it will
only serve to light up a match for somebody else. The young
woman's a handsome young woman, I can't deny it; but, father, if
I might be your pilot in this case, you should not marry her. It's
just the same thing as if so be you should sail so far as the Straits[8]
without provision.

SIR SAMPSON: Who gave you authority to speak, sirrah? To your
element, fish; be mute, fish, and to sea; rule your helm, sirrah,
don't direct me.

BEN: Well, well, take you care of your own helm, or you mayn't
keep your own vessel steady.

SIR SAMPSON: Why you impudent tarpaulin! Sirrah, do you bring

7. *Via Lactea*: the Milky Way.
8. *Straits*: of Gibraltar.

your forecastle jests upon your father? But I shall be even with you, I won't give you a groat. Mr Buckram, is the conveyance so worded that nothing can possibly descend to this scoundrel? I would not so much as have him have the prospect of an estate, though there were no way to come to it but by the North-East Passage.[9]

BUCKRAM: Sir, it is drawn according to your directions; there is not the least cranny of the law unstopped.

BEN: Lawyer, I believe there's many a cranny and leak unstopped in your conscience. If so be that one had a pump to your bosom, I believe we should discover a foul hold. They say a witch will sail in a sieve, but I believe the devil would not venture aboard o' your conscience. And that's for you.

SIR SAMPSON: Hold your tongue, sirrah. How now, who's there?

[*Enter* TATTLE *and* MRS FRAIL.]

MRS FRAIL: O sister, the most unlucky accident!

MRS FORESIGHT: What's the matter?

TATTLE: O, the two most unfortunate poor creatures in the world we are.

FORESIGHT: Bless us! How so?

MRS FRAIL: Ah, Mr Tattle and I, poor Mr Tattle and I are – I can't speak it out.

TATTLE: Nor I – but poor Mrs Frail and I are –

MRS FRAIL: Married.

MRS FORESIGHT: Married! How?

TATTLE: Suddenly – before we knew where we were – that villain Jeremy, by the help of disguises, tricked us into one another.

FORESIGHT: Why, you told me just now you went hence in haste to be married.

ANGELICA: But I believe Mr Tattle meant the favour to me; I thank him.

TATTLE: I did; as I hope to be saved, madam, my intentions were good. – But this is the most cruel thing, to marry one does not know how, nor why, nor wherefore. – The devil take me if ever I was so much concerned at anything in my life.

9. *North-East Passage*: route to the East over the top of Russia.

ANGELICA: 'Tis very unhappy, if you don't care for one another.

TATTLE: The least in the world – that is, for my part; I speak for myself. Gad, I never had the least thought of serious kindness – I never liked anybody less in my life. Poor woman! Gad, I'm sorry for her too, for I have no reason to hate her neither; but I believe I shall lead her a damned sort of a life.

MRS FORESIGHT [*aside to* MRS FRAIL]: He's better than no husband at all, though he's a coxcomb.

MRS FRAIL [*to her*]: Ay, ay, it's well it's no worse. [*Aloud.*] Nay, for my part I always despised Mr Tattle of all things; nothing but his being my husband could have made me like him less.

TATTLE: Look you there, I thought as much. – Pox on't, I wish we could keep it secret. Why, I don't believe any of this company would speak of it.

MRS FRAIL: But, my dear, that's impossible; the parson and that rogue Jeremy will publish it.

TATTLE: Ay, my dear, so they will, as you say.

ANGELICA: Oh, you'll agree very well in a little time; custom will make it easy to you.

TATTLE: Easy! Pox on't, I don't believe I shall sleep tonight.

SIR SAMPSON: Sleep, quotha! No, why you would not sleep o' your wedding night? I'm an older fellow than you, and don't mean to sleep.

BEN: Why, there's another match now, as tho'f a couple of privateers were looking for a prize, and should fall foul of one another. I'm sorry for the young man with all my heart. Look you, friend, if I may advise you – when she's going, for that you must expect, I have experience of her – when she's going, let her go. For no matrimony is tough enough to hold her, and if she can't drag her anchor along with her, she'll break her cable, I can tell you that. Who's here? the madman?

[*Enter* VALENTINE *dressed*, SCANDAL, *and* JEREMY.]

VALENTINE: No, here's the fool; and if occasion be, I'll give it under my hand.

SIR SAMPSON: How now?

VALENTINE: Sir, I'm come to acknowledge my errors, and ask your pardon.

SIR SAMPSON: What, have you found your senses at last then? In good time, sir.

VALENTINE: You were abused, sir; I never was distracted.

FORESIGHT: How! Not mad! Mr Scandal?

SCANDAL: No really, sir; I'm his witness, it was all counterfeit.

VALENTINE: I thought I had reasons. – But it was a poor contrivance, the effect has shown it such.

SIR SAMPSON: Contrivance, what, to cheat me? To cheat your father! Sirrah, could you hope to prosper?

VALENTINE: Indeed, I thought, sir, when the father endeavoured to undo the son, it was a reasonable return of nature.

SIR SAMPSON: Very good, sir! Mr Buckram, are you ready? – Come, sir, will you sign and seal?

VALENTINE: If you please, sir; but first I would ask this lady one question.

SIR SAMPSON: Sir, you must ask my leave first. That lady, no, sir; you shall ask that lady no questions till you have asked her blessing, sir; that lady is to be my wife.

VALENTINE: I have heard as much, sir, but I would have it from her own mouth.

SIR SAMPSON: That's as much as to say I lie, sir, and you don't believe what I say.

VALENTINE: Pardon me, sir. But I reflect that I very lately counterfeited madness; I don't know but the frolic may go round.

SIR SAMPSON: Come, chuck, satisfy him, answer him. – Come, come, Mr Buckram, the pen and ink.

BUCKRAM: Here it is, sir, with the deed; all is ready.

[VALENTINE goes to ANGELICA.]

ANGELICA: 'Tis true, you have a great while pretended love to me; nay, what if you were sincere? Still you must pardon me, if I think my own inclinations have a better right to dispose of my person, than yours.

SIR SAMPSON: Are you answered now, sir?

VALENTINE: Yes, sir.

SIR SAMPSON: Where's your plot, sir, and your contrivance now, sir? Will you sign, sir? Come, will you sign and seal?

VALENTINE: With all my heart, sir.

SCANDAL: 'S'death, you are not mad indeed, to ruin yourself?

VALENTINE: I have been disappointed of my only hope; and he that loses hope may part with anything. I never valued fortune but as it was subservient to my pleasure; and my only pleasure was to please this lady. I have made many vain attempts, and find at last that nothing but my ruin can effect it: which, for that reason, I will sign to – give me the paper.

ANGELICA [aside]: Generous Valentine!

BUCKRAM: Here is the deed, sir.

VALENTINE: But where is the bond by which I am obliged to sign this?

BUCKRAM: Sir Sampson, you have it.

ANGELICA: No, I have it; and I'll use it as I would everything that is an enemy to Valentine.

[Tears the paper.]

SIR SAMPSON: How now!

VALENTINE: Ha!

ANGELICA [to VALENTINE]: Had I the world to give you, it could not make me worthy of so generous and faithful a passion: here's my hand, my heart was always yours, and struggled very hard to make this utmost trial of your virtue.

VALENTINE: Between pleasure and amazement, I am lost – but on my knees I take the blessing.

SIR SAMPSON: Oons, what is the meaning of this?

BEN: Mess, here's the wind changed again. Father, you and I may make a voyage together now.

ANGELICA: Well, Sir Sampson, since I have played you a trick, I'll advise you how you may avoid such another. Learn to be a good father, or you'll never get a second wife. I always loved your son, and hated your unforgiving nature. I was resolved to try him to the utmost; I have tried you too, and know you both. You have not more faults than he has virtues; and 'tis hardly more pleasure to me, that I can make him and myself happy, than that I can punish you.

VALENTINE: If my happiness could receive addition, this kind surprise would make it double.

SIR SAMPSON: Oons, you're a crocodile.

FORESIGHT: Really, Sir Sampson, this is a sudden eclipse –

SIR SAMPSON: You're an illiterate fool, and I'm another, and the stars are liars; and if I had breath enough, I'd curse them and you, myself and everybody. – Oons, cullied, bubbled, jilted, woman-bobbed at last. – I have not patience.

    [*Exit* SIR SAMPSON.]

TATTLE: If the gentleman is in this disorder for want of a wife, I can spare him mine. [*To* JEREMY.] Oh, are you there, sir? I'm indebted to you for my happiness.

JEREMY: Sir, I ask you ten thousand pardons; 'twas an errant mistake. – You see, sir, my master was never mad, nor anything like it. – Then how could it be otherwise?

VALENTINE: Tattle, I thank you; you would have interposed between me and heaven; but Providence laid purgatory in your way. – You have but justice.

SCANDAL: I hear the fiddles that Sir Sampson provided for his own wedding; methinks 'tis pity they should not be employed when the match is so much mended. Valentine, though it be morning, we may have a dance.

VALENTINE: Anything, my friend, everything that looks like joy and transport.

SCANDAL: Call 'em, Jeremy.

ANGELICA: I have done dissembling now, Valentine; and if that coldness which I have always worn before you should turn to an extreme fondness, you must not suspect it.

VALENTINE: I'll prevent that suspicion – for I intend to dote on at that immoderate rate, that your fondness shall never distinguish itself enough to be taken notice of. If ever you seem to love too much, it must be only when I can't love enough.

ANGELICA: Have a care of large promises; you know you are apt to run more in debt than you are able to pay.

VALENTINE: Therefore I yield my body as your prisoner, and make your best on't.

SCANDAL: The music stays for you.

    [*Dance.*]

SCANDAL: Well, madam, you have done exemplary justice, in punishing an inhuman father, and rewarding a faithful lover; but there is a third good work, which I, in particular, must thank you for; I was an infidel to your sex, and you have converted me. – For now I am convinced that all women are not like fortune, blind in bestowing favours either on those who do not merit, or who do not want 'em.

ANGELICA: 'Tis an unreasonable accusation that you lay upon our sex: you tax us with injustice, only to cover your own want of merit. You would all have the reward of love, but few have the constancy to stay till it becomes your due. Men are generally hypocrites and infidels; they pretend to worship, but have neither zeal nor faith. How few, like Valentine, would persevere even unto martyrdom, and sacrifice their interest to their constancy! In admiring me, you misplace the novelty.

> The miracle today is that we find
> A lover true, not that a woman's kind.

[Exeunt omnes.]

FINIS.

EPILOGUE

Spoken at the opening of the new house,
by Mrs Bracegirdle.

Sure Providence at first designed this place
To be the player's refuge in distress;
For still in every storm they all run hither,
As to a shed that shields 'em from the weather.
But thinking of this change which last befell us,
It's like what I have heard our poets tell us:
For when behind our scenes their suits are pleading,
To help their love, sometimes they show their reading;
And wanting ready cash to pay for hearts,
They top their learning on us, and their parts.
Once of philosophers they told us stories,
Whom, as I think they called – Py – Pythagories,

I'm sure 'tis some such Latin name they give 'em,
And we, who know no better, must believe 'em.
Now to these men (say they) such souls were given,
That after death ne'er went to Hell, nor Heaven,
But lived, I know not how, in beasts; and then,
When many years were past, in men again.
Methinks, we players resemble such a soul,
That, does from bodies, we from houses stroll.
Thus Aristotle's soul, of old that was,
May now be damned to animate an ass;
Or in this very house, for aught we know,
Is doing painful penance in some beau;
And this our audience, which did once resort
To shining theatres to see our sport,
Now find us tossed into a tennis court.[1]
These walls but t'other day were filled with noise
Of roaring gamesters, and your *damme* boys.
Then bounding balls and rackets they encompassed,
And now they're filled with jests, and flights, and bombast!
I vow, I don't much like this transmigration,
Strolling from place to place, by circulation.
Grant Heaven, we don't return to our first station.
I know not what these think, but for my part,
I can't reflect without an aching heart,
How we should end in our original, a cart.
But we can't fear, since you're so good to save us,
That you have only set us up, to leave us.
Thus from the past, we hope for future grace,
I beg it –
And some here know I have a begging face.
Then pray continue this your kind behaviour,
For a clear stage[2] won't do, without your favour.

1. *tennis court*: the newly re-opened theatre had also functioned as an (indoor) tennis court.
2. *clear stage*: one free from debt.

The Way
of the World

TO THE RIGHT HONOURABLE RALPH
EARL OF MOUNTAGUE ETC.[1]

My Lord,

Whether the world will arraign me of vanity or not, that I have presumed to dedicate this comedy to your Lordship, I am yet in doubt: though it may be it is some degree of vanity even to doubt of it. One who has at any time had the honour of your Lordship's conversation, cannot be supposed to think very meanly of that which he would prefer to your perusal; yet it were to incur the imputation of too much sufficiency to pretend to such a merit as might abide the test of your Lordship's censure.

Whatever value may be wanting to this play while yet it is mine, will be sufficiently made up to it when it is once become your Lordship's; and it is my security that I cannot have overrated it more by my dedication than your Lordship will dignify it by your patronage.

That it succeeded on the stage was almost beyond my expectation; for but little of it was prepared for that general taste which seems now to be predominant in the palates of our audience.

Those characters which are meant to be ridiculous in most of our comedies are of fools so gross that, in my humble opinion, they should rather disturb than divert the well-natured and reflecting part of an audience; they are rather objects of charity than contempt; and instead of moving our mirth, they ought very often to excite our compassion.

This reflection moved me to design some characters which should appear ridiculous not so much through a natural folly (which is incorrigible, and therefore not proper for the stage) as through an affected wit; a wit, which at the same time that it is affected, is also false. As there is some difficulty in the formation of a character of this nature, so there is some hazard which attends the progress of its

---

1. *Montague*: Ralph Montagu (1638?–1709), courtier and diplomat.

success upon the stage. For many come to a play so over-charged with criticism that they very often let fly their censure, when through their rashness they have mistaken their aim. This I had occasion lately to observe; for this play had been acted two or three days, before some of these hasty judges could find the leisure to distinguish betwixt the character of a Witwoud and a Truewit.

I must beg your Lordship's pardon for this digression from the true course of this epistle; but that it may not seem altogether impertinent, I beg that I may plead the occasion of it, in part of that excuse of which I stand in need for recommending this comedy to your protection. It is only by the countenance of your Lordship, and the few so qualified, that such who write with care and pains can hope to be distinguished, for the prostituted name of poet promiscuously levels all that bear it.

Terence, the most correct writer in the world, had a Scipio and a Lelius,[2] if not to assist him, at least to support him in his reputation; and notwithstanding his extraordinary merit, it may be their countenance was not more than necessary.

The purity of his style, the delicacy of his turns, and the justness of his characters, were all of them beauties which the greater part of his audience were incapable of tasting; some of the coarsest strokes of Plautus, so severally censured by Horace, were more likely to affect the multitude; such who come with expectation to laugh out the last act of a play, and are better entertained with two or three unseasonable jests, than with the artful solution of the fable.

As Terence excelled in his performances, so had he great advantages to encourage his undertakings; for he built most on the foundations of Menander: his plots were generally modelled, and his characters ready drawn to his hand. He copied Menander; and Menander had no less light in the formation of his characters from the observations of Theophrastus,[3] of whom he was a disciple; and Theophrastus it is known was not only the disciple but the immedi-

2. *Scipio . . . Lelius*: Scipio Africanus the younger and Gaius Laelius were both patrons of Terence.
3. *Theophrastus*: Greek writer (*c*.372–287 B.C.), best known for his *Characters*.

ate successor of Aristotle, the first and greatest judge of poetry. These were great models to design by; and the further advantage which Terence possessed, towards giving his plays the due ornaments of purity of style, and justness of manners, was not less considerable from the freedom of conversation which was permitted him with Lelius and Scipio, two of the greatest and most polite men of his age. And indeed, the privilege of such a conversation is the only certain means of attaining to the perfection of dialogue.

If it has happened in any part of this comedy, that I have gained a turn of style, or expression more correct, or at least more corrigible than in those which I have formerly written, I must, with equal pride and gratitude, ascribe it to the honour of your Lordship's admitting me into your conversation, and that of a society where everybody else was so well worthy of you, in your retirement last summer from the town, for it was immediately after that this comedy was written. If I have failed in my performance, it is only to be regretted, where there were so many not inferior either to a Scipio or a Lelius, that there should be one wanting equal to the capacity of a Terence.

If I am not mistaken, poetry is almost the only art which has not yet laid claim to your Lordship's patronage. Architecture, and painting, to the great honour of our country, have flourished under your influence and protection. In the mean time, poetry, the eldest sister of all arts, and parent of most, seems to have resigned her birthright by having neglected to pay her duty to your Lordship, and by permitting others of a later extraction to prepossess that place in your esteem to which none can pretend a better title. Poetry, in its nature, is sacred to the good and great; the relation between them is reciprocal, and they are ever propitious to it. It is the privilege of poetry to address to them, and it is their prerogative alone to give it protection.

This received maxim is a general apology for all writers who consecrate their labours to great men. But I could wish at this time that this address were exempted from the common pretence of all dedications; and that, as I can distinguish your Lordship even among the most deserving, so this offering might become remarkable by some particular instance of respect, which should assure your

Lordship that I am, with all due sense of your extreme worthiness and humanity,

> MY LORD,
> Your Lordship's most obedient
> and most obliged humble servant,
>   WILL. CONGREVE.

PROLOGUE

Spoken by Mr Betterton.

Of those few fools, who with ill stars are cursed,
Sure scribbling fools, called poets, fare the worst;
For they're a sort of fools which Fortune makes,
And after she has made 'em fools, forsakes.
With Nature's oafs 'tis quite a diff'rent case,
For Fortune favours all her idiot race;
In her own nest the cuckoo eggs we find,
O'er which she broods to hatch the changeling kind.
No portion for her own she has to spare,
So much she dotes on her adopted care.
 Poets are bubbles,[1] by the town drawn in,
Suffered at first some trifling stakes to win;
But what unequal hazards do they run!
Each time they write, they venture all they've won;
The squire that's buttered[2] still, is sure to be undone.
This author, heretofore, has found your favour,
But pleads no merit from his past behaviour.
To build on that might prove a vain presumption,
Should grants to poets made admit resumption;
And in Parnassus he must lose his seat,
If that be found a forfeited estate.
 He owns, with toil he wrought the following scenes,
But if they're naught ne'er spare him for his pains;
Damn him the more; have no commiseration
For dullness on mature deliberation.
He swears he'll not resent one hissed-off scene,

1. *bubbles*: dupes.
2. *buttered*: flattered.

Nor, like those peevish wits, his play maintain,
Who, to assert their sense, your taste arraign.
Some plot we think he has, and some new thought;
Some humour too, no farce; but that's a fault.
Satire, he thinks, you ought not to expect;
For so reformed a town who dares correct?
To please, this time, has been his sole pretence;
He'll not instruct, lest it should give offence.
Should he by chance a knave or fool expose,
That hurts none here, sure here are none of those.
In short, our play, shall (with your leave to show it)
Give you one instance of a passive poet.
Who to your judgments yields all resignation;
So save or damn, after your own discretion.

DRAMATIS PERSONAE

MEN

FAINALL, *in love with* MRS MARWOOD

MIRABELL, *in love with* MRS MILLAMANT

WITWOUD, ⎱ *followers of* ⎱
PETULANT, ⎰ MRS MILLAMANT ⎰

SIR WILFULL WITWOUD, *half-brother to* WITWOUD, *and nephew to* LADY WISHFORT

WAITWELL, *servant to* MIRABELL

WOMEN

LADY WISHFORT, *enemy to* MIRABELL, *for having falsely pretended love to her*

MRS MILLAMANT, *a fine lady, niece to* LADY WISHFORT, *and loves* MIRABELL

MRS MARWOOD, *friend to* MR FAINALL, *and likes* MIRABELL

MRS FAINALL, *daughter to* LADY WISHFORT, *and wife to* FAINALL, *formerly friend to* MIRABELL

FOIBLE, *woman to* LADY WISHFORT

MINCING, *woman to* MRS MILLAMANT

Dancers, Footmen, and Attendants.

The scene
LONDON
The time equal to that of the presentation.

ACT ONE

SCENE ONE

A chocolate-house

[MIRABELL *and* FAINALL *rising from cards.* BETTY *waiting.*]

MIRABELL: You are a fortunate man, Mr Fainall.

FAINALL: Have we done?

MIRABELL: What you please. I'll play on to entertain you.

FAINALL: No, I'll give you your revenge another time, when you are not so indifferent; you are thinking of something else now, and play too negligently. The coldness of a losing gamester lessens the pleasure of the winner. I'd no more play with a man that slighted his ill fortune, than I'd make love to a woman who undervalued the loss of her reputation.

MIRABELL: You have a taste extremely delicate, and are for refining on your pleasures.

FAINALL: Prithee, why so reserved? Something has put you out of humour.

MIRABELL: Not at all. I happen to be grave today, and you are gay; that's all.

FAINALL: Confess, Millamant and you quarrelled last night after I left you; my fair cousin has some humours that would tempt the patience of a Stoic. What, some coxcomb came in and was well received by her, while you were by?

MIRABELL: Witwoud and Petulant, and what was worse, her aunt, your wife's mother, my evil genius; or to sum up all in her own name, my old Lady Wishfort came in.

FAINALL: Oh there it is then – she has a lasting passion for you, and with reason. – What, then my wife was there?

MIRABELL: Yes, and Mrs Marwood, and three or four more whom I never saw before. Seeing me, they all put on their grave faces, whispered one another; then complained aloud of the vapours, and after fell into a profound silence.

FAINALL: They had a mind to be rid of you.

MIRABELL: For which reason I resolved not to stir. At last the good old lady broke through her painful taciturnity with an invective against long visits. I would not have understood her, but Millamant joining in the argument, I rose and with a constrained smile told her, I thought nothing was so easy as to know when a visit began to be troublesome. She reddened and I withdrew, without expecting her reply.

FAINALL: You were to blame to resent what she spoke only in compliance with her aunt.

MIRABELL: She is more mistress of herself than to be under the necessity of such a resignation.

FAINALL: What? Though half her fortune depends upon her marrying with my lady's approbation?

MIRABELL: I was then in such a humour that I should have been better pleased if she had been less discreet.

FAINALL: Now I remember, I wonder not they were weary of you; last night was one of their cabal[1] nights; they have 'em three times a week, and meet by turns at one another's apartments, where they come together like the coroner's inquest, to sit upon the murdered reputations of the week. You and I are excluded; and it was once proposed that all the male sex should be excepted; but somebody moved that to avoid scandal there might be one man of the community; upon which motion Witwoud and Petulant were enrolled members.

MIRABELL: And who may have been the foundress of this sect? My Lady Wishfort, I warrant, who publishes her detestation of mankind, and full of the vigour of fifty-five, declares for a friend and ratafia,[2] and let posterity shift for itself, she'll breed no more.

1. *cabal*: a secret group for private or political ends.
2. *ratafia*: flavoured cordial or liqueur.

FAINALL: The discovery of your sham addresses to her, to conceal your love to her niece, has provoked this separation. Had you dissembled better, things might have continued in the state of nature.

MIRABELL: I did as much as man could, with any reasonable conscience; I proceeded to the very last act of flattery with her, and was guilty of a song in her commendation. Nay, I got a friend to put her into a lampoon, and compliment her with the imputation of an affair with a young fellow, which I carried so far that I told her the malicious town took notice that she had grown fat of a sudden; and when she lay in of a dropsy, persuaded her she was reported to be in labour. The devil's in't, if an old woman is to be flattered further, unless a man should endeavour downright personally to debauch her; and that my virtue forbad me. But for the discovery of that amour I am indebted to your friend, or your wife's friend, Mrs Marwood.

FAINALL: What should provoke her to be your enemy, without she has made you advances which you have slighted? Women do not easily forgive omissions of that nature.

MIRABELL: She was always civil to me till of late. I confess I am not one of those coxcombs who are apt to interpret a woman's good manners to her prejudice, and think that she who does not refuse 'em everything, can refuse 'em nothing.

FAINALL: You are a gallant man, Mirabell; and though you may have cruelty enough not to satisfy a lady's longing, you have too much generosity not to be tender of her honour. Yet you speak with an indifference which seems to be affected, and confesses you are conscious of a negligence.

MIRABELL: You pursue the argument with a distrust that seems to be unaffected, and confesses you are conscious of a concern for which the lady is more indebted to you than your wife.

FAINALL: Fie, fie, friend, if you grow censorious I must leave you. — I'll look upon the gamesters in the next room.

MIRABELL: Who are they?

FAINALL: Petulant and Witwoud. [*To* BETTY.] Bring me some chocolate.

[*Exit.*]

MIRABELL: Betty, what says your clock?

BETTY: Turned of the last canonical hour,[3] sir.

[*Exit.*]

MIRABELL: How pertinently the jade answers me! [*Looking on his watch.*] Ha? almost one o'clock! Oh, y'are come –

[*Enter a* SERVANT.]

Well, is the grand affair over? You have been something tedious.

SERVANT: Sir, there's such coupling at Pancras[4] that they stand behind one another, as 'twere in a country dance. Ours was the last couple to lead up, and no hopes appearing of dispatch, besides the parson growing hoarse, we were afraid his lungs would have failed before it came to our turn; so we drove round to Duke's Place,[5] and there they were riveted in a trice.

MIRABELL: So, so, you are sure they are married.

SERVANT: Married and bedded, sir; I am witness.

MIRABELL: Have you the certificate?

SERVANT: Here it is, sir.

MIRABELL: Has the tailor brought Waitwell's clothes home, and the new liveries?

SERVANT: Yes, sir.

MIRABELL: That's well. Do you go home again, d'ye hear, and adjourn the consummation till farther order; bid Waitwell shake his ears, and Dame Partlet[6] rustle up her feathers, and meet me at one o'clock by Rosamond's Pond,[7] that I may see her before she returns to her lady; and as you tender your ears, be secret.

[*Exit* SERVANT.]

[*Re-enter* FAINALL.]

FAINALL: Joy of your success, Mirabell; you look pleased.

MIRABELL: Ay; I have been engaged in a matter of some sort of mirth, which is not yet ripe for discovery. I am glad this is not a cabal night. I wonder, Fainall, that you who are married, and of

3. *canonical hour*: one of the hours in which it was legal to perform a marriage in church.

4. *Pancras*: St Pancras, where unlicensed marriages were performed.

5. *Duke's Place*: St James's Church, Duke Place, Aldgate.

6. *Partlet*: Pertlelote, wife of Chanticleer; see Chaucer, *The Nun's Priest's Tale.*

7. *Rosamond's Pond*: in St James's Park.

consequence should be discreet, will suffer your wife to be of such a party.

FAINALL: Faith, I am not jealous. Besides, most who are engaged are women and relations; and for the men, they are of a kind too contemptible to give scandal.

MIRABELL: I am of another opinion. The greater the coxcomb, always the more the scandal; for a woman who is not a fool can have but one reason for associating with a man that is.

FAINALL: Are you jealous as often as you see Witwoud entertained by Millamant?

MIRABELL: Of her understanding I am, if not of her person.

FAINALL: You do her wrong; for to give her her due, she has wit.

MIRABELL: She has beauty enough to make any man think so, and complaisance enough not to contradict him who shall tell her so.

FAINALL: For a passionate lover, methinks you are a man somewhat too discerning in the failings of your mistress.

MIRABELL: And for a discerning man, somewhat too passionate a lover; for I like her with all her faults; nay, like her for her faults. Her follies are so natural, or so artful, that they become her; and those affectations which in another woman would be odious, serve but to make her more agreeable. I'll tell thee, Fainall, she once used me with that insolence, that in revenge I took her to pieces; sifted her, and separated her failings; I studied 'em, and got 'em by rote. The catalogue was so large that I was not without hopes one day or other to hate her heartily: to which end I so used myself to think of 'em that at length, contrary to my design and expectation, they gave me every hour less and less disturbance; till in a few days it became habitual to me to remember 'em without being displeased. They are now grown as familiar to me as my own frailties; and in all probability, in a little time longer I shall like 'em as well.

FAINALL: Marry her, marry her; be half as well acquainted with her charms as you are with her defects, and my life on't, you are your own man again.

MIRABELL: Say you so?

FAINALL: Ay, ay, I have experience; I have a wife, and so forth.

[*Enter* MESSENGER.]

MESSENGER: Is one Squire Witwoud here?

BETTY: Yes; what's your business?

MESSENGER: I have a letter for him, from his brother Sir Wilfull, which I am charged to deliver into his own hands.

BETTY: He's in the next room, friend; that way.

[*Exit* MESSENGER.]

MIRABELL: What, is the chief of that noble family in town, Sir Wilfull Witwoud?

FAINALL: He is expected today. Do you know him?

MIRABELL: I have seen him. He promises to be an extraordinary person; I think you have the honour to be related to him.

FAINALL: Yes; he is half-brother to this Witwoud by a former wife, who was sister to my Lady Wishfort, my wife's mother. If you marry Millamant, you must call cousins too.

MIRABELL: I had rather be his relation than his acquaintance.

FAINALL: He comes to town in order to equip himself for travel.

MIRABELL: For travel! Why, the man that I mean is above forty.

FAINALL: No matter for that; 'tis for the honour of England, that all Europe should know we have blockheads of all ages.

MIRABELL: I wonder there is not an act of parliament to save the credit of the nation, and prohibit the exportation of fools.

FAINALL: By no means, 'tis better as 'tis; 'tis better to trade with a little loss than to be quite eaten up with being overstocked.

MIRABELL: Pray, are the follies of this knight-errant and those of the squire his brother anything related?

FAINALL: Not at all; Witwoud grows by the knight, like a medlar grafted on a crab.[8] One will melt in your mouth, and t'other set your teeth on edge; one is all pulp, and the other all core.

MIRABELL: So one will be rotten before he be ripe, and the other will be rotten without ever being ripe at all.

FAINALL: Sir Wilfull is an odd mixture of bashfulness and obstinacy. – But when he's drunk, he's as loving as the monster in *The Tempest*,[9] and much after the same manner. To give the t'other his

8. *medlar . . . crab*: the medlar is a fruit eaten when it is soft and pulpy but the crab-apple remains hard and sour.

9. *monster . . . Tempest*: the allusion is to the Dryden–Davenant opera based on Shakespeare's play.

due, he has something of good nature and does not always want
wit.

MIRABELL: Not always; but as often as his memory fails him, and
his commonplace[10] of comparisons. He is a fool with a good
memory and some few scraps of other folks' wit. He is one whose
conversation can never be approved, yet it is now and then to be
endured. He has indeed one good quality, he is not exceptious; for
he so passionately affects the reputation of understanding raillery,
that he will construe an affront into a jest, and call downright
rudeness and ill language, satire and fire.

FAINALL: If you have a mind to finish his picture, you have an
opportunity to do it at full length. Behold the original!

[*Enter* WITWOUD.]

WITWOUD: Afford me your compassion, my dears! Pity me,
Fainall, Mirabell, pity me!

MIRABELL: I do from my soul.

FAINALL: Why, what's the matter?

WITWOUD: No letters for me, Betty?

BETTY: Did not the messenger bring you one but now, sir?

WITWOUD: Ay, but no other?

BETTY: No, sir.

WITWOUD: That's hard, that's very hard. – A messenger, a mule, a
beast of burden, he has brought me a letter from the fool my
brother, as heavy as a panegyric in a funeral sermon, or a copy of
commendatory verses from one poet to another. And what's
worse, 'tis as sure a forerunner of the author as an epistle
dedicatory.

MIRABELL: A fool, and your brother, Witwoud!

WITWOUD: Ay, ay, my half-brother. My half-brother he is, no
nearer upon honour.

MIRABELL: Then 'tis possible he may be but half a fool.

WITWOUD: Good, good, Mirabell, *le drôle!* Good, good, hang him,
don't let's talk of him. – Fainall, how does your lady? Gad, I say
anything in the world to get this fellow out of my head. I beg
pardon that I should ask a man of pleasure and the town, a

10. *commonplace*: commonplace book.

question at once so foreign and domestic. But I talk like an old maid at a marriage, I don't know what I say; but she's the best woman in the world.

FAINALL: 'Tis well you don't know what you say, or else your commendation would go near to make me either vain or jealous.

WITWOUD: No man in town lives well with a wife but Fainall. Your judgment, Mirabell?

MIRABELL: You had better step and ask his wife, if you would be credibly informed.

WITWOUD: Mirabell.

MIRABELL: Ay.

WITWOUD: My dear, I ask ten thousand pardons. – Gad, I have forgot what I was going to say to you.

MIRABELL: I thank you heartily, heartily.

WITWOUD: No, but prithee excuse me; my memory is such a memory.

MIRABELL: Have a care of such apologies, Witwoud; for I never knew a fool but he affected to complain either of the spleen or his memory.

FAINALL: What have you done with Petulant?

WITWOUD: He's reckoning his money – my money it was. I have no luck today.

FAINALL: You may allow him to win of you at play, for you are sure to be too hard for him at repartee; since you monopolize the wit that is between you, the fortune must be his of course.

MIRABELL: I don't find that Petulant confesses the superiority of wit to be your talent, Witwoud.

WITWOUD: Come, come, you are malicious now, and would breed debates. – Petulant's my friend, and a very honest fellow, and a very pretty fellow, and has a smattering – faith and troth, a pretty deal of an odd sort of a small wit; nay, I'll do him justice. I'm his friend, I won't wrong him neither. – And if he had but any judgment in the world, – he would not be altogether contemptible. Come come, don't detract from the merits of my friend.

FAINALL: You don't take your friend to be over-nicely bred?

WITWOUD: No, no, hang him, the rogue has no manners at all, that

I must own. – No more breeding than a bum-baily,[11] that I grant you. – 'Tis pity, faith; the fellow has fire and life.

MIRABELL: What, courage?

WITWOUD: Hum, faith, I don't know as to that; I can't say as to that. – Yes, faith, in a controversy he'll contradict anybody.

MIRABELL: Though 'twere a man whom he feared, or a woman whom he loved.

WITWOUD: Well, well, he does not always think before he speaks; we have all our failings. You are too hard upon him, you are, faith. Let me excuse him; I can defend most of his faults, except one or two; one he has, that's the truth on't; if he were my brother, I could not acquit him. – That, indeed, I could wish were otherwise.

MIRABELL: Ay, marry, what's that, Witwoud?

WITWOUD: O, pardon me. – Expose the infirmities of my friend? – No, my dear, excuse me there.

FAINALL: What, I warrant he's unsincere, or 'tis some such trifle.

WITWOUD: No, no, what if he be? 'Tis no matter for that, his wit will excuse that. A wit should no more be sincere than a woman constant; one argues a decay of parts, as t'other of beauty.

MIRABELL: Maybe you think him too positive?

WITWOUD: No, no, his being positive is an incentive to argument, and keeps up conversation.

FAINALL: Too illiterate?

WITWOUD: That! that's his happiness; his want of learning gives him the more opportunities to show his natural parts.

MIRABELL: He wants words.

WITWOUD: Ay, but I like him for that now; for his want of words gives me the pleasure very often to explain his meaning.

FAINALL: He's impudent.

WITWOUD: No, that's not it.

MIRABELL: Vain.

WITWOUD: No.

MIRABELL: What, he speaks unseasonable truths sometimes, because he has not wit enough to invent an evasion?

11. *bum-baily*: 'a bailiff of the meanest kind; one employed in arrests' (Dr Johnson's *Dictionary*).

WITWOUD: Truths! Ha, ha, ha! No, no, since you will have it, – I mean he never speaks truth at all, – that's all. He will lie like a chambermaid, or a woman of quality's porter. Now that is a fault.

[*Enter* COACHMAN.]

COACHMAN: Is Master Petulant here, mistress?

BETTY: Yes.

COACHMAN: Three gentlewomen in the coach would speak with him.

FAINALL: O brave Petulant; three!

BETTY: I'll tell him.

COACHMAN: You must bring two dishes of chocolate and a glass of cinnamon-water.[12]

[*Exit* BETTY *and* COACHMAN.]

WITWOUD: That should be for two fasting strumpets, and a bawd troubled with wind. Now you may know what the three are.

MIRABELL: You are very free with your friend's acquaintance.

WITWOUD: Ay, ay, friendship without freedom is as dull as love without enjoyment, or wine without toasting. But to tell you a secret, these are trulls that he allows coach-hire, and something more, by the week, to call on him once a day at public places.

MIRABELL: How!

WITWOUD: You shall see he won't go to 'em because there's no more company here to take notice of him. – Why this is nothing to what he used to do; before he found out this way, I have known him call for himself.

FAINALL: Call for himself? What dost thou mean?

WITWOUD: Mean, why he would slip you out of this chocolate-house, just when you had been talking to him; as soon as your back was turned – whip, he was gone. Then trip to his lodging, clap on a hood and scarf and mask, slap into a hackney-coach, and drive hither to the door again in a trice, where he would send in for himself, that I mean, call for himself, wait for himself, nay, and what's more, not finding himself, sometimes leave a letter for himself.

MIRABELL: I confess this is something extraordinary. – I believe he

12. *cinnamon-water*: 'an aromatic beverage prepared from cinnamon' (*O.E.D.*).

waits for himself now, he is so long a-coming. Oh, I ask his
pardon.

[*Enter* PETULANT.]

BETTY: Sir, the coach stays.

PETULANT: Well, well, I come. – 'Sbud, a man had as good be a
professed midwife as a professed whoremaster, at this rate! To be
knocked up and raised at all hours, and in all places. Pox on 'em, I
won't come. – D'ye hear, tell 'em I won't come. – Let 'em snivel
and cry their hearts out.

FAINALL: You are very cruel, Petulant.

PETULANT: All's one, let it pass. – I have a humour to be cruel.

MIRABELL: I hope they are not persons of condition that you use at
this rate.

PETULANT: Condition! Condition's a dried fig, if I am not in
humour. – By this hand, if they were your – a – a – your
what-d'ye-call-'ems themselves, they must wait or rub off, if I
want appetite.

MIRABELL: What-d'ye-call-'ems! What are they, Witwoud?

WITWOUD: Empresses, my dear; by your what-d'ye-call-'ems he
means Sultana queens.

PETULANT: Ay, Roxolanas.[13]

MIRABELL: Cry you mercy.

FAINALL: Witwoud says they are –

PETULANT: What does he say th'are?

WITWOUD: I? Fine ladies, I say.

PETULANT: Pass on, Witwoud. – Hearkee, by this light his relations: two co-heiresses his cousins, and an old aunt that loves
caterwauling better than a conventicle.[14]

WITWOUD: Ha, ha, ha! I had a mind to see how the rogue would
come off. – Ha, ha, ha! Gad, I can't be angry with him, if he said
they were my mother and my sisters.

MIRABELL: No!

WITWOUD: No; the rogue's wit and readiness of invention charm
me; dear Petulant!

13. *Roxolanas*: Roxolana is the Sultana in Davenant's *Siege of Rhodes*.
14. *conventicle*: clandestine gathering of Dissenters.

BETTY: They are gone, sir, in great anger.

PETULANT: Enough, let 'em trundle. Anger helps complexion, saves paint.

FAINALL: This continence is all dissembled; this is in order to have something to brag of the next time he makes court to Millamant, and swear he has abandoned the whole sex for her sake.

MIRABELL: Have you not left your impudent pretensions there yet? I shall cut your throat sometime or other, Petulant, about that business.

PETULANT: Ay, ay, let that pass. – There are other throats to be cut –

MIRABELL: Meaning mine, sir?

PETULANT: Not I – I mean nobody – I know nothing. But there are uncles and nephews in the world, and they may be rivals – what then? All's one for that.

MIRABELL: How! Hearkee Petulant, come hither. – Explain, or I shall call your interpreter.

PETULANT: Explain! I know nothing. – Why, you have an uncle, have you not, lately come to town, and lodges by my Lady Wishfort's?

MIRABELL: True.

PETULANT: Why, that's enough. – You and he are not friends; and if he should marry and have a child, you may be disinherited, ha?

MIRABELL: Where hast thou stumbled upon all this truth?

PETULANT: All's one for that; why then, say I know something.

MIRABELL: Come, thou art an honest fellow, Petulant, and shalt make love to my mistress, thou shalt faith. What hast thou heard of my uncle?

PETULANT: I? Nothing I. If throats are to be cut, let swords clash. Snug's the word; I shrug and am silent.

MIRABELL: O raillery, raillery. Come, I know thou art in the women's secrets. – What, you're a cabalist; I know you stayed at Millamant's last night, after I went. Was there any mention made of my uncle, or me? Tell me. If thou hadst but good nature equal to thy wit, Petulant, Tony Witwoud, who is now thy competitor in fame, would show as dim by thee as a dead whiting's eye by a pearl of orient; he would no more be seen by thee than Mercury is by the sun. Come, I'm sure thou wilt tell me.

PETULANT: If I do, will you grant me common sense then, for the future?

MIRABELL: Faith, I'll do what I can for thee; and I'll pray that heaven may grant it thee in the meantime.

PETULANT: Well, hearkee.

[MIRABELL *and* PETULANT *talk apart.*]

FAINALL: Petulant and you both will find Mirabell as warm a rival as a lover.

WITWOUD: Pshaw! pshaw! That she laughs at Petulant is plain. And for my part, but that it is almost a fashion to admire her, I should. – Hearkee, to tell you a secret, but let it go no further; between friends, I shall never break my heart for her.

FAINALL: How!

WITWOUD: She's handsome; but she's a sort of an uncertain woman.

FAINALL: I thought you had died for her.

WITWOUD: Umh – no –

FAINALL: She has wit.

WITWOUD: 'Tis what she will hardly allow anybody else. Now, demme, I should hate that, if she were as handsome as Cleopatra. Mirabell is not so sure of her as he thinks for.

FAINALL: Why do you think so?

WITWOUD: We stayed pretty late there last night, and heard something of an uncle to Mirabell, who is lately come to town, – and is between him and the best part of his estate. Mirabell and he are at some distance, as my Lady Wishfort has been told; and you know she hates Mirabell worse than a Quaker hates a parrot, or than a fishmonger hates a hard frost. Whether this uncle has seen Mrs Millamant or not, I cannot say; but there were items of such a treaty being in embryo, and if it should come to life, poor Mirabell would be in some sort unfortunately fobbed, i'faith.

FAINALL: 'Tis impossible Millamant should hearken to it.

WITWOUD: Faith, my dear, I can't tell; she's a woman, and a kind of a humorist.

MIRABELL: And this is the sum of what you could collect last night?

PETULANT: The quintessence. Maybe Witwoud knows more; he stayed longer. – Besides, they never mind him; they say anything before him.

MIRABELL: I thought you had been the greatest favourite.

PETULANT: Ay, *tête à tête*, but not in public, because I make remarks.

MIRABELL: Do you?

PETULANT: Ay, ay, pox, I'm malicious, man. Now he's soft you know; they are not in awe of him. – The fellow's well-bred; he's what you call a – what-d'ye-call-'em. A fine gentleman, but he's silly withal.

MIRABELL: I thank you, I know as much as my curiosity requires. – Fainall, are you for the Mall?

FAINALL: Ay, I'll take a turn before dinner.

WITWOUD: Ay, we'll all walk in the park; the ladies talked of being there.

MIRABELL: I thought you were obliged to watch for your brother Sir Wilfull's arrival.

WITWOUD: No, no, he comes to his aunt's, my Lady Wishfort. Pox on him, I shall be troubled with him too; what shall I do with the fool?

PETULANT: Beg him for his estate, that I may beg you afterwards; and so have but one trouble with you both.

WITWOUD: O rare Petulant! Thou art as quick as a fire in a frosty morning; thou shalt to the Mall with us, and we'll be very severe.

PETULANT: Enough, I'm in a humour to be severe.

MIRABELL: Are you? Pray then walk by yourselves: let not us be accessory to your putting the ladies out of countenance with your senseless ribaldry, which you roar out aloud as often as they pass by you; and when you have made a handsome woman blush, then you think you have been severe.

PETULANT: What, what? Then let 'em either show their innocence by not understanding what they hear, or else show their discretion by not hearing what they would not be thought to understand.

MIRABELL: But hast not thou then sense enough to know that thou ought'st to be most ashamed thyself, when thou hast put another out of countenance?

PETULANT: Not I, by this hand. – I always take blushing either for a sign of guilt, or ill breeding.

MIRABELL: I confess you ought to think so. You are in the right, that you may plead the error of your judgment in defence of your practice.

> Where modesty's ill manners, 'tis but fit
> That impudence and malice pass for wit.

[*Exeunt.*]

ACT TWO

SCENE ONE

St James's Park.

[*Enter* MRS FAINALL *and* MRS MARWOOD.]

MRS FAINALL: Ay, ay, dear Marwood, if we will be happy, we must find the means in ourselves, and among ourselves. Men are ever in extremes; either doting or averse. While they are lovers, if they have fire and sense, their jealousies are insupportable; and when they cease to love, (we ought to think at least) they loathe; they look upon us with horror and distaste; they meet us like the ghosts of what we were, and as such, fly from us.

MRS MARWOOD: True, 'tis an unhappy circumstance of life, that love should ever die before us; and that the man so often should outlive the lover. But say what you will, 'tis better to be left than never to have been loved. To pass our youth in dull indifference, to refuse the sweets of life because they once must leave us, is as preposterous as to wish to have been born old, because we one day must be old. For my part, my youth may wear and waste, but it shall never rust in my possession.

MRS FAINALL: Then it seems you dissemble an aversion to mankind, only in compliance with my mother's humour.

MRS MARWOOD: Certainly. To be free, I have no taste of those insipid dry discourses with which our sex of force must entertain themselves, apart from men. We may affect endearments to each other, profess eternal friendships, and seem to dote like lovers; but 'tis not in our natures long to persevere. Love will resume his empire in our breasts, and every heart, or soon or late, receive and readmit him as its lawful tyrant.

MRS FAINALL: Bless me, how have I been deceived! Why you profess a libertine!

MRS MARWOOD: You see my friendship by my freedom. Come, be as sincere, acknowledge that your sentiments agree with mine.

MRS FAINALL: Never.

MRS MARWOOD: You hate mankind?

MRS FAINALL: Heartily, inveterately.

MRS MARWOOD: Your husband?

MRS FAINALL: Most transcendently; ay, though I say it, meritoriously.

MRS MARWOOD: Give me your hand upon it.

MRS FAINALL: There.

MRS MARWOOD: I join with you; what I have said has been to try you.

MRS FAINALL: Is it possible? Dost thou hate those vipers, men?

MRS MARWOOD: I have done hating 'em, and am now come to despise 'em; the next thing I have to do, is eternally to forget 'em.

MRS FAINALL: There spoke the spirit of an Amazon, a Penthesilea.[1]

MRS MARWOOD: And yet I am thinking sometimes to carry my aversion further.

MRS FAINALL: How?

MRS MARWOOD: Faith, by marrying; if I could but find one that loved me very well and would be thoroughly sensible of ill usage, I think I should do myself the violence of undergoing the ceremony.

MRS FAINALL: You would not make him a cuckold?

MRS MARWOOD: No; but I'd make him believe I did, and that's as bad.

MRS FAINALL: Why, had not you as good do it?

MRS MARWOOD: Oh, if he should ever discover it, he would then know the worst, and be out of his pain; but I would have him ever to continue upon the rack of fear and jealousy.

MRS FAINALL: Ingenious mischief! Would thou wert married to Mirabell.

MRS MARWOOD: Would I were.

1. *Penthesilea*: Queen of the Amazons.

MRS FAINALL: You change colour.

MRS MARWOOD: Because I hate him.

MRS FAINALL: So do I; but I can hear him named. But what reason have you to hate him in particular?

MRS MARWOOD: I never loved him; he is, and always was, insufferably proud.

MRS FAINALL: By the reason you give for your aversion, one would think it dissembled; for you have laid a fault to his charge of which his enemies must acquit him.

MRS MARWOOD: Oh, then it seems you are one of his favourable enemies. Methinks you look a little pale, and now you flush again.

MRS FAINALL: Do I? I think I am a little sick o' the sudden.

MRS MARWOOD: What ails you?

MRS FAINALL: My husband. Don't you see him? He turned short upon me unawares, and has almost overcome me.

[*Enter* FAINALL *and* MIRABELL.]

MRS MARWOOD: Ha, ha, ha; he comes opportunely for you.

MRS FAINALL: For you, for he has brought Mirabell with him.

FAINALL: My dear.

MRS FAINALL: My soul.

FAINALL: You don't look well today, child.

MRS FAINALL: D'ye think so?

MIRABELL: He is the only man that does, madam.

MRS FAINALL: The only man that would tell me so at least; and the only man from whom I could hear it without mortification.

FAINALL: Oh, my dear, I am satisfied of your tenderness; I know you cannot resent anything from me; especially what is an effect of my concern.

MRS FAINALL: Mr Mirabell, my mother interrupted you in a pleasant relation last night; I would fain hear it out.

MIRABELL: The persons concerned in that affair have yet a tolerable reputation. – I am afraid Mr Fainall will be censorious.

MRS FAINALL: He has a humour more prevailing than his curiosity and will willingly dispense with the hearing of one scandalous story, to avoid giving an occasion to make another by being seen to walk with his wife. This way Mr Mirabell, and I dare promise you will oblige us both.

[*Exeunt* MRS FAINALL *and* MIRABELL.]

FAINALL: Excellent creature! Well sure if I should live to be rid of my wife, I should be a miserable man.

MRS MARWOOD: Ay!

FAINALL: For having only that one hope, the accomplishment of it, of consequence, must put an end to all my hopes; and what a wretch is he who must survive his hopes! Nothing remains when that day comes but to sit down and weep like Alexander, when he wanted other worlds to conquer.

MRS MARWOOD: Will you not follow 'em?

FAINALL: Faith, I think not.

MRS MARWOOD: Pray let us; I have a reason.

FAINALL: You are not jealous?

MRS MARWOOD: Of whom?

FAINALL: Of Mirabell.

MRS MARWOOD: If I am, is it inconsistent with my love to you that I am tender of your honour?

FAINALL: You would intimate then, as if there were a fellow-feeling between my wife and him.

MRS MARWOOD: I think she does not hate him to that degree she would be thought.

FAINALL: But he, I fear, is too insensible.

MRS MARWOOD: It may be you are deceived.

FAINALL: It may be so. I do now begin to apprehend it.

MRS MARWOOD: What?

FAINALL: That I have been deceived madam, and you are false.

MRS MARWOOD: That I am false! What mean you?

FAINALL: To let you know I see through all your little arts. – Come, you both love him, and both have equally dissembled your aversion. Your mutual jealousies of one another have made you clash till you have both struck fire. I have seen the warm confession reddening on your cheeks and sparkling from your eyes.

MRS MARWOOD: You do me wrong.

FAINALL: I do not. – 'Twas for my ease to oversee and wilfully neglect the gross advances made him by my wife; that by permitting her to be engaged, I might continue unsuspected in my pleasures, and take you oftener to my arms in full security. But could you think, because the nodding husband would not wake, that e'er the watchful lover slept?

MRS MARWOOD: And wherewithal can you reproach me?

FAINALL: With infidelity, with loving of another, with love of Mirabell.

MRS MARWOOD: 'Tis false. I challenge you to show an instance that can confirm your groundless accusation. I hate him.

FAINALL: And wherefore do you hate him? He is insensible, and your resentment follows his neglect. An instance? The injuries you have done him are a proof: your interposing in his love. What cause had you to make discoveries of his pretended passion? To undeceive the credulous aunt, and be the officious obstacle of his match with Millamant?

MRS MARWOOD: My obligations to my lady urged me; I had professed a friendship to her, and could not see her easy nature so abused by that dissembler.

FAINALL: What, was it conscience then? Professed a friendship! O the pious friendships of the female sex!

MRS MARWOOD: More tender, more sincere, and more enduring than all the vain and empty vows of men, whether professing love to us, or mutual faith to one another.

FAINALL: Ha, ha, ha! You are my wife's friend too.

MRS MARWOOD: Shame and ingratitude! Do you reproach me? You, you upbraid me! Have I been false to her, through strict fidelity to you, and sacrificed my friendship to keep my love inviolate? And have you the baseness to charge me with the guilt, unmindful of the merit! To you it should be meritorious that I have been vicious. And do you reflect that guilt upon me, which should lie buried in your bosom?

FAINALL: You misinterpret my reproof. I meant but to remind you of the slight account you once could make of strictest ties, when set in competition with your love to me.

MRS MARWOOD: 'Tis false, you urged it with deliberate malice. — 'Twas spoke in scorn, and I never will forgive it.

FAINALL: Your guilt, not your resentment, begets your rage. If yet you loved, you could forgive a jealousy; but you are stung to find you are discovered.

MRS MARWOOD: It shall be all discovered. You too shall be discovered; be sure you shall. I can but be exposed. – If I do it myself, I shall prevent your baseness.

FAINALL: Why, what will you do?

MRS MARWOOD: Disclose it to your wife; own what has passed between us.

FAINALL: Frenzy!

MRS MARWOOD: By all my wrongs I'll do't. – I'll publish to the world the injuries you have done me, both in my fame and fortune. With both I trusted you, you bankrupt in honour, as indigent of wealth.

FAINALL: Your fame I have preserved. Your fortune has been bestowed as the prodigality of your love would have it, in pleasures which we both have shared. Yet had not you been false, I had ere this repaid it. 'Tis true! Had you permitted Mirabell with Millamant to have stolen their marriage, my lady had been incensed beyond all means of reconcilement; Millamant had forfeited the moiety[2] of her fortune, which then would have descended to my wife. – And wherefore did I marry, but to make lawful prize of a rich widow's wealth, and squander it on love and you?

MRS MARWOOD: Deceit and frivolous pretence.

FAINALL: Death, am I not married? What's pretence? Am I not imprisoned, fettered? Have I not a wife? Nay a wife that was a widow, a young widow, a handsome widow; and would be again a widow, but that I have a heart of proof, and something of a constitution to bustle through the ways of wedlock and this world. Will you yet be reconciled to truth and me?

MRS MARWOOD: Impossible. Truth and you are inconsistent. – I hate you, and shall for ever.

FAINALL: For loving you?

MRS MARWOOD: I loathe the name of love after such usage; and next to the guilt with which you would asperse me, I scorn you most. Farewell.

FAINALL: Nay, we must not part thus.

2. *moiety*: half.

MRS MARWOOD: Let me go.

FAINALL: Come, I'm sorry.

MRS MARWOOD: I care not – let me go. – Break my hands, do. – I'd leave 'em to get loose.

FAINALL: I would not hurt you for the world. Have I no other hold to keep you here?

MRS MARWOOD: Well, I have deserved it all.

FAINALL: You know I love you.

MRS MARWOOD: Poor dissembling! Oh, that – well, it is not yet –

FAINALL: What? What is it not? What is it not yet? It is not yet too late –

MRS MARWOOD: No, it is not yet too late – I have that comfort.

FAINALL: It is to love another.

MRS MARWOOD: But not to loathe, detest, abhor mankind, myself and the whole treacherous world.

FAINALL: Nay, this is extravagance. – Come, I ask your pardon. – No tears. – I was to blame; I could not love you and be easy in my doubts. – Pray, forbear. – I believe you; I'm convinced I've done you wrong, and any way, every way will make amends. I'll hate my wife yet more, damn her. – I'll part with her, rob her of all she's worth, and we'll retire somewhere, anywhere, to another world. I'll marry thee; be pacified. – 'Sdeath, they come; hide your face, your tears. – You have a mask; wear it a moment. This way, this way. Be persuaded.

[Exeunt.]

[Enter MIRABELL and MRS FAINALL.]

MRS FAINALL: They are here yet.

MIRABELL: They are turning into the other walk.

MRS FAINALL: While I only hated my husband, I could bear to see him; but since I have despised him, he's too offensive.

MIRABELL: Oh, you should hate with prudence.

MRS FAINALL: Yes, for I have loved with indiscretion.

MIRABELL: You should have just so much disgust for your husband as may be sufficient to make you relish your lover.

MRS FAINALL: You have been the cause that I have loved without bounds, and would you set limits to that aversion of which you have been the occasion? Why did you make me marry this man?

MIRABELL: Why do we daily commit disagreeable and dangerous actions? To save that idol, reputation. If the familiarities of our loves had produced that consequence of which you were apprehensive, where could you have fixed a father's name with credit, but on a husband? I knew Fainall to be a man lavish of his morals, an interested and professing friend, a false and a designing lover; yet one whose wit and outward fair behaviour have gained a reputation with the town enough to make that woman stand excused who has suffered herself to be won by his addresses. A better man ought not to have been sacrificed to the occasion; a worse had not answered to the purpose. When you are weary of him, you know your remedy.

MRS FAINALL: I ought to stand in some degree of credit with you, Mirabell.

MIRABELL: In justice to you, I have made you privy to my whole design, and put it in your power to ruin or advance my fortune.

MRS FAINALL: Whom have you instructed to represent your pretended uncle?

MIRABELL: Waitwell, my servant.

MRS FAINALL: He is an humble servant to Foible, my mother's woman, and may win her to your interest.

MIRABELL: Care is taken for that – she is won and worn by this time. They were married this morning.

MRS FAINALL: Who?

MIRABELL: Waitwell and Foible. I would not tempt my servant to betray me by trusting him too far. If your mother, in hopes to ruin me, should consent to marry my pretended uncle, he might, like Mosca in *The Fox*,[3] stand upon terms; so I made him sure beforehand.

MRS FAINALL: So, if my poor mother is caught in a contract, you will discover the imposture betimes, and release her by producing a certificate of her gallant's former marriage.

MIRABELL: Yes, upon condition she consent to my marriage with her niece, and surrender the moiety of her fortune in her possession.

3. *Mosca . . . Fox*: Mosca is the servant in Ben Jonson's *Volpone*.

MRS FAINALL: She talked last night of endeavouring at a match between Millamant and your uncle.

MIRABELL: That was by Foible's direction, and my instruction, that she might seem to carry it more privately.

MRS FAINALL: Well, I have an opinion of your success, for I believe my lady will do anything to get a husband; and when she has this, which you have provided for her, I suppose she will submit to anything to get rid of him.

MIRABELL: Yes, I think the good lady would marry anything that resembled a man, though 'twere no more than what a butler could pinch out of a napkin.

MRS FAINALL: Female frailty! We must all come to it, if we live to be old and feel the craving of a false appetite when the true is decayed.

MIRABELL: An old woman's appetite is depraved like that of a girl. – 'Tis the green sickness of a second childhood, and, like the faint offer of a latter spring, serves but to usher in the fall, and withers in an affected bloom.

MRS FAINALL: Here's your mistress.

[*Enter* MRS MILLAMANT, WITWOUD, *and* MINCING.]

MIRABELL: Here she comes, i'faith, full sail, with her fan spread and her streamers[4] out, and a shoal of fools for tenders. – Ha, no, I cry her mercy.

MRS FAINALL: I see but one poor empty sculler, and he tows her woman after him.

MIRABELL: You seem to be unattended, madam. You used to have the *beau monde* throng after you, and a flock of gay, fine perukes hovering round you.

WITWOUD: Like moths about a candle. – I had like to have lost my comparison for want of breath.

MILLAMANT: Oh, I have denied myself airs today. I have walked as fast through the crowd –

WITWOUD: As a favourite in disgrace, and with as few followers.

MILLAMANT: Dear Mr Witwoud, truce with your similitudes; for I am as sick of 'em –

4. *streamers*: ribbons.

WITWOUD: As a physician of a good air. – I cannot help it madam, though 'tis against myself.

MILLAMANT: Yet again! Mincing, stand between me and his wit.

WITWOUD: Do, Mrs Mincing, like a screen before a great fire. I confess I do blaze today; I am too bright.

MRS FAINALL: But dear Millamant, why were you so long?

MILLAMANT: Long! Lord, have I not made violent haste? I have asked every living thing I met for you; I have enquired after you as after a new fashion.

WITWOUD: Madam, truce with your similitudes. No, you met her husband, and did not ask him for her.

MIRABELL: By your leave, Witwoud, that were like enquiring after an old fashion, to ask a husband for his wife.

WITWOUD: Hum, a hit, a hit, a palpable hit, I confess it.

MRS FAINALL: You were dressed before I came abroad.

MILLAMANT: Ay, that's true. – Oh, but then I had – Mincing, what had I? Why was I so long?

MINCING: Oh mem, your la'ship stayed to peruse a pecquet of letters.

MILLAMANT: Oh, ay, letters – I had letters – I am persecuted with letters – I hate letters. Nobody knows how to write letters, and yet one has 'em, one does not know why. They serve one to pin up one's hair.

WITWOUD: Is that the way? Pray madam, do you pin up your hair with all your letters? I find I must keep copies.

MILLAMANT: Only with those in verse, Mr Witwoud. I never pin up my hair with prose. I fancy one's hair would not curl if it were pinned up with prose. I think I tried once, Mincing.

MINCING: O mem, I shall never forget it.

MILLAMANT: Ay, poor Mincing tift and tift[5] all the morning.

MINCING: Till I had the cremp in my fingers I'll vow, mem. And all to no purpose. But when your la'ship pins it up with poetry, it sits so pleasant the next day as anything, and is so pure and so crips.[6]

WITWOUD: Indeed, so crips?

MINCING: You're such a critic Mr Witwoud.

5. *tift*: arranged.
6. *crips*: crisp.

MILLAMANT: Mirabell, did not you take exceptions last night? Oh, ay, and went away. – Now I think on't, I'm angry. – No, now I think on't I'm pleased, for I believe I gave you some pain.

MIRABELL: Does that please you?

MILLAMANT: Infinitely; I love to give pain.

MIRABELL: You would affect a cruelty which is not in your nature; your true vanity is in the power of pleasing.

MILLAMANT: Oh, I ask your pardon for that. One's cruelty is one's power, and when one parts with one's cruelty, one parts with one's power; and when one has parted with that, I fancy one's old and ugly.

MIRABELL: Ay, ay, suffer your cruelty to ruin the object of your power, to destroy your lover – and then how vain, how lost a thing you'll be! Nay, 'tis true: you are no longer handsome when you've lost your lover; your beauty dies upon the instant. For beauty is the lover's gift; 'tis he bestows your charms, your glass is all a cheat. The ugly and the old, whom the looking-glass mortifies, yet after commendation can be flattered by it, and discover beauties in it; for that reflects our praises, rather than your face.

MILLAMANT: Oh, the vanity of these men! Fainall, d'ye hear him? If they did not commend us, we were not handsome! Now you must know they could not commend one, if one was not handsome. Beauty the lover's gift – Lord, what is a lover, that it can give? Why, one makes lovers as fast as one pleases, and they live as long as one pleases, and they die as soon as one pleases; and then, if one pleases, one makes more.

WITWOUD: Very pretty. Why, you make no more of making of lovers, madam, than of making so many card-matches.[7]

MILLAMANT: One no more owes one's beauty to a lover, than one's wit to an echo. They can but reflect what we look and say; vain empty things if we are silent or unseen, and want a being.

MIRABELL: Yet to those two vain empty things you owe two of the greatest pleasures of your life.

MILLAMANT: How so?

7. *card-matches*: cardboard matches.

MIRABELL: To your lover you owe the pleasure of hearing yourselves praised; and to an echo the pleasure of hearing yourselves talk.

WITWOUD: But I know a lady that loves talking so incessantly, she won't give an echo fair play; she has that everlasting rotation of tongue, that an echo must wait till she dies before it can catch her last words.

MILLAMANT: Oh, fiction! Fainall, let us leave these men.

MIRABELL [aside to MRS FAINALL]: Draw off Witwoud.

MRS FAINALL: Immediately. – I have a word or two for Mr Witwoud.

MIRABELL: I would beg a little private audience too –
    [Exit WITWOUD and MRS FAINFALL.]
You had the tyranny to deny me last night, though you knew I came to impart a secret to you that concerned my love.

MILLAMANT: You saw I was engaged.

MIRABELL: Unkind. You had the leisure to entertain a herd of fools; things who visit you from their excessive idleness, bestowing on your easiness that time which is the encumbrance of their lives. How can you find delight in such society? It is impossible they should admire you; they are not capable. Or if they were, it should be to you as a mortification; for sure, to please a fool is some degree of folly.

MILLAMANT: I please myself. – Besides, sometimes to converse with fools is for my health.

MIRABELL: Your health! Is there a worse disease than the conversation of fools?

MILLAMANT: Yes, the vapours; fools are physics for it, next to assafoetida.[8]

MIRABELL: You are not in a course of fools?

MILLAMANT: Mirabell, if you persist in this offensive freedom you'll displease me. – I think I must resolve, after all, not to have you; we shan't agree.

MIRABELL: Not in our physic, it may be.

MILLAMANT: And yet our distemper in all likelihood will be the

---

8. *assafoetida*: a medicinal gum.

same; for we shall be sick of one another. I shan't endure to be reprimanded, nor instructed; 'tis so dull to act always by advice, and so tedious to be told of one's faults – I can't bear it. Well, I won't have you Mirabell – I'm resolved – I think – you may go. Ha, ha, ha! What would you give that you could help loving me?

MIRABELL: I would give something that you did not know I could not help it.

MILLAMANT: Come, don't look grave then. Well, what do you say to me?

MIRABELL: I say that a man may as soon make a friend by his wit, or a fortune by his honesty, as win a woman with plain dealing and sincerity.

MILLAMANT: Sententious Mirabell! Prithee, don't look with that violent and inflexible wise face, like Solomon at the dividing of the child in an old tapestry hanging.

MIRABELL: You are merry, madam, but I would persuade you for one moment to be serious.

MILLAMANT: What, with that face? No, if you keep your countenance, 'tis impossible I should hold mine. Well, after all, there is something very moving in a love-sick face. Ha, ha, ha! – Well, I won't laugh; don't be peevish. Heigho! Now I'll be melancholy, as melancholy as a watch-light.[9] Well, Mirabell, if ever you will win me, woo me now. – Nay, if you are so tedious, fare you well; I see they are walking away.

MIRABELL: Can you not find in the variety of your disposition one moment –

MILLAMANT: To hear you tell me that Foible's married, and your plot like to speed? – No.

MIRABELL: But how came you to know it?

MILLAMANT: Unless by the help of the devil, you can't imagine; unless she should tell me herself. Which of the two it may have been, I will leave you to consider; and when you have done thinking of that, think of me.

[Exit.]

MIRABELL: I have something more – gone! Think of you? To think

9. watch-light: night-light.

of a whirlwind, though 'twere in a whirlwind, were a case of more steady contemplation; a very tranquillity of mind and mansion. A fellow that lives in a windmill has not a more whimsical dwelling than the heart of a man that is lodged in a woman. There is no point of the compass to which they cannot turn, and by which they are not turned; and by one as well as another, for motion, not method is their occupation. To know this, and yet continue to be in love, is to be made wise from the dictates of reason, and yet persevere to play the fool by the force of instinct. – Oh, here come my pair of turtles.[10] – What, billing so sweetly? Is not Valentine's day over with you yet?

[*Enter* WAITWELL *and* FOIBLE.]

Sirrah Waitwell, why sure you think you were married for your own recreation, and not for my conveniency.

WAITWELL: Your pardon, sir. With submission, we have indeed been solacing in lawful delights; but still with an eye to business, sir. I have instructed her as well as I could. If she can take your directions as readily as my instructions, sir, your affairs are in a prosperous way.

MIRABELL: Give you joy, Mrs Foible.

FOIBLE: Oh las, sir, I'm so ashamed. – I'm afraid my lady has been in a thousand inquietudes for me. But I protest, sir, I made as much haste as I could.

WAITWELL: That she did indeed, sir. It was my fault that she did not make more.

MIRABELL: That I believe.

FOIBLE: But I told my lady as you instructed me, sir: that I had a prospect of seeing Sir Rowland your uncle, and that I would put her ladyship's picture in my pocket to show him; which I'll be sure to say has made him so enamoured of her beauty, that he burns with impatience to lie at her ladyship's feet and worship the original.

MIRABELL: Excellent Foible! Matrimony has made you eloquent in love.

WAITWELL: I think she has profited, sir. I think so.

10. *turtles*: turtledoves.

FOIBLE: You have seen Madam Millamant, sir?

MIRABELL: Yes.

FOIBLE: I told her, sir, because I did not know that you might find an opportunity; she had so much company last night.

MIRABELL: Your diligence will merit more. In the meantime –
[*Gives money.*]

FOIBLE: Oh dear sir, your humble servant.

WAITWELL: Spouse.

MIRABELL: Stand off, sir, not a penny – Go on and prosper, Foible; the lease shall be made good and the farm stocked, if we succeed.

FOIBLE: I don't question your generosity, sir; and you need not doubt of success. If you have no more commands, sir, I'll be gone; I'm sure my lady is at her toilet, and can't dress till I come. [*Looking out.*] Oh dear, I'm sure that was Mrs Marwood that went by in a mask; if she has seen me with you I'm sure she'll tell my lady. I'll make haste home and prevent her. Your servant, sir. B'w'y,[11] Waitwell.
[*Exit* FOIBLE.]

WAITWELL: Sir Rowland, if you please. The jade's so pert upon her preferment she forgets herself.

MIRABELL: Come sir, will you endeavour to forget yourself, and transform into Sir Rowland?

WAITWELL: Why sir, it will be impossible I should remember myself – Married, knighted, and attended all in one day! 'Tis enough to make any man forget himself. The difficulty will be how to recover my acquaintance and familiarity with my former self, and fall from my transformation to a reformation into Waitwell. Nay, I shan't be quite the same Waitwell, neither – for now I remember me, I am married, and can't be my own man again.

> Ay there's the grief; that's the sad change of life;
> To lose my title, and yet keep my wife.

[*Exeunt.*]

---

11. *B'w'y*: [God] be with you.

ACT THREE

SCENE ONE

A Room in Lady Wishfort's House.

[LADY WISHFORT *at her toilet,* PEG *waiting.*]

LADY WISHFORT: Merciful, no news of Foible yet?

PEG: No, madam.

LADY WISHFORT: I have no more patience. – If I have not fretted myself till I am pale again, there's no veracity in me. Fetch me the red – the red, do you hear, sweet-heart? An errant ash colour, as I'm a person. Look you how this wench stirs! Why dost thou not fetch me a little red? Did'st thou not hear me, mopus?[1]

PEG: The red ratifia does your ladyship mean, or the cherry brandy?

LADY WISHFORT: Ratifia, fool? No, fool. Not the ratifia, fool – grant me patience! I mean the Spanish paper,[2] idiot; complexion, darling. Paint, paint, paint; dost thou understand that, changeling, dangling thy hands like bobbins before thee? Why dost thou not stir, puppet? thou wooden thing upon wires!

PEG: Lord, madam, your ladyship is so impatient – I cannot come at the paint, madam; Mrs Foible has locked it up, and carried the key with her.

LADY WISHFORT: A pox take you both – fetch me the cherry brandy then. [*Exit* PEG.] I'm as pale and as faint, I look like Mrs Qualmsick, the curate's wife, that's always breeding. Wench, come, come, wench, what art thou doing? Sipping? Tasting? Save thee, dost thou not know the bottle?

---

1. *mopus*: somebody dull and stupid.
2. *Spanish paper*: for applying rouge.

[*Enter* PEG *with a bottle and china cup.*]

PEG: Madam, I was looking for a cup.

LADY WISHFORT: A cup, save thee, and what a cup hast thou brought! Dost thou take me for a fairy, to drink out of an acorn? Why didst thou not bring thy thimble? Hast thou ne'er a brass thimble clinking in thy pocket with a bit of nutmeg? I warrant thee. Come, fill, fill. So – again. [*One knocks.*] See who that is. Set down the bottle first. Here, here, under the table. – What, wouldst thou go with the bottle in thy hand like a tapster? As I'm a person, this wench has lived in an inn upon the road before she came to me, like Maritornes the Asturian in *Don Quixote*. No Foible yet?

PEG: No, madam, Mrs Marwood.

LADY WISHFORT: Oh, Marwood, let her come in. Come in, good Marwood.

[*Enter* MRS MARWOOD.]

MRS MARWOOD: I'm surprised to find your ladyship in *dishabilie* at this time of day.

LADY WISHFORT: Foible's a lost thing; has been abroad since morning, and never heard of since.

MRS MARWOOD: I saw her but now, as I came masked through the park, in conference with Mirabell.

LADY WISHFORT: With Mirabell! You call my blood into my face with mentioning that traitor. She durst not have the confidence. I sent her to negotiate an affair in which, if I'm detected, I'm undone. If that wheedling villain has wrought upon Foible to detect me, I'm ruined. Oh my dear friend, I'm a wretch of wretches if I'm detected.

MRS MARWOOD: Oh madam, you cannot suspect Mrs Foible's integrity.

LADY WISHFORT: Oh, he carries poison in his tongue that would corrupt integrity itself. If she has given him an opportunity, she has as good as put her integrity into his hands. Ah, dear Marwood, what's integrity to an opportunity? Hark! I hear her. – Go, you thing, and send her in. [*Exit* PEG.] Dear friend, retire into my closet, that I may examine her with more freedom. – You'll pardon me, dear friend; I can make bold with you. – There are books over the chimney – Quarles and Prynne,[3] and the *Short View of the Stage*,[4] with Bunyan's works, to entertain you.

[*Exit* MARWOOD.]

[*Enter* FOIBLE.]

O Foible, where hast thou been? What hast thou been doing?

FOIBLE: Madam, I have seen the party.

LADY WISHFORT: But what hast thou done?

FOIBLE: Nay, 'tis your ladyship has done, and are to do; I have only promised. But a man so enamoured – so transported! Well, here it is, all that is left; all that is not kissed away. Well, if worshipping of pictures be a sin, poor Sir Rowland, I say.

LADY WISHFORT: The miniature has been counted like. – But hast thou not betrayed me, Foible? Hast thou not detected me to that faithless Mirabell? What hadst thou to do with him in the park? Answer me, he has got nothing out of thee?

FOIBLE [*aside*]: So, the devil has been beforehand with me. What shall I say? – Alas, madam, could I help it, if I met that confident thing? Was I in fault? If you had heard how he used me, and all upon your ladyship's account, I'm sure you would not suspect my fidelity. Nay, if that had been the worst, I could have borne; but he had a fling at your ladyship too, and then I could not hold, but i'faith I gave him his own.

LADY WISHFORT: Me? What did the filthy fellow say?

FOIBLE: Oh madam, 'tis a shame to say what he said, with his taunts and his fleers, tossing up his nose. 'Humh!' says he, 'what, you are a-hatching some plot,' says he, 'you are so early abroad, or catering,' says he, 'ferreting for some disbanded officer, I warrant. Half-pay is but thin subsistence,' says he. 'Well, what pension does your lady propose? Let me see,' says he. 'What, she must come down pretty deep, now she's superannuated,' says he, 'and –'

LADY WISHFORT: Ods my life, I'll have him, I'll have him murdered. I'll have him poisoned. Where does he eat? I'll marry a

3. *Quarles . . . Prynne*: Francis Quarles was the author of *Emblems, Divine and Moral* (1635) and William Prynne of *Histriomastix* (1635), a Puritan attack on the stage.
4. *Short View of the Stage*: Jeremy Collier's recent (1698) attack on the stage.

drawer to have him poisoned in his wine. I'll send for Robin from Locket's[5] immediately.

FOIBLE: Poison him? Poisoning's too good for him. Starve him madam, starve him; marry Sir Rowland and get him disinherited. Oh, you would bless yourself to hear what he said.

LADY WISHFORT: A villain! 'Superannuated!'

FOIBLE: 'Humh,' says he, 'I hear you are laying designs against me too,' says he, 'and Mrs Millamant is to marry my uncle' (he does not suspect a word of your ladyship); 'but,' says he, 'I'll fit you for that, I warrant you,' says he. 'I'll hamper you for that,' says he, 'you and your old frippery[6] too,' says he, 'I'll handle you –'

LADY WISHFORT: Audacious villain! 'handle' me, would he durst! – 'Frippery? old frippery!' Was there ever such a foul-mouthed fellow? I'll be married tomorrow, I'll be contracted tonight.

FOIBLE: The sooner the better, madam.

LADY WISHFORT: Will Sir Rowland be here, say'st thou? When, Foible?

FOIBLE: Incontinently,[7] madam. No new sheriff's wife expects the return of her husband after knighthood with that impatience in which Sir Rowland burns for the dear hour of kissing your ladyship's hands after dinner.

LADY WISHFORT: 'Frippery! Superannuated frippery!' I'll frippery the villain; I'll reduce him to frippery and rags! A tatterdemalion! – I hope to see him hung with tatters, like a Long Lane penthouse[8] or a gibbet thief. A slander-mouthed railer: I warrant the spend-thrift prodigal's in debt as much as the million lottery,[9] or the whole court upon a birthday. I'll spoil his credit with his tailor. Yes, he shall have my niece with her fortune, he shall.

FOIBLE: He! I hope to see him lodge in Ludgate[10] first, and angle into Blackfriars for brass farthings with an old mitten.[11]

5. *Locket's*: well-known restaurant and tavern.
6. *frippery*: worn-out clothes.
7. *incontinently*: immediately.
8. *Long Lane penthouse*: stall in Long Lane, where the rag trade flourished.
9. *million lottery*: Davis identifies this as the government lottery of 1694.
10. *Ludgate*: Ludgate prison.
11. *angle . . . mitten*: as a way of retrieving offerings from passers-by.

LADY WISHFORT: Ay dear Foible; thank thee for that, dear Foible. He has put me out of all patience. I shall never recompose my features to receive Sir Rowland with any economy of face. This wretch has fretted me that I am absolutely decayed. Look, Foible.

FOIBLE: Your ladyship has frowned a little too rashly, indeed, madam. There are some cracks discernible in the white varnish.

LADY WISHFORT: Let me see the glass. – Cracks, say'st thou? Why I am arrantly flayed; I look like an old peeled wall. Thou must repair me Foible, before Sir Rowland comes, or I shall never keep up to my picture.

FOIBLE: I warrant you, madam; a little art once made your picture like you, and now a little of the same art must make you like your picture. Your picture must sit for you, madam.

LADY WISHFORT: But art thou sure Sir Rowland will not fail to come? Or will a' not fail when he does come? Will he be importunate, Foible, and push? For if he should not be importunate, I shall never break decorums. I shall die with confusion, if I am forced to advance. – Oh no, I can never advance. – I shall swoon if he should expect advances. No, I hope Sir Rowland is better bred than to put a lady to the necessity of breaking her forms. I won't be too coy neither. – I won't give him despair – but a little disdain is not amiss; a little scorn is alluring.

FOIBLE: A little scorn becomes your ladyship.

LADY WISHFORT: Yes, but tenderness becomes me best – a sort of a dyingness. You see that picture has a sort of a – ha, Foible? A swimminess in the eyes. Yes, I'll look so. – My niece affects it, but she wants features. Is Sir Rowland handsome? Let my toilet be removed – I'll dress above. I'll receive Sir Rowland here. Is he handsome? Don't answer me. I won't know; I'll be surprised. I'll be taken by surprise.

FOIBLE: By storm, madam. Sir Rowland's a brisk man.

LADY WISHFORT: Is he! Oh, then he'll importune, if he's a brisk man. I shall save decorums if Sir Rowland importunes. I have a mortal terror at the apprehension of offending against decorums. Nothing but importunity can surmount decorums. Oh, I'm glad he's a brisk man. Let my things be removed, good Foible.

[*Exit.*]

[*Enter* MRS FAINALL.]

MRS FAINALL: Oh Foible, I have been in a fright, lest I should come
    too late. That devil Marwood saw you in the park with Mirabell,
    and I'm afraid will discover it to my lady.

FOIBLE: Discover what, madam?

MRS FAINALL: Nay, nay, put not on that strange face. I am privy to
    the whole design, and know that Waitwell, to whom thou wert
    this morning married, is to personate Mirabell's uncle, and as
    such, winning my lady, to involve her in those difficulties from
    which Mirabell only must release her, by his making his con-
    ditions to have my cousin and her fortune left to her own
    disposal.

FOIBLE: O dear madam, I beg your pardon. It was not my confi-
    dence in your ladyship that was deficient; but I thought the
    former good correspondence between your ladyship and Mr
    Mirabell might have hindered his communicating this secret.

MRS FAINALL: Dear Foible, forget that.

FOIBLE: O dear madam, Mr Mirabell is such a sweet winning
    gentleman – but your ladyship is the pattern of generosity. Sweet
    lady, to be so good! Mr Mirabell cannot choose but be grateful. I
    find your ladyship has his heart still. Now, madam, I can safely
    tell your ladyship our success. Mrs Marwood had told my lady,
    but I warrant I managed myself. I turned it all for the better. I told
    my lady that Mr Mirabell railed at her. I laid horrid things to his
    charge, I'll vow; and my lady is so incensed, that she'll be
    contracted to Sir Rowland tonight, she says. I warrant I worked
    her up, that he may have her for asking for, as they say of a Welsh
    maidenhead.

MRS FAINALL: O rare Foible!

FOIBLE: Madam, I beg your ladyship to acquaint Mr Mirabell of his
    success. I would be seen as little as possible to speak to him.
    Besides, I believe Madam Marwood watches me. – She has a
    month's mind,[12] but I know Mr Mirabell can't abide her. [*Enter*
    FOOTMAN.] John, remove my lady's toilet. Madam, your ser-
    vant. My lady is so impatient, I fear she'll come for me if I stay.

12. *month's mind*: strong desire.

MRS FAINALL: I'll go with you up the back stairs, lest I should meet her.

[*Exeunt.*]

[*Enter* MRS MARWOOD.]

MRS MARWOOD: Indeed Mrs Engine, is it thus with you? Are you become a go-between of this importance? Yes, I shall watch you. Why this wench is the *passe-partout*, a very master key to everybody's strong-box. My friend Fainall, have you carried it so swimmingly? I thought there was something in it; but it seems it's over with you. Your loathing is not from a want of appetite then, but from a surfeit. Else you could never be so cool to fall from a principal to be an assistant; to procure for him! 'A pattern of generosity,' that I confess. Well, Mr Fainall, you have met with your match. – O man, man! Woman, woman! The devil's an ass; if I were a painter, I would draw him like an idiot, a driveller, with a bib and bells. Man should have his head and horns, and woman the rest of him. Poor simple fiend! 'Madam Marwood has a month's mind, but he can't abide her.' – 'Twere better for him you had not been his confessor in that affair, without you could have kept his counsel closer. I shall not prove another pattern of generosity and stalk for him, till he takes his stand to aim at a fortune. He has not obliged me to that with those excesses of himself; and now I'll have none of him. Here comes the good lady, panting ripe; with a heart full of hope, and a head full of care, like any chemist[13] upon the day of projection.

[*Enter* LADY WISHFORT.]

LADY WISHFORT: O dear Marwood, what shall I say for this rude forgetfulness? But my dear friend is all goodness.

MRS MARWOOD: No apologies, dear madam. I have been very well entertained.

LADY WISHFORT: As I'm a person, I am in a very chaos to think I should so forget myself. – But I have such an olio[14] of affairs really I know not what to do. [*Calls.*] Foible! I expect my nephew, Sir Wilfull, every moment too – why, Foible! He means to travel for improvement.

13. *chemist*: alchemist.
14. *olio*: mixture or medley.

MRS MARWOOD: Methinks Sir Wilfull should rather think of marrying than travelling at his years. I hear he is turned of forty.

LADY WISHFORT: Oh, he's in less danger of being spoiled by his travels. I am against my nephew's marrying too young. It will be time enough when he comes back and has acquired discretion to choose for himself.

MRS MARWOOD: Methinks Mrs Millamant and he would make a very fit match. He may travel afterwards. 'Tis a thing very usual with young gentlemen.

LADY WISHFORT: I promise you I have thought on't; and since 'tis your judgment, I'll think on't again, I assure you I will; I value your judgment extremely. On my word, I'll propose it.

　　[Enter FOIBLE.]

Come, come Foible, I had forgot my nephew will be here before dinner. I must make haste.

FOIBLE: Mr Witwoud and Mr Petulant are come to dine with your ladyship.

LADY WISHFORT: Oh dear, I can't appear till I'm dressed. Dear Marwood, shall I be free with you again, and beg you to entertain 'em? I'll make all imaginable haste. Dear friend, excuse me.

　　[Exit LADY WISHFORT and FOIBLE.]
　　[Enter MRS MILLAMANT and MINCING.]

MILLAMANT: Sure never anything was so unbred as that odious man. – Marwood, your servant.

MRS MARWOOD: You have a colour; what's the matter?

MILLAMANT: That horrid fellow, Petulant, has provoked me into a flame. I have broke my fan – Mincing, lend me yours; is not all the powder out of my hair?

MRS MARWOOD: No. What has he done?

MILLAMANT: Nay, he has done nothing; he has only talked – nay, he has said nothing neither; but he has contradicted everything that has been said. For my part, I thought Witwoud and he would have quarrelled.

MINCING: I vow mem, I thought once they would have fit.[15]

15. *fit*: fought.

MILLAMANT: Well, 'tis a lamentable thing, I'll swear, that one has not the liberty of choosing one's acquaintance as one does one's clothes.

MRS MARWOOD: If we had the liberty, we should be as weary of one set of acquaintance, though never so good, as we are of one suit, though never so fine. A fool and a doily stuff[16] would now and then find days of grace, and be worn for variety.

MILLAMANT: I could consent to wear 'em, if they would wear alike, but fools never wear out – they are such *drap-du-Berry*[17] things, without one could give 'em to one's chambermaid after a day or two.

MRS MARWOOD: 'Twere better so indeed. Or what think you of the play-house? A fine gay glossy fool should be given there, like a new masking habit, after the masquerade is over, and we have done with the disguise. For a fool's visit is always a disguise, and never admitted by a woman of wit but to blind her affair with a lover of sense. If you would but appear bare-faced now, and own Mirabell, you might as easily put off Petulant and Witwoud as your hood and scarf. And indeed 'tis time, for the town has found it; the secret is grown too big for the pretence. 'Tis like Mrs Primly's great belly; she may lace it down before, but it burnishes on her hips. Indeed, Millamant, you can no more conceal it than my Lady Strammel can her face, that goodly face, which in defiance of her Rhenish-wine tea,[18] will not be comprehended in a mask.

MILLAMANT: I'll take my death, Marwood, you are more censorious than a decayed beauty, or a discarded toast; Mincing, tell the men they may come up. My aunt is not dressing; their folly is less provoking than your malice. [*Exit* MINCING.] 'The town has found it.' What has it found? That Mirabell loves me is no more a secret than it is a secret that you discovered it to my aunt, or than the reason why you discovered it is a secret.

MRS MARWOOD: You are nettled.

16. *doily stuff*: light woollen material.
17. *drap-du-Berry*: woollen cloth from Berry, France.
18. *Rhenish-wine tea*: Rhine wines were thought to be slimming.

MILLAMANT: You're mistaken. Ridiculous!

MRS MARWOOD: Indeed my dear, you'll tear another fan if you don't mitigate those violent airs.

MILLAMANT: Oh silly! Ha, ha, ha! I could laugh immoderately. Poor Mirabell! His constancy to me has quite destroyed his complaisance for all the world beside. I swear, I never enjoined it him to be so coy. – If I had the vanity to think he would obey me, I would command him to show more gallantry. – 'Tis hardly well bred to be so particular on one hand, and so insensible on the other. But I despair to prevail, and so let him follow his own way. Ha, ha, ha. Pardon me, dear creature, I must laugh, ha, ha, ha, though I grant you 'tis a little barbarous, ha, ha, ha.

MRS MARWOOD: What pity 'tis, so much fine raillery, and delivered with so significant gesture, should be so unhappily directed to miscarry.

MILLAMANT: Ha? Dear creature, I ask your pardon – I swear I did not mind you.

MRS MARWOOD: Mr Mirabell and you both may think it a thing impossible, when I shall tell him, by telling you –

MILLAMANT: Oh dear, what? For it is the same thing if I hear it, ha, ha, ha.

MRS MARWOOD: That I detest him, hate him, madam.

MILLAMANT: Oh madam, why so do I – and yet the creature loves me, ha, ha, ha. How can one forbear laughing to think of it. – I am a sybil if I am not amazed to think what he can see in me. I'll take my death, I think you are handsomer – and within a year or two as young. If you could but stay for me, I should overtake you – but that cannot be. Well, that thought makes me melancholy. – Now I'll be sad.

MRS MARWOOD: Your merry note may be changed sooner than you think.

MILLAMANT: D'ye say so? Then I'm resolved I'll have a song to keep up my spirits.

[*Enter* MINCING.]

MINCING: The gentlemen stay but to comb, madam, and will wait on you.

MILLAMANT: Desire Mrs —, that is in the next room, to sing the

song I would have learned yesterday. You shall hear it madam –
not that there's any great matter in it, but 'tis agreeable to my
humour.

[*Set by Mr John Eccles, and sung by Mrs Hodgson.*[19]]

(*Song*)

I

Love's but the frailty of the mind,
    When 'tis not with ambition joined;
A sickly flame, which if not fed, expires;
And feeding, wastes in self-consuming fires.

II

'Tis not to wound a wanton boy
    Or am'rous youth, that gives the joy;
But 'tis the glory to have pierced a swain,
For whom inferior beauties sighed in vain.

III

Then I alone the conquest prize,
    When I insult a rival's eyes;
If there's delight in love, 'tis when I see
That heart which others bleed for, bleed for me.

[*Enter* PETULANT *and* WITWOUD.]

MILLAMANT: Is your animosity composed, gentlemen?

WITWOUD: Raillery, raillery, madam; we have no animosity. – We
hit off a little wit now and then, but no animosity. – The falling
out of wits is like the falling out of lovers; we agree in the main,
like treble and bass. Ha, Petulant?

PETULANT: Ay, in the main – but when I have a humour to
contradict.

WITWOUD: Ay, when he has a humour to contradict, then I
contradict too. What, I know my cue. Then we contradict one
another like two battledores; for contradictions beget one another
like Jews.

19. *Mrs Hodgson*: popular singer of the day.

PETULANT: If he says black's black, if I have a humour to say 'tis blue, let that pass; all's one for that. If I have a humour to prove it, it must be granted.

WITWOUD: Not positively must – but it may, it may.

PETULANT: Yes, it positively must, upon proof positive.

WITWOUD: Ay, upon proof positive it must; but upon proof presumptive it only may. That's a logical distinction now, madam.

MRS MARWOOD: I perceive your debates are of importance and very learnedly handled.

PETULANT: Importance is one thing, and learning's another; but a debate's a debate, that I assert.

WITWOUD: Petulant's an enemy to learning; he relies altogether on his parts.

PETULANT: No, I'm no enemy to learning; it hurts not me.

MRS MARWOOD: That's a sign indeed it's no enemy to you.

PETULANT: No, no, it's no enemy to anybody but them that have it.

MILLAMANT: Well, an illiterate man's my aversion. I wonder at the impudence of any illiterate man to offer to make love.

WITWOUD: That I confess I wonder at too.

MILLAMANT: Ah! to marry an ignorant that can hardly read or write.

PETULANT: Why should a man be ever the further from being married though he can't read, any more than he is from being hanged? The Ordinary's[20] paid for setting the psalm, and the parish priest for reading the ceremony. And for the rest which is to follow in both cases, a man may do it without book – so all's one for that.

MILLAMANT: D'ye hear the creature? Lord, here's company; I'll be gone.

[*Exeunt* MILLAMANT *and* MINCING.]

WITWOUD: In the name of Bartlemew and his fair,[21] what have we here?

MRS MARWOOD: 'Tis your brother, I fancy. Don't you know him?

20. *Ordinary*: prison chaplain.
21. *Bartlemew . . . fair*: the annual fair, full of strange sights, which was held in Smithfield on St Bartholomew's day.

WITWOUD: Not I. – Yes, I think it is he. – I've almost forgot him; I have not seen him since the Revolution.[22]

[*Enter* SIR WILFULL WITWOUD *in a country riding habit, and* SERVANT *to* LADY WISHFORT.]

SERVANT: Sir, my lady's dressing. Here's company, if you please to walk in, in the mean time.

SIR WILFULL: Dressing! What, it's but morning here, I warrant with you, in London; we should count it towards afternoon in our parts, down in Shropshire. Why then, belike my aunt han't dined yet – ha, friend?

SERVANT: Your aunt, sir?

SIR WILFULL: My aunt, sir, yes my aunt, sir, and your lady, sir; your lady is my aunt, sir. – Why, what, dost thou not know me, friend? Why then send somebody here that does. How long hast thou lived with thy lady, fellow, ha?

SERVANT: A week, sir; longer than anybody in the house, except my lady's woman.

SIR WILFULL: Why then, belike thou dost not know thy lady if thou seest her, ha, friend?

SERVANT: Why truly, sir, I cannot safely swear to her face in a morning, before she is dressed. 'Tis like I may give a shrewd guess at her by this time.

SIR WILFULL: Well, prithee try what thou canst do; if thou canst not guess, enquire her out, dost hear fellow? And tell her, her nephew, Sir Wilfull Witwoud, is in the house.

SERVANT: I shall, sir.

SIR WILFULL: Hold ye, hear me, friend; a word with you in your ear. Prithee who are these gallants?

SERVANT: Really sir, I can't tell; here come so many here, 'tis hard to know 'em all.

[*Exit* SERVANT.]

SIR WILFULL: Oons, this fellow knows less than a starling; I don't think a' knows his own name.

MRS MARWOOD: Mr Witwoud, your brother is not behindhand in forgetfulness; I fancy he has forgot you too.

22. *the Revolution*: that of 1688.

WITWOUD: I hope so. – The devil take him that remembers first, I say.

SIR WILFUL: Save you, gentlemen and lady.

MRS MARWOOD: For shame, Mr Witwoud; why won't you speak to him? – And you, sir.

WITWOUD: Petulant, speak.

PETULANT: And you, sir.

SIR WILFULL: No offence, I hope.

[Salutes MRS MARWOOD.]

MRS MARWOOD: No sure, sir.

WITWOUD: This is a vile dog, I see that already. No offence! Ha, ha, ha! To him, to him, Petulant; smoke[23] him.

PETULANT: It seems as if you had come a journey, sir, hem, hem.

[Surveying him round.]

SIR WILFULL: Very likely, sir, that it may seem so.

PETULANT: No offence, I hope, sir.

WITWOUD: Smoke the boots, the boots, Petulant, the boots. Ha, ha, ha.

SIR WILFULL: Maybe not, sir; thereafter as 'tis meant, sir.

PETULANT: Sir, I presume upon the information of your boots.

SIR WILFULL: Why, 'tis like you may, sir. If you are not satisfied with the information of my boots, sir, if you will step to the stable, you may enquire further of my horse, sir.

PETULANT: Your horse, sir! Your horse is an ass, sir!

SIR WILFULL: Do you speak by way of offence, sir?

MRS MARWOOD: The gentleman's merry, that's all, sir. [Aside.] 'Slife, we shall have a quarrel betwixt an horse and an ass, before they find one another out. [Aloud.] You must not take anything amiss from your friends, sir. You are among your friends here, though it may be you don't know it. If I am not mistaken, you are Sir Wilfull Witwoud.

SIR WILFULL: Right, lady; I am Sir Wilfull Witwoud, so I write myself; no offence to anybody, I hope; and nephew to the Lady Wishfort of this mansion.

MRS MARWOOD: Don't you know this gentleman, sir?

23. *smoke*: make fun of, ridicule.

SIR WILFULL: Hum! What, sure 'tis not – yea, by'r lady, but 'tis. –
'S'heart, I know not whether 'tis or no – yea but 'tis by the
Rekin.[24] Brother Anthony! What Tony, i'faith! What, dost thou
not know me? By'r Lady, nor I thee, thou art so becravatted, and
beperiwigged. – 'S'heart, why dost not speak? Art thou o'er-
joyed?

WITWOUD: Odso, brother, is it you? Your servant, brother.

SIR WILFULL: Your servant! Why, yours, sir. Your servant again,
's'heart, and your friend and servant to that, and a (*puff*) and a
flapdragon for your service, sir; and a hare's foot, and a hare's
scut[25] for your service, sir, an you be so cold and so courtly!

WITWOUD: No offence, I hope, brother.

SIR WILFULL: 'S'heart, sir, but there is, and much offence. – A pox,
is this your Inns o' Court breeding, not to know your friends and
your relations, your elders, and your betters?

WITWOUD: Why, brother Wilfull of Salop,[26] you may be as short
as a Shrewsbury cake, if you please. But I tell you, 'tis not modish
to know relations in town. You think you're in the country,
where great lubberly brothers slabber and kiss one another when
they meet, like a call of serjeants.[27] – 'Tis not the fashion here; 'tis
not indeed, dear brother.

SIR WILFULL: The fashion's a fool; and you're a fop, dear brother.
'S'heart, I've suspected this. – By'r Lady I conjectured you were a
fop, since you began to change the style of your letters, and write
in a scrap of paper gilt round the edges, no broader than a
subpoena. I might expect this, when you left off 'Honoured
Brother', and 'hoping you are in good health', and so forth, to
begin with a 'Rat me, knight, I'm so sick of a last night's debauch'
– ods heart, and then tell a familiar tale of a cock and a bull, and a
whore and a bottle, and so conclude. – You could write news
before you were out of your time, when you lived with honest
Pumplenose the attorney of Furnival's Inn; you could entreat to
be remembered then to your friends round the Rekin. We could

24. *Rekin*: the Wrekin, a prominent hill in Shropshire.
25. *scut*: tail.
26. *Salop*: Shropshire.
27. *call of serjeants*: group called to the Bar at the same time.

have gazettes then, and *Dawk's Letter*,[28] and the weekly bill,[29] till of late days.

PETULANT: 'Slife, Witwoud, were you ever an attorney's clerk? Of the family of the Furnivals? Ha, ha, ha!

WITWOUD: Ay, ay, but that was for a while. Not long, not long; pshaw, I was not in my own power then. An orphan, and this fellow was my guardian; ay, ay, I was glad to consent to that man to come to London. He had the disposal of me then. If I had not agreed to that, I might have been bound 'prentice to a felt-maker in Shrewsbury; this fellow would have bound me to a maker of felts.

SIR WILFULL: 'S'heart, and better than to be bound to a maker of fops, where, I suppose, you have served your time; and now you may set up for yourself.

MRS MARWOOD: You intend to travel, sir, as I'm informed.

SIR WILFULL: Belike I may, madam. I may chance to sail upon the salt seas, if my mind hold.

PETULANT: And the wind serve.

SIR WILFULL: Serve or not serve, I shan't ask licence of you, sir; nor the weather-cock your companion. I direct my discourse to the lady, sir. 'Tis like my aunt may have told you, madam. – Yes, I have settled my concerns, I may say now, and am minded to see foreign parts. If an how that the peace[30] holds, whereby, that is, taxes abate.

MRS MARWOOD: I thought you had designed for France at all adventures.

SIR WILFULL: I can't tell that; 'tis like I may, and 'tis like I may not. I am somewhat dainty in making a resolution, because when I make it I keep it. I don't stand shill I, shall I, then; if I say't, I'll do't. But I have thoughts to tarry a small matter in town, to learn somewhat of your lingo first, before I cross the seas. I'd gladly have a spice of your French, as they say, whereby to hold discourse in foreign countries.

MRS MARWOOD: Here is an academy in town for that use.

28. *Dawk's Letter*: a newspaper.
29. *weekly bill*: weekly record of the deaths in the City of London.
30. *the peace*: the Peace of Ryswick (1697).

SIR WILFULL: There is? 'Tis like there may.

MRS MARWOOD: No doubt you will return very much improved.

WITWOUD: Yes, refined, like a Dutch skipper from a whale-fishing.

[*Enter* LADY WISHFORT *and* FAINALL.]

LADY WISHFORT: Nephew, you are welcome.

SIR WILFULL: Aunt, your servant.

FAINALL: Sir Wilfull, your most faithful servant.

SIR WILFULL: Cousin Fainall, give me your hand.

LADY WISHFORT: Cousin Witwoud, your servant; Mr Petulant, your servant. – Nephew, you are welcome again. Will you drink anything after your journey, nephew, before you eat? Dinner's almost ready.

SIR WILFULL: I'm very well, I thank you, aunt; however, I thank you for your courteous offer. 'S'heart, I was afraid you would have been in the fashion too, and have remembered to have forgot your relations. Here's your cousin Tony, belike I mayn't call him brother for fear of offence.

LADY WISHFORT: Oh he's a rallier, nephew – my cousin's a wit, and your great wits always rally their best friends to choose.[31] When you have been abroad, nephew, you'll understand raillery better.

[FAINALL *and* MRS MARWOOD *talk apart.*]

SIR WILFULL: Why then let him hold his tongue in the meantime, and rail when that day comes.

[*Enter* MINCING.]

MINCING: Mem, I come to acquaint your la'ship that dinner is impatient.

SIR WILFULL: Impatient? Why then belike it won't stay till I pull off my boots. Sweetheart, can you help me to a pair of slippers? – My man's with his horses, I warrant.

LADY WISHFORT: Fie, fie, nephew, you would not pull off your boots here. – Go down into the hall; dinner shall stay for you. – My nephew's a little unbred; you'll pardon him, madam. – Gentlemen, will you walk? Marwood?

---

31. *to choose*: by choice.

MRS MARWOOD: I'll follow you, madam, before Sir Wilfull is ready.

[*Manent* MRS MARWOOD *and* FAINALL.]

FAINALL: Why then, Foible's a bawd, an errant, rank, matchmaking bawd. And I it seems am a husband, a rank husband; and my wife a very arrant, rank wife, – all in the way of the world. 'Sdeath, to be an anticipated cuckold, a cuckold in embryo! Sure I was born with budding antlers like a young satyr, or a citizen's child. 'Sdeath to be out-witted, to be out-jilted, – out-matrimonied! If I had kept my speed like a stag, 'twere somewhat, but to crawl after, with my horns, like a snail, and out-stripped by my wife – 'tis scurvy wedlock.

MRS MARWOOD: Then shake it off. You have often wished for an opportunity to part, and now you have it. But first prevent their plot; the half of Millamant's fortune is too considerable to be parted with, to a foe, to Mirabell.

FAINALL: Damn him! that had been mine – had you not made that fond discovery. That had been forfeited, had they been married. My wife had added lustre to my horns by that increase of fortune; I could have worn 'em tipped with gold, though my forehead had been furnished like a deputy-lieutenant's hall.

MRS MARWOOD: They may prove a cap of maintenance[32] to you still, if you can away with your wife. And she's no worse than when you had her – I dare swear she had given up her game before she was married.

FAINALL: Hum! That may be. – She might throw up her cards; but I'll be hanged if she did not put Pam[33] in her pocket.

MRS MARWOOD: You married her to keep you; and if you can contrive to have her keep you better than you expected, why should you not keep her longer than you intended?

FAINALL: The means, the means.

MRS MARWOOD: Discover to my lady your wife's conduct; threaten to part with her. – My lady loves her, and will come to

32. *cap of maintenance*: 'a kind of cap, with two points like horns behind, borne in the arms of certain families' (*O.E.D.*).

33. *Pam*: the Jack of Clubs; in the game of Loo it is the highest card.

any composition to save her reputation. Take the opportunity of breaking it, just upon the discovery of this imposture. My lady will be enraged beyond bounds, and sacrifice niece and fortune and all at that conjuncture. And let me alone to keep her warm; if she should flag in her part, I will not fail to prompt her.

FAINALL: Faith, this has an appearance.

MRS MARWOOD: I'm sorry I hinted to my lady to endeavour a match between Millamant and Sir Wilfull; that may be an obstacle.

FAINALL: Oh, for that matter leave me to manage him; I'll disable him for that. He will drink like a Dane; after dinner, I'll set his hand in.

MRS MARWOOD: Well, how do you stand affected towards your lady?

FAINALL: Why, faith, I'm thinking of it. – Let me see – I am married already, so that's over. – My wife has played the jade with me; well, that's over too. – I never loved her, or if I had, why that would have been over too by this time. – Jealous of her I cannot be, for I am certain; so there's an end of jealousy. Weary of her I am, and shall be. – No, there's no end of that; no, no, that were too much to hope. Thus far concerning my repose. Now for my reputation. – As to my own, I married not for it; so that's out of the question. – And as to my part in my wife's – why she had parted with hers before; so bringing none to me, she can take none from me. 'Tis against all rule of play that I should lose to one who has not wherewithal to stake.

MRS MARWOOD: Besides, you forget, marriage is honourable.

FAINALL: Hum! Faith, and that's well thought on; marriage is honourable as you say; and if so, wherefore should cuckoldom be a discredit, being derived from so honourable a root?

MRS MARWOOD: Nay I know not; if the root be honourable, why not the branches?

FAINALL: So, so; why this point's clear. – Well, how do we proceed?

MRS MARWOOD: I will contrive a letter which shall be delivered to my lady at the time when that rascal who is to act Sir Rowland is with her. It shall come as from an unknown hand – for the less I appear to know of the truth, the better I can play the incendiary. Besides, I would not have Foible provoked if I could help it, because you know she knows some passages. Nay, I expect all will come out; but let the mine be sprung first, and then I care not if I'm discovered.

FAINALL: If the worst come to the worst, I'll turn my wife to grass. – I have already a deed of settlement of the best part of her estate, which I wheedled out of her; and that you shall partake at least.

MRS MARWOOD: I hope you are convinced that I hate Mirabell now; you'll be no more jealous?

FAINALL: Jealous, no – by this kiss. Let husbands be jealous; but let the lover still believe. Or if he doubt, let it be only to endear his pleasure and prepare the joy that follows, when he proves his mistress true. But let husbands' doubts convert to endless jealousy; or if they have belief, let it corrupt to superstition and blind credulity. I am single, and will herd no more with 'em. True, I wear the badge; but I'll disown the order. And since I take my leave of 'em, I care not if I leave 'em a common motto to their common crest.

> All husbands must or pain or shame endure;
> The wise too jealous are, fools too secure.

[*Exeunt.*]

ACT FOUR

SCENE ONE

Scene continues.

[*Enter* LADY WISHFORT *and* FOIBLE.]

LADY WISHFORT: Is Sir Rowland coming, say'st thou, Foible? and are things in order?

FOIBLE: Yes, madam. I have put wax-lights in the sconces, and placed the footmen in a row in the hall, in their best liveries, with the coachman and postilion to fill up the equipage.

LADY WISHFORT: Have you pullvilled[1] the coachman and postilion, that they may not stink of the stable when Sir Rowland comes by?

FOIBLE: Yes, madam.

LADY WISHFORT: And are the dancers and the music ready, that he may be entertained in all points with correspondence to his passion?

FOIBLE: All is ready, madam.

LADY WISHFORT: And – well – and how do I look, Foible?

FOIBLE: Most killing well, madam.

LADY WISHFORT: Well, and how shall I receive him? In what figure shall I give his heart the first impression? There is a great deal in the first impression. Shall I sit? No, I won't sit – I'll walk; ay, I'll walk from the door upon his entrance, and then turn full upon him. – No, that will be too sudden. I'll lie – ay, I'll lie down. – I'll receive him in my little dressing-room; there's a couch – yes, yes, I'll give the first impression on a couch. – I won't lie neither, but loll and lean upon one elbow, with one foot a little dangling off,

1. *pullvilled*: dusted with perfumed powder.

jogging in a thoughtful way. – Yes – and then as soon as he appears, start, ay, start and be surprised, and rise to meet him in a pretty disorder. – Yes – oh, nothing is more alluring than a levée from a couch in some confusion. – It shows the foot to advantage, and furnishes with blushes and re-composing airs beyond comparison. Hark! There's a coach.

FOIBLE: 'Tis he, madam.

LADY WISHFORT: Oh dear, has my nephew made his addresses to Millamant? I ordered him.

FOIBLE: Sir Wilfull is set in to drinking, madam, in the parlour.

LADY WISHFORT: Ods my life, I'll send him to her. Call her down, Foible; bring her hither. I'll send him as I go. – When they are together, then come to me, Foible, that I may not be too long alone with Sir Rowland.

[Exit.]

[Enter MRS MILLAMANT, and MRS FAINALL.]

FOIBLE: Madam, I stayed here to tell your ladyship that Mr Mirabell has waited this half hour for an opportunity to talk with you, though my lady's orders were to leave you and Sir Wilfull together. Shall I tell Mr Mirabell that you are at leisure?

MILLAMANT: No – what would the dear man have? I am thoughtful, and would amuse myself – bid him come another time.

> There never yet was woman made,
> Nor shall, but to be curs'd.[2]

[Repeating and walking about.]

That's hard!

MRS FAINALL: You are very fond of Sir John Suckling today, Millamant, and the poets.

MILLAMANT: He? Ay, and filthy verses; so I am.

FOIBLE: Sir Wilfull is coming, madam. Shall I send Mr Mirabell away?

MILLAMANT: Ay, if you please, Foible, send him away – or send him hither – just as you will, dear Foible. I think I'll see him; shall I? Ay, let the wretch come.

---

2. *There . . . cursed*: opening lines of a lyric by Sir John Suckling (1609–42).

Thyrsis a youth of the inspir'd train[3] –

[*Repeating.*]

Dear Fainall, entertain Sir Wilfull. – Thou hast philosophy to undergo a fool, thou art married and hast patience. – I would confer with my own thoughts.

MRS FAINALL: I am obliged to you, that you would make me your proxy in this affair; but I have business of my own.

[*Enter* SIR WILFULL.]

O Sir Wilfull, you are come at the critical instant. There's your mistress up to the ears in love and contemplation; pursue your point, now or never.

SIR WILFULL: Yes; my aunt would have it so. – I would gladly have been encouraged with a bottle or two, because I'm somewhat wary at first, before I am acquainted. – But I hope after a time, I shall break my mind – that is, upon further acquaintance. – So for the present, cousin, I'll take my leave. – If so be you'll be so kind to make my excuse, I'll return to my company – [*This while* MILLAMANT *walks about repeating to herself.*]

MRS FAINALL: Oh fie, Sir Wilfull! What, you must not be daunted.

SIR WILFULL: Daunted, no, that's not it, it is not so much for that – for if so be that I set on't, I'll do't. But only for the present, 'tis sufficient till further acquaintance, that's all – your servant.

MRS FAINALL: Nay, I'll swear you shall never lose so favourable an opportunity, if I can help it. I'll leave you together and lock the door.

[*Exit.*]

SIR WILFULL: Nay, nay cousin – I have forgot my gloves. – What d'ye do? 'S'heart, a' has locked the door indeed, I think. – Nay, cousin Fainall, open the door. – Pshaw, what a vixen trick is this? – Nay, now a' has seen me too. – Cousin, I made bold to pass through as it were. – I think this door's enchanted. –

MILLAMANT [*repeating*].

> *I prithee spare me, gentle boy,*
> *Press me no more for that slight toy.*[4]

3. *Thyrsis . . . train*: opening line of *The Story of Phoebus and Daphne, Applied*, by Edmund Waller (1606–87).
4. *I prithee . . . .* : Millamant continues to quote from Suckling.

SIR WILFULL: Anan? Cousin, your servant.

MILLAMANT: *That foolish trifle of a heart* – Sir Wilfull!

SIR WILFULL: Yes – your servant. No offence I hope, cousin.

MILLAMANT [*repeating*].

> *I swear it will not do its part,*
> *Tho' thou dost thine, employ'st the power and art.*

Natural, easy Suckling!

SIR WILFULL: Anan? Suckling? No such suckling neither, cousin, nor stripling; I thank heaven, I'm no minor.

MILLAMANT: Ah rustic! ruder than Gothic.

SIR WILFULL: Well, well, I shall understand your lingo one of these days, cousin; in the meanwhile, I must answer in plain English.

MILLAMANT: Have you any business with me, Sir Wilfull?

SIR WILFULL: Not at present, cousin. – Yes, I made bold to see, to come and know if that how you were disposed to fetch a walk this evening, if so be that I might not be troublesome, I would have sought a walk with you.

MILLAMANT: A walk? What then?

SIR WILFULL: Nay, nothing – only for the walk's sake, that's all –

MILLAMANT: I nauseate walking; 'tis a country diversion, I loathe the country and everything that relates to it.

SIR WILFULL: Indeed! Hah! Look ye, look ye, you do? Nay, 'tis like you may. – Here are choice of pastimes here in town, as plays and the like; that must be confessed indeed.

MILLAMANT: Ah, *l'étourdie!* I hate the town too.

SIR WILFULL: Dear heart, that's much. – Hah! that you should hate 'em both! Hah! 'tis like you may; there are some can't relish the town, and others can't away with the country. – 'Tis like you may be one of those, cousin.

MILLAMANT: Ha, ha, ha. Yes, 'tis like I may. – You have nothing further to say to me?

SIR WILFULL: Not at present, cousin. – 'Tis like when I have an opportunity to be more private, I may break my mind in some measure. – I conjecture you partly guess – however, that's as time shall try; but spare to speak and spare to speed, as they say.

MILLAMANT: If it is of no great importance, Sir Wilfull, you will
oblige me to leave me; I have just now a little business –

SIR WILFULL: Enough, enough, cousin; yes, yes, all a case – when
you're disposed, when you're disposed. Now's as well as another
time; and another time as well as now. All's one for that. – Yes,
yes, if your concerns call you, there's no haste; it will keep cold, as
they say. – Cousin, your servant. – I think this door's locked.

MILLAMANT: You may go this way, sir.

SIR WILFULL: Your servant; then with your leave I'll return to my
company.

[*Exit.*]

MILLAMANT: Ay, ay; ha, ha, ha!

Like Phoebus sung the no less am'rous boy.

[*Enter* MIRABELL.]

MIRABELL: – *Like Daphne she as lovely and as coy.*[5] Do you lock
yourself up from me, to make my search more curious? Or is this
pretty artifice contrived, to signify that here the chase must end
and my pursuit be crowned, for you can fly no further –

MILLAMANT: Vanity! No – I'll fly and be followed to the last
moment. Though I am upon the very verge of matrimony, I
expect you should solicit me as much as if I were wavering at the
grate of a monastery, with one foot over the threshold. I'll be
solicited to the very last, nay and afterwards.

MIRABELL: What, after the last?

MILLAMANT: Oh, I should think I was poor and had nothing to
bestow, if I were reduced to an inglorious ease, and freed from the
agreeable fatigues of solicitation.

MIRABELL: But do not you know that when favours are conferred
upon instant and tedious solicitation, that they diminish in their
value, and that both the giver loses the grace, and the receiver
lessens his pleasure?

MILLAMANT: It may be in things of common application, but never
sure in love. Oh, I hate a lover that can dare to think he draws a
moment's air independent on the bounty of his mistress. There is

5. *Like . . . coy*: Mirabell completes a couplet (113–14) of the Waller poem quoted
earlier.

not so impudent a thing in nature as the saucy look of an assured man, confident of success. The pedantic arrogance of a very husband has not so pragmatical an air. Ah! I'll never marry, unless I am first made sure of my will and pleasure.

MIRABELL: Would you have 'em both before marriage? Or will you be contented with the first now, and stay for the other till after grace?

MILLAMANT: Ah, don't be impertinent. – My dear liberty, shall I leave thee? My faithful solitude, my darling contemplation, must I bid you then adieu? ay-h adieu, my morning thoughts, agreeable wakings, indolent slumbers, all ye *douceurs*, ye *sommeils du matin*, adieu. – I can't do't, 'tis more than impossible. – Positively Mirabell, I'll lie a-bed in a morning as long as I please.

MIRABELL: Then I'll get up in a morning as early as I please.

MILLAMANT: Ah, idle creature, get up when you will – and d'ye hear, I won't be called names after I'm married; positively I won't be called names.

MIRABELL: Names!

MILLAMANT: Ay, as wife, spouse, my dear, joy, jewel, love, sweetheart and the rest of that nauseous cant in which men and their wives are so fulsomely familiar; I shall never bear that. – Good Mirabell, don't let us be familiar or fond, nor kiss before folks, like my Lady Fadler and Sir Francis; nor go to Hyde Park together the first Sunday in a new chariot, to provoke eyes and whispers, and then never to be seen there together again, as if we were proud of one another the first week, and ashamed of one another for ever after. Let us never visit together, nor go to a play together, but let us be very strange and well-bred; let us be as strange as if we had been married a great while, and as well bred as if we were not married at all.

MIRABELL: Have you any more conditions to offer? Hitherto your demands are pretty reasonable.

MILLAMANT: Trifles. – As liberty to pay and receive visits to and from whom I please; to write and receive letters, without interrogatories or wry faces on your part. To wear what I please, and choose conversation with regard only to my own taste; to have no obligation upon me to converse with wits that I don't like, because they are your acquaintance, or to be intimate with fools, because they may be your relations. Come to dinner when I please; dine in my dressing-room when I'm out of humour, without giving a reason. To have my closet inviolate; to be sole empress of my tea-table, which you must never presume to approach without first asking leave. And lastly, wherever I am, you shall always knock at the door before you come in. These articles subscribed, if I continue to endure you a little longer, I may by degrees dwindle into a wife.

MIRABELL: Your bill of fare is something advanced in this latter account. Well, have I liberty to offer conditions – that when you are dwindled into a wife, I may not be beyond measure enlarged into a husband?

MILLAMANT: You have free leave; propose your utmost, speak and spare not.

MIRABELL: I thank you. *Inprimis* then, I covenant that your ac-quaintance be general; that you admit no sworn confidante, or intimate of your own sex; no she-friend to screen her affairs under your countenance and tempt you to make trial of a mutual secrecy. No decoy-duck to wheedle you a fop, scrambling to the play in a mask; then bring you home in a pretended fright, when you think you shall be found out – and rail at me for missing the play, and disappointing the frolic, which you had to pick me up and prove my constancy.

MILLAMANT: Detestable *inprimis!* I go to the play in a mask!

MIRABELL: *Item*, I article that you continue to like your own face, as long as I shall. And while it passes current with me, that you endeavour not to new coin it. To which end, together with all vizards for the day, I prohibit all masks for the night, made of oiled skins and I know not what – hog's-bones, hare's-gall, pig-water, and the marrow of a roasted cat. In short, I forbid all commerce with the gentlewoman in what-d'ye-call-it Court. *Item*, I shut my doors against all bawds with baskets, and penny-worths of muslin, china, fans, atlases,[6] etc, etc. – *Item*, when you shall be breeding –

6. *atlases*: atlas is 'a silk-satin manufactured in the East' (*O.E.D.*).

MILLAMANT: Ah! Name it not.

MIRABELL: Which may be presumed, with a blessing on our endeavours –

MILLAMANT: Odious endeavours!

MIRABELL: I denounce against all strait-lacing, squeezing for a shape, till you mould my boy's head like a sugar-loaf; and instead of a man-child, make me the father to a crooked billet. Lastly, to the dominion of the tea-table I submit – but with proviso that you exceed not in your province, but restrain yourself to native and simple tea-table drinks, as tea, chocolate and coffee. As likewise to genuine and authorized tea-table talk, such as mending of fashions, spoiling reputations, railing at absent friends, and so forth; but that on no account you encroach upon the men's prerogative, and presume to drink healths, or toast fellows; for prevention of which, I banish all foreign forces, all auxiliaries to the tea-table, as orange-brandy, all aniseed, cinnamon, citron and Barbadoes waters, together with ratifia and the most noble spirit of clary.[7] But for cowslip wine, poppy-water and all dormitives, those I allow. – These provisos admitted, in other things I may prove a tractable and complying husband.

MILLAMANT: Oh horrid provisos! Filthy strong waters! I toast fellows, odious men! I hate your odious provisos.

MIRABELL: Then we're agreed. Shall I kiss your hand upon the contract? And here comes one to be a witness to the sealing of the deed.

[Enter MRS FAINALL.]

MILLAMANT: Fainall, what shall I do? Shall I have him? I think I must have him.

MRS FAINALL: Ay, ay, take him, take him, what should you do?

MILLAMANT: Well then – I'll take my death I'm in a horrid fright. – Fainall, I shall never say it. – Well – I think – I'll endure you.

MRS FAINALL: Fie, fie, have him, have him, and tell him so in plain terms; for I am sure you have a mind to him.

MILLAMANT: Are you? I think I have – and the horrid man looks as if he thought so too. – Well, you ridiculous thing you, I'll have

7. *orange-brandy . . . clary*: all of these were strong, fortified drinks.

you. – I won't be kissed, nor I won't be thanked. – Here, kiss my hand though. – So, hold your tongue now, and don't say a word.

MRS FAINALL: Mirabell, there's a necessity for your obedience; you have neither time to talk nor stay. My mother is coming; and in my conscience if she should see you, would fall into fits, and maybe not recover time enough to return to Sir Rowland, who as Foible tells me is in a fair way to succeed. Therefore spare your ecstasies for another occasion, and slip down the backstairs, where Foible waits to consult you.

MILLAMANT: Ay, go, go. In the meantime I suppose you have said something to please me.

MIRABELL: I am all obedience.

[Exit MIRABELL.]

MRS FAINALL: Yonder Sir Wilfull's drunk, and so noisy that my mother has been forced to leave Sir Rowland to appease him; but he answers her only with singing and drinking. What they have done by this time I know not, but Petulant and he were upon quarrelling as I came by.

MILLAMANT: Well, if Mirabell should not make a good husband, I am a lost thing – for I find I love him violently.

MRS FAINALL: So it seems, when you mind not what's said to you. – If you doubt him, you had best take up with Sir Wilfull.

MILLAMANT: How can you name that superannuated lubber, foh!

[Enter WITWOUD from drinking.]

MRS FAINALL: So, is the fray made up, that you have left 'em?

WITWOUD: Left 'em? I could stay no longer. – I have laughed like ten christenings – I am tipsy with laughing. – If I had stayed any longer I should have burst – I must have been let out and pieced[8] in the sides like an unsized camlet.[9] Yes, yes, the fray is composed; my lady came in like a *noli prosequi*[10] and stopped their proceedings.

MILLAMANT: What was the dispute?

WITWOUD: That's the jest, there was no dispute, they could neither

8. *pieced*: enlarged with extra pieces.
9. *camlet*: costly eastern fabric.
10. *noli prosequi*: nolle prosequi, a term for ending legal proceedings.

of 'em speak for rage, and so fell a-sputtering at one another like two roasting apples.

[*Enter* PETULANT *drunk.*]

Now Petulant, all's over, all's well? Gad, my head begins to whim it about – why dost thou not speak? Thou art both as drunk and as mute as a fish.

PETULANT: Look you, Mrs Millamant, if you can love me, dear nymph – say it – and that's the conclusion. – Pass on, or pass off – that's all.

WITWOUD: Thou hast uttered volumes, folios, in less than decimo sexto,[11] my dear Lacedemonian.[12] Sirrah Petulant, thou art an epitomizer of words.

PETULANT: Witwoud, – you are an annihilator of sense.

WITWOUD: Thou art a retailer of phrases, and dost deal in remnants of remnants, like a maker of pincushions – thou art in truth (metaphorically speaking) a speaker of shorthand.

PETULANT: Thou art (without a figure) just one half of an ass, and Baldwin[13] yonder, thy half-brother, is the rest. – A gemini of asses split would make just four of you.

WITWOUD: Thou dost bite, my dear mustard-seed; kiss me for that.

PETULANT: Stand off. – I'll kiss no more males. – I have kissed your twin yonder in a humour of reconciliation, till he [*hiccup*] rises upon my stomach like a radish.

MILLAMANT: Eh, filthy creature – what was the quarrel?

PETULANT: There was no quarrel – there might have been a quarrel.

WITWOUD: If there had been words enow between 'em to have expressed provocation, they had gone together by the ears like a pair of castanets.

PETULANT: You were the quarrel.

MILLAMANT: Me!

PETULANT: If I have a humour to quarrel, I can make less matters conclude premises. – If you are not handsome, what then, if I have

11. *decimo sexto*: a book that is only one-eighth the size of a folio.
12. *Lacedemonian*: Spartan – noted for brevity.
13. *Baldwin*: the ass in the beast-epic *Reynard the Fox*.

a humour to prove it? If I shall have my reward, say so; if not, fight for your face the next time yourself – I'll go sleep.

WITWOUD: Do, wrap thyself up like a wood-louse and dream revenge; and hear me, if thou canst learn to write by tomorrow morning, pen me a challenge. – I'll carry it for thee.

PETULANT: Carry your mistress's monkey a spider – go flea dogs, and read romances – I'll go to bed to my maid.

[*Exit.*]

MRS FAINALL: He's horridly drunk – how came you all in this pickle?

WITWOUD: A plot, a plot, to get rid of the knight, – your husband's advice; but he sneaked off.

[*Enter* LADY WISHFORT *and* SIR WILFULL *drunk.*]

LADY WISHFORT: Out upon't, out upon't, at years of discretion, and comport yourself at this rantipole[14] rate.

SIR WILFULL: No offence, aunt.

LADY WISHFORT: Offence? As I'm a person, I'm ashamed of you. – Fogh! how you stink of wine! D'ye think my niece will ever endure such a borachio![15] you're an absolute borachio.

SIR WILFULL: Borachio!

LADY WISHFORT: At a time when you should commence an amour and put your best foot foremost –

SIR WILFULL: 'S'heart, an you grutch me your liquor, make a bill. – Give me more drink, and take my purse.

[*Sings*].

> Prithee fill me the glass
> Till it laugh in my face,
> With ale that is potent and mellow;
> He that whines for a lass,
> Is an ignorant ass,
> For a bumper has not its fellow.

But if you would have me marry my cousin, – say the word, and I'll do't. – Wilfull will do't, that's the word – Willfull will do't; that's my crest – my motto I have forgot.

14. *rantipole*: ill-behaved.
15. *borachio*: drunkard.

LADY WISHFORT: My nephew's a little overtaken, cousin – but 'tis with drinking your health. – O' my word you are obliged to him.

SIR WILFULL: *In vino veritas* aunt. – If I drunk your health today cousin – I am a borachio. But if you have a mind to be married, say the word, and send for the piper, Wilfull will do't. If not, dust it away, and let's have t'other round – Tony! Ods-heart, where's Tony? Tony's an honest fellow, but he spits after a bumper, and that's a fault.

[*Sings.*]

> We'll drink, and we'll never ha' done, boys,
> Put the glass then around with the sun, boys,
> Let Apollo's example invite us;
> For he's drunk every night,
> And that makes him so bright,
> That he's able next morning to light us.

The sun's a good pimple, an honest soaker, he has a cellar at your Antipodes. If I travel, aunt, I touch at your Antipodes – your Antipodes are a good rascally sort of topsy-turvy fellows. – If I had a bumper, I'd stand upon my head and drink a health to 'em. – A match or no match, cousin with the hard name? Aunt, Wilfull will do't; if she has her maidenhead, let her look to't, – if she has not, let her keep her own counsel in the meantime, and cry out at the nine months' end.

MILLAMANT: Your pardon, madam, I can stay no longer. – Sir Wilfull grows very powerful. Egh, how he smells! I shall be overcome if I stay. Come, cousin.

[*Exeunt* MILLAMANT *and* MRS FAINALL.]

LADY WISHFORT: Smells! He would poison a tallow-chandler[16] and his family. Beastly creature, I know not what to do with him. – Travel, quoth 'a! Ay, travel, travel, get thee gone, get thee but far enough, to the Saracens or the Tartars or the Turks – for thou are not fit to live in a Christian commonwealth, thou beastly pagan.

SIR WILFULL: Turks, no; no Turks, aunt: your Turks are infidels,

16. *tallow-chandler*: maker and seller of tallow candles.

and believe not in the grape. Your Mahometan, your Mussulman, is a dry stinkard – no offence, aunt. My map says that your Turk is not so honest a man as your Christian. – I cannot find by the map that your Mufti is orthodox – whereby it is a plain case, that orthodox is a hard word, aunt, and [*hiccup*] Greek for claret.

   [*Sings.*]

>   To drink is a Christian diversion,
>   Unknown to the Turk and the Persian:
>   Let Mahometan fools
>   Live by heathenish rules,
> And be damned over tea cups and coffee.
>   But let British lads sing,
>   Crown a health to the king,
> And a fig for your Sultan and Sophy.[17]

Ah Tony!
   [*Enter* FOIBLE, *and whispers* LADY WISHFORT.]

LADY WISHFORT: Sir Rowland impatient? Good lack! what shall I do with this beastly tumbril? – Go lie down and sleep, you sot, or as I'm a person, I'll have you bastinadoed with broom-sticks. Call up the wenches.

   [*Exit* FOIBLE.]

SIR WILFULL: Ahey! Wenches, where are the wenches?

LADY WISHFORT: Dear cousin Witwoud, get him away, and you will bind me to you inviolably. I have an affair of moment that invades me with some precipitation. – You will oblige me to all futurity.

WITWOUD: Come, knight. – Pox on him, I don't know what to say to him. – Will you go to a cock-match?

SIR WILFULL: With a wench, Tony? Is she a shake-bag,[18] sirrah? Let me bite your cheek for that.

WITWOUD: Horrible! He has a breath like a bagpipe – ay, ay, come, will you march, my Salopian?

SIR WILFULL: Lead on, little Tony – I'll follow thee, my Anthony,

17. *Sophy*: a ruler of the (Persian) Sufi dynasty.
18. *shake-bag*: name of a large breed of fowl.

my Tantony, sirrah, thou shalt be my Tantony, and I'll be thy
pig.[19]

– And a fig for your Sultan and Sophy.

[*Exit singing with* WITWOUD.]

LADY WISHFORT: This will never do. It will never make a match –
at least before he has been abroad.

[*Enter* WAITWELL, *disguised as* SIR ROWLAND.]

Dear Sir Rowland, I am confounded with confusion at the retro-
spection of my own rudeness, – I have more pardons to ask than
the Pope distributes in the year of Jubilee.[20] But I hope where
there is likely to be so near an alliance, – we may unbend the
severity of decorum – and dispense with a little ceremony.

WAITWELL: My impatience madam, is the effect of my transport;
and till I have the possession of your adorable person, I am
tantalized on a rack, and do but hang, madam, on the tenter of
expectation.

LADY WISHFORT: You have excess of gallantry, Sir Rowland, and
press things to a conclusion with a most prevailing vehemence. –
But a day or two for decency of marriage –

WAITWELL: For decency of funeral, madam. The delay will break
my heart – or if that should fail, I shall be poisoned. My nephew
will get an inkling of my designs and poison me, and I would
willingly starve him before I die – I would gladly go out of the
world with that satisfaction. – That would be some comfort to
me, if I could but live so long as to be revenged on that unnatural
viper.

LADY WISHFORT: Is he so unnatural say you? Truly I would
contribute much both to the saving of your life and the accomplishment of your revenge. – Not that I respect myself; though he
has been a perfidious wretch to me.

WAITWELL: Perfidious to you!

LADY WISHFORT: Oh Sir Rowland, the hours that he has died away
at my feet, the tears that he has shed, the oaths that he has sworn,

19. *Tantony . . . pig*: Tantony is a shortened form of St Antony who was often
depicted as accompanied by a pig.
20. *year of Jubilee*: when the Pope grants a special remission of punishments for sin.

the palpitations that he has felt, the trances, and the tremblings, the ardours and the ecstasies, the kneelings and the risings, the heart-heavings and the hand-grippings, the pangs and the pathetic regards of his protesting eyes! Oh, no memory can register.

WAITWELL: What, my rival! Is the rebel my rival? A' dies.

LADY WISHFORT: No, don't kill him at once Sir Rowland, starve him gradually, inch by inch.

WAITWELL: I'll do't. In three weeks he shall be barefoot; in a month out at knees with begging alms. – He shall starve upward and upward, till he has nothing living but his head, and then go out in a stink like a candle's end upon a save-all.[21]

LADY WISHFORT: Well, Sir Rowland, you have the way. – You are no novice in the labyrinth of love; you have the clue. – But as I am a person, Sir Rowland, you must not attribute my yielding to any sinister appetite, or indigestion of widowhood; nor impute my complacency to any lethargy of continence. – I hope you do not think me prone to any iteration of nuptials –

WAITWELL: Far be it from me –

LADY WISHFORT: If you do, I protest I must recede – or think that I have made a prostitution of decorums, but in the vehemence of compassion, and to save the life of a person of so much importance –

WAITWELL: I esteem it so –

LADY WISHFORT: Or else you wrong my condescension –

WAITWELL: I do not, I do not –

LADY WISHFORT: Indeed you do.

WAITWELL: I do not, fair shrine of virtue.

LADY WISHFORT: If you think the least scruple of carnality was an ingredient –

WAITWELL: Dear madam, no. You are all camphire[22] and frankincense, all chastity and odour.

LADY WISHFORT: Or that –

[Enter FOIBLE.]

FOIBLE: Madam, the dancers are ready, and there's one with a letter, who must deliver it into your own hands.

21. *save-all*: small holder with a central pin for candle-ends.
22. *camphire*: camphor.

LADY WISHFORT: Sir Rowland, will you give me leave? Think
favourably, judge candidly, and conclude you have found a
person who would suffer racks in honour's cause, dear Sir
Rowland, and will wait on you incessantly.
    [*Exit.*]

WAITWELL: Fie, fie! – What a slavery have I undergone. Spouse,
hast thou any cordial? – I want spirits.

FOIBLE: What a washy rogue art thou, to pant thus for a quarter of
an hour's lying and swearing to a fine lady!

WAITWELL: Oh, she is the antidote to desire. Spouse, thou wilt fare
the worse for't. – I shall have no appetite to iteration of nuptials
this eight-and-forty hours. – By this hand I'd rather be a chair-
man in the dog-days[23] than act Sir Rowland till this time
tomorrow.
    [*Enter* LADY WISHFORT *with a letter.*]

LADY WISHFORT: Call in the dancers. – Sir Rowland, we'll sit if
you please, and see the entertainment.
    [*Dance.*]
Now with your permission Sir Rowland, I will peruse my letter. –
I would open it in your presence, because I would not make
you uneasy. If it should make you uneasy, I would burn it –
speak, if it does – but you may see by the superscription it is like a
woman's hand.

FOIBLE [*to him*]: By heaven! Mrs Marwood's, – I know it – my heart
aches – get it from her.

WAITWELL: A woman's hand? No, madam, that's no woman's
hand; I see that already. That's somebody whose throat must be
cut.

LADY WISHFORT: Nay Sir Rowland, since you give me a proof of
your passion by your jealousy, I promise you I'll make you a
return, by a frank communication. – You shall see it – we'll open
it together. – Look you here.

[*Reads.*] – *Madam, though unknown to you* (look you there, 'tis from
nobody that I know) – *I have that honour for your character, that I
think myself obliged to let you know you are abused. He who pretends to
be Sir Rowland is a cheat and a rascal –*

23. *chair-man in the dog-days*: sedan-chair carrier in the hottest time of summer.

Oh heavens! what's this?

FOIBLE: Unfortunate, all's ruined.

WAITWELL: How, how, let me see, let me see – [*reading.*] *A rascal, and disguised and suborned for that imposture.* – O villainy, O villainy! – *by the contrivance of* –

LADY WISHFORT: I shall faint, I shall die, I shall die, oh!

FOIBLE [*to him*]: Say 'tis your nephew's hand – quickly – his plot, swear, swear it –

WAITWELL: Here's a villain! madam, don't you perceive it, don't you see it?

LADY WISHFORT: Too well, too well! I have seen too much.

WAITWELL: I told you at first I knew the hand. – A woman's hand? The rascal writes a sort of a large hand, your Roman hand. – I saw there was a throat to be cut presently. If he were my son, as he is my nephew, I'd pistol him –

FOIBLE: O treachery! But are you sure, Sir Rowland, it is his writing?

WAITWELL: Sure? Am I here? Do I live? Do I love this pearl of India? I have twenty letters in my pocket from him, in the same character.

LADY WISHFORT: How!

FOIBLE: Oh, what luck it is, Sir Rowland, that you were present at this juncture! This was the business that brought Mr Mirabell disguised to Madam Millamant this afternoon. I thought something was contriving, when he stole by me and would have hid his face.

LADY WISHFORT: How, how! – I heard the villain was in the house indeed, and now I remember, my niece went away abruptly, when Sir Wilfull was to have made his addresses.

FOIBLE: Then, then, madam, Mr Mirabell waited for her in her chamber, but I would not tell your ladyship to discompose you when you were to receive Sir Rowland.

WAITWELL: Enough, his date is short.

FOIBLE: No, good Sir Rowland, don't incur the law.

WAITWELL: Law? I care not for law. I can but die, and 'tis in a good cause. – My lady shall be satisfied of my truth and innocence, though it cost me my life.

LADY WISHFORT: No, dear Sir Rowland, don't fight, if you should be killed I must never show my face, or be hanged. – Oh, consider my reputation, Sir Rowland. – No, you shan't fight. – I'll go in and examine my niece; I'll make her confess. I conjure you Sir Rowland, by all your love, not to fight.

WAITWELL: I am charmed madam, I obey. But some proof you must let me give you; I'll go for a black box which contains the writings of my whole estate, and deliver that into your hands.

LADY WISHFORT: Ay, dear Sir Rowland, that will be some comfort; bring the black box.

WAITWELL: And may I presume to bring a contract to be signed this night? May I hope so far?

LADY WISHFORT: Bring what you will; but come alive, pray come alive. Oh this is a happy discovery.

WAITWELL: Dead or alive I'll come – and married we will be in spite of treachery; ay, and get an heir that shall defeat the last remaining glimpse of hope in my abandoned nephew. Come, my buxom widow.

> Ere long you shall substantial proof receive
> That I'm an arrant knight –

FOIBLE [aside]: Or arrant knave.
  [Exeunt.]

ACT FIVE

SCENE ONE

Scene continues.

[LADY WISHFORT *and* FOIBLE.]

LADY WISHFORT: Out of my house, out of my house, thou viper,
thou serpent, that I have fostered, thou bosom traitress, that I
raised from nothing – begone, begone, begone, go, go – that I
took from washing of old gauze and weaving of dead hair, with a
bleak blue nose, over a chafing-dish of starved embers and dining
behind a traverse rag, in a shop no bigger than a bird-cage – go,
go, starve again, do, do.

FOIBLE: Dear madam, I'll beg pardon on my knees.

LADY WISHFORT: Away, out, out, go set up for yourself again –
do, drive a trade, do, with your three penny-worth of small ware,
flaunting upon a pack-thread, under a brandy-seller's bulk,[1] or
against a dead wall by a ballad-monger. Go hang out an old
frisoneer-gorget,[2] with a yard of yellow colberteen[3] again, do; an
old gnawed mask, two rows of pins and a child's fiddle; a glass
necklace with the beads broken, and a quilted night-cap with one
ear. Go, go, drive a trade – these were your commodities, you
treacherous trull, this was your merchandise you dealt in when I
took you into my house, placed you next myself, and made you
governante of my whole family. You have forgot this, have you,
now you have feathered your nest?

1. *bulk*: stall.
2. *frisoneer-gorget*: woollen covering for the neck.
3. *colberteen*: a kind of lace.

FOIBLE: No, no, dear madam. Do but hear me, have but a moment's patience – I'll confess all. Mr Mirabell seduced me; I am not the first that he has wheedled with his dissembling tongue. Your ladyship's own wisdom has been deluded by him, then how should I, a poor ignorant, defend myself? O madam, if you knew but what he promised me, and how he assured me your ladyship should come to no damage. – Or else the wealth of the Indies should not have bribed me to conspire against so good, so sweet, so kind a lady as you have been to me.

LADY WISHFUL: 'No damage?' What, to betray me, to marry me to a cast servingman; to make me a receptacle, an hospital for a decayed pimp? 'No damage?' O thou frontless impudence, more than a big-bellied actress.

FOIBLE: Pray do but hear me madam, he could not marry your ladyship, madam. – No indeed, his marriage was to have been void in law, for he was married to me first, to secure your ladyship. He could not have bedded your ladyship; for if he had consummated with your ladyship, he must have run the risk of the law and been put upon his clergy.[4] – Yes indeed, I enquired of the law in that case before I would meddle or make.

LADY WISHFORT: What, then I have been your property, have I? I have been convenient to you it seems, while you were catering for Mirabell; I have been broker for you? What, have you made a passive bawd of me? This exceeds all precedent; I am brought to fine uses, to become a botcher of second-hand marriages between Abigails and Andrews![5] I'll couple you. Yes, I'll baste you together, you and your Philander. I'll Duke's Place you, as I'm a person. Your turtle is in custody already; you shall coo in the same cage, if there be constable or warrant in the parish.

[*Exit.*]

FOIBLE: O that ever I was born! O that I was ever married! – A bride, ay, I shall be a Bridewell[6] bride. Oh!

[*Enter* MRS FAINALL.]

4. *put upon his clergy*: those able to read and write could escape the death penalty by claiming 'benefit of clergy'.

5. *Abigails and Andrews*: female and male servants.

6. *Bridewell*: a prison for women.

MRS FAINALL: Poor Foible, what's the matter?

FOIBLE: O madam, my lady's gone for a constable; I shall be had to a justice, and put to Bridewell to beat hemp. Poor Waitwell's gone to prison already.

MRS FAINALL: Have a good heart, Foible; Mirabell's gone to give security for him. This is all Marwood's and my husband's doing.

FOIBLE: Yes, yes, I know it, madam; she was in my lady's closet, and overheard all that you said to me before dinner. She sent the letter to my lady, and that missing effect, Mr Fainall laid this plot to arrest Waitwell when he pretended to go for the papers; and in the meantime Mrs Marwood declared all to my lady.

MRS FAINALL: Was there no mention made of me in the letter? – My mother does not suspect my being in the confederacy? I fancy Marwood has not told her, though she has told my husband.

FOIBLE: Yes, madam, but my lady did not see that part. We stifled the letter before she read so far. Has that mischievous devil told Mr Fainall of your ladyship then?

MRS FAINALL: Ay, all's out, my affair with Mirabell, everything discovered. This is the last day of our living together, that's my comfort.

FOIBLE: Indeed madam, and so 'tis a comfort if you knew all. – He has been even with your ladyship; which I could have told you long enough since, but I love to keep peace and quietness by my good will; I had rather bring friends together than set 'em at distance. But Mrs Marwood and he are nearer related than ever their parents thought for.

MRS FAINALL: Say'st thou so, Foible? Canst thou prove this?

FOIBLE: I can take my oath of it, madam; so can Mrs Mincing. We have had many a fair word from Madam Marwood, to conceal something that passed in our chamber one evening when you were at Hyde Park and we were thought to have gone a-walking; but we went up unawares, though we were sworn to secrecy too. Madam Marwood took a book and swore us upon it, but it was but a book of verses and poems. – So as long as it was not a Bible oath, we may break it with a safe conscience.

MRS FAINALL: This discovery is the most opportune thing I could wish. Now, Mincing?

[*Enter* MINCING.]

MINCING: My lady would speak with Mrs Foible, mem. Mr Mirabell is with her; he has set your spouse at liberty, Mrs Foible, and would have you hide yourself in my lady's closet till my old lady's anger is abated. Oh, my old lady is in a perilous passion at something Mr Fainall has said. He swears, and my old lady cries. There's a fearful hurricane, I vow. He says, mem, how that he'll have my lady's fortune made over to him, or he'll be divorced.

MRS FAINALL: Does your lady and Mirabell know that?

MINCING: Yes, mem; they have sent me to see if Sir Wilfull be sober, and to bring him to them. My lady is resolved to have him, I think, rather than lose such a vast sum as six thousand pound. Oh, come Mrs Foible, I hear my old lady.

MRS FAINALL: Foible, you must tell Mincing that she must prepare to vouch when I call her.

FOIBLE: Yes, yes madam.

MINCING: Oh yes, mem, I'll vouch anything for your ladyship's service, be what it will.

[*Exeunt* MINCING *and* FOIBLE.]

[*Enter* LADY WISHFORT *and* MARWOOD.]

LADY WISHFORT: O my dear friend, how can I enumerate the benefits that I have received from your goodness? To you I owe the timely discovery of the false vows of Mirabell; to you the detection of the impostor Sir Rowland. And now you are become an intercessor with my son-in-law, to save the honour of my house, and compound for the frailties of my daughter. Well, friend, you are enough to reconcile me to the bad world, or else I would retire to deserts and solitudes, and feed harmless sheep by groves and purling streams. Dear Marwood, let us leave the world, and retire by ourselves and be shepherdesses.

MRS MARWOOD: Let us first dispatch the affair in hand, madam; we shall have leisure to think of retirement afterwards. Here is one who is concerned in the treaty.

LADY WISHFORT: O daughter, daughter, is it possible thou shouldst be my child, bone of my bone, and flesh of my flesh, and as I may say, another me, and yet transgress the most minute particle of severe virtue? Is it possible you should lean aside to iniquity, who have been cast in the direct mould of virtue? I have not only been a mould but a pattern for you, and a model for you, after you were brought into the world.

MRS FAINALL: I don't understand your ladyship.

LADY WISHFORT: Not understand? Why, have you not been naught? Have you not been sophisticated?[7] Not understand? Here I am ruined to compound for your caprices and your cuckoldoms. I must pawn my plate and my jewels and ruin my niece, and all little enough –

MRS FAINALL: I am wronged and abused, and so are you. 'Tis a false accusation, as false as hell, as false as your friend there, ay, or your friend's friend, my false husband.

MRS MARWOOD: My friend, Mrs Fainall? Your husband my friend? What do you mean?

MRS FAINALL: I know what I mean madam, and so do you; and so shall the world at a time convenient.

MRS MARWOOD: I am sorry to see you so passionate, madam. More temper would look more like innocence. But I have done. I am sorry my zeal to serve your ladyship and family should admit of misconstruction, or make me liable to affronts. You will pardon me, madam, if I meddle no more with an affair in which I am not personally concerned.

LADY WISHFORT: O dear friend, I am so ashamed that you should meet with such returns – you ought to ask pardon on your knees, ungrateful creature; she deserves more from you than all your life can accomplish. – Oh, don't leave me destitute in this perplexity! No, stick to me, my good genius.

MRS FAINALL: I tell you, madam, you're abused. – Stick to you? Ay, like a leech, to suck your best blood – she'll drop off when she's full. Madam, you shan't pawn a bodkin, nor part with a brass counter in composition for me. I defy 'em all. Let 'em prove their aspersions; I know my own innocence, and dare stand a trial.
    [*Exit.*]

LADY WISHFORT: Why, if she should be innocent, if she should be wronged after all, ha? I don't know what to think – and I promise

7. *sophisticated*: corrupted.

you, her education has been unexceptionable. I may say it; for I chiefly made it my own care to initiate her very infancy in the rudiments of virtue, and to impress upon her tender years a young odium and aversion to the very sight of men. – Ay, friend, she would ha' shrieked if she had but seen a man, till she was in her teens. As I'm a person 'tis true. – She was never suffered to play with a male child, though but in coats; nay, her very babies[8] were of the feminine gender. – Oh, she never looked a man in the face but her own father, or the chaplain, and him we made a shift to put upon her for a woman, by the help of his long garments and his sleek face, till she was going in her fifteen.

MRS MARWOOD: 'Twas much she should be deceived so long.

LADY WISHFORT: I warrant you, or she would never have borne to have been catechized by him; and have heard his long lectures against singing and dancing, and such debaucheries, and going to filthy plays, and profane music meetings, where the lewd trebles squeak nothing but bawdy, and the bases roar blasphemy. Oh, she would have swooned at the sight or name of an obscene play-book – and can I think after all this, that my daughter can be naught? What, a whore? And thought it excommunication to set her foot within the door of a play-house. O my dear friend, I can't believe it, no, no. As she says, let him prove it, let him prove it.

MRS MARWOOD: Prove it madam? What, and have your name prostituted in a public court? Yours and your daughter's reputation worried at the bar by a pack of bawling lawyers? To be ushered in with an *Oyez* of scandal, and have your case opened by an old fumbling lecher in a quoif[9] like a man-midwife to bring your daughter's infamy to light; to be a theme for legal punsters and quibblers by the statute, and become a jest against a rule of court, where there is no precedent for a jest in any record, not even in Doomsday Book; to discompose the gravity of the bench, and provoke naughty interrogatories in more naughty law Latin, while the good judge, tickled with the proceeding, simpers under

8. *babies*: dolls.
9. *quoif*: white cap then worn by lawyers.

a grey beard, and fidges off and on his cushion as if he had swallowed cantharides,[10] or sat upon cow-itch.[11]

LADY WISHFORT: Oh, 'tis very hard!

MRS MARWOOD: And then to have my young revellers of the Temple[12] take notes, like 'prentices at a conventicle; and after, talk it all over again in commons,[13] or before drawers in an eating-house.

LADY WISHFORT: Worse and worse.

MRS MARWOOD: Nay, this is nothing; if it would end here, 'twere well. But it must after this be consigned by the shorthand writers to the public press; and from thence be transferred to the hands, nay into the throats and lungs of hawkers, with voices more licentious than the loud flounder-man's or the woman that cries 'grey peas'. And this you must hear till you are stunned; nay, you must hear nothing else for some days.

LADY WISHFORT: Oh, 'tis insupportable. No, no, dear friend, make it up, make it up; ay, ay, I'll compound. I'll give up all, myself and my all, my niece and her all, – anything, everything for composition.

MRS MARWOOD: Nay madam, I advise nothing, I only lay before you as a friend the inconveniencies which perhaps you have overseen. Here comes Mr Fainall. If he will be satisfied to huddle up all in silence, I shall be glad. You must think I would rather congratulate than condole with you.

[Enter FAINALL.]

LADY WISHFORT: Ay, ay, I do not doubt it, dear Marwood; no, no, I do not doubt it.

FAINALL: Well, madam, I have suffered myself to be overcome by the importunity of this lady your friend, and am content you shall enjoy your own proper estate during life, on condition you oblige yourself never to marry, under such penalty as I think convenient.

LADY WISHFORT: Never to marry?

10. *cantharides*: Spanish Fly, considered a diuretic and aphrodisiac.
11. *cow-itch*: a stinging plant.
12. *of the Temple*: students at the Inns of Court.
13. *in commons*: in the dining-hall.

FAINALL: No more Sir Rowlands – the next imposture may not be so timely detected.

MRS MARWOOD: That condition, I dare answer, my lady will consent to without difficulty; she has already but too much experienced the perfidiousness of men. Besides, madam, when we retire to our pastoral solitude, we shall bid adieu to all other thoughts.

LADY WISHFORT: Ay, that's true; but in case of necessity, as of health, or some such emergency –

FAINALL: Oh, if you are prescribed marriage, you shall be considered; I will only reserve to myself the power to choose for you. If your physic be wholesome, it matters not who is your apothecary. Next, my wife shall settle on me the remainder of her fortune not made over already, and for her maintenance depend entirely on my discretion.

LADY WISHFORT: This is most inhumanly savage, exceeding the barbarity of a Muscovite husband.

FAINALL: I learned it from his Czarish majesty's retinue,[14] in a winter evening's conference over brandy and pepper, amongst other secrets of matrimony and policy, as they are at present practised in the Northern hemisphere. But this must be agreed unto, and that positively. Lastly, I will be endowed, in right of my wife, with that six thousand pound which is the moiety of Mrs Millamant's fortune in your possession; and which she has forfeited (as will appear by the last will and testament of your deceased husband, Sir Jonathan Wishfort) by her disobedience in contracting herself against your consent or knowledge, and by refusing the offered match with Sir Wilfull Witwoud, which you, like a careful aunt, had provided for her.

LADY WISHFORT: My nephew was *non compos*, and could not make his addresses.

FAINALL: I come to make demands. – I'll hea- no objections.

LADY WISHFORT: You will grant me time to consider.

FAINALL: Yes, while the instrument is drawing, to which you must set your hand till more sufficient deeds can be perfected; which I

14. *Czarish majesty's retinue*: Peter the Great had visited London in 1697.

will take care shall be done with all possible speed. In the meanwhile, I will go for the said instrument, and till my return, you may balance this matter in your own discretion.

[*Exit* FAINALL.]

LADY WISHFORT: This insolence is beyond all precedent, all parallel; must I be subject to this merciless villain?

MRS MARWOOD: 'Tis severe indeed, madam, that you should smart for your daughter's wantonness.

LADY WISHFORT: 'Twas against my consent that she married this barbarian, but she would have him, though her year[15] was not out. – Ah! her first husband, my son Languish, would not have carried it thus. Well, that was my choice, this is hers; she is matched now with a witness.[16] I shall be mad; dear friend, is there no comfort for me? Must I live to be confiscated at this rebel rate? – Here come two more of my Egyptian plagues too.

[*Enter* MILLAMANT *and* SIR WILFULL.]

SIR WILFULL: Aunt, your servant.

LADY WISHFORT: Out caterpillar, call not me aunt; I know thee not.

SIR WILFULL: I confess I have been a little in disguise, as they say. – 'S'heart! and I'm sorry for't. What would you have? I hope I committed no offence, aunt, – and if I did, I am willing to make satisfaction; and what can a man say fairer? If I have broke anything, I'll pay for't, an it cost a pound. And so let that content for what's past, and make no more words. For what's to come, to pleasure you I'm willing to marry my cousin. So pray let's all be friends, she and I are agreed upon the matter before a witness.

LADY WISHFORT: How's this, dear niece? Have I any comfort? Can this be true?

MILLAMANT: I am content to be a sacrifice to your repose, madam; and to convince you that I had no hand in the plot, as you were misinformed, I have laid my commands on Mirabell to come in person, and be a witness that I give my hand to this flower of knighthood; and for the contract that passed between Mirabell and me, I have obliged him to make a resignation of it, in your

15. *her year*: her year of mourning.
16. *with a witness*: with a vengeance.

ladyship's presence. He is without, and waits your leave for admittance.

LADY WISHFORT: Well, I'll swear I am something revived at this testimony of your obedience; but I cannot admit that traitor. – I fear I cannot fortify myself to support his appearance. He is as terrible to me as a Gorgon; if I see him, I fear I shall turn to stone, petrify incessantly.

MILLAMANT: If you disoblige him, he may resent your refusal and insist upon the contract still. Then 'tis the last time he will be offensive to you.

LADY WISHFORT: Are you sure it will be the last time? – If I were sure of that. – Shall I never see him again?

MILLAMANT: Sir Wilfull, you and he are to travel together, are you not?

SIR WILFULL: 'S'heart, the gentleman's a civil gentleman, aunt; let him come in. Why, we are sworn brothers and fellow travellers. – We are to be Pylades and Orestes,[17] he and I. He is to be my interpreter in foreign parts. He has been overseas already; and with proviso that I marry my cousin will cross 'em once again, only to bear me company. – 'S'heart, I'll call him in – an I set on't once, he shall come in; and see who'll hinder him.

  [*Exit.*]

MRS MARWOOD: This is precious fooling, if it would pass, but I'll know the bottom of it.

LADY WISHFORT: O dear Marwood, you are not going?

MARWOOD: Not far, madam; I'll return immediately.

  [*Exit.*]

  [*Re-enter* SIR WILFULL *and* MIRABELL.]

SIR WILFULL: Look up man, I'll stand by you; 'sbud an she do frown, she can't kill you; besides, hearkee, she dare not frown desperately, because her face is none of her own; 's'heart, an she should, her forehead would wrinkle like the coat of a cream-cheese, but mum for that, fellow traveller.

MIRABELL: If a deep sense of the many injuries I have offered to so good a lady, with a sincere remorse, and a hearty contrition, can

17. *Pylades and Orestes*: representative figures of faithful friendship.

402 THE WAY OF THE WORLD

but obtain the least glance of compassion I am too happy. – Ah madam, there was a time – but let it be forgotten. I confess I have deservedly forfeited the high place I once held, of sighing at your feet; nay, kill me not by turning from me in disdain, I come not to plead for favour; nay, not for pardon. I am a suppliant only for your pity. – I am going where I never shall behold you more –

SIR WILFULL: How, fellow traveller! You shall go by yourself then.

MIRABELL: Let me be pitied first, and afterwards forgotten – I ask no more.

SIR WILFULL: By'r Lady, a very reasonable request, and will cost you nothing, aunt. – Come, come, forgive and forget, aunt, why you must, an you are a Christian.

MIRABELL: Consider, madam, in reality you could not receive much prejudice; it was an innocent device; though I confess it had a face of guiltiness. It was at most an artifice which love contrived, and errors which love produces have ever been accounted venial. At least think it is punishment enough that I have lost what in my heart I hold most dear, that to your cruel indignation I have offered up this beauty, and with her my peace and quiet; nay, all my hopes of future comfort.

SIR WILFULL: An he does not move me, would I might never be o' the Quorum.[18] An it were not as good a deed as to drink, to give her to him again, I would I might never take shipping. Aunt, if you don't forgive quickly, I shall melt, I can tell you that. My contract went no further than a little mouth-glue,[19] and that's hardly dry; one doleful sigh more from my fellow traveller, and 'tis dissolved.

LADY WISHFORT: Well, nephew, upon your account – ah, he has a false insinuating tongue! Well, sir, I will stifle my just resentment at my nephew's request. I will endeavour what I can to forget, but on proviso that you resign the contract with my niece immediately.

MIRABELL: It is in writing, and with papers of concern; but I have sent my servant for it, and will deliver it to you, with all acknowledgments for your transcendent goodness.

18. *o' the Quorum*: a Justice of the Peace.
19. *mouth-glue*: an oral promise.

LADY WISHFORT [*apart*]: Oh, he has witchcraft in his eyes and tongue. When I did not see him, I could have bribed a villain to his assassination; but his appearance rakes the embers which have so long lain smothered in my breast.

[*Enter* FAINALL *and* MRS MARWOOD.]

FAINALL: Your date of deliberation, madam, is expired. Here is the instrument; are you prepared to sign?

LADY WISHFORT: If I were prepared, I am not empowered. My niece exerts a lawful claim, having matched herself by my direction to Sir Wilfull.

FAINALL: That sham is too gross to pass on me, though 'tis imposed on you, madam.

MILLAMANT: Sir, I have given my consent.

MIRABELL: And, sir, I have resigned my pretensions.

SIR WILFULL: And, sir, I assert my right; and will maintain it in defiance of you, sir, and of your instrument. 'S'heart an you talk of an instrument, sir, I have an old fox[20] by my thigh shall hack your instrument of ram vellum to shreds, sir. It shall not be sufficient for a mittimus[21] or a tailor's measure.[22] Therefore withdraw your instrument, sir, or by'r Lady, I shall draw mine.

LADY WISHFORT: Hold nephew, hold.

MILLAMANT: Good Sir Wilfull, respite your valour.

FAINALL: Indeed? Are you provided of a guard, with your single Beefeater there? But I'm prepared for you, and insist upon my first proposal. You shall submit your own estate to my management, and absolutely make over my wife's to my sole use, as pursuant to the purport and tenor of this other covenant. [*To* MILLAMANT.] I suppose, madam, your consent is not requisite in this case; nor, Mr Mirabell, your resignation; nor, Sir Wilfull, your right. – You may draw your fox if you please, sir, and make a bear-garden flourish[23] somewhere else, for here it will not avail. This, my Lady Wishfort, must be subscribed, or your darling

20. *fox*: sword.
21. *mittimus*: a warrant for imprisonment.
22. *tailor's measure*: then often made out of parchment.
23. *bear-garden flourish*: bear-gardens were notorious for riotous and unseemly behaviour.

daughter's turned adrift, like a leaky hulk to sink or swim, as she and the current of this lewd town can agree.

LADY WISHFORT: Is there no means, no remedy, to stop my ruin? Ungrateful wretch! dost thou not owe thy being, thy subsistence, to my daughter's fortune?

FAINALL: I'll answer you when I have the rest of it in my possession.

MIRABELL: But that you would not accept of a remedy from my hands – I own I have not deserved you should owe any obligation to me; or else perhaps I could advise –

LADY WISHFORT: Oh what? what? To save me and my child from ruin, from want, I'll forgive all that's past; nay I'll consent to anything to come, to be delivered from this tyranny.

MIRABELL: Ay, madam; but that is too late, my reward is intercepted. You have disposed of her who only could have made me a compensation for all my services. But be it as it may, I am resolved I'll serve you; you shall not be wronged in this savage manner.

LADY WISHFORT: How! Dear Mr Mirabell, can you be so generous at last? But it is not possible. Hearkee, I'll break my nephew's match; you shall have my niece yet, and all her fortune, if you can but save me from this imminent danger.

MIRABELL: Will you? I take you at your word. I ask no more. I must have leave for two criminals to appear.

LADY WISHFORT: Ay, ay, anybody, anybody.

MIRABELL: Foible is one, and a penitent.

[Enter MRS FAINALL, FOIBLE, and MINCING.]

MRS MARWOOD [To FAINALL]: O my shame! [MIRABELL and LADY WISHFORT go to MRS FAINALL and FOIBLE.] These corrupt things are bought and brought hither to expose me.

FAINALL: If it must all come out, why let 'em know it, 'tis but the way of the world. That shall not urge me to relinquish or abate one tittle of my terms; no, I will insist the more.

FOIBLE: Yes indeed, madam; I'll take my Bible oath of it.

MINCING: And so will I, mem.

LADY WISHFORT: O Marwood, Marwood, art thou false? My friend deceive me? Hast thou been a wicked accomplice with that profligate man?

MRS MARWOOD: Have you so much ingratitude and injustice, to give credit against your friend to the aspersions of two such mercenary trulls?

MINCING: 'Mercenary', mem? I scorn your words. 'Tis true we found you and Mr Fainall in the blue garret; by the same token, you swore us to secrecy upon Messalina's poems.[24] 'Mercenary?' No, if we would have been mercenary, we should have held our tongues; you would have bribed us sufficiently.

FAINALL: Go, you are an insignificant thing. Well, what are you the better for this? Is this Mr Mirabell's expedient? I'll be put off no longer. – You thing, that was a wife, shall smart for this. I will not leave thee wherewithal to hide thy shame; your body shall be naked as your reputation.

MRS FAINALL: I despise you and defy your malice. You have aspersed me wrongfully. – I have proved your falsehood. Go you and your treacherous – I will not name it, but starve together – perish.

FAINALL: Not while you are worth a groat, indeed my dear. Madam, I'll be fooled no longer.

LADY WISHFORT: Ah Mr Mirabell, this is small comfort, the detection of this affair.

MIRABELL: Oh, in good time. – Your leave for the other offender and penitent to appear, madam.

[Enter WAITWELL with a box of writings.]

LADY WISHFORT: Oh, Sir Rowland! – Well, rascal?

WAITWELL: What your ladyship pleases. I have brought the black box at last, madam.

MIRABELL: Give it me. Madam, you remember your promise.

LADY WISHFORT: Ay, dear sir.

MIRABELL: Where are the gentlemen?

WAITWELL: At hand sir, rubbing their eyes; just risen from sleep.

FAINALL: 'Sdeath, what's this to me? I'll not wait your private concerns.

[Enter PETULANT and WITWOUD.]

PETULANT: How now? What's the matter? Whose hand's out?

24. *Messalina's poems*: as suggested by Dobrée and others, Mincing probably means 'miscellany poems'. Messalina was renowned for her immorality.

WITWOUD: Heyday! what, are you all got together, like players at the end of the last act?

MIRABELL: You may remember, gentlemen, I once requested your hands as witnesses to a certain parchment.

WITWOUD: Ay, I do, my hand I remember. – Petulant set his mark.

MIRABELL: You wrong him, his name is fairly written, as shall appear. You do not remember, gentlemen, anything of what that parchment contained?

[Undoing the box.]

WITWOUD: No.

PETULANT: Not I. I writ. I read nothing.

MIRABELL: Very well; now you shall know. Madam, your promise.

LADY WISHFORT: Ay, ay, sir, upon my honour.

MIRABELL: Mr Fainall, it is now time that you should know that your lady, while she was at her own disposal, and before you had by your insinuations wheedled her out of a pretended settlement of the greatest part of her fortune –

FAINALL: Sir! Pretended!

MIRABELL: Yes, sir. I say that this lady while a widow, having it seems received some cautions respecting your inconstancy and tyranny of temper, which from her own partial opinion and fondness of you, she could never have suspected – she did, I say, by the wholesome advice of friends and of sages learned in the laws of this land, deliver this same as her act and deed to me in trust, and to the uses within mentioned. You may read if you please [holding out the parchment] though perhaps what is inscribed on the back may serve your occasions.

FAINALL: Very likely, sir. What's here? Damnation! [Reads.] A deed of conveyance of the whole estate real of Arabella Languish, widow, in trust to Edward Mirabell. Confusion!

MIRABELL: Even so, sir; 'tis the way of the world, sir, of the widows of the world. I suppose this deed may bear an elder date than what you have obtained from your lady.

FAINALL: Perfidious fiend! Then thus I'll be revenged. [Offers to run at MRS FAINALL.]

SIR WILFULL: Hold, sir, now you may make your bear-garden flourish somewhere else, sir.

FAINALL: Mirabell, you shall hear of this, sir; be sure you shall. Let me pass, oaf!

    [*Exit.*]

MRS FAINALL: Madam, you seem to stifle your resentment; you had better give it vent.

MRS MARWOOD: Yes, it shall have vent – and to your confusion, or I'll perish in the attempt.

    [*Exit.*]

LADY WISHFORT: O daughter, daughter, 'tis plain thou hast inherited thy mother's prudence.

MRS FAINALL: Thank Mr Mirabell, a cautious friend, to whose advice all is owing.

LADY WISHFORT: Well, Mr Mirabell, you have kept your promise, and I must perform mine. First, I pardon for your sake, Sir Rowland there, and Foible. The next thing is to break the matter to my nephew – and how to do that –

MIRABELL: For that, madam, give yourself no trouble; let me have your consent. Sir Wilfull is my friend; he has had compassion upon lovers and generously engaged a volunteer in this action, for our service, and now designs to prosecute his travels.

SIR WILFULL: 'S'heart aunt, I have no mind to marry. My cousin's a fine lady, and the gentleman loves her and she loves him, and they deserve one another; my resolution is to see foreign parts. I have set on't – and when I'm set on't, I must do't. And if these two gentlemen would travel too, I think they may be spared.

PETULANT: For my part, I say little; – I think things are best off or on.

WITWOUD: Egad I understand nothing of the matter – I'm in a maze yet, like a dog in a dancing school.

LADY WISHFORT: Well sir, take her, and with her all the joy I can give you.

MILLAMANT: Why does not the man take me? Would you have me give myself to you over again.

MIRABELL: Ay, and over and over again; for I would have you as often as possibly I can. [*Kisses her hand.*] Well, heaven grant I love you not too well, that's all my fear.

SIR WILFULL: 'S'heart, you'll have him time enough to toy after you're married; or if you will toy now, let us have a dance in the meantime, that we who are not lovers may have some other employment besides looking on.

MIRABELL: With all my heart, dear Sir Wilfull. What shall we do for music?

FOIBLE: Oh, sir, some that were provided for Sir Rowland's entertainment are yet within call.

[*A dance.*]

LADY WISHFORT: As I am a person I can hold out no longer. I have wasted my spirits so today already that I am ready to sink under the fatigue; and I cannot but have some fears upon me yet that my son Fainall will pursue some desperate course.

MIRABELL: Madam, disquiet not yourself on that account. To my knowledge his circumstances are such, he must of force comply. For my part, I will contribute all that in me lies to a reunion. [*To* MRS FAINALL.] In the meantime, madam, let me before these witnesses restore to you this deed of trust. It may be a means, well managed, to make you live easily together.

> From hence let those be warned, who mean to wed,
> Lest mutual falsehood stain the bridal bed;
> For each deceiver to his cost may find,
> That marriage frauds too oft are paid in kind.

[*Exeunt omnes.*]

EPILOGUE

Spoken by Mrs Bracegirdle.

After our epilogue this crowd dismisses,
I'm thinking how this play'll be pulled to pieces.
But pray consider ere you doom its fall,
How hard a thing 'twould be to please you all.
There are some critics so with spleen diseased,
They scarcely come inclining to be pleased;
And sure he must have more than mortal skill,
Who pleases anyone against his will.
Then, all bad poets we are sure are foes,
And how their number's swelled the town well knows;
In shoals I've marked 'em judging in the pit;
Though they're on no pretence for judgment fit,
But that they have been damned for want of wit.
Since when, they, by their own offences taught,
Set up for spies on plays, and finding fault.
Others there are whose malice we'd prevent;
Such who watch plays with scurrilous intent
To mark out who by *characters* are meant.
And though no perfect likeness they can trace,
Yet each pretends to know the copied face.
These with false glosses feed their own ill nature,
And turn to libel, what was meant a satire.
May such malicious fops this fortune find,
To think themselves alone the fools designed;
If any are so arrogantly vain,
To think they singly can support a scene,
And furnish fool enough to entertain.
For well the learned and the judicious know,
That satire scorns to stoop so meanly low
As any one abstracted fop to shew.
For, as when painters form a matchless face,

They from each fair one catch some differerent grace,
And shining features in one portrait blend,
To which no single beauty must pretend;
So poets oft do in one piece expose
Whole *belles assemblées* of coquettes and beaux.

FINIS.

THE STORY OF PENGUIN CLASSICS

Before 1946 ...'Classics' are mainly the domain of academics and students, without readable editions for everyone else. This all changes when a little-known classicist, E. V. Rieu, presents Penguin founder Allen Lane with the translation of Homer's *Odyssey* that he has been working on and reading to his wife Nelly in his spare time.

1946 *The Odyssey* becomes the first Penguin Classic published, and promptly sells three million copies. Suddenly, classic books are no longer for the privileged few.

1950s Rieu, now series editor, turns to professional writers for the best modern, readable translations, including Dorothy L. Sayers's *Inferno* and Robert Graves's *The Twelve Caesars*, which revives the salacious original.

1960s The Classics are given the distinctive black jackets that have remained a constant through the series's various looks. Rieu retires in 1964, hailing the Penguin Classics list as 'the greatest educative force of the 20th century'.

1970s A new generation of translators arrives to swell the Penguin Classics ranks, and the list grows to encompass more philosophy, religion, science, history and politics.

1980s The Penguin American Library joins the Classics stable, with titles such as *The Last of the Mohicans* safeguarded. Penguin Classics now offers the most comprehensive library of world literature available.

1990s The launch of Penguin Audiobooks brings the classics to a listening audience for the first time, and in 1999 the launch of the Penguin Classics website takes them online to a larger global readership than ever before.

The 21st Century Penguin Classics are rejacketed for the first time in nearly twenty years. This world famous series now consists of more than 1300 titles, making the widest range of the best books ever written available to millions – and constantly redefining the meaning of what makes a 'classic'.

The Odyssey continues ...

The best books ever written

PENGUIN (🐧) CLASSICS

SINCE 1946

Find out more at www.penguinclassics.com

PENGUIN CLASSICS

THE COMPLETE PLAYS   CHRISTOPHER MARLOWE

DIDO, QUEEN OF CARTHAGE / TAMBURLAINE THE
GREAT, *Parts One and Two* / THE JEW OF MALTA / DOCTOR
FAUSTUS / EDWARD THE SECOND / THE MASSACRE AT
PARIS

'When I behold the heavens, then I repent,
And curse thee, wicked Mephistopheles'

Christopher Marlowe – a possible spy with a reputation for atheism who
was murdered in mysterious circumstances – courted danger throughout
his life. A sense of dark forces operating in all social and political
relationships underlies his work. In *Dr Faustus*, a man of great intellect
and even greater ambition craves knowledge, and is prepared to sell his
soul to the Devil to achieve it. Tamburlaine attempts to satisfy his desire
for greatness through his domination over an ever-growing empire, while
Edward II upsets the delicate balance of power in the land and plants the
seed of his own murder. All the plays here show Marlowe's fascination
with the tension between weak and strong, sacred and profane.

Frank Romany's introduction relates the plays to Marlowe's turbulent
religious world. The fully modernized texts have been newly edited from
the earliest editions, and the full commentary on each play is
supplemented with a glossary and an appendix of mythological and
historical allusions.

Edited by Frank Romany and Robert Lindsey

PENGUIN CLASSICS

PLAYS PLEASANT   BERNARD SHAW

ARMS AND THE MAN / CANDIDA / THE MAN OF DESTINY / YOU NEVER CAN TELL

'Soldiering, my dear madam, is the coward's art of attacking mercilessly when you are strong, and keeping out of harm's way when you are weak'

One of Bernard Shaw's most glittering comedies, *Arms and the Man* is a burlesque of Victorian attitudes to heroism, war and empire. In the contrast between Bluntschli, the mercenary soldier, and the brave leader, Sergius, the true nature of valour is revealed. Shaw mocks deluded idealism in *Candida*, when a young poet becomes infatuated with the wife of a Socialist preacher. *The Man of Destiny* is a witty war of words between Napoleon and a 'strange lady', while in the exuberant farce *You Never Can Tell* a divided family is reunited by chance. Although Shaw intended *Plays Pleasant* to be gentler comedies than those in their companion volume, *Plays Unpleasant*, their prophetic satire is sharp and provocative.

This is the definitive text under the editorial supervision of Dan H. Laurence. This volume includes Shaw's Preface of 1898.

Introduced by W. J. McCormack

PENGUIN CLASSICS

PYGMALION   BERNARD SHAW

'Yes, you squashed cabbage leaf . . . you incarnate insult to the English language: I could pass you off as the Queen of Sheba'

Pygmalion both delighted and scandalized its first audiences in 1914. A brilliantly witty reworking of the classical tale of the sculptor Pygmalion, who falls in love with his perfect female statue, it is also a barbed attack on the British class system and a statement of Shaw's feminist views. In Shaw's hands, the phoneticist Henry Higgins is the Pygmalion figure who believes he can transform Eliza Doolittle, a cockney flower girl, into a duchess at ease in polite society. The one thing he overlooks is that his 'creation' has a mind of her own.

This is the definitive text under the editorial supervision of Dan H. Laurence, with an illuminating introduction by Nicholas Grene, discussing the language and politics of the play. Included in this volume is Shaw's preface, as well as his 'sequel' written for the first publication in 1916, to rebut public demand for a more conventionally romantic ending.

Edited by Dan H. Laurence with an introduction by Nicholas Grene

---